The
MEGAYACHTS
USA

Volume Five ★ 2004

A BOAT INTERNATIONAL PUBLICATION

The MEGAYACHTS USA

Volume Five ★ 2004

is published by
EDISEA LIMITED
a subsidiary of

BOAT INTERNATIONAL PUBLICATIONS LIMITED
5-7 Kingston Hill, Kingston-upon-Thames, Surrey KT2 7PW, UK
Tel: +44 (0) 20 8547 2662 Fax: +44 (0) 20 8547 1201

EDITORIAL & DESIGN OFFICE
EDISEA USA, INC.
P.O. Box 1066 or Bridge Street Marketplace
Waitsfield, VT 05673
Tel: (802) 496-6948 Fax: (802) 496-6958
Email: info@boatiusa.com

Copyright © 2004 Edisea Ltd.

ISBN 1 8985245 64

★ ★ ★

PUBLISHER	Christian Chalmin
CHIEF OPERATING OFFICER	Ben Hudson
EDITOR	Jill Bobrow
MANAGING EDITOR	Rebecca Cahilly
EDITOR / LUXURY YACHT MARKET	Matthew Esposito
DESIGN / PRODUCTION	Stacey Hood / Big Eyedea Visual Design
GENERAL ACCOMMODATION DRAWINGS	Don Beeck
COPY EDITOR	Lauri Grotstein
HEAD OF SALES	Malcolm MacLean
GROUP ADVERTISEMENT MANAGER	Charles Finney
ADVERTISEMENT MANAGER	Douglas Hunter
ADVERTISEMENT SALES	Ben Farnborough
	Andy Howell
ADVERTISEMENT ADMINISTRATION	Caren Lewis
ADVERTISEMENT DESIGNER	Craig Shuttlewood
ADVERTISEMENT COORDINATOR	Heidi Parrott
PRODUCTION MANAGER	Francis Ransom
PRODUCTION ASSISTANT	Alice Purser
PRE PRESS	AdHoc, Canada
PRINTING & BINDING	Toppan, Hong Kong

M/Y Andrea

206 763 2383

www.deltamarine.com

Contents

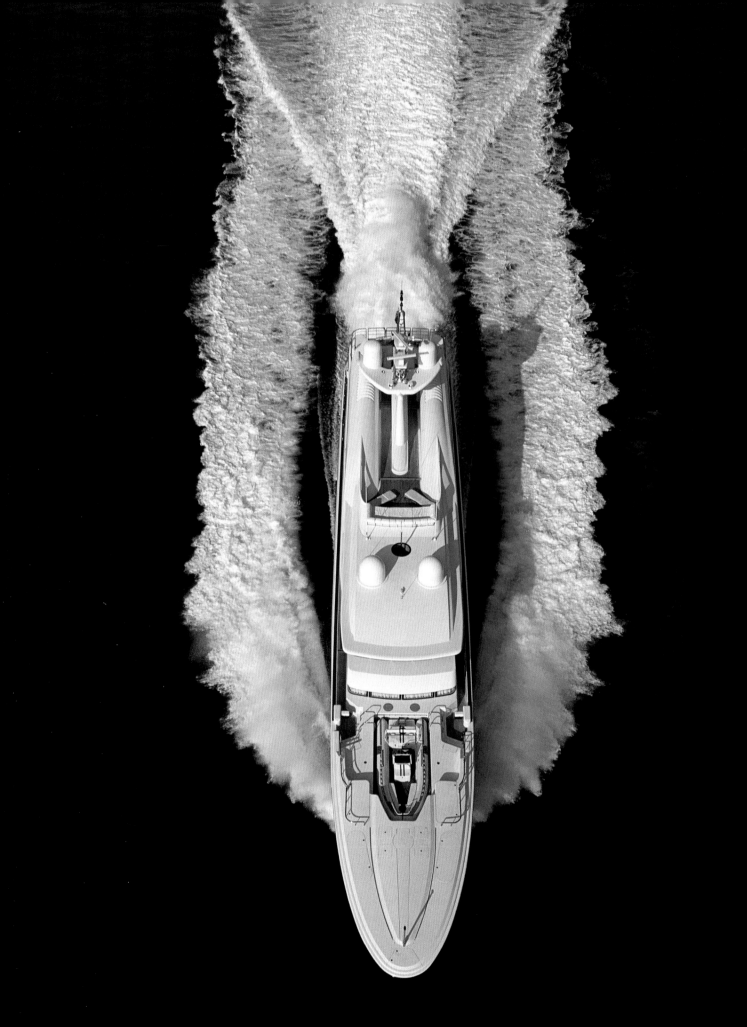

MEGA YACHT MANAGEMENT FROM THE ESSENTIAL AGENT.

Edmiston is the essential agent for mega yachts. With offices in London, Monte Carlo and Los Angeles, we are always open to deliver the necessary backup worldwide. Each and every yacht gets an individual solution to suit her particular needs, be it full yacht management, charter management or just the reassurance of having our expertise and resources on call. Not satisfied being your central agent, we want to be your essential agent. Edmiston – world leaders in the sale and charter of large yachts.

FOREWORD ──────────────────────────────────── ★

Many people wonder why in the world I started construction on a 127ft tri-deck motoryacht at the young age of 95! The answer lies in my past and in my true love of water and yachting. I've had boats in my blood since the age of nine, when I was taken to Seattle to visit my grandmother. Her brother—my uncle—owned a fleet of ferry boats in Puget Sound. Realizing that I'd better save my pennies if I wanted a boat of my own someday, I sold candy bars and peanuts aboard his boats.

I wasn't the only one in the family with a passion for boating. My father, Charles Walgreen Sr., who started the Walgreen pharmacy chain in 1901, purchased his first boat in 1935—a 136ft steel ship named *Dixonia*. He and I loved to fish and took that boat on many trips to Canada, often into uncharted waters where the fishing was best. We loved the cruise north from Chicago as much as the fishing.

During World War II, *Dixonia* was leased by the U.S. Army. It's rumored that General Eisenhower and his top staff planned the D-Day invasion while sailing on our yacht. *Dixonia* was returned to us after the war, and in 1947 I sold it and purchased *Dixonia II*, a 63ft wooden boat.

The rest is history: I bought my first Burger in 1956, naming her *Sis W* after my first wife, Mary Ann. My appetite for yachting was insatiable and I went on to own two more Burgers. I am especially proud of the time logged on my boats. Let's put it this way—they rarely sat at the dock. My philosophy: "If you own a boat, use it!"

Time passed, and in our nineties health problems confined both me and my second wife, Jean, to wheelchairs. During recovery from a stroke, I called with great enthusiasm for my grandson, Casey Pratt—a yacht broker—to discuss a new boat. The family nurses blamed this fixation on heavy medication. My grandson tried to reason with me and suggested chartering a yacht, or buying a used one and converting it to be wheelchair-accessible.

But more than anything in the world, I wanted to build a new *Sis W*! Finally, everyone started to believe me. We did our homework and met with various builders, but Burger was the 'natural' fit. They immediately started on the design of a fully wheelchair-accessible boat, including an elevator and a myriad of other amenities. Next, we simply had to pull together our favorite crew—Captain Jim Bean and his wife, Beth, accepted the challenge.

I have realized a dream at the age of 97. Jean and I plan to spend the rest of our lives on this boat cruising with family and friends. It has everything we need and want, from a gourmet galley to a piano keyboard to a fireplace. And, like my other boats, it can sail the oceans. My next dream is to see the 'Walgreen Coast,' a 1,000ft stretch of the north coast of Antarctica named for my dad by Admiral Richard E. Byrd in 1933. I've seen it from the air, but never from sea.

Over the years, my philosophy has neither changed nor dimmed: "If you own a boat," I say, "especially one as beautiful as this – use it!" We certainly will … and with much joy.

[signature: C R Walgreen Jr]

Charles R. Walgreen Jr.
Owner, *Sis W*

Evolution of *Sis W*
Burger Boat Company built four *Sis W*s for the Walgreen family between 1956 and 2003.

126' Aluminum Tri-Deck 2003

86' Aluminum House Boat 1971

72' Aluminum Cruiser 1961

65' Steel Cruiser 1956

INTRODUCTION ── ★

This year marks the Fifth Anniversary of *The MegaYachts USA*. Since the book's inception, it has grown in concept and in execution. I remember producing the first volume and how difficult it was to explain to people the difference between *The MegaYachts USA* and our more established book, *The Superyachts*. While we are sister publications belonging to the same parent company, *MegaYachts* initially suffered the younger sibling syndrome: upstart, raw, untested. It is often a struggle to get the marine industry to take notice of something new. However, a mere four years later, I am happy to say that *MegaYachts* is definitely well established. At 332 pages, this is our biggest edition ever!

Each year we include 21 feature yachts. The extraordinary vessels chosen for this book are generally new builds 85ft and above in length. On occasion we choose to represent a special classic yacht that has undergone a major refit. All of the entrants have something to do with this side of the pond. The criteria is simply that there be some American rationale: American owned, designed, built or conceived for the American (including North and South American) market.

In Volume Five we are pleased to include the exquisitely refitted 258ft vessel *Delphine*, built originally as a steam yacht in 1921 for automotive magnate Horace Dodge. She made a stunning comeback debut in Monaco in September 2003. Additionally, this year seems to be the year of the Expedition Vessel: we have three, varying from Feadship's first ever expedition yacht, the 140ft *Andiamo*, belonging to an American woman from California; to the Newcastle Explorer 125, a spec boat classically designed by Luiz de Basto and built by Newcastle Marine, and then there is *Amarellla*, a sturdy, no nonsense Inace Exploration Vessel. On the modern wild side, we have the likes of Azimut's 98 Leonardo, a stunning Italian creation, slick as they come. For sailing we have the largest aluminum-built Perini Navi, *Felicitá west*, designed by Ron Holland, as well as the Rivolta 90, a new design by American-based Italian designer Piero Rivolta. Also, we have an impressive contingent of tri-deck vessels including Delta Marine's 124ft *Defiant*, Burger Boat Company with their largest ever, 127ft *Sis W*, and, Christensen's magnificent 150ft *Mystic*.

Every year our recent launches in the Luxury Yacht Market section, Builders and Designers, grows, bolstering our confidence in the industry and creating much excitement. Destination features this year take us to the Spanish Virgin Islands aboard the 90ft *MJ* and around the Long Island Sound aboard the 114ft superfast *MITseaAH*. To increase value to our readers and to the marine industry, we have instituted two new aspects to the book this year: A Registry of all the featured boats that have appeared in our previous volumes and a listing of the Top 100 North American-built boats. We strive to keep our Directory up to date and send out informational questionnaires months before publication. However, sometimes we don't get responses to repeated queries, so if something is askew, don't blame us, call us with corrections and additions! We welcome suggestions and count on you, our readers, to help keep us on our toes and informed.

It has been a difficult time for the American economy, but check out the new projects in The Luxury Yacht market section—judging by the new designs and new builds in play, I'd say things are looking up.

Jill Bobrow

Jill Bobrow
Editor
The MegaYachts USA, Volume Five

Benetti

Italian Excellence since 1873

Shipyard: Via M. Coppino, 104 · 55049 Viareggio · Italy · tel. +39 0584 3821 · fax +39 0584 396232
Benetti Germany: Herbert Dahm KG, Bendemannstr. 9, D-40210 Dusseldorf · tel. +49 211 3555100 · mobil +49 172 2064188 · fax +49 211 3555112

AZIMUT
YACHTS

The best eye-shot about your wishes

Advanced technologies and materials for the new seaworthy full displacement motor yacht: the first CBI NAVI 37m/122' semi-custom project

C.B.I. NAVI

C.B.I. NAVI SPA - 55049 Viareggio ITALY - Via Giannessi Via Pescatori
Tel. +39-0584-388192 - Fax +39-0584-388060
20100 Milano ITALY - Via Della Spiga, 52
Tel. +39-02-76394086 - fax +39-02-76397503
E-Mail: info@cbinavi.com - Internet: http://www.cbinavi.com

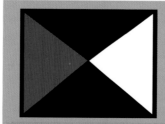

It's your vision...

...exclusively

Sensation Composite Series

Imagine a superyacht that reflects your personal style, sophistication and taste.

Sensation New Zealand can build your dream.

Volare Series - 95ft, 115ft

Allegro Series - 115ft, 130ft

Heritage Series - 120ft, 135ft, 150ft

SENSATION
NEW ZEALAND

11 Selwood Road, Henderson, Auckland, New Zealand **Phone**: +64 9 837-2210 **Email**: sensation@sensation.co.nz **Website**: www.sensation.co.nz

WE HAVE HAND CRAFTED AN

EXQUISITELY DESIGNED

"NEXT GENERATION" 102' YACHT

IN BAVARIA (GERMANY)

EVERYTHING EXTRAORDINARY

COMES AS STANDARD

C'EST LA VIE IS AVAILABLE

FOR AN EXCLUSIVE PRESENTATION

Felicità west Image *Carlo Borlenghi*

PERINI NAVI, *Blue-Water Sailing Yachts*

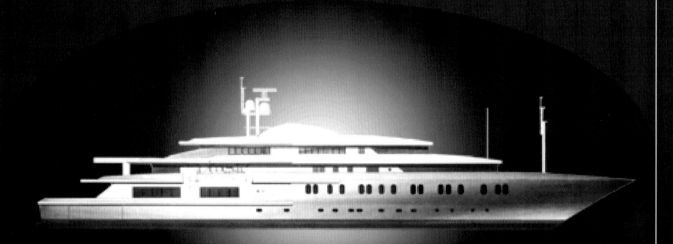

At International Yacht Collection we take pride in creating a full complement of yachting experiences, tailored to your unique specifications and discriminating tastes. Unsurpassed personalization, service and integrity from a worldwide industry leader. Allow us to deliver your experience of a lifetime. Relax…enjoy.

enjoy! the Total Yachting Experience

INTERNATIONAL YACHT COLLECTION
Specializing in World Class Megayachts

1850 SE 17th St, Ste 301 • Fort Lauderdale, FL 33316 • (954) 522-2323 • (888) 213-7577 • www.yachtcollection.com • info@yachtcollection.co

FORT LAUDERDALE • ST. MAARTEN • NEWPOR

YACHT SALES | YACHT CHARTERS | CHARTER MARKETING | YACHT MANAGEMENT | CREW PLACEMENT | NEW CONSTRUCTIC

LADY SHERIDAN PHOTO: SCOTT PEARSON

It's the most beautiful things are made still more beautiful by us ...

Especially with Refit & Repair there is an above average level of
- very highly skilled crafts-manship
- finding solutions in con-junction with the customer and organisation
- reliability in keeping to the time schedule and flexibi-lity together with the tech-nological know-how which represents the qualities, distinguishing our Refit & Repair team. No challenge is to daunting and we offer you technological and visual solutions into the smallest details.

metrica
INTERIOR

YACHTS   AIRCRAFTS   RESIDENCES

metrica INTERIOR by Rudolf Rincklake van Endert

Germany: Bahnhofstr. 73 · D-48308 Senden · Tel. +49 (0) 2536 / 330900 · Fax 330930
Switzerland: Terrassenweg 17 · CH-6315 Oberägeri/ZG · Tel. +41 (0) 41 750 90 89 · Fax 750 62 70
Turkey: Serbest Bölge · TR-07070 Antalya · Tel. +90 (0) 242 259 2847 · Fax 1673
info@metrica.de · www.metrica-interior.com

STUDY IN WHITE

From any angle, the sweeping lines and meticulous detailing
of every Amels superyacht are the work of pure craftsmanship.

SUPERSTRUCTURE – DETAIL. AMELS 62M.

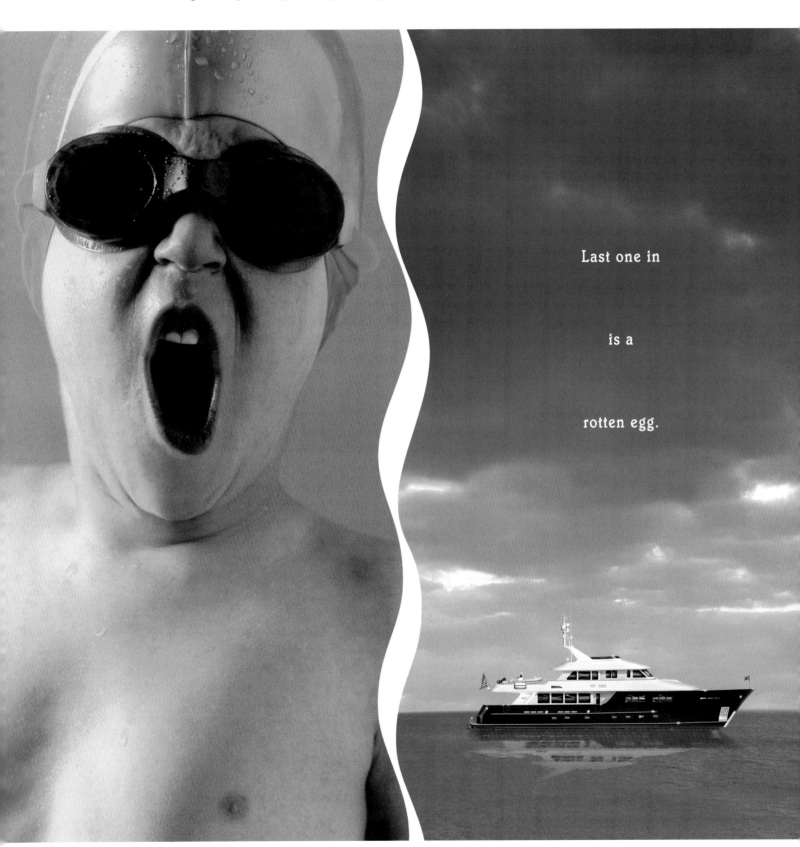

ONE PORT OF CALL

Devonport produces and re-configures some of the world's most admired yachts.
Our blend of traditional craftsmanship and advanced technology provides a unique
combination of exquisite luxury and the finest engineering.
For the yacht of your dreams, there is only one port of call.

DEVONPORT

EXPERTISE...YACHTSPERTISE

DEVONPORT ROYAL DOCKYARD LIMITED DEVONPORT PLYMOUTH ENGLAND PL1 4SG
T +44 (0)1752 323311 F +44 (0)1752 323247 E YACHTS@DEVONPORT.CO.UK

FALCON

FALCON YACHTS s.r.l.

55049 Viareggio
Via Petrarca
Tel. +39 0584 388027
Fax +39 0584 383412
E. Mail: info@falconyachts.com
Internet: www.falconyachts.com

Cielo Terra Mare s.a.s.
Milano
Tel. + 39 02 66985133
Fax + 39 02 66986013

France
Mr. Alain Nicaud
Tel. +33 493012340
Fax +33 493012133

Greece
Atalanta Marine S.A.
Tel. +30210 4174669
Fax +30210 4112951

The 107 SonShip is the jewel in West Bay's crown. It incorporates every design and engineering innovation they've developed and their unprecedented attention to detail is in evidence everywhere. From her sleek, Mediterranean-style exterior to her precision handcrafted joinery and elegant appointments, this is one Flagship that will have the competition in a flap. For more information about SonShip yachts, click on www.west-bay.com or email: marketing@west-bay.com

West Bay SONSHIP Yachts Ltd.

A FAMILY TRADITION FOR MORE THAN 35 YEARS.

CHEOY LEE
SHIPYARDS

130 YEARS OF WISDOM

QUALITY, INTEGRITY AND VALUE YOU CAN RELY ON

A WIDE RANGE OF CHOICE AWAIT YOU

GOOD FORTUNE
BRINGS EXCITING CHOICES. Diversity and value come together at Cheoy Lee. The recently launched, 172' steel and fiberglass displacement yacht, "Seashaw", joins the fleet. Come and see the new 68' Sport motoryacht and 125' pilot house, debuting at the Fort Lauderdale International Boat Show. Whether you're looking for something 60'-200'; expedition, long range or motoryacht in alloy, steel, fiberglass or a combination thereof, we have probably built it. Send us a "bid package" or call today. You will be amazed at our value and know **YOU'VE MADE A WISE DECISION.**

SHIP BUILDERS TO THE WORLD FOR MORE THAN A CENTURY
www.cheoyleena.com

HONG KONG 852.2.307.6333
info@cheoylee.com

UNITED STATES 954.527.0999
info@cheoyleena.com

W. COAST UNITED STATES 206.625.1580
info.sea@compasspointyachts.com

CODECASA

CANTIERI NAVALI CODECASA S.p.A. Via Amendola - 55049 VIAREGGIO ITALIA Tel. 0584 383221 - Fax 0584 383531
www.codecasayachts.com   e-mail: info@codecasayachts.com

Sunny side up.

The exciting new Lazzara 106E open bridge.

LAZZARA YACHTS

68   80C   80E   80SC   106E   106SC

Seabeam.

Sleek and darting like the first ray of morning the 112'
cuts through the waves with exceptional cruising performance.
The interiors are spacious allowing one to live the sea
in an airy sense of total freedom.

CUSTOM LINE 112'

0 — 94' | **112'** | 128'

mpr - Italy

the SAINT-TROPEZ book

The fame of St-Tropez as a world leader in cosmopolitan chic has led to many misunderstandings about this most fascinating of towns. Here, for the first time, is a fully illustrated large format book that traces the history of St-Tropez from its foundation during the days of the Roman Empire, its growth to become the most important fishing port on the Cote d'Azur and its suffering at the hands of the Moorish invasion.

Its rise to prominence as a gathering-place each summer of celebrities from the fields of music, film and the arts is well documented with scores of previously unpublished photographs. And, of course, St-Tropez is an idyllic setting for the most elegant of the world's sailing regattas, Les Voiles de Saint-Tropez.

This is a book of delights to savour slowly.

Illustrated by 284 photos, paintings, drawings, plans and maps. Printed in full colour throughout.

MAGNIFICA
PROFILE IN LUXURY

mpr - Italy

Need to locate long lost friends and relatives? We can help.

Alexa C²

The truth is nothing brings a family together like a gorgeous, customized yacht. In fact you might even discover that you have more friends than you ever knew. All of which is something you can ponder while basking in the profound luxury of a boat built to your exacting specifications and tastes. Oh, and you might also consider getting caller ID.

NORDLUND
CUSTOM BOAT BUILDERS

www.nordlundboat.com

Nordlund Boat Company, 1626 Marine View Drive, Tacoma, WA 98422, Tel:253.627.0605

500 foot PRIVATE SHIP

There's a reason why owners keep coming back to Hargrave.

HARGRAVE
CUSTOM YACHTS

Pictured above is the 100' Raised Pilothouse "LA MARCHESA" $4,975,750 Delivered

"If you come to the boat shows and talk to our owners the first thing you'll realize is that many of them are building their second or third custom yacht with us. They talk about the excitement of building as much as cruising. From space planning and interior design choices to electronics and water toys, it's all part of the fun in building your dream boat.

When we use the phrase "custom boat" at Hargrave we're talking about making those kind of difficult engineering changes like moving engine rooms, and crew forward and aft, changing the profile from sport deck to raised pilothouse or skylounge or changing the draft. We're not just selecting blue or beige carpets. We make those changes because they are necessary to create the perfect boat for you and your family. At Hargrave our total focus and commitment is on building your dream boat, not ours!

In case you haven't noticed, there has been a major shakeup in the 80'-130' segment of the yachting industry during the past couple of years. If you compare you'll notice the best part about the 100' Hargrave is its price. Amazingly enough, you can own this boat for a million dollars less than any of the competition's and it can be custom equipped the way you want. Just imagine what you could do with a million extra bucks in your pocket!"

There *is* a reason why owners keep coming back to Hargrave

-Michael Joyce, President

DESIGNERS, BUILDERS, & DISTRIBUTORS OF WORLD CLASS YACHTS

1887 WEST STATE ROAD 84 • FT. LAUDERDALE, FL 33315 • TEL 954.463.0555 • FAX 954.463.8621 • WWW.HARGRAVE.ORG • SALES@HARGRAVE.ORG

The
Luxury Yacht Market

Builders

The Luxury Yacht Market

Builders

ABEKING & RASMUSSEN

Founded in 1907, Abeking & Rasmussen has continuously developed from a specialized wooden boatbuilder into a modern, hi-tech shipyard. Their 90 years of experience have served them well, seeing the delivery of numerous sailing and motoryachts, designed in cooperation with some of the world's leading naval architects and designers. Ranging from 98 to 262ft, the yard has gained a reputation for substantial, complex, and technically advanced vessels, meeting the highest standards in the market. Keeping the owner's wishes at the forefront, A & R strives for the union of func-

ABEKING & RASMUSSEN
Excellence III

tionality and style when crafting the interior and exterior of their vessels. The yard also specializes in the refit of megayachts, a process conducted to meet the most discriminating standards.

ABEKING & RASMUSSEN
Alithia

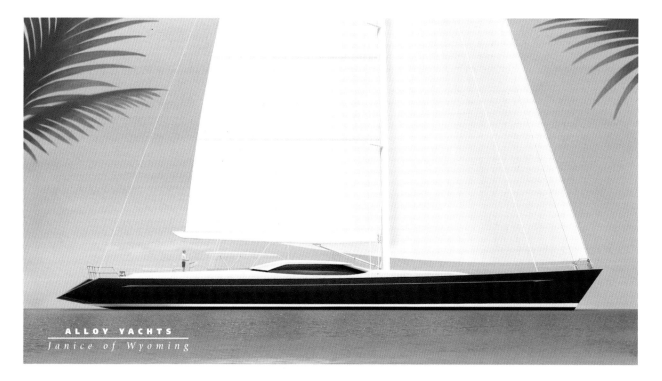

ALLOY YACHTS
Janice of Wyoming

ALLOY YACHTS

Alloy Yachts has seen a substantial body of work completed this past year, including several vessels designed in conjunction with Dubois Naval Architects. Amongst recent launches from the collaborators are the 134ft sloop *Destination Fox Harb'r* and the 128ft *S.Q.N.*, a motoryacht delivered to Alloy Chairman Gary Lane. Another sloop at 130ft has also begun construction with styling from Dubois. Built for an American owner she will be called *Janice of Wyoming*, and will be launched in early 2005. Interior styling is being completed by the owner and the Alloy Yachts design team, and will feature walnut fielded panels with detailed molding. Current projects underway are the 178ft Dubois sloop *Tiara*, and a 108ft Fontaine Design Group sloop due for launch summer 2004.

AMELS

Two megayachts have recently been launched from Amels in Vlissingen, comprised of a 202ft Michael Leach-designed motoryacht (featuring innovations such as a two-deck owner's suite) and a 171ft Terence Disdale 'classic'. The latter delivered just in time to vacate her space for the next 171ft Disdale project, a stunningly laid-out yacht designed by Alberto Pinto and Laura Sessa. At their Makkum facility, Amels has launched a new Disdale 174ft—somewhat unconventionally through the yard's back door—to make room for the sleek *Ilona*, a 242ft Redman Whitely Dixon design. *Ilona* has been described as 'having it all,' from an aft helicopter hanger with full refueling station to a battery of 65 underwater lights. New builds are also taking shape, with an elegant, 190ft Andrew Winch design destined for a 2005 delivery and a Disdale 212ft due for early 2006. In the true fashion of growth and evolution, the shipyard has added key personnel in the areas of engineering, refit/repair, and design to keep pace with their expanding capacity.

AMELS
242ft Five Deck
Motoryacht

AZIMUT

After more than 30 years of experience in the yachting industry, Azimut-Benetti is the one of the world's leading builders—and Europe's supreme producer—of yachts in the range of 39 to 100ft. The Azimut 116 is a new motoryacht featuring a gliding keel, presently under construction at their Viareggio boatyard. External lines and concept are by Stefano Righini, with interior from Carlo Galeazzi. The yacht is available in several versions: either with two owner's suites on the main deck and four guest cabins lower or with all five cabins below and ample space for entertaining on the main deck (with an option for a 'country style' galley). Anticipated furnishings include limed oak and walnut, while a stern garage is able to accommodate an array of water toys and tenders or can be configured for an extra crew cabin with head.

BAGLIETTO

The latest creation from Baglietto is a 100ft all-aluminum megayacht launched recently from their Varazze facility. *Saramour* is quite notable for her avant-garde design and extreme comfort, even at speeds approaching 30 knots. Naval architecture on *Saramour* was provided by A. Sculati, while exteriors and interiors were designed respectively by F. Paszkowski and Studio Aiello. The unmistakably modern Baglietto has a range of 900nm at 26 knots and boasts spacious living areas on the main deck, conventional stateroom arrangements below, and a bow garage for tender stowage. Her capacious flybridge includes a helm and several relaxation areas for guests, made possible by the clever bow compartment. The yacht also comes equipped with RINA Class certification and the 100-A-1.1 "Y" Maltese Cross. Baglietto has also launched the 138ft *Blue Scorpion* this past year, designed again by F. Paszkowski, with a sleek yet soft styling. Light oak and dark wenge compose her supple interior.

BAGLIETTO
Blue Scorpion

BENETTI
More

BENETTI

Twenty-five yachts in composite and/or steel are on the order books at Benetti Shipyard, with vessels ranging from 100 to 213 feet in build or on order, for deliveries up until May of 2006. The new line of Benetti Tradition 100ft motoryachts is showing signs of equal success to her bigger sister—the 115ft Benetti Classic series—with seven sold of the former and twenty-two of the latter. The Benetti Vision (145ft) is also in demand with four under contract, all with completely different interiors. As not to discriminate, the yard still participates in many custom builds, including nine steel construction yachts currently underway from 164 to 213ft. Four are being built for repeat clients, with delivery expected by 2006. The next two to be launched are the 180ft *Amnesia*, with interior by Stefano Natucci, and *Sai Ram*, 170ft

with a minimalist interior from Lazzarini & Pickering.

BLOEMSMA & VAN BREEMEN

Bloemsma & van Breemen have set a new benchmark in quality with their delivery of the 100ft *Patriot*, featuring naval architecture and interior design from Vripack Yachting. Designed for exploration and adventure, she has a 5,500 mile range, ice-strengthened hull, and is the most extensively equipped Doggersbank Offshore built to date. With specs reading like a 'What's What' of tomorrow's technologies, the vessel has been stretched to unprecedented levels of sophistication, and includes not-so-standard items such as night-vision cameras, 11 touch-screen monitors, five helm stations, and a NATO-standard watermaker. In addition to what she holds inside, *Patriot* is defined by her elegant explorer profile with exceptional stain-

less-steel work and custom-made glass, as well as by her virtually silent and luxurious interior. Ready for anything, Bloemsma & Van Breemen's *Patriot* represents the very latest in boat design and engineering.

BURGER

In the works at Burger Boat Company is an unprecedented development, marking a first for the strictly custom builder. To complement their successful, well-established design/build megayacht division, the boatyard will be adding a new semi-production, mid-size yacht range from 65-80ft. The company's strategy calls for designing, engineering, and building limited edition, high-quality, semi-custom yachts, kicking off with the 70ft Timeless Cruiser Series. This series marks the revival of the extremely popular and very successful cruiser style yacht originally made famous by the company. Since its introduction in the mid 1950s, Burger built 72 cruiser yachts through 1990, making it one of the most prolific yacht styles ever. Throughout its 35-year run it has become one of the most highly sought after yachts in the secondary marketplace. This new series will blend traditional exterior styling with state-of-the-art technology and performance, and is ideally suited for owner/operator situations and/or shorthanded cruising.

BURGER
603 Classic

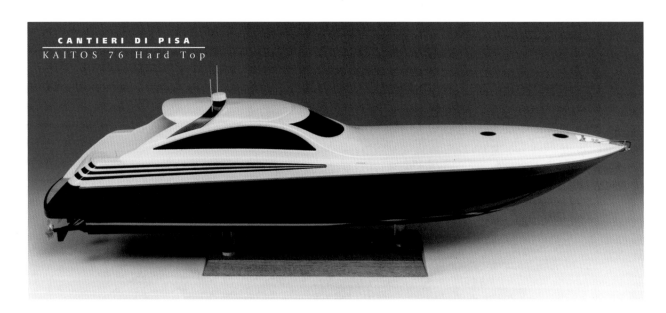

CANTIERI DI PISA
KAITOS 76 Hard Top

CANTIERI DI PISA

The new line of KAITOS open yachts from Cantieri di Pisa is undoubtedly the most interesting building going on at this Italian shipyard. The yard plans to initially produce two models, a 64ft and 76ft (open and hard top versions), which will be joined shortly by a 95ft model with hard top only. The KAITOS range features innovative interiors with spacious solutions uncommon in boats of this size. The architects of Lazzarini & Pickering have pioneered originality with such inventions as the master cabin in the 76-footer that contains a fold-away berth, and subsequently creates a voluminous two-level suite. The KAITOS 64 will be proposed with two different layouts (two or three cabins), and the option of two different engine types.

CAPE HORN

The Cape Horn Trawler Corporation builds one type of vessel: full displacement, extremely safe, strong and comfortable trans-oceanic

motoryachts. Over 20 have been sold to date and are cruising the world's seas. Cape Horn models range from 55 to 120 feet and are designed for those who might wish to veer off the beaten track, keeping Marriotts and Marinas out of mind. Recently, Cape Horn has worked with Sparkman & Stephens to perfect the design of the CH65, conceived as an ultimate cruiser that live-aboard yachting couples can maintain on their own with relative ease. It is ideal for coastal waters, with a 6ft draft, and has also been proven comfortable and highly stable as a trans-oceanic boat. This semi-production builder is very flexible to any owner's need, and can accommodate almost anything— as evidenced by their completion of an 81ft handicap-accessible yacht.

C.B.I. NAVI

Located in Viareggio, Italy, C.B.I. Navi is a total facility shipbuilder special-

ized in luxury long-range full or semi-displacement custom yachts in steel or aluminum, ranging from 92ft to 197ft. Their motoryachts are characterized by high quality standards and special consideration for noise reduction and vibration insulation. From their experience with custom production, the yard has recently introduced a new semi-custom concept product. The first vessel of the new generation is a 125ft full displacement motoryacht, designed as usual to Lloyd's, RINA, MCA, and 'Registro Navale Italiano' specifications. Again, great importance has been given to the sound and thermal insulation by applying the most innovative materials on the market. The vessels' interiors have also been carefully studied to respect important ergonomic principles, and are designed to obtain maximum comfort at sea when cruising worldwide. Each interior will also be customized, following the needs and taste of her respective owner.

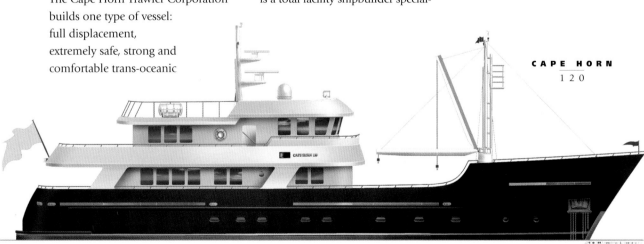

CAPE HORN
120

CHEOY LEE SHIPYARDS

Well-established for their fiberglass yachts, Cheoy Lee is now diversifying into both steel and aluminum yacht construction—witnessed by the recently launched 172ft steel displacement motoryacht *Seashaw*. Built to ABS classing, *Seashaw* has a steel hull with composite fiberglass superstructure, and is replacing the owner's previous 145ft fiberglass Cheoy Lee. Other features include Quantum Zero speed stabilzers and a high fog system throughout the accommodations, as well as an interior by Dee Robinson. The shipyard, which currently has 15 commercial projects underway, is now capable of building yachts to any class up to 197ft, in any construction medium or combination thereof. Other recent launches include a 125ft composite motoryacht, with work still continuing on a 164ft project.

CHRISTENSEN SHIPYARDS

Christensen has established itself as a world leader in building composite yachts. Continuing to grow with the launch of the 150ft tri-deck *Mystic*, current construction counts three other yachts underway. Christensen is capable of virtually unlimited design possibilities, by combining their superstructure tooling techniques with a fully adjustable hull design.

As with other Christensen Yachts, their latest 155ft hull utilizes a unique design that joins a full-displacement bow section with a semi-displacement aft section. The combination provides a seaworthy ride and a wide range of speed/power options without sacrificing overall performance. Inside, the 155ft offers generous floor spaces, elegant owner and guest accommodations, crew's quarters for 10, and an elevator servicing all levels.

CODECASA

Codecasa Shipyard of Viareggio is getting ready to bring their first 'Open' on to the market, a 115-footer, built entirely in aluminum light alloy. The yacht will enjoy a top speed of 38 knots and a cruising speed of 34 knots, with a range of 450 miles. Accommodations are located on the lower deck with owner and VIP cabins featuring ensuites. On the main deck, the wheelhouse and the wide saloon with dining room fill the interior beam, while exterior aft areas will be designated for sunbathing or enjoying the spa pool. In the forward area of the main deck two jet skis can be stowed in a covered recess served by a crane. The 'Open,' adding to Codecasa's wide range of prestigious vessels, will be ready for presentation Spring 2004. In addition to new builds, the Codecasa Due Shipyard

has the necessary facilities and equipment to repair and refit both motor and sailing yachts in their facility which builds steel and aluminum vessels up to 115ft. The Codecasa Ugo and Codecasa Tre facilities build steel and aluminum vessels from 100ft to 300ft, specializing in luxury motoryachts.

CRESCENT CUSTOM YACHTS

Under construction at Crescent Custom Yachts is the second of two speculative projects begun at their all-new Vancouver facilities. The 125ft vessel envisioned and started by company president Jack Charles Sr. is due for delivery in August 2004, while her predecessor, the 121ft *Crescent Lady*, is cruising in South Florida after transiting from British Columbia last spring. As the first hull from Crescent's new expandable mold, *Crescent Lady* has performed flawlessly, surpassing her builder's performance expectations with top speeds approaching 23 knots (fully loaded with water, fuel, and 28 guests). In addition to the 125, the shipyard is also working on a 119ft project for a US client from the east coast. This 119ft custom vessel is anticipated to launch in early 2004, and, similar to the prior spec projects designed with a 26ft overall beam, she will feature a spacious interior from Robin Rose & Associates.

CUSTOM LINE
112

CUSTOM LINE

The Custom Line 112 is once again a harmonious blend of speed, comfort, elegance, and performance, this time from the joint efforts of the CRN Engineering Division and Zuccon International Project. In true Custom Line fashion, the interiors of this motoryacht are comprised of only the finest leathers and sought-after woods, with contrasting tones in each material meticulously complementing the other. Attention to detail and total functionality overall define the vessel, with each yacht truly unique, encompassing the contributions of their individual owners. Several arrangements are available on the 112, from main deck or lower deck master suites, double master suites, a VIP stateroom and two large living area suites, to a five-stateroom configuration. As a Ferretti Group Company, owners of Custom Line vessels can rest assured that with the Ferretti Group USA Product Manager System, someone with extensive knowledge of the vessel is on call day and night.

DELTA MARINE

Delta's deliveries this year include the 124ft semi-displacement motoryacht *Defiant* and the 126ft expedition yacht, *Andrea*. *Andrea* is the first composite megayacht in North America to be both Lloyd's and MCA classed. In addition to the usual regulation stability standards, she also meets the "international severe wind and roll criterion," a classification bestowed on few yachts. *Andrea* also features Michael Kirschstein interiors, contemporary and elegant with extensive use of glass, light veneers, and Art Deco appointments. Current projects under construction include 163ft and 164ft full displacement composite motoryachts, designed and engineered by the in-house Delta Design Group. In addition, they are working on several projects over 200ft with steel hulls and composite superstructures. Outside the realm of new builds, Delta continues to expand its refit and repair capabilities with the addition of a new 400-ton Marine Travelift.

DERECKTOR SHIPYARDS

Derecktor Shipyards continues the tradition of creating highly custom sailing and motoryachts, as begun 55 years ago by founder Bob Derecktor. Maintaining a team of talented craftsmen skilled in all areas of shipbuilding—including aluminum, wood, steel, and fiberglass—is the key to the Derecktor reputation for quality. Current projects include a 150ft Frers designed sailing yacht and two 235ft high speed passenger ferries. The recent addition of a 600 metric ton Travelift (the largest in North America) greatly complements the yard's service and new construction capabilities. Derecktor locations include Ft. Lauderdale, FL, Mamaroneck, NY, and Bridgeport, CT.

DERECKTOR
SHIPYARDS
150ft Frers

DEVONPORT

Devonport specializes in the build, conversion, and restoration of large yachts, with a primary focus on constructing megayachts of the highest caliber. Several projects underway for the yard include a 250ft displacement motoryacht, as well as a 164ft high speed vessel. The 250ft project incorporates five decks, with accommodations for an owner plus 14 guests, and is capable of cruising worldwide. She is built to full MCA standards for chartering up to 12 guests, with a crew of twenty and four staff. The interior includes a spectacular glass main stair rising through four decks to a fully-fitted gymnasium and spa. A helicopter deck is capable of receiving a wide range of helicopters, and a large enclosed garage aft in the hull can handle the docking of a 43ft tender. The yacht also carries two 25ft tenders, a separate rescue boat, and a three ton crane to stow a mini-submarine.

FALCON YACHTS

The next step for the Falcon range will be a new 114-footer, due for delivery early this year. She will embody the essence of all the successful Falcon Yachts that have been delivered over the past twenty years. Entirely in reinforced fiberglass, she will exhibit the careful craftsmanship of their first wooden vessels, accented with fine finishing and detailing and the most sophisticated technology. The Falcon 114ft features a spacious and comfortable interior utilizing her full-beam whenever possible, and providing a versatile environment for which to personalize the vessel. The raised pilothouse is also of considerable size, offering a convenient work space combined with the finest in navigation instrumentation. An ample cockpit, vast flybridge, and comfortable forward sun bathing area allows for full enjoyment of the outdoors onboard.

FEADSHIP
Blue Moon

FEADSHIP

Combining the talents and traditions of the De Vries and Royal Van Lent Shipyards with the design prowess of De Voogt Naval Architects, Feadship remains a benchmark for custom-built motoryachts. Recently launched vessels in contrasting styles are: the largest Feadship launched to date, *Wedge Too*; the first expedition-type Feadship, *Andiamo*; and the extraordinary new *Katrion* and *Dream*. Due for delivery in the summer of 2005 from Feadship is the new *Blue Moon* at 198ft, replacing the owner's previous 165ft vessel of the same name. The latter, the largest aluminum Feadship built to date, is being replaced with a design offering more space and volume within the same concept, and a steel hull—as a shallow draft is no

longer a priority. While the owner relishes the prospect of being intimately involved once again with another new build, he also wishes to push the envelope in terms of form and function and technical perfection. To achieve this the triumvirate responsible for his first vessel has been reassembled, including Royal Van Lent, De Voogt Naval Architects, and designer Donald Starkey. A central glass elevator surrounded by a floating staircase will be an aesthetic highlight, as well as one of the various practical changes based on the owner's past experiences and possible future needs.

FIPA GROUP

Under the mark of Maiora, the Fipa Group features a product range that

includes fiberglass flybridge motoryachts from 65 to 125ft. However, recently the group has received a very important commission for a motoryacht of 144ft, constructed of stainless-steel and aluminum and set to be launched in 2005. In addition to the Maiora line, Fipa is also in control of AB Yachts, a line that emphasizes speed and technology. With AB, the shipyard made its debut in the field of open motoryachts, particularly water-jet vessels that can achieve speeds of 55 knots. At present, models are available from 57ft to 88ft, with the latter their latest construction endeavor. Fipa Group now boast 10 factories and 400 employees dedicated to forming structural and refined works of art from simple origins, just as the company itself was built.

FEADSHIP
Wedge Too

HARGRAVE

Bringing the best of past and present together for the future, Hargrave Custom Yachts is proud to deliver their 81ft enclosed bridge motoryacht, embracing technology without succumbing to it. As everything is made-to-order these days, CEO Mike Joyce felt production yachts should be the same. The new 81ft has taken the notion of custom design to new heights by being one of the first, and certainly one of the finest, handicap-accessible yachts conceived. With a brief that specified a solid, spacious, well-planned, and comfortable yacht, Hargrave has created a lovely and practical vessel without sacrificing aesthetic concerns. Her overall effect is subtle and delightful all at once, and, most importantly, a realization of her owner's dream.

HEESEN YACHTS

Built in accordance with the latest nautical thinking, equipped with state-of-the-art control, navigation and communications technology, fitted with powerful engines, and furnished with every conceivable luxury, each Heesen Yacht gives new meaning to the concept of custom-built. No two Heesen Yachts are alike, each ship being the realization of an owner's ideas and wishes, a challenge which keeps the yard continually in-tune and excited. Three recent launches from Heesen include *Sweet Doll*, a 151ft semi-displacement motoryacht distinctive in her hull color of pearl gloss lacquer. She features a colorful contemporary interior with natural accents of leather and wood veneers. Other deliveries are the 100ft *Amigo*, designed especially by Pieter Beeldsnijder for northern European waters and climates and for operation without a crew, and *Sorted H*, a MCA compliant 144ft megayacht, with interior by Terence Disdale.

HELIYACHTS
Senses Refit

HELIYACHTS

Increasing in number, refit projects of all kinds have been going on at Heliyachts this year. Recently finished was the conversion of the 60ft motoryacht *Camenga*, completely gutted leaving only the engine and hull. After renewing her shell plates and tanks, the yard installed new electrical systems, pipes, air-conditioning, water makers, and a new interior. Also refit was the 69ft John Alden schooner *Etesian*, that spent her winter in Croatia receiving full paint and varnish work inside and out, new electrical systems, a new engine room, and new rigging. An increasing number of large yachts visited the yard as well for a variety of repairs, of note was the 193ft *Senses* which received technical support while at Heliyachts. Bolstering new construction for the builders is the recent signing for a 193ft motoryacht designed by Studio Starkel in Trieste, Italy. The hull and superstructure are of steel and in accordance with Bureau Veritas, her interior will be completed in-house.

HODGDON YACHTS

Scheherazade, a Bruce King designed ketch with interior by Andrew Winch is the most technologically advanced vessel this yard has ever built, and at 154ft she is the largest sailboat currently under construction in the United States. Her bow and low freeboard are classic King trademarks, though delicately contrasted by a reverse transom and low-slung pilothouse—a reflection of the modern technology that is at the heart of this vessel. Her contemporary interior features fiddleback sycamore and black walnut, though hidden beneath the beautifully hand-crafted furniture and walnut soles is the latest in modern equipment. The integrated bridge system allows captive winches to handle the powerful rigging with the touch of a button, and similarly the anchors, passarelle, and boarding stairs are all deployed by a touch screen interface. Navigation, climate control, entertainment and other vessel systems are also integrated and controlled by 17 touch screens placed throughout the yacht.

HOLLAND JACHTBOUW

Dutch builder Holland Jachtbouw has seen a busy season this past year with several exciting launches, new builds, and refits underway. The 152ft *Windrose*, designed by Gerard Dijkstra was launched in the beginning of the year, debuting gloriously at Antigua Classic Race Week and breaking the 97 year old transatlantic record by more than 17 hours (completing the crossing in just 11 days, 10 hours, 25 minutes, and 10 seconds). Other launches include the 106ft plumb-bowed classic cutter, *Christoffel's Lighthouse*, also designed by Dijkstra and equipped for arctic sailing with a reinforced hull for ice and extra watertight compartments for safety; and the 116ft pilothouse sloop *Whisper* with hull lines and profile by Ted Fontaine, featuring a very detailed and refined interior from Andrew Winch. A special project for Holland Jachtbouw has been their first motoryacht ever, the 105ft Bill Langan designed *Cassiopeia*. A semi-displacement fast cruiser with top speed of 27 knots, *Cassiopeia* is a traditionally styled vessel with classic lines.

HODGDON YACHTS
Scheherazade

HORIZON

New from Horizon is the 82ft cockpit motoryacht *5 Shining Stars*, a stretched version of the builder's 76-footer. The addition of a full cockpit at water level greatly improves the functionality of the yacht, providing easy access to and from the tender, into the water for swimming, and even for fishing. At the request of the client not only was the hull stretched six feet in length, but the beam was widened to 20ft rather than 19ft. In turn, a one foot difference has created a geometrically larger yacht, well worth the investment. The yacht still features wide side decks and the basic John Lindblom hull design, but such areas as the saloon can now accommodate a greater variety of furniture and entertaining. The interior is finished in a warm red makoré with high-gloss finish, and burled accents are used throughout. With a surprising six stateroom layout, and overall inflated design, Horizon has certainly risen to the occasion, in this case the occasion being customer satisfaction.

INACE

Located in Fortaleza, Brazil, Inace has been building military, commercial and pleasure vessels since 1969. In 1984 the company began their motor-yacht division and since have constructed more than sixteen yachts ranging from 66 to 100 feet. Currently

INACE
Zembra

Inace is focusing energies on their new line of Trawler Explorer vessels—the Forward House 85 and all-aluminum Bucaneiro 60, which are gaining popularity worldwide as tough steel and aluminum expedition yachts with cleverly designed interiors. As testament to the builder's quality and performance, a fourth Explorer series vessel is already under construction (the 90ft *Zembra*), following the recent delivery of the 83ft *Amarellla*, the third Explorer built by Inace. All have been designed by Michael Kirschstein, keeping the mantra of maximum space in a medium-sized yacht in mind.

INSIGNIA YACHTS

Greek shipbuilders Insignia Yachts is almost ready to deliver the new *Insignia*, an impressive 183ft vessel

in steel and aluminum that has recently undergone complete exterior and interior restyling. With painstaking attention to detail, the interior has been completely redesigned, including a vast and open main saloon in honey-brown Tanganyika wood and rich upholstered wall panels. A stylish yet modern bar is also finished in wood and Portoro marble, while the dining room comfortably accommodates 14. Visually separating the main saloon and dining area is a freestanding ornamental stairway accessing more casual entertaining areas on the upper deck. New to the field, Insignia Yachts' latest delivery (featuring the styling of Luiz de Basto Designs) should certainly leave its mark.

INSIGNIA YACHTS
183ft *Insignia*

IZAR
147ft Tri-deck
Motoryacht

IZAR

Spanish shipbuilder Izar is delighted to be building their third megayacht since the construction and launch of the Royal Yacht *Fortuna*. This 147ft motoryacht is larger than her two predecessors and can accommodate ten guests and nine crew in her steel hull and aluminum superstructure. The interior, designed by French architect Jean Michel Wilmotte, reflects state-of-the-art styling and construction throughout the luxury vessel. Atop the superstructure is an ample flybridge, arranged to provide three different yet interconnected living spaces: a spa pool forward, dining area in the center, and a sunbathing area aft. The yacht will be classified by Lloyd's and will fulfill MCA standards, contributing to Izar's stature as a builder of fine megayachts.

JONGERT

With their new shipyard in Waterpark Wieringermeer complete, technology and innovation will form the basis of this 21st Century facility, enabling Jongert to extend capacity and to accommodate the ever-increasing demand for larger yachts, as well as the constant onslaught of refit projects. As one of the largest yards in the world to build and market megayachts under a single brand name, Jongert offers three choices: traditional, modern, or custom-built. Unique and individually created for each owner, their yacht-building skills can be shaped into any type of yacht. Recently the yard launched a Jongert 3200M and a Jongert 40T. Four yachts are presently under construction including a custom-built Jongert 45, a Jongert 2700 and 2900M and a traditional Jongert 40T. Three more are confirmed for delivery in the next two years. Full steam ahead, the yard is looking forward to their 50th Jubilee at the turn of the year, with projects in 2004 inspiring confidence all around.

KAISERWERFT

KaiserWerft is a custom builder of high quality yachts ranging from 100 to 197ft, as well as the builder of the BARON semi-custom line of 103ft GRP-construction vessels. Their facilities in Bavaria have been building custom yachts for 11 years and currently employ 80 skilled craftsmen, giving them the ability to create most projects in-house. This past year has seen the launch of three BARON yachts, with orders already filling up for the coming year. Plans are also underway for a custom 125-footer set for delivery in 2005.

LAZZARA

This past year has marked the introduction of several new products from Lazzara Yachts, a company that builds a somewhat limited number of personalized yachts each year. The Lazzara 106 is currently the largest yacht the builder offers to the megayacht market, although the 80 C has gained popularity with its full-beam 100sqft cockpit completely outfitted for fishing and diving. The E, or Euro, class ranges in size from 68 to 106ft and features a 'European' styled open bridge and swept back radar arch. The quickest of the E class is the 80 E, equipped with twin Caterpillar 1550hp engines and a top speed of 30 knots. 2004 will welcome the debut of several larger yachts from Lazzara, including two in the 120ft to 160ft range.

LAZZARA
80 E

LÜRSSEN
Phoenix

LÜRSSEN

A complete facility shipbuilder located in Germany, Lürssen has been building high-quality custom megayachts and other specialized vessels for over 125 years. The combination of constant innovation, superior quality work, discretion, and close interaction with the client are highly valued amongst their customers. At four facilities in northern Germany, Lürssen currently has nine new-builds of 177ft and upwards underway. *Phoenix*, due for delivery in April, will feature a revolutionary Andrew Winch design. Special attention has been given to the master suite on this 200ft vessel, including a duplex arrangement running over two decks and 1,450 square feet. A stateroom will occupy the main deck, with a study above, whilst anticipation of this remarkable design will occupy our curiosities.

LYMAN-MORSE

This year's star launch at Lyman-Morse was the 85ft elaborate classic motor-yacht *Acadia*, custom designed by Ward Setzer as the perfect live-aboard vessel, featuring every possible amenity. The attention to details, joiner work, and

thoughtful design make this project one of their most exquisite to date. In addition, Lyman-Morse is also launching a 30ft jet boat and a custom designed Westmac 50. Now under construction is an 80ft version of the popular Ward Setzer series designed exclusively for Lyman-Morse. The new design will be 6.5ft longer and 1.5ft wider than *Magpie*, the first in the series launched in 2001. On the sailing side, Hull #1 of the Sparkman & Stephens designed new series of Seguin 52s will start construction with an aft classic cockpit version. The yard has also completed a full-scale mockup of the newly

designed Seguin 58 series as well, which features a pilothouse version.

NAVITAS

Navitas is the exclusive dealer and distributor for Posillipo Yachts, a luxurious line of custom-built vessels by well-known Italian boat manufacturer Rizzardi. As true masterpieces of art and technology, the Posillipo line has gained great attention in the megayacht marketplace. A wide array of sizes and styles can be built to order and shipped to the US after completion.

NORDLUND

The sounds of progress are ever present at the Nordlund Boat Company, with three new boats under construction. Launching this fall will be *Phantasma*, a 94ft vessel designed by Edwin Monk of Nolan Marine Design, with interior by Nordlund. With two Detroit/MTU 12V2000 engines, her top speed will be 23 knots. Also under construction is the second *Southern Way*, a 114ft new and improved version by the same owner who built the first *Southern Way*. The third vessel is yet to be named, but measures 110ft. Recent past launches include the 114ft *Alexa C²*, the largest boat to be built by Nordlund to date. She too was designed by Ed Monk, with the engineering and drawing package provided by Nolan Marine Design.

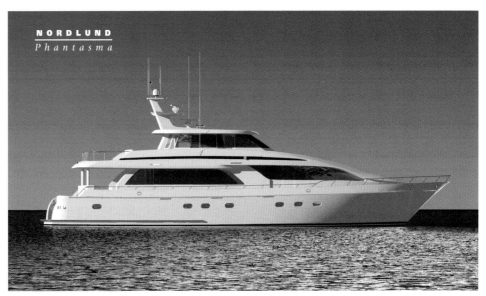

NORDLUND
Phantasma

NORTHERN MARINE

Premium builder of Expedition Trawlers and motoryachts, Northern Marine will see another round of custom yachts delivered before the end of 2004. With five Trawler yachts delivered by the end of last year (bringing the total delivered to 20) and three larger projects scheduled this year, the yard is certainly in full swing. Extremely heavy-duty components and systems have proven the worldwide circumnavigation and sea keeping capabilities of all Northern Marine's Trawlers, which range in size from 57ft to 84ft. The use of exotic woods, etched granite, soft leathers, and quality fabrics characterize the interiors of these sturdy vessels, assuring the owner safety and elegance. With gaining popularity in the Trawler market, Northern Marine has introduced another Expedition model of 105ft to accommodate every type of client. Custom vessels such as the 127ft tri-deck *Magic* and 150ft world-class Expedition Trawler *Lai Fail* are also available from Northern.

NORTH STAR YACHTS

North Star Yachts recently launched the North Star 105, the latest in a series of tank-tested designs by Jack Sarin. With a 24ft beam, innovative main deck arrangement, and third level sky lounge, the vessel offers the accommodations and comfort of a much larger yacht. The 'eclectic contemporary' Sylvia Bolton interior includes four staterooms below, accessed by a central foyer, with additional berthing for either crew or family aft. The cockpit provides safety and comfort for various water sports and activities, as well as ease of boarding for tender and personal watercraft use. Crowning the tri-deck arrangement is a capacious flybridge that offers the utmost in outdoor cruising. The 105ft tri-deck will be the seventh launch from North Star Yachts in less than five years, and with no signs of slowing down they will soon be launching a 100ft motoryacht this year, as well as starting a new series of raised pilothouse models of 100 and 110 feet.

PACIFIC MARINER

Pacific Mariner is widely acknowledged for their premier owner-operated motoryachts, most notably the Pacific Mariner 65. The new 65 Diamond edition boasts all the attributes of the original, plus an even more extensive list of standard features. More than 35 of these vessels have been built, as promising testimony to the company's newest flagship, the Pacific Mariner 85. The 85 embodies a new level of comfort and convenience, with the galley placed at pilothouse level, so captain, chef, and guests can enjoy cruising together. Four staterooms accommodate eight guests in this William Garden designed hull, while twin 1500hp MTU diesels propel the vessel to a top speed of 30 knots, with cruising range in the mid-20s.

PACIFIC MARINER

PHILBROOK'S

Philbrook's Boatyard in British Columbia has recently built and launched *Chinook Post*, a new 65ft aluminum express cruiser based on the Canadian Fisheries Patrol A Post Class hull series. Originally designed over 30 years ago by William Garden, the lines were re-drawn by Greg Marshall to suit the vessel's patrol-like appearance and to incorporate functionality, elegance and comfort in the overall design. The yacht has been built to Lloyd's Special Service Class Rules and is powered by two Detroit Diesel Series 60 engines, giving her a top speed of 24 knots and cruising speed of 20 knots. Furthermore, *Chinook Post* will have a range of over 1,000 nautical miles at 18 knots, allowing her owner to journey non-stop from Southern Vancouver Island to Alaska.

RIVOLTA MARINE

Rivolta Marine is part of a long European legacy of designing and building automobiles and yachts that combine tradition with innovation. Headquartered in Sarasota, Florida, Rivolta has created a strong market presence in both the sail and power market. Their flagship sailboat is the Rivolta 90, created to fill a void in the maxi sailboat market, while keeping in mind the most important key for creative yacht design: simplicity. Easy to sail and maintain no matter what the conditions may be, the Rivolta 90's retractable keel can enter ports with just six feet of water. Though fast and light, she is designed for the rigors of blue-water sailing. The new PT Runner also breaks ground in design and function. Available in either waterjet or propeller versions and easily towed, the PT Runner makes an ideal tender or secondary yacht. Featuring speeds of 40 knots and a draft of just 18in, this 38ft center console/express can deliver even the most discerning yacht owner and guests to the dock or beach in true European-yacht style.

PHILBROOK'S
Chinook Post

RIVOLTA MARINE
Rivolta 90

RMK MARINE
1 2 0 f t   T r a w l e r

RMK MARINE

RMK Marine has recently received an order for the construction of a 120ft Trawler Yacht, due for delivery in 2005. The vessel incorporates the full design and engineering of Vripack Yachting International, interior by R. Tansu-Troy, and is being constructed with a steel hull and aluminum flybridge. She is powered by a pair of Caterpillar 3406E's, 600hp each to achieve a maximum speed of 13 knots, with cruising speed at 10 knots for a range of 4,000 miles. Special custom features include a full-beam owner's cabin on the main deck with four full height windows to port and starboard, mahogany and lacquered panels throughout the interior, and boat deck accommodating four tenders and leisure equipment which also transforms for entertaining when the vessels are launched. Although the yacht will be built for a private owner, she is designed and engineered in compliance with MCA rules.

ROYAL DENSHIP

New from Royal Denship is a 135ft trideck, an innovative world cruiser built using tried-and-true shipbuilding techniques, as well as cutting-edge technology. The interior was designed by François Zuretti and features a blend of Danish crafted interior joinery with custom Italian furniture by Provasi in Milan and accents of the finest Italian marble. Her sophisticated propulsion system incorporates Schottel drives, powered by Caterpillar diesels, that rotate 360 degrees for maximum maneuverability. While increasing efficiency compared to conventional shaft

ROYAL HUISMAN
Antares

and propeller systems, they do not effect the 8ft draft of the vessel. Royal Denship, together with Lantic Systems, has also created a yacht management and entertainment system soon to be the envy of the industry. The ship's management system is class approved and provides a detailed display of every significant system on the vessel. The entertainment system allows each flat screen monitor to access movies, television, music, as well as the ship's monitoring system and navigation electronics.

ROYAL HUISMAN

Several awe-inspiring projects are underway at Royal Huisman Shipyards, a builder which has gained a reputation for combining innovative engineering principles

with traditional Dutch craftsmanship. The 131ft Bruce King-designed classic cutter *Maria Cattiva* debuted with excellent turns of speed under sail and a whisper quiet interior while under power. Rigged as a classic three-masted schooner, the 298ft *Athena* continues to take shape. The massive sailing vessel combines the naval architecture of Gerard Dijkstra and the interior and exterior styling of Pieter Beeldsnijder. Initial design work has also been completed for the 131ft ketch *Antares*, a project that blends an exterior by Bill Dixon with an interior by the equally talented Dick Young design team. While in most recent news, the yard has signed a contract to build a stately 118ft motoryacht designed by Tony Castro, the Dick Young interior will be finished in paneled mahogany.

SAN JUAN

Following the SanJuan 38, the second boat in San Juan Composites' fast-cruising motoryacht series is the similarly Downeast-style SanJuan 48. Working with Gregory C. Marshall Naval Architects, the company has combined the appeal of the traditional lobster boat with cutting-edge design. Quality engineering and resin-infused Kevlar composite construction create a comfortable, dry-riding boat with excellent sea-keeping. No effort has been spared in the detail, and the 48 has an impressive standard inventory that includes bow and stern thrusters and a transom garage for a tender. Top speeds approach 40 knots. Currently the builder is working on a SanJuan 30, adding yet another option to this already classic line of runabouts.

SOVEREIGN YACHTS

Sovereign Yachts is a first-class, award-winning, megayacht builder offering clients a global construction presence. The company has facilities in Auckland, New Zealand as well as in Vancouver, Canada. Recently their New Zealand facility delivered an ABS-classed, MCA-compliant 138ft motoryacht to an American client on the east coast. Both Sovereign's facilities offer on-site deep water launching and state-of-the-art capabilities.

Each has 60,000sqft of floor space, with additional 15,000sqft mezzanine levels. New to the yacht line is a Sportfish fleet designed by the renown naval architects of Warwick Yacht Design. Two 103 sportfish yachts are scheduled for launch in the coming years. With the combined talents of both Canadian and New Zealand operations, Sovereign brings an unparalleled perspective to every yacht's design, innovation, performance, and resplendent luxury.

TRINITY YACHTS

Trinity Yachts is completing work on the 155ft tri-deck motoryacht *White Star*. Drawing on past experience, Trinity has incorporated a number of advanced design elements into this yacht, taking it to a new level. The yacht will be capable of 22 knots, and will cruise around 18 knots, with a 7ft shallow draft that will allow her access to many ports uncommon for a yacht of this size. The notable owner's suite, located on the pilothouse deck, is complete with his-and-hers ensuite baths that include a whirlpool tub and large marble shower, cedar-lined closets, and a private aft deck with a spa pool. An open main saloon and dining area allows for a casual or formal atmosphere, with an expansive aft deck equipped with a bar and grill for dining *al fresco*.

TRINITY
White Star

VENTURE YACHTS

In response to the growing demand for technically advanced fast luxury powercats, New Zealand-based Venture Yachts is continuing to develop its range of European styled vessels. A new 65ft Sportfisher is being added to the range to join the ultimate 80ft Sportfisher. The 80ft is a long range warrior able to travel quickly and safely in any sea. With every conceivable amenity onboard, she is happily self-sufficient for long periods in the most remote locations. Superyacht Society winner Craig Loomes is responsible for her naval architecture. Specific design features include a fully air-conditioned enclosed flybridge with bar and entertainment area, as well as an all-business aft cockpit with two fighting chairs, fridge/freezer, commercial icemaker, live bait tanks, and an oversized barbecue. Clearly the 65ft and 80ft Venture Yachts Sportfishers are destined to take sportfishing to a new level.

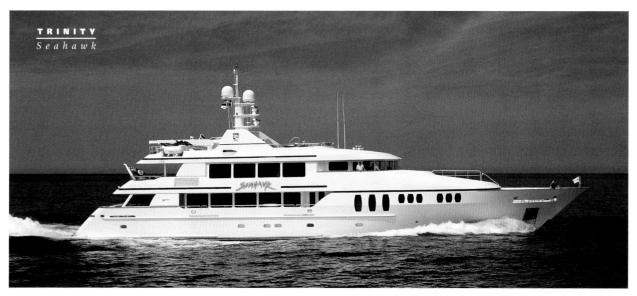
TRINITY
Seahawk

WALLY

In this past season Wally has completed an array of beautifully designed boats in all shapes and sizes. The breakthrough 118ft Wally Power met expectations of speed and sea-worthiness, combined with a unique styling of the hull, deck, and interior. In the sailing yacht genre, the Wally 98 designed by Javier Soto Acebal evolved as a sleek cruising sloop with maxi-racer performance, while the Wally 94 designed by German Frers combines the builder's intrinsic style with long distance cruising and ocean passage capabilities. The Wally 80 flush-deck version is the first of a new semi-cus-tom line in this range, lines are at the hand of Farr Yacht Design–resulting in a performance cruiser with large interior volumes. In addition to featuring a central skylight extending from the companionway to the mast base, the 80ft flush-deck is offered in 16 different combinations. Production of the WallyTender is an equally successful endeavor for the builder, twelve were delivered in 2003 with a present delivery schedule of one every month.

WEST BAY SONSHIP YACHTS

The largest yacht built to date by the Canadian builder is the SonShip 107, debuting this coming year along with the SonShip 68 and SonShip 1, a 78-footer originally built for the yard's founders. Currently in design and under construction at their yard in British Columbia are three 61ft vessels, three 72ft vessels, and one 86ft custom yacht with an enclosed climate controlled aft deck, custom-joinery, and master suite with attached nursery. Also underway is *Alicia*, an 89ft custom yacht with an enclosed sky lounge, formal dining, and a fishing cockpit. Completion of a new 35,000sqft building facility will increase the yard's production capacity by 15 percent, allowing them to enter the new year well-equipped for growing demand.

WESTPORT YACHTS

The Westport fleet of yachts offers eloquent testimony to the power of innovative design and advanced composite technology, encompassing three models: the Westport 130 tri-deck motoryacht, the Westport 112 raised-pilothouse motoryacht, and the Westport 98, also a raised-pilothouse. On the way is the Westport 164 tri-deck, destined to lead the fleet not only in size, but also in design and technology. As one of North America's largest builders of composite yachts, they have built more than fifty vessels. The builder offers the advantages of lightweight strength for greater efficiency and longer cruising range, superior thermal and acoustic insulation, and low maintenance for reduced operating costs. Their yachts are built with precision tooling developed by the industry's most respected naval architects and marine engineers, with premier components selected for all systems. MTU engines are matched to each hull for exceptional performance and a premium electronics package includes Westport's proprietary Vessel Information and Control System for reliable monitoring and operation of the yacht's functions.

WESTPORT

www.andrew-winch-designs.co.uk

The Old Fire Station, 123 Mortlake High Street, London SW14 8SN, Telephone: +44 (0) 20 8392 8400, Fax: +44 (0) 20 8392 8401, Email: info@andrew-winch-designs.co.uk

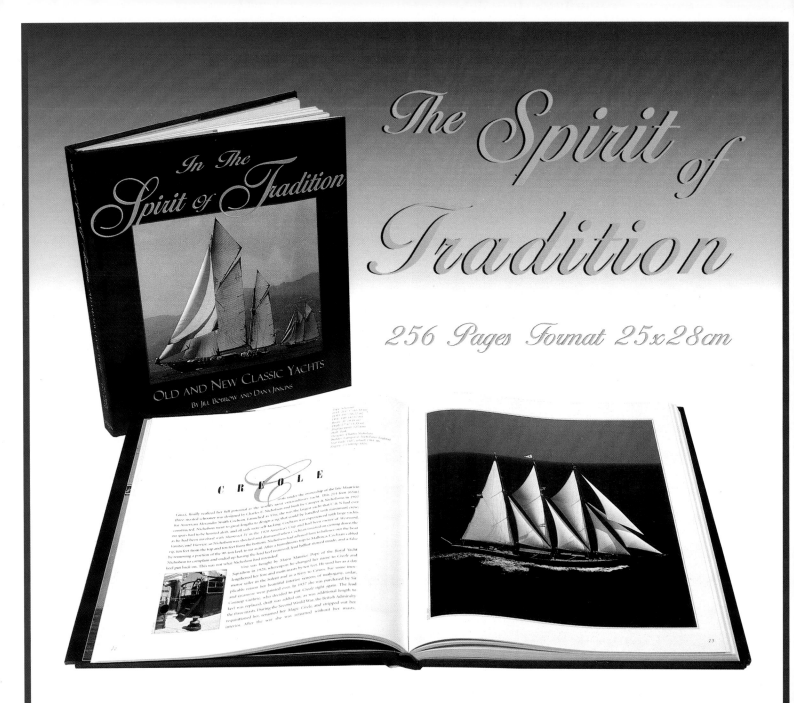

The Spirit of Tradition

256 Pages Format 25x28cm

This lush, beautiful volume by the authors of *Classic Yacht Interiors* and *The World's Most Extraordinary Yachts*, is the most complete and up-to-date book on classic yachts ever produced. Featured are 48 sailing vessels and motor yachts depicted with hundreds of colour photographs (both exterior and interior), line drawings, and anecdotal histories. World-famous vintage yachts as well as "new classics" are all included.

Additionally, there are essays by classic yacht professionals such as Bruce King, John Munford and Duncan Walker, who are involved in designing, preserving and restoring traditional boats. Classic Yacht Regattas: Monaco Classic Week, The Nioulargue, Cannes Régates Royales, Antigua Classic Yacht Regatta, and the New England Wooden Boat Series are some of the venues for the exciting photography in this book.

The following yachts are featured in the book:

Adela • Agneta • Alejandra • Altair • Alzavola • Arawak • Avel • Bolero • Borkumriff III • Classique • Creole • Endeavour • Henry Morgan • Hetairos • Kathleen • Kathryn B. • Kentra • La Cle De Sol • Land's End • Lelantina • MacNab • Magic Carpet • Mariette • Miss Asia • Neith • Pauline • Principia • Puritan • Radiance • Shamrock V • Signe • Sintra • So Fong • Stephen Taber • Thendara • Ticonderoga • Tuiga • Vela • Violet • When and If • Whitehawk • Windigo • Zaca • Zaca a te Moana • Zanna • Zapala.

Motor Yacht Kiss the Sky

Chesler Photography

PATRICK ★ KNOWLES
DESIGNS

YACHT • AIRCRAFT • SPECIALISTS

2030 Northeast 18th Street • Fort Lauderdale, Florida 33305
954-832-0108 • Fax: 954-537-7766
WWW.PATRICKKNOWLESDESIGNS.COM
ID. No. - 0003607, ASID, NCIDQ

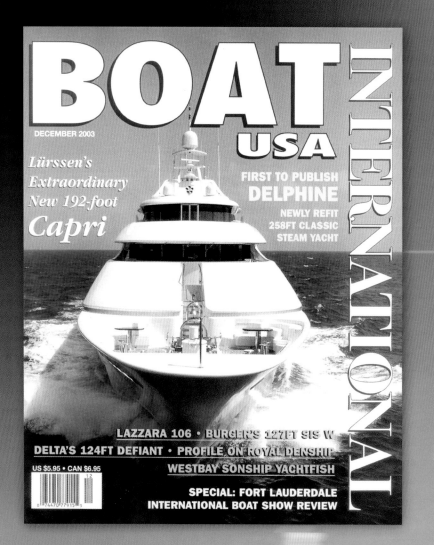

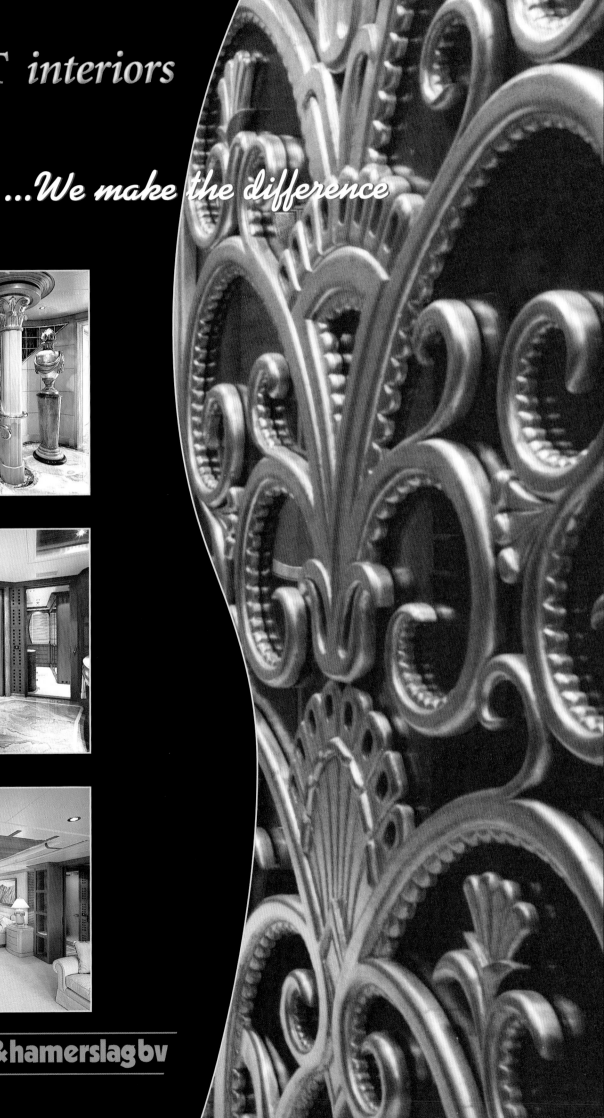

Terence Disdale Design

Creators of distinguished yachts

Sussurro

Mipos (140m), Pelorus (115m), Tatoosh (92m), Montkaj (75m), Boadicea (70.5m), Awal (65m), Il Vagabondo (64m), Pegasus IV (63m), Cacique (57m), Paris (56m), Varmar Ve (55m), Sea Sedan (55m), Wedge One (53m), Rio Rita (52m), Leocrie III (52m), Destiny (52m), Tigre D'Or (52m), Toinie (52m), Amevi (52m), Tommy (50m), Sahab IV (50m), Queen M (50m), Sussurro (50m), Thunder Gulch (50m), Tigre D'Os (50m), Kermit (50m), Alexandra K (50m), Tricat (47m), Rahal (46.5m), Maupiti (46m), Rima (45m), Joalmi (45m), Princess Magna (45m), Amorazur (45m), Sea Jewel (44m), Shenandoah (43m), Paraffin (43m), Sorted (43m), Faribana (42m), Lady Suffolk(42m), Matanthar (42m), Sea Sedan (42m), Sahab III (39m), Libra Star (39m), Taramber (36m), Azimut 118 (36m), Yankee Too (35m), Kiring (34m), Quest (32m), Azimut 96 (30m), Azimut 100 (30m), La Masquerade (30m), Vagrant (28m), Alize (28m)

31 The Green, Richmond, Surrey TW9 1LX
Telephone: +44 (0) 20 8940 1452 Fax: +44 (0) 20 8940 5964
E-mail: terencedisdale@terencedisdale.co.uk

The Luxury Yacht Market

Designers

The Luxury Yacht Market

Designers

AC.T STUDIO
Jasmin

AC.T STUDIO

The Turkish-based AC.T Studio was established in 1999 in response to a local demand for interior design work. Since then Eva Cadio and Rima Abi Chahine have been working closely (with technical support from French Industrial designers Pascal Pommier and Didier Duffuler) to provide a full range of services from initial interior design to decoration and accessories. Of recent AC.T is celebrating the launch of *Jasmin*, a 121ft motoryacht with styling by Vripack. Her interior is a classical combination of sipo wood and brass, with all fabrics in silk. The studio also completed the interior styling and design for the 128ft sailing yacht *MuMu*, launched in the summer of 2003, with a complex blend of pearwood, aluminum, and leather—accented by linen and silk furnishings to create a light and modern feel.

JOHN G. ALDEN NAVAL ARCHITECTS

After the recent successful delivery of the 164ft traditional schooner *Borkumriff IV* from the Royal Huisman Shipyard, John G. Alden Naval Architects is working on another traditionally styled schooner

project. *Arbella* is 114ft on deck, with a waterline length of 85ft. Her design brief called for a graceful looking, efficient, aft cockpit, two-masted schooner set up for easy handling and minimum upkeep. For her interior volumes, the general arrangement called for below deck access to the aft cockpit from the owner's cabin, two double cabins, and a raised saloon and crew accommodations for four. All working sails are furling, with in-boom furling for the main and fore sail and in-mast furling for the topsail. Hydraulically powered concealed captive reel winches and deck mounted drum winches control the running rigging. High maintenance bright work is also a fixture on deck, applied sparsely to enhance the traditional look. In addition to *Arbella*, the firm is completing work on two other schooner projects.

JOHN G. ALDEN
NAVAL ARCHITECTS
114ft *Arbella*

JOSEPH ARTESE DESIGN
Davidson Refit

ALAN ANDREWS YACHT DESIGN, INC

Combining high-performance with state-of-the-art engineering, Alan Andrews Yacht Design creates superior sailing vessels, both racing and cruising. Andrews racing designs have won throughout the world at many prestigious events including Key West Race Week and the Kenwood Cup in Hawaii, while his Maxis and Turbo-sleds have set records or secured first to finish honors in the Transpac, both Mackinacs, and a host of other notable races. The same sailing performance is also bred into Andrews performance cruisers, along with the necessary addition of comfort. Their performance cruisers have traveled around the globe and satisfied clients and their passengers with comfort and speed. Launched in 2003 from Alan Andrews was *Alchemy*, after a quick ten month design and build schedule achieving the client's goal of a lightning-quick racer with comfortable interior and clean lines. Already this Andrews 77 has finished first in five of six races. Next off the boards is the Andrews 80 canting keel racer, already under construction at Dencho Marine for the 2004 season.

ANITA'S INTERIORS

The second half of 2003 proved extremely busy for South Florida design team Anita's Interiors. In addition to work on an 85ft

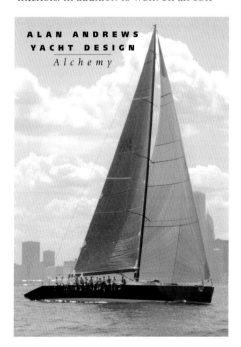

ALAN ANDREWS YACHT DESIGN
Alchemy

new build tri-deck from Passage Maker Shipyard in Portugal, the firm was also preoccupied with a major interior refit of the 130ft Oceanfast, *Sounds of the Pacific*, as well as in the final stages of the extension and interior refit of the 105ft motoryacht *Solace IV*. *Sounds of the Pacific* features a new interior arrangement plan for the saloon and dining area with new joinery in high-gloss, flush-filled, figured cherry wood. Anita's will also be responsible for the interior design of the Passage Maker Marine series of yachts from 75 to 150ft.

APOLLONIO NAVAL ARCHITECTURE

Apollonio Naval Architecture offers leading edge yacht and commercial vessel design, engineering, styling, and space planning for a wide variety of unique and advanced craft. Their licensed professional engineers are well-versed specialists in hull form, ride comfort, propulsion, structure, and noise control—familiar with most every type of vessel on the water from monohulls to hydrofoils. Apollonio's current projects include two Wavepiercer catamaran motoryachts, 55ft and 92ft; a 67ft cat cruising yacht; three series of fast passenger catamarans; several patrol boats; and a trawler yacht series. As if that wasn't sufficient, the firm is also involved with several models of production series yachts under construction at PAMA Yachts and McKinna Yachts, and is awaiting orders for a 130ft motoryacht as well as unique large trimaran motoryacht. Apollonio subjects their varied and many designs to extensive research and development to ensure a constantly praiseworthy product. Aiding in the development of the 92ft Wavepiercer and 67ft tri-deck cat motoryacht were several studies and tank-testing, eventually allowing the latter to sustain cruising speeds at 35 knots with the assistance of hydrofoil and waterjet propulsion.

ARDEO DESIGN, INC

In addition to crafting a high-tech stainless steel interior (replete with waterproof leather) for the first 40ft private

ARDEO DESIGNS
Souvenir Saloon

submarine of its kind, Ardeo Design is also busy completing several projects above water. Recent designs include a custom interior for the 'new' classic motoryacht *Souvenir*, an 87ft flush deck vessel with exterior styling and naval architecture from Tom Fexas, as well as an 'arts and crafts'-themed interior for the 80ft expedition style *Meander* from Northern Marine. Currently in production is the 130ft motoryacht *Magic*, also from Northern Marine, featuring an Ardeo interior with raised mahogany paneling and marble soles. The firm looks forward to future design work on a new series from Nordhavn of semi-production expedition style trawlers.

JOSEPH ARTESE DESIGN

Joseph Artese Design is a highly creative design office based in Seattle, Washington that has been specializing in the styling of yacht interiors and exteriors for over 20 years. Equally versed with sail or power, his custom yachts have been recognized by the International Superyacht Society and have been awarded several prestigious design awards. Two megayacht projects with which they have been involved are from Venture Pacific Marine, including the just completed interior architecture for the 178ft *Revelation*, as well as a total exterior/interior refit of a 178ft NOAA research vessel, stretched and renamed *Centurion* at 188ft. Additionally they have participated in extensive exterior styling changes to the 65ft motoryacht *Cinnabar VI*, and worked closely on San Juan Composite's new San Juan 48 flybridge.

BELINA
Primadonna

JONATHAN QUINN BARNETT, LTD

JQB Ltd, a Seattle-based yacht design firm specializing in interior and exterior design, recently completed the interior for *Octopus*, a 410ft Lürssen owned by an undisclosed client. With an aggressive schedule the mammoth project was completed in three years. The steel vessel with an ice-classed hull incorporates cutting edge entertainment systems throughout her stunning interior. Also keeping JQB hard at work is the exterior and interior design of a new 151ft expedition-style motoryacht, with an innovative design to allow the client enjoyment of Northwest sport fishing aboard a vessel designed for safety and world-class comfort in potentially hostile marine environs. Off the water JQB has been involved in such illustrious projects as the detailed renovation of an 1880s Victorian mansion for the legendary film director Francis Coppola, utilizing 3D computer modeling software to orchestrate the task.

BELINA

Well established for the construction and installation of yacht interiors, Belina Interiors continues to expand after a successful season. Completed projects include the refit of the 150ft *Life of Riley*, and major participation in the 145ft *Gran*

Finale and the 126ft *Sinbad*. Of recent they have completed the interior for the 124ft *Defiant* and cabinetry and furniture for several other large boats. Still underway is a 163ft project, with several others scheduled to begin shortly. Belina's metalwork division has continued to support various shipyards with handrails, custom hardware, furniture, and fixtures. Of particular note is the showpiece handrail of the 145ft *Primadonna*. In keeping with their full-service approach to the yacht building industry, Belina has upgraded its veneer plant, providing numerous shops with architectural panels, tabletops, and custom veneered items. Additionally, their upholstery department has been expanded to now offer custom couches and furniture, included in an already wide range of soft good items.

DONALD L. BLOUNT AND ASSOCIATES

An innovative design firm, recognized for their high-performance motoryacht designs, Donald L. Blount is currently developing two projects in excess of 165ft in length. One vessel will be capable of speeds exceeding 50 knots, while the larger of the two will achieve speeds surpassing 40 knots, with both projects utilizing a gas turbine and water jet propulsion system. Additionally, the design firm has six projects ranging from 60 to 84ft in length, all destined to break 40 knots. Well established in their designs, the firm has continuously produced successful yachts that incorporate owner's specifications and styling requirements, while achieving classification society rules and possessing superior ride qualities.

JONATHAN
QUINN BARNETT

SYLVIA BOLTON DESIGN

A busy year for Sylvia Bolton Design, the firm has completed several new build and refit projects of much acclaim. Launched in the summer of 2003 was a 105ft Northstar with a contemporary styled interior, finished in cherry, tropical brown granite, and black and olive accents. A total refit of the 92ft Stephens motoryacht *Alexis* was also completed, with interior appointments including custom hand-woven carpets and glass blown light fixtures, mahogany and woven leather finishes in the owner's suite, and a formal al fresco dining area on the former aft deck. An 85ft Le Clercq custom yacht will also feature a distinctive and modern interior from Sylvia Bolton, with an innovative layout taking full advantage of the vessel's opened interior space. Sylvia has also teamed with Ocean Alexander of Taiwan in their newest venture to produce a deluxe version of their 68-footer.

CLAUDETTE BONVILLE ASSOCIATES, INC

Using advanced computer programs, designer Claudette Bonville revolutionizes the process of interior design by allowing her clients to first 'see' or 'walk through' the interior before it begins construction. This gives the owner the important opportunity to make decisions regarding essential design elements early on in the process. With such attention to her craft, it is no surprise the firm has won several international design awards for such

BRAY YACHT DESIGN
76ft Working Yacht

vessel as *Lady Linda* (Delta Marine), *Cakewalk* (Feadship), and *Seahawk* (Trinity Yachts). Recent launches include the new 155ft *Seahawk*, again from Trinity, the 145ft *Silverfox* under construction at the NQEA yard in Australia, and the 142ft *Regency* built by Palmer Johnson. They are currently under contract to design six new-build yachts that will launch in 2004, 2005, and 2006.

BRAY YACHT DESIGN

Bray Yacht Design has delivered its first Working Yachts 76, a tough steel cruiser that reached its home port after an 8,300 mile journey through Panama to San Diego. A second of the 76ft Working Yachts series is currently underway for a Vancouver client. Each vessel is built to order on a standard hull form and machinery package. Both the interior and superstructure layout are customized based on client input and preferences. The first 76 was specifically designed for

serious fishing and included two refrigerated fish holds, a built-in live bait tank, and rod holders throughout the cockpit and along the aft deck boat rail. The second vessel called for an aft master stateroom, large exercise room and spacious main saloon—made possible by the 22ft beam. Standard features for Working Yachts include heavy-steel construction in excess of ABS requirements, a bulbous bow, fixed or fixed/active stabilizers, and full collision and watertight bulkheads. Construction has already begun for 80ft Expediton and 85ft Pilothouse versions.

PHILIPPE BRIAND YACHT DESIGN

Philippe Briand has been designing sailing yachts since 1978, with at least eight yachts over five campaigns for the America's Cup and more than 20 yachts over 70ft around the world—the most renowned being the *Mari-Cha III*. This year they have launched several cruisers including a CNB 77, CNB 95 (*Grand Bleu V*), and the 145ft racing yacht *Mari-Cha IV*. Another 130ft cruiser was launched in Turkey in the autumn. Their office has been currently working on several large sailing yachts, which includes a 115ft with Andrew Winch interior at CNB; composites in 78ft and 132ft; and a 140ft aluminum cruiser/racer. The 132 is destined to be one of the most hi-tech megayachts of her size (and one of the biggest sloops currently available), built completely out of carbon composite. In addition to these, a variety of other large megayacht projects are also in discussion.

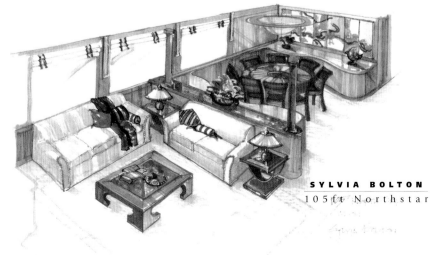

SYLVIA BOLTON
105ft Northstar

BRILLIANT BOATS

While the name Brilliant Boats may be somewhat obscure, their products are certainly cutting edge and mainstream in the megayacht market this year. Recently completed endeavors include the motoryacht *Forty Love*, a pair of all carbon fiber sailing catamarans, the Blubay 100ft and 72ft, and the interior of US Submarine's latest Seattle 1000. All projects are developed entirely in 3D, tank-tested and designed to FEA methods delivering maximum efficiency in hull forms and diverse construction packages. Current projects for Brilliant Boats comprise a 125ft Yacht Fisherman, design and engineering for the world's first underwater hotel and entertainment complex, a 50ft trimaran cruiser/racer in carbon fiber and Nomex, and a 30 knot, 100ft catamaran motoryacht.

TONY CASTRO LTD

Tony Castro continues to expand his repertoire with a new 118ft 'classic look' motoryacht for a US client, scheduled for production at the Royal Huisman Shipyard in Holland. The hull of this vessel is being pre-designed with the help of the latest CFD and Seakeeping computer tools and a full complement of conventional tank tests, while the remainder of the design is being totally developed in 3D with the help of the firm's in-house CAD packages. Simultaneously, Castro is working on a 131ft ketch, sistership to the US yacht *Islandia*, and two new 100ft sailing yachts at Jongert. The latter are quite modern, combining luxury and proven performance. Additionally at 82ft, they are working on an all-carbon fiber super-fast cruising sloop in production at CNB, in France. Still on paper are designs from 147ft to 213ft waiting to come to fruition, while the firm is now centering their work around an increasing demand for all-inclusive design packages including exterior and interior design, as well as naval architecture.

LUIZ DE BASTO DESIGNS, INC

Luiz de Basto is presently working on the interior design of a new 138ft vessel from Izar. The aluminum hull is scheduled to be launched this year. The interior is warm and comfortable with clean, elegant lines and a mix of the classic and the contemporary. Most notable is the splendid master stateroom. The entrance is through a spacious walk-in closet to a room which features dark cherrywood walls combined with exquisitely upholstered panels. A chic sitting room with suede armchairs faces the king-size bed, and floor to ceiling windows provide amazing views. An elaborate wall panel in a two-color wood weave serves as a headboard to accent the back of the bed, while sandblasted double glass doors opposite divide the room and bathroom. The bath is finished with lacquered walls, Calacata Luccioso marble counters and back splashes, and dark cherry cabinets.

LUIZ DE BASTO DESIGNS
138ft Izar

GUIDO DE GROOT DESIGN

Guido de Groot Design is ecstatic with the honor of being the main designer for both the interior and exterior of the just-delivered, first-ever Russian megayacht. The 104ft modern luxury yacht *Pallada* is the first out of a new series of yachts being built according to western standards by Moscow Shipyard. Other interesting and ambitious projects include a 288ft megayacht for an Asian client, with naval architecture by Alpha Marine in Greece. The voluminous yacht will have six decks, two of which feature 10ft high ceilings, and will be built to SOLAS regulations. Also in the works at Guido de Groot is a new series of pocket luxury motoyachts for both Mulder Shipyard and Inmarcon in Holland. Several interior projects in Italy, as well as a 115ft Dutch tugboat conversion, are also keeping the firm busy.

ROEL DE GROOT

This young design firm first achieved fame with an award-winning series of interiors for Moody sailboats. Recently relocated to the South of England, work continues at its normal frenzied pace on projects including interior design for Princess Yachts (Viking in the USA) production powerboats and the conversion of a 88ft 1955 French harbor tug. Ongoing for some time have been a variety of projects with naval architect Christian Stimson of the Isle of Wight. Their latest joint project reflects the owner's somewhat unconventional and interrogative brief: what would happen if a substantial sailing yacht was combined with the amenities of a private beach club? Short of cabanas on the boat deck, there are several beach club-like amenities including an aft deck that opens to become a pontoon for laser dinghies and windsurfers, while at the same time revealing the hot tub. So far results are exciting, as this project exposes the limits to which a sailing yacht can be pushed.

DESIGN UNLIMITED

This studio is currently working alongside Baltic Yachts in Finland and America's Cup winning Naval Architects Judel Vrolijk Design on a 150ft high performance sloop. Due for completion in 2006, this yacht will have an interior featuring a combination of finishes to lend a uniquely modern look. Also being developed is a 125ft Reichel

GUIDO DE GROOT
288-footer

ROEL DE GROOT
80ft Performance
Sloop

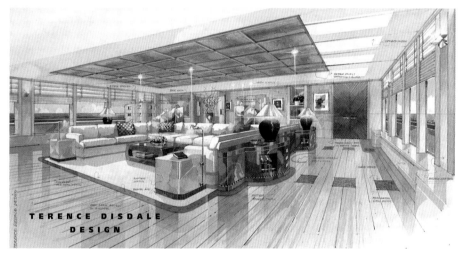

TERENCE DISDALE
DESIGN

Pugh Sloop, which will form part of a three yacht collection, the others at 100ft and 150ft. Recently launched was the Farr 115 performance cruising ketch, replete with a luxurious interior combining mahogany paneling and sumptuous soft furnishings and finishes. While in the megayacht genre, the firm recently completed a refit of the 108ft Feadship *Heavenly Daze*, which now features a stylish and relaxing contemporary interior, inherently enhancing her timeless elegance.

TERENCE DISDALE DESIGN

Terence Disdale Design delivered five yachts in the first six months of 2003 alone, keeping the talented design team finely tuned for a myriad of upcoming projects. Delivered amongst the five were the 377ft *Pelorus* from Lürssen with interior by Disdale, the 180ft *La Masquarade,* the 170ft *Amevi* from Amels with complete interior and exterior from the firm, the 150ft *Rahal* from Royal Van Lent (interior and exterior collaboration), and the interior for the 141ft *Sorted* from Heesen. In the coming year they will be delivering a 295ft yacht with a clean modern interior, a fast 282ft gas turbine powered yacht, a 236ft with casual interior, and a 164ft for a repeat customer. As if that doesn't seem like quite enough, they have recently been commissioned to design two yachts nearing 213ft, for delivery in the next three years at two different Dutch Shipyards.

DUBOIS NAVAL ARCHITECTS

Following the successful launches of such notable (and massive) sailing yachts as *Salperton, Squall,* and *Red Dragon,* this past year has seen several impressive feats from Dubois Naval Architects. Amongst those in 2003 were the 134ft sloop *Destination Fox Harb'r* and the 128ft *SQN,* both built at Alloy Yachts in New Zealand. Turquoise-Proteksan in Turkey has also launched its latest Dubois-designed 174ft motoryacht, with a second on the way. In Europe Vitters Shipyard has launched two more sloops at 141ft, *Whirlaway* and *Gimla.* Current projects include a 95ft sloop under construction at Pendennis Shipyard in the UK, the new SeaStream 650 also in the UK, and several additional sloops between 120 and 180ft in New Zealand. In addition, 125ft sloops are also underway at Perini Navi and Kha Shing in Taiwan, with a 90ft all-out racing yacht mid-construction at McConaghy Boats in Sydney, the latter the subject of the firm's most extensive research program.

IVAN ERDEVICKI

Ivan Erdevicki Naval Architecture and Yacht Design is a Canadian-based design office offering a diverse range of styling, engineering, and detailing options to the megayacht sector. The company strives to achieve the perfect balance of classical design methods with the most recent computer software technology available. The result: beautiful and elegant sail and power vessels supported with uncompromised engineering in every detail. Currently on the drawing boards is the 153ft motoryacht *Diamond* designed for an American client. Her modern exterior

ESPINOSA
Tajin

appearance bears Erdevicki's distinctive styling, incorporating never before seen three-dimensional triangular windows, positioned in such a way to each other so as to form special lighting effects in the main saloon. The yacht's accommodations are spread over three decks and the flybridge, with the owner's stateroom, galley, and main saloon on the main deck, and sky lounge and pilot-house on the boat deck. *Diamond*'s semi-displacement hull will provide the vessel minimum resistance and good overall performance for her intended horsepower and cruising specifications.

ESPINOSA, INC

The past season has kept Florida-based design firm Espinosa, Inc. busy as ever with several new projects ranging from 87 to 170 feet. While in the midst of accepting much deserved acclaim for the innovative design and outstanding interiors of *Gran Finale,* one of their latest projects, Espinosa has begun work styling two new series of yachts as well as a 164ft tri-deck motoryacht. The latter is an elegant vessel in the preliminary stages of design commissioned for a repeat client—the owner's previous vessel of 147ft was also designed by Espinosa. The sleek but elegant superstructure will contain an expansive interior designed to accommodate the client's extensive art collection. Working with naval architect Jon Overing, Espinosa is also in the final stages of a new series of 100ft pilothouse motoryachts that will feature full-displacement steel hulls. Work continues for them with yet another new series of yachts with architect Arthur Barbeito, including an 82ft and 125ft tri-deck for the first two models.

FONTAINE DESIGN GROUP

Recently launched Fontaine designs include the 116ft *Whisper* from Holland Jachtbouw and the 65ft *Sarah Jane* from Dana Robes Boat Builders. Additionally the group has many projects under construction internationally including the 110ft *Paraiso* at Alloy Yachts, the 109ft *Aventura* at Danish Yacht, and the 92ft *Cabochon* at Ta Chou Yacht Builders. Fontaine Design Group has also introduced a line of technologically advanced sailing yachts, a series led by the innovative Friendship 40 featuring the SailStick integrated sail control system. The SailStick system provides coordinated single lever controls for the furling and sheeting of sails, enabling fingertip control of a modern sailing rig. All of the group's designs illustrate the continuation of the shallow draft, high performance design philosophy perfected by Fontaine while chief designer at Ted Hood Design Group. Designed to sail to the distant corners of the earth, this studio's projects continue to meet the most exacting demands of discriminating yachtsmen.

KEN FREIVOKH DESIGN

Work continues for Ken Freivokh Design on the completion of detailed drawings for the 286ft Perini Navi Clipper Yacht *Maltese Falcon* and her tenders. The Dijkstra design features an innovative ultra-light Freivokh interior, with extensive use of carbon, honeycomb, leather, and billet aluminum. Other projects near completion for the firm are the 190ft *Ocean One*, a high-speed, all-aluminum motoryacht and *Vega*, a 148ft exploration yacht. As with *Maltese Falcon*,

103' KETCH   108' SLOOP

these projects have been styled externally and internally by the Ken Freivokh Design studio. With the aforementioned in their final stages, the firm has begun preliminary work on two displacement yachts of 164 and 108 feet, as well as detail design for the 118ft *Metsuyan IV*—a full displacement motoryacht with naval architecture by Jaron Ginton.

RON HOLLAND DESIGN

After their recent successful collaboration on the 210ft *Felicitá west*, Perini Navi has invited Ron Holland Design to work with them again on a series of projects ranging from 141ft to 223ft. In the interim, work continues on the 245ft *Mirabella V*, still under construction at Vosper Thornycroft. The studio is also preoccupied with the

creation of a 138ft ocean-going motoryacht, and with a series of production and semi-production yachts in the 40-50ft range. Prior to his work on this ocean going motoryacht, Holland's most recent design was for the 151ft Delta, *Affinity*.

IK YACHT DESIGN, INC

IK Yacht Design provides the unique experience of 'stop, dock, and shop' interior yacht design, with furniture and accessories located at their store directly on the water in Fort Lauderdale, Florida. A 10,000sqft showroom allows the connoisseur to browse an extensive collection of yacht furnishings and accessories and select fabric from an enormous library for custom built sofas and chairs built in-house at the company's workshop. IK has the ability to refit any size and type vessel from sportfish to megayachts, and are open seven days at week at their dockside Florida location. Currently they are working on a 105ft Cheoy Lee and an 85ft Burger, with contracts underway for a 58ft Bertram and 212ft Vickers Expedition Yacht.

KEN FREIVOKH
DESIGN
Ocean One

IK YACHT
DESIGN

BRUCE KING
YACHT DESIGN
123ft Motoryacht

GLADE JOHNSON DESIGN

A 150ft motoryacht is the latest project from Glade Johnson Design, scheduled to be launched by Hakvoort in Holland. Her exterior is styled in a modern, aggressive manner, with a complementary warm, contemporary interior featuring generous use of high-gloss rich sapele and mahogany woods, with accents of polished metal. Johnson has also developed the exterior styling and interior design of a 135ft 'J-Class' sailing yacht built to Lloyds and MCA standards by Danish Yacht in Denmark, a vessel destined to be a benchmark in classic design and quality. Recent deliveries include *Capri*, a 190ft five-deck motoryacht by Lürssen in Germany, externally and internally styled by Johnson, with an elaborate, highly detailed, soft contemporary interior.

BRUCE KING YACHT DESIGN

After completion of the 154ft ketch *Scheherazade* at Hodgdon Yachts, Bruce King is currently working on a 123ft motoryacht, styled in the fashion of a turn-of-the-century, clipper bow, fantail stern steam yacht. This vessel was commissioned by a US client who currently owns a large contemporary style megayacht, though has switched his tastes to something more traditional.

PATRICK KNOWLES DESIGNS

Patrick Knowles does not discriminate when it comes to fine interiors. In addition to current work on several mega-yachts, the firm is also busy with non-marine projects such as a DC6-B Aircraft in Europe and a private tour bus. The aircraft is to feature an Orient Express interior with a 17ft long bar and social area, while the tour bus is finished in mahogany paneling with a leather coffered ceiling. In collaboration with Bill Sanderson of Camper & Nicholsons and Don Tracey, Patrick Knowles Designs is in the process of developing a 189ft speculation project at CMN. The designer is responsible for complete general arrangement as well as exterior styling. Additionally, at Burger Boat Company, a 94ft tri-deck is set to feature a PKD interior, accents include lace wood, Amboyna burl, and Ciricote Rosewood.

REYMOND LANGTON

While a recent addition to the field of luxury yacht designers, this firm has harnessed youth and passion to complete an array of stunning interiors on mega-yachts worldwide. Currently underway—in addition to several other projects in production throughout Europe—are exterior styling and interior design for a 158ft megayacht from Bloemsma and Van Breemen. The striking and powerful looking vessel is being built for an American client, with naval architecture and engineering by Vripack. The interior is a blend of European sophistication with a classical atmosphere and strong flavor of the Orient. Traditional finishes such as rich Cuban crown-cut mahogany and leather paneling complement the more exotic hand-burnished laquers and silk appointments. Other projects underway for Reymond Langton include two 148ft motoryachts from Abeking and Rasmussen, and three vessels over 140ft from Izar.

LIEBOWITZ AND PRITCHARD

The award-winning architects of Liebowitz and Pritchard offer their clients designs of architectural distinction, geared toward the subtleties necessary for living comfortably. As a primarily creative team, LP combines elements of yachting's rich past with forward thinking to inspire both innovative and practical solutions. Their design team is foremost concerned with the vessel's configuration, balancing the outside to inside proportions so as to create special spaces that can belong to only the yacht under design. Current projects include an innovative 155ft high performance motorsailer, due for delivery early next year at Pendennis Shipyard, UK. As principal designer (with Pedrick Yacht Designs as naval architects) LP has created a completely custom vessel, reflected in the boat's intricate spaces and aesthetics. Other projects for Liebowitz and Pritchard include several heavy displacement world cruisers, uniquely designed with an uncommon arrangement of decks and open mezzanines.

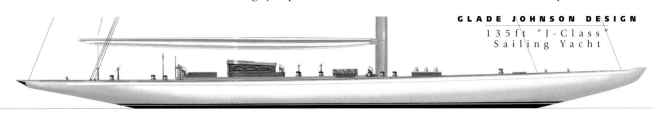

GLADE JOHNSON DESIGN
135ft "J-Class"
Sailing Yacht

MANGIA ONDA

Mangia Onda's newest design, the Wave Eater 65, offers amazing stability, speed, and comfort even in rough offshore environments. It features a double M-hull with an exceptional beam of 32ft, allotting a remarkable amount of space for the interior. The hull exhibits superior long-range capabilities, surpassing monohull and catamaran designs with a cruising speed of 40 knots. Mangia Onda was formed as a design firm to develop the innovative M-hull technology, a challenge which evolved to help combat the serious problem of wave erosion to the ancient buildings of Venice. As a solution, this environmentally friendly hull form was introduced. It combines the best features of displacement and planing to offer low wash, superior seakeeping, and enhanced propulsion efficiency. The M-hull is currently being developed for the US Navy and is now available to the general public.

MANGIA ONDA
Wave Eater 65

EVAN K. MARSHALL

Evan Marshall is presently involved with several projects of a very interesting nature. The first two are for the same owner who has recently invested in a once top-secret Ukranian shipyard, which will be constructing the vessels. The Morye Yard was once responsible for groundbreaking hydrofoils and surface effect military vessels, a technology that Marshall plans to build upon in this uniquely styled yacht, called *Terra*. With the assistance of naval architect Paolo Scanu, this project is meant to showcase the capabilities of the yard to build a megayacht that will achieve speeds up to 23 knots. Also being constructed at the yard for the same private client is the Hydro 28. This unique yacht will incorporate the latest modern hydrofoil technology and achieve a top speed of 50 knots, while requiring considerably less power than a comparable non-hydrofoil craft. The Hydro 28 will be the first in a series of similar yachts, designed with new technology that will allow the craft to perform efficiently at all speeds. Marshall has also completed the interior and exterior refit for a private and extremely important Middle Eastern client on the *Moonlight III*, and designed the interiors for the one-of-a-kind Luxus Cruise Ship, in its final stages of development and negotiations.

GREGORY C. MARSHALL

Located on the west coast of Canada, Gregory C. Marshall has been working for 25 years designing a large array of both custom yachts, as well as production type vessels. The firm of Gregory C. Marshall Naval Architects is thoroughly experienced, working with such disciplines as interior and exterior styling, advanced hull design, state-of-the-art computer modeling, and the development of a cost-effective Vacuum Infusion Process. Greg has worked extensively with William Garden as well as Ed Fry, both of whom have greatly contributed to his expertise in the design of luxury yachts. His ultimate goal is to create a cost-effective 'good-looking' yacht that the client enjoys from the beginning of the design process to the final voyage.

RODGER MARTIN DESIGN

From their office at the Newport Shipyard, Rodger Martin Design has been extremely busy is the past year. Their main projects have included a 66ft fast, though comfortable, cruising yacht with lifting keel, as the beginning of a sailing yacht series for a major shipyard. An ideal rally yacht or circumnavigator, the brief for the 66 specified a capable offshore cruiser which family and friends could take on transoceanic voyages. Her hull is to be aluminum, with a composite deck and interior. The office has also completed considerable development on a one-design sailboat now nearing construction, and the conversion of a 50ft IMS boat into a very comfortable single-handed cruiser for a Dutch client.

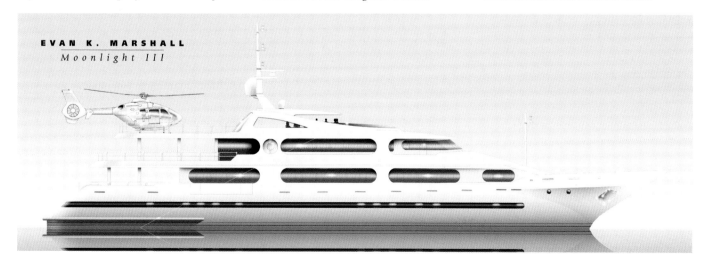

EVAN K. MARSHALL
Moonlight III

OVERING YACHT DESIGNS
100ft RPH Explorer

OVERING YACHT DESIGNS

Two major projects are underway at Overing Yacht Designs, a 100ft RPH Explorer that is well into the engineering phase and a 112ft Tri-deck Explorer that is in the preliminary stage. UK-based Dauntless Yachts has contracted the full design and engineering package on the 100ft and will follow with the 112ft after completion of the preliminary stage. As testament to the worthy design, Hull Numbers 1 and 2 of the 100ft Explorer are already under contract. The layout of the 100ft is the result of collaboration with Juan Carlos Espinosa, for an extremely elegant cherry panel interior. The spacious four-stateroom arrangement has an interior volume typically found on yachts much larger in size, and other features such as a forward lounge provide ample living/entertaining areas as well. Safe and elegant (boasting a Lloyd's-and-MCA-classed steel hull/aluminum superstructure) this impressive yacht will achieve a 4,000 mile range at 10 knots, and will reach a top speed of 14 knots.

PEDRICK YACHT DESIGNS

As masters of innovation, Pedrick Yacht Designs applies its creative and engineering skills to the individual wishes expressed by each client. Three of the firm's designs satisfying very different requirements are: the 90ft classic-styled sloop *Savannah*—a superyacht award winner combining 1930s elegance with modern performance and engineering; the 75ft raised-saloon sloop *Shanakee II*—a comfortable cruiser that sped to line honors in the 2001 Transpac Race; and the new, breakthrough motorsailer *MITseaAH*—a light, luxury sailing yacht designed to motor at an unprecedented 25 knots. Created in collaboration with principal designers Liebowitz & Pritchard Architects, Pedrick Yacht Designs has shaped a dinghy-like hull for *MITseaAH* that

incorporates retractable keel and rudders, planing flaps, recessed, controllable pitch propellers and 7,000 hp in twin diesel engines to maximize performance under both power and sail.

DEE ROBINSON INTERIORS, INC.

In the demanding marketplace of megayacht interior design, Dee Robinson prides herself on having built a career on small and thoughtful steps. Always putting the client's interests first, she has designed and refit myriad yachts since

her inception in the industry twenty-five years ago. After achieving the position of the first in-house designer for Hatteras of Lauderdale, she re-established an independent office, with the assistance of a full staff to aid in new construction and refit projects in the yachting sector, as well as residential design. Dee Robinson has delivered over 125 yachts, and received much acclaim for her work in the yachting industry. Most recently she has been involved with the interior design for a 172ft composite yacht, *Sea Shaw II*, being built in China for an Asian client, as well as a 103ft Cheoy Lee, recently delivered.

ROBIN M. ROSE & ASSOCIATES

The team of Robin M. Rose & Associates is at full capacity dealing with several Crescent Custom Yachts projects. Delivered at the end of last year, the 119ft *Impetuous* is finished in gorgeous mahogany, with a finely crafted dining saloon, and capacious VIP and master staterooms. Also from

PEDRICK YACHT DESIGNS
MITseaAH Hull

Crescent, featuring a Robin Rose interior, is a 121ft raised-pilothouse motoryacht. Inside she is accented with an Asian and Oriental influence, including a hand-painted mural on a curved, oversized starboard foyer wall. Other innovations include rubbed suede woven wall coverings and carved Asian panels inlaid with shell. This third project is the private vessel of the yard's owner, Jack Charles, Sr. The 115ft *Hotei* underwent a partial refit by Robin M. Rose & Associates, including complete re-planning of the master suite. The tone is also Oriental on this vessel, delicately complemented by hammered-brass hardware, rich burnt red fabrics, and ebony cabinetry.

COR D. ROVER

Cor D. Rover has designed the new 132ft *Blue Belle* built by Mondomarine and currently featured in this volume. After her success, Mondomarine has ordered another design, this time for a 115ft fast motoryacht. All-aluminum construction, MTU engines and a top speed of 30 knots are specified. On the drawing boards for Rover is a 155ft displacement motoryacht for an American client to replace their present 142-footer. Construction will encompass a steel hull and aluminum superstructure. Caterpillar main engines and gensets will be installed for propulsion, with extra attention devoted to stability both while stationary and when underway.

SETZER DESIGN GROUP

Setzer Design Group is presently monitoring the progress and construction of six vessels from 82ft to 155ft, with designs ranging from classic cruisers to contemporary megayachts. The majority of the vessels represent turnkey projects, where Setzer is providing the yacht design, naval architecture, and interior design services. All designs continue to be classic with modern twists of style and technology, overall affecting a timeless aesthetic. New projects include the development of a series of Expedition Yachts from 98 to 130ft, a classic motoryacht at 108ft for extended cruising and charter, and designs for a semi-custom series of tender/fishing Carolina boats to be 'tow behinds' for current larger designs underway. These larger vessels comprise a series of full displacement designs ranging from 185ft to 205ft on the drawing boards. Setzer Design Group's Interior Design department continues to develop complete décor and design packages, including highly organized systems of material specification and tracking for countless décor and architectural details.

SIEWERT DESIGN, LLC

Yacht designer Greg Siewert has partnered with Sterling Yachts to develop and import a complete line of classic style motor cruisers, beginning with the Sterling Atlantic 43. Embodying the essence of yachts from the early 20th Century, the graceful and elegant Sterling Atlantic series incorporates modern design, materials, and technology. Anticipated additions to the series include a 39ft open layout weekender, and a 49ft pilothouse cruiser. Siewert specializes in incorporating distinctive and functional yacht styling with contemporary production methods and materials, a strategy for which he has won numerous industry awards and patents for manufacturers. Several US production builders currently retain Siewert Design's services, with projects ranging in size from 40 to 60ft. In addition, megayacht refit projects still occupy a large part of business for the office, with successful full interior and exterior redesigns constantly generating further commissions.

SHARP DESIGN

Under construction for Sharp Design is the 150ft *Summit One* project, a complete refit of the yacht originally known as *LAC III* and launched in 1973. The refit involves changes to the hull and upper deck configurations, a structural update, new propulsion, and a completely refreshed interior with all spaces given a new arrangement. The yacht will be fully classed Lloyd's and MCA and will go into charter service immediately upon completion. Also in preliminary design stages are two projects for Royal Denship, a 134ft classic-styled yacht and a 203ft modern-styled vessel. Both will employ steel hulls with FRP composite superstructures and are slated for a 2005 delivery. In addition, Sharp Design is working with a group in Mexico to develop a line of 100ft+ yachts, specifically designed and constructed for the requirements of the yacht cruising market in that country.

SPARKMAN & STEPHENS

Founded in 1929, Sparkman & Stephens has developed a legacy for designing strong offshore cruising boats, trophy-winning racing boats, large megayachts, and America's Cup winners. The firm's designs, while aesthetically pleasing, also have a strong foundation or basis in science.

Model testing, velocity program predictions, and computer fluid dynamics are an integral part of the design process for any vessel in the firm's incredibly versatile range. The latest design on the boards is a rugged 120ft explorer yacht being developed for the The Cape Horn Trawler Corporation. This new vessel will incorporate the best of both companies' strengths, in the hopes of creating the ultimate world cruising motoryacht. With all engineering and design by S&S, the yacht will be built by Cape Horn at its Canadian facility. The general arrangement will be customized to the owner's requirements, though a standard general arrangement has been developed. Innovative features include a private convertible study off the master stateroom, easily converted to a fifth stateroom, and an elaborate wet bar nestled within the sky lounge.

DONALD STARKEY DESIGNS

Donald Starkey Designs is nearing completion on three new yachts over 150ft for the coming year. The first, the 162ft *Larissa*, is in construction at Amels, while a 213ft full displacement yacht, *The White Rose of Drachs*, will be completed by Kusch Yachts in Germany in the Spring. A 230ft Lürssen featuring a Starkey interior is soon to launch as well. Designs still being

detailed on the drawing boards include a new 198ft *Blue Moon*, being built by Royal Van Lent, a 236ft full displacement 'modern classic' at Delta Marine, and the Westport 501, a 164ft composite style from Westport's new facility. Still in progress are plans for a 205ft full displacement yacht for a European owner and a massive 425ft private pleasure ship with strikingly modern lines being built in Europe for a retired industrialist.

TR DESIGN

Current Projects at TR Design include a 55ft steel trawler yacht for Christensen Yachts, a fast 40ft aluminum powercat designed for cruising the west coast from Alaska to San Francisco, and continuing development of the Passagemaker Lite Series. Newest versions of the series include the 46ft in cold-molded wood, a 39ft in aluminum, and the 65ft in wood, composite, and aluminum. Also from the firm is a 108ft aluminum centerboard cutter designed to cruise with charter parties of up to four couples. Comfortable and easy to handle, the design features many striking elements including Herreshoff-inspired oval cockpits and transom. Combining high-performance and ease under sail, she is defined by her classic exterior and stunning Art Nouveau interior.

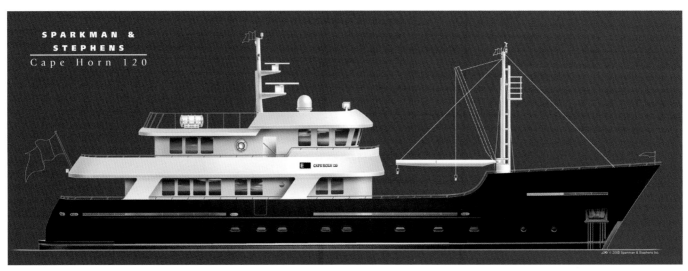

TRIPP DESIGN
Alithia

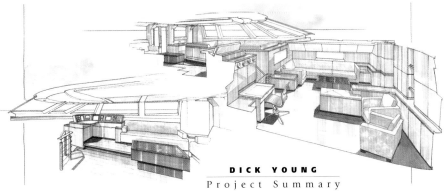

DICK YOUNG
Project Summary

TRIPP DESIGN

Tripp Design specializes in the design of high performance cruising and racing yachts. Tripp's largest launch to date is the 130ft *Alithia*, with clean lines, speed, and seaworthiness at the forefront of her design. The vessel traveled 15,000 miles in her first eight months, visiting some of the most diverse parts of the planet. Recent launches for the firm include a new Baltic 50, a lifting keel 60ft racer/cruiser, a 77ft world cruising ketch from New Zealand, and a 79ft carbon lifting keel cruiser/racer from Italy. For the future, Tripp design is focusing their energy toward a custom 119ft composite lift cruiser and a 100ft design for series build, with several very large yet high performance sailing yachts on the horizon.

VRIPACK YACHTING

With 35 experts on naval architecture, marine engineering, and exterior and interior design, Vripack Yachting has numerous projects ranging in size from 16 to 280ft. Well-known from the firm are the Doggersbank, Research Vessel Yacht, and the Explorer and Expedition Vessel designs. These no-nonsense, go-anywhere series meet the increasing desire of many owners to explore the more extreme areas around the world. Vripack's reputation for design encompasses sturdiness, large and comfortable accommodation spaces, well arranged technical layouts, and amazing hull performances and maneuvering. Vripack works closely with many well-known yards worldwide, providing complete design and drawing packages and the ability to offer production information directly to the shop floors for builders.

ANDREW WINCH DESIGNS

This past year has been quite exciting for Andrew Winch Designs, which has seen the launch of Holland Jachtbouw's 116ft sloop *Whisper*, Lufthansa's 737 boeing business jet, Magnum Marine's 60ft high-speed motoryacht *Ronin*, and Hodgdon Yachts' 154ft ketch *Scheherazade*. Among new projects are five motoryachts being built at Oceanco, Lürssen, Amels, and CMN, along with a 115ft sailing yacht at CNB. The design and styling of the 182ft motoryacht *Fascination*, under construction at CMN Shipyard, has also kept Andrew Winch Designs quite occupied. The project once again calls together the partnership of Winch and CMN, after their successful collaboration on *Bermie*. Notable features include her huge open plan sun deck which allows for myriad arrangements and a full-beam sky lounge designed in the essence of panorama opening onto the aft deck.

DICK YOUNG DESIGNS

With 15 years experience to guide his way, Dick Young has compiled and led a highly talented design team to a position of international prominence. The company has projects underway at several of the most prestigious yards around the world, and is currently working with Royal Huisman on their third collaborative endeavor. After the successful launch of *Maria Cattiva*, the 130ft Bruce King designed classic, work has begun on *Antares*, a modern performance ketch of 130ft. Also under construction at Vitters is an ultra-modern 144ft Dubois cruising sloop. Work is also set to begin soon with Vripack for a 141ft classic motoryacht. Other projects in various stages keep the firm busy internationally, with vessels in production in New Zealand, California, the UK, Italy, and Greece. Collaborations with production yards have included a recent commission for a new Millenium Joinery style for the entire Oyster Marine fleet and two 112ft yachts for Nautor Swan.

ZURN YACHT DESIGN

Douglas Zurn is the designer of the entire range of Marlow Explorer Series motoryachts, and the 38ft Shelter Island runabout, of which thirty six sisterships have been built to date. First apprenticing with established naval architects Dieter Empacher and Chuck Paine, he moved on to work with the in-house design staff at Able Marine and Tartan Yachts before embarking on his own independent career. Though ironically concentrating initially on sailboats, his first commission was for the 48 knot Shelter Island for client Billy Joel. Today new and current projects range from the Gloucester 20, a center console pocket rocket, to the Vanguard 24 runabout. Upcoming launches include the C.W. Hood 50 and a 57ft fast commuter for a certain former client, the Piano Man himself.

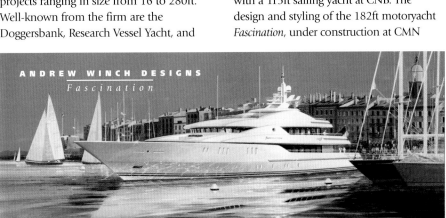

ANDREW WINCH DESIGNS
Fascination

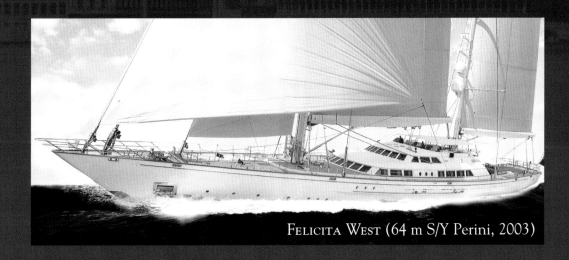

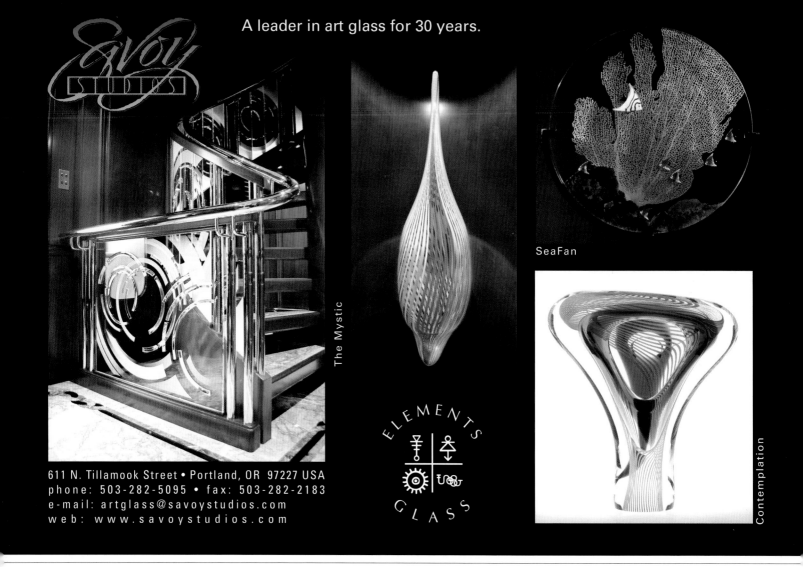

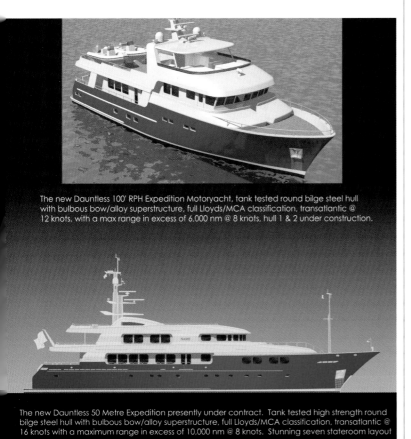

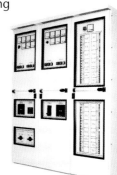

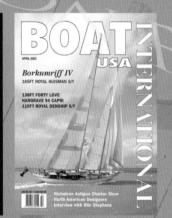
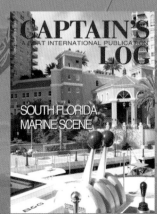

A PLACE TO DREAM

INTERIOR DESIGN

Creators of exclusive interiors for luxury yachts and prestige projects worldwide.
Whatever and wherever your dreams are, we specialise in making them come true.

INTERIORS

THREE ENGINES ARE BETTER THAN ONE.

It is commonly accepted that Cavendish White has one of the most successful charter departments in yachting. Amongst those who know, Wilson Yacht Management is recognised as one of the most efficient of yacht managers. Few would dispute that Merle Wood Associates is one of the strongest names in brokerage.

With the three companies linking up to form a new association, yacht owners have the best of all worlds. Three independent companies bringing you their specialist strengths, allied to the power, scope and resources of one organisation.

You can talk to any one of these companies and receive a seamless service across the group worldwide. Regardless of whether you need to sell in Spain, manage in Mexico or charter in Corsica, we have the answer.

One engine can power your yacht, two is better and three just gives you the edge.

Tel: +1 954 525 5111
mail@merlewood.com
www.merlewood.com

Tel: +44 (0)1482 648322
admin@wilsonyachtmanagement.com
www.wilsonyachtmanagement.com

Tel: +44 (0)20 7381 7600
yachts@cavendishwhite.com
www.cavendishwhite.com

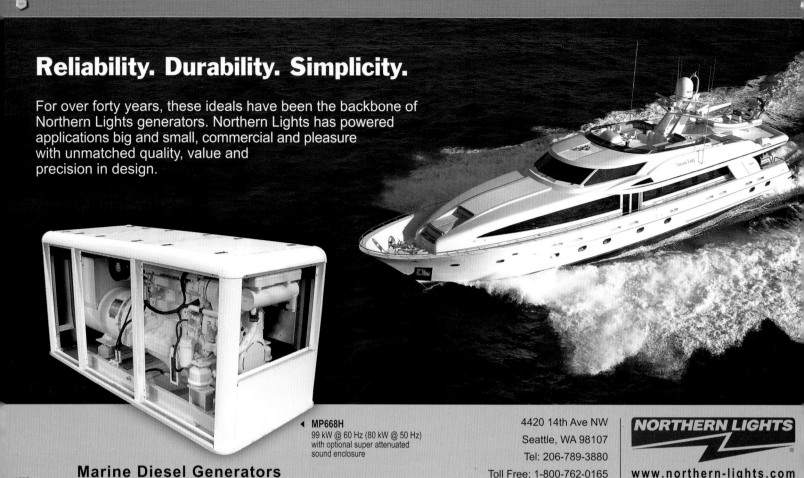

Glass Deco International designs, develops, produces and installs exclusive interior products in among others glass, marble and metal or a combination of these elements. Products like stairs, decorated hard-glass doors, dining tables, dressers, decorated floors, etc.

With use of several techniques as blasting, etching, waterjet cutting, fused application, moulding and blowing, we are able to live up to your expectations, eventually in combination with metal or wood.

Our in-house designers can, in cooperation with external architects, develop a custom-made product for you if desired.

If any information is required, please contact us.

GLASS DECO
I N T E R N A T I O N A L

Glass Deco - Mierloseweg 126 - 5707 AR Helmond - The Netherlands
Phone: +31(0) 492 - 524261 - Internet: www.glass-deco.com - E-mail: info@glass-deco.com

Alegria

95-FOOT HARGRAVE CUSTOM MOTORYACHT

The explosive growth of the yacht charter market has brought a welcome source of income to yacht owners who once might never have considered such an endeavor. Even a few weeks of charter a year can help allay the expenses of a large yacht as well as provide significant tax advantages. Regardless of where the yacht is registered, or to which country the owner writes his tax checks, chartering has become a commonplace activity and astute owners consider chartering even as they are planning to build a new yacht

That is the case with *Alegria*, a new Hargrave 95 recently delivered to first-time yacht owners. In the process of searching for a builder, they realized that chartering was a way that the yacht could help pay for itself. However, unlike many owners who build to suit their own needs, *Alegria*'s owners consulted charter brokers to determine what qualities would make their future yacht particularly viable for the charter market. They were advised that, for a yacht in the 88ft to 100ft range, four cabins were needed, a good supply of water toys should be available, and the crew quarters should be above average. Crew quarters? Why would a potential charterer care about crew quarters? The answer is simple: a happy crew makes for a successful charter, so *Alegria* was given crew cabins that rival the guest staterooms of many yachts for comfort and amenities.

The owners only found what they wanted when they reached Hargrave Custom Yachts. This yard has grown under the stewardship of Michael Joyce from the former

Jack Hargrave naval architectural design firm to become a major contender in yacht construction. With everything from design and construction to interior design under one roof, Hargrave has become known as a 'can do' builder for whom no request is too difficult to realize.

In the case of *Alegria*, the owners had seen *High Cotton*, the first of the Hargrave 95ft raised pilothouse motor-yachts, and liked what they saw—with one exception. *High Cotton* was built for an owner who enjoys fishing, so it was fitted with a large cockpit, but the owners of *Alegria* wanted full motoryacht styling. "No problem" was the answer from Hargrave, which stretched the saloon aft and created a raised aft deck that would be perfect for alfresco meals protected by the overhanging boatdeck. In the process, they also added that all-important charter ingredient: two comfortable crew cabins each with its own head.

Alegria has proven such a success, both for her owners and charter clients, that in her first eight months she has clocked more than 700 hours on the engines and around 6,000 nautical miles from New England to the Caribbean under her keel.

The interior of *Alegria*, a collaboration between interior designer Shelley Higgins and the owner's wife, has an emphasis on comfort. The cherrywood joinery is warm and inviting, with burled accents on the window and mirrored ceiling surrounds. A pair of leather settees is aft while a floral-print overstuffed two-seater settee and ottoman completes the sitting area. A pop-up television and a pair of chairs lie to starboard, where seated guests have good views through large side windows and the electrically-operated sliding glass door.

A circular ceiling treatment with an antique chandelier delineates the dining area with its circular table for up to

Porthole ★ The pilothouse is on a separate mezzanine level.

Top ★ This raised pilothouse has proven to be a very successful charter yacht.

Opp. bottom ★ The flybridge is designed for entertaining with bar and barbecue.

Right ★ Protected aft maindeck dining.

eight accented with inlays and burled wood. The table is round because, although it takes up more space than a conventional rectangular shape, it is a more 'democratic' table where all the guests can converse easily. An interesting feature is the built-in desk on the port side of the dining area, providing a place for the owner or guests to work while still enjoying the main deck views.

Hargrave is a proponent of the country-style galley arrangement, which is reached from a starboard passageway, past the day head. Considering the American affinity for casual living, this is an area which has proven popular both with the chef (who isn't left out) and with guests who can gather on the comfortable settee to watch television or enjoy the scenery and a snack or two. The galley is a gourmet's dream—from the gray granite counters with high backsplashes and center island, to the easily-cleaned teak-and-holly sole and stainless steel appliances. A plethora of drawers and lockers provide ample storage and the center island doubles as a breakfast bar with three stools that swivel underneath when not in use.

The guest accommodations are divided, with the forward VIP reached via stairs from the galley, and the master and two additional guest cabins accessed down stairs forward

of the dining area. The VIP fills the bow with a queen-size berth beneath a headboard of cherrywood and bevelled mirrors. The ensuite shower room is particularly spacious, with a wood-framed glass shower door and matching granite on the sole and countertops.

The stairs amidships curve down into a pleasant hall with oval overhead treatment of mirrors and rope lights. Here is a hidden washer/dryer and a shelf for breakfast rolls and coffee. Twin doors open into the full-beam master suite with the overhead raised to nearly seven feet to create an open and airy getaway. The king-size berth is on the center-line between granite-topped bedside tables and bevelled mirrors. A long settee is to port and built-in storage units fill the starboard side, while both aft corners have oversized wardrobes. The his-and-hers ensuite shower room spans the full beam forward, with its large glass-doored shower dividing the two marbled dressing areas with heads.

Aft of the hall is a pair of identically-sized guest cabins. These house queen-size beds but, by moving the bedside table and sliding the bases apart, the double beds can easily convert into a pair of singles with Pullman berths overhead. Each cabin has a television hidden behind a tambour door and the ensuite shower rooms have teak soles and oversized showers.

On a separate mezzanine level, the pilothouse has the helmstation forward and a settee aft, and relies simply on an upholstered leaning post rather than a conventional helm chair. The full-width instrument panel displays Nobeltec navigation software on flat screens, as well as an array of Furuno, Raytheon and Simrad electronics.

The flybridge is designed for entertaining, with a vast curved settee to port with twin adjustable tables and a large barbecue area. A fully-equipped granite-topped bar with three stools is to starboard, providing guests with a view over the three Pompanette helm seats forward. The helm is covered by a soft top on a rigid framework for all-season protection. Aft, the boatdeck easily handles the 16ft Nautica RIB tender which is launched via a Quicklift davit with powered rotation. There is also a pair of SkiDoos.

The crew quarters are reached through a watertight door in the transom and consist of a captain's double cabin to port and a crew cabin to starboard with bunks—both have ensuite shower rooms. The area also has a second washer/dryer and a work area.

Alegria is powered by twin Caterpillar 3412 diesels of 1,400hp and, with chartering in mind, many of the systems have been upgraded, including the Onan 27kW and 35kW gensets. As Caribbean cruising is planned, the CruiseAir air-conditioning has been increased to 180,000 BTU and

Above ★ The vast country-style galley—perfect for a casual lifestyle.

Opp. top and below ★ The saloon and sociable dining area provide a convivial grouping and are surrounded by large windows.

Above ★ The master has a king-size berth between granite-topped bedside tables and a beveled mirror.

Left ★ The VIP queen-size guestroom is forward in the bow and accessed via the galley.

Below ★ The his-and-hers master bath spans the full-beam forward.

Opp. page ★ Many systems upgrades have prepared *Alegria* for serious Caribbean cruising.

the Naiad stabilizers have fins. In the interests of noise reduction, all the insulation in the engine-room has been doubled or tripled above standard. Other systems include a Village Marine watermaker and Trace inverter.

During her 6,000 nautical mile cruise, she encountered considerable bad weather, but her captain reports that she is solid and stable, with a 22.5 knot top speed and a comfortable cruise of 19 knots. With a draft of just over five feet, *Alegria* has full access to areas in the Bahamas.

Planning ahead for chartering and using a builder for which no request is impossible has brought nothing but rewards for *Alegria*'s owners.

SPECIFICATIONS

LOA:	95ft (28.9m)
LWL:	83ft 2in (25.3m)
Beam:	20ft (6.1m)
Draft:	5ft 3in (1.6m)
Displacement:	177,000lbs
Engines:	2 x 1,400hp Caterpillar 3412
Gears:	ZF Marine
Speed (max/cruise):	22.5 knots/18 knots
Fuel capacity:	3,200gal
Range @ 12 knots:	1,100nm
Electrical generation:	2 x Onan 27kW & 35kW
Water pressure system:	Headhunter Jet Pack
Sanitation:	Headhunter
Air-conditioning:	180,000 BTU Cruise Air
Accommodation:	8 guests plus 4 crew
Construction:	FRP
Naval architecture:	Hargrave Design
Builder/Year:	Hargrave Custom Yachts/2002

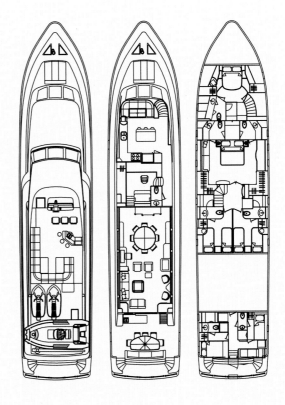

Alexa C²

114-FOOT NORDLUND MOTORYACHT

tanding on the proud bow of the 114ft *Alexa C²*, I let my eyes sweep up the streamlined foredeck to the broad brow overhanging dark-tinted port and starboard windows and the weatherdecks, the whole in turn topped by the sky lounge. Small steps carved into the fore-deck's center lead up to the sky lounge windows. "We call it the 'eagle look,'" says the vessel's captain, John Carlisle. He's right: the glossy fiberglass arching up to the mast evokes the imperious and disdainful raptor hunting prey in the Pacific Northwest, where *Alexa C²* was conceived and built.

Naval architect Ed Monk, who designed her, calls himself a 'Bauhaus man.' "That was the 1920s German art and architectural movement that concentrated on functional craftsmanship, where form follows function," he explains. Monk has a strong distaste for what he calls 'frou-frou boats.' Functionality is one of the hallmarks of his designs as reflected in *Alexa C²*'s flared, semi-displacement hull, fiberglass over Airex core, fuel-efficient propulsion, full

bulwarks, highly accessible engine room and the many practical details and safety features. Even Monk's styling has a function: there's no styling for styling's sake. The 'eagle' brow, for example, protects the wing bridges whose hide-away controls allow the skipper to maneuver the vessel when docking. Nevertheless, the exterior is an evolution of Monk's designs: this latest vessel is less angular than his usual work—more fluid, her curves more ample.

Alexa C² is the largest custom vessel yet constructed by Nordlund Boat Company of Tacoma, Washington. Although the owners, Noel and Alexa Coon, specified that above all, the boat should have a comfortable, family feel, the interior design is daring, artistic and incorporates elements of *feng shui*, the ancient Chinese art whose princi-ples determine how the positioning and shapes of rooms and objects help create a harmonious life. Many of the design features and furnishings are curved rather than recti-

linear; rooms are open rather than enclosed which, *feng shui* practitioners believe, allow energy to flow freely.

Alexa Coon is of Japanese descent and grew up in Hawaii. Proud of her heritage, she introduced many other Asian touches: the master and two guest staterooms use translucent *shoji* screens that hide portholes yet allow filtered natural light to seep into each cabin. The *shoji* motif is repeated in the honey-colored carpeting that defines the saloon, staterooms and sky lounge. Various vases, sculptures and artifacts (held fast with earthquake wax) also evoke Japanese artistry.

Boarding *Alexa C²* takes place via aluminum, self-leveling, port and starboard ladders, or astern onto the ample swim platform. From this platform which, like all exterior decks, is covered with flawlessly laid teak, twin curved companionways connect to the cockpit. From here the captain can dock the ship from a slave control station, with its B&G wind and current repeater and bow-and-stern-thruster controls. Two more curved stairs lead to the Cal deck with comfortable seating around an oval, New Vyana polished granite table. Noel Coon, a Texan, quips that this cheerful eating place serves as 'his back porch.'

The *Alexa C²* is the Coons' second Nordlund vessel and the couple values both the quality construction and the relationship they've developed with brothers Gary and Paul Nordlund, low-key, second-generation boat builders.

Although the Coons enjoyed their previous 74ft motor-yacht, they felt its size offered too few amenities for guests. With this latest acquisition, they radically changed the approach to the interior. "In our previous boat, we focused on strong colors, like raspberry reds and purples," explains Alexa Coon. "But this time, we wanted something calmer, warmer—earthtones with splashes of color." They hired interior designer Jon Pokela to carry out their wishes and he achieved "a layered look with the same color tones but different textures."

Porthole ★ A circular staircase connects the various deck levels.

Opp. bottom ★ Two black leather helm seats face a bridge with four 20in pop-up screens that manage the ship's systems.

Top ★ Sleek and functional Ed Monk exterior styling is evident on the *Alexa C²*.

The saloon, accessible from the Cal deck, features two gold-toned sofas that tempt you to curl up with a cup of coffee and a good book. A matching footstool doubles as a storage bin, a first indication of the way all space has been maximized on this vessel—the owners' summer home. A tower dividing the saloon from the dining room, hides the first of the plasma-screen televisions installed in each room, and stores the hand-made, glass, Japanese-inspired dinnerware. The tower is clad with quilted sapeli, an African tropical rainforest wood. Several differently shaped occasional tables are made of cherry, beechwood, and oak-burl veneers, melding various browns, tans and golds, which contrast sharply with the common practice of installing matching wood throughout a boat.

Forward of the saloon, the dining room is furnished with a magnificent, round sapeli table complemented by French yew Biedermeier chairs. The cone-shaped ceiling light fixture is made of hand-blown, fiery red and gold glass created by glass artist Scott Curry, the first of many such colorful fixtures throughout the boat. To starboard of the dining area, a small foyer with an abstract painting by Jon Pokela provides a splash of color. Across is a day head with a spectacular azure glass washbowl perched on a black granite pedestal.

Ahead, past the wine cooler, the galley serves as one of the vessel's central gathering places. The spacious room again combines an unusual array of woods. The walls are clad with blonde English sycamore with horizontal undulations ("like rippled sand under water," says Noel Coon), while the cupboards and center island's sides are made of figured sapeli. At floor level, the kickplate and inlaid border use a neutral pearwood as a counterpoint; a black feature strip demarcates it in turn from the solid bamboo-planked floor with its endless repetition of nodes. The inlay patterns are repeated at the room's edges, separating one space from another. The center island's top and twin dining tables are made from absolute-black Indian granite with the countertops and settee backdrop using contrasting madura-gold granite. The mullions and dividing pillars are finished with a golden-brown polyurethane metallic paint. Several cupboards use *shoji* screen doors. The stainless twin Subzero refrigerator/freezers, Dacor double ovens and microwaves occupy one side of the galley. More stainless can be found in the GE fanhood floating above the central island. This mix of woods, (three of them highly figured) different granites, stainless steel, metallic paint and cream

Opp. top ★ The main saloon in accordance with Jon Pokela's interior design concept incorporates the same color tones but with different textures.

Opp. bottom ★ The sky lounge and bridge are connected in an open plan.

Right ★ One of the vessel's central gathering places is the stunning galley.

Below ★ The sapeli dining table is surrounded by French yew Biedermeier chairs.

shoji screens might seem like a mishmash, perhaps a bit over the top. It isn't. The galley has a clean, elegant look, a place where you can feel happy chowing down fish and chips or feasting on a rich boeuf bourguignon prepared by chef Michael Winning.

Crew quarters with a separate galley lie forward of the main galley. The captain has a cabin with head, while the chef, steward and mate share two cabins and head.

Two spiral staircases—one rising to the sky lounge, the other descending to the staterooms—are embellished with hand-crafted, polished stainless rails and open-filigreed stair rises. The curves and openwork again follow *feng shui* tenets. The down staircase leads to a circular foyer with three arched doors opening into the master and two guest state-

Left ★ Spiral staircases rise to the sky lounge and descend to the staterooms.

Opp. top ★ Guests have a choice of either the 'gold' or the 'blue' stateroom—each have queen-size beds.

Opp. middle ★ Dayhead with azure glass washbowl perched on a black granite pedestal.

Below ★ Sapeli and sycamore veneers highlighted by inlays enhance the serene quality of the master stateroom.

rooms. The foyer's ceiling is covered by a shatterproof A-Look mirror. Two circular art niches contain sculptures, but a third holds a surprise. Located between the two guest suites, the nook accommodates a coffeemaker encouraging guests to grab a cup of early-morning java. The master stateroom continues the mix of figured sapeli and sycamore veneers, highlighted by additional wood inlays, and a circular ceiling canopy overhangs the elegant island bed. The bed hides the access to the master bilge with its filters, bow thruster and other equipment. His and her bathrooms, each with toilet and sink, are centrally joined by a glass walled, madura-gold granite lined shower room with dual heads and steam jets.

Next door, guests have a choice of either the 'gold' or 'blue' stateroom, so called for their décor. Their queen-size island beds are flanked by built-in, black-granite nightstands, and each has a separately designed head where the unusual mix of sapeli, sycamore, pear and bamboo woods continues. The blue room also hides an access to the 'garage,' an ample storage place to squirrel away bins with extra T-shirts, golf clubs and luggage. The 'gold' room also has an extra door which leads a second, watertight engine room door.

The twin 16V 2000 Detroit Diesel engines at 1800hp each are the centerpieces of the spotless engine room and are started hydraulically. All engine room equipment is 360 degree accessible, making maintenance and repairs easy tasks. The floor consists of plastic-coated, non-slip grating, allowing for full visibility of the equipment installed in the bilge. "This way," says Captain Carlisle, "I can see the slightest ingress of oil or water and detect heat or smoke instantly." Two 60kW Kohler generators provide electricity for the vessel's hotel load, the Aqua Air air-conditioning, Keypower thrusters, Naiad stabilizers and the US watermakers. The *Alexa C²* is also equipped with Racor filters for fuel polishing, fuel transfer systems, Headhunter wastewater treatment and an FM200 fire-suppression system. With a 5500-gallon fuel capacity, the vessel has a 2400 nautical mile range at 12 knots.

The aft engine-room door leads to a utility room with freezer, two Maytag Neptune washer-dryer stacks, a workshop with tool cabinets, and the ship's electrical panels. Further aft lies the lazarette, a roomy area storing the two US watermakers, dive gear and air compressor, hot-water tanks, battery banks and a variety of provisions.

The vessel's third-level deck houses the sky lounge and a massive aft deck which stores the owners' 600 HP Novurania tender and the 15ft Rendova crew tender as well as the crane to lower them to the waterline. Fire safety equipment and survival suits are stowed in lockers aft of the sky lounge. Early in the design process, the owners eliminated the flybridge and opted to open the sky

lounge's aft wall to allow for a 360° view. Only the equipment tower with its antennas, communication domes, radars and eight flute horns rise above it. Unlike the standard bridge, with a settee and table aft, this sky lounge is rounded, with magnificent views, a curved banquette and easy-chair seating areas, and a desk-like console behind the navigation station. The console houses a satellite phone, a computer linked to all on-board computers, a fax and other communication electronics.

The bridge is impressive. Two black leather captain's chairs face a dashboard with four 20-inch pop-up screens, which can interchangeably show Nobeltec charts, depth and wind instruments, radars, views from the security cameras, and a Simon ship's management system. "Simon" monitors the engines, coolant, air, alarms, cameras, tanks and generators. The ARPA-enabled Furuno radars can plot multiple targets. Eight security cameras pan 360° of the ship's exterior and the engine and utility rooms.

Alexa C² is a superb, stylish, yet comfortable yacht, which took much planning and teamwork from the owners, designers and builders to bring together. It combines luxury, artistic daring, and layered textures without rococo embellishments, while maintaining a high degree of seaworthiness and safety. One of Noel Coon's dreams is to take *Alexa C²* south, transit the Panama Canal and the Caribbean, cruise up the Atlantic seaboard to the St. Lawrence and eventually explore the Great Lakes as far as Lake Superior. "Whether I actually make this trip is not important though," he muses. "It's not the destination that counts—it's the voyage."

Opp. top ★ *Alexa C²* is the largest custom vessel yet constructed by Nordlund.

Right ★ With a 5,500 gallon fuel capacity, she has a 2,400 nautical mile range at 12 knots.

SPECIFICATIONS

LOA:	114ft (34.8m)
Beam:	24ft (7.3m)
Draft:	6ft (1.8m)
Displacement (light ship):	265,000lbs
Propulsion:	2 x 16V 2000 Detroit Diesel (1800 hp each)
Speed (max/cruise):	24k/18k
Fuel capacity:	5,500 gal
Range @ 12 knots:	2,400 nautical miles
Electrical generation:	2 x 60kw Kohler
Bow thruster:	Keypower
Hydraulics:	Keypower (Dean Yule)
Stabilizers:	Naiad
Watermaker:	US Watermaker
Water pressure system:	Gould Aquavar
Sanitation:	Headhunter
Entertainment systems:	Mckee Design
Paint/painters:	Sterling/Seaworthy Services
Air-conditioning:	Aqua Air
Electronics:	J&G Marine
Communications:	Thrane F77
Tenders:	600 HP Novurania/15' Rendova
Construction:	Cored FRP
Project management:	Richard Gladych
Naval architecture:	Edwin Monk/Nolan Marine Design
Exterior styling:	Edwin Monk
Interior design:	Pokela Design
Builder/Year:	Nordlund Boat Co. /2003

Amarellla

83-FOOT INACE MOTORYACHT

*I*t's no surprise that a tough expedition yacht would come from a Brazilian boatbuilder—the coastline of South America is rocks, reefs, rivers, and impenetrable jungle. This is not the place that a wimpy cocktail cruiser would find comfortable.

Amarellla, on the other hand, is *the* yacht for such an inhospitable area and, yes, her name has three Ls, but the explanation falls in the realm of "does not translate well." The three Ls are a symbol for the yacht—a triple-L is proudly inlaid in the saloon bar. Go figure.

Built in steel by Inace and designed by Michael Kirschstein, this 83-footer has the purposeful look of a yacht that won't be spending much time in marinas. As a boatbuilder, Inace is, like the tired Hollywood joke, an overnight success after more than thirty years in the business. With more than 800 fishing trawlers, offshore support vessels, and naval patrol vessels, this company knows what works and what doesn't when you're a long way from homeport.

Standing dockside next to *Amarellla*, there are things you notice, giveaways that say this isn't an ordinary motoryacht. There are no teak caps on the rails and, by the way, there aren't any of those pretty stainless steel rails—*Amarellla* has husky welded and painted rails that look like they could fence in a herd of Caterpillar tractors. Lean against one, and there's no flex. In fact, there's no flex anywhere on this yacht.

Another telling feature is the oversized freeing ports along the main deck. Most yachts rely on pretty little drains like the one in your bathtub to handle spray and washdown, but

a freeing port, on the other hand, is meant to dump, as quickly as possible, that six-foot wall of blue-green water that floods the main deck when a ship sticks her bow into a thundering comber somewhere in the Roaring Forties. Water weighs tons, so you don't want it lingering on deck because it can seriously compromise stability. Inace built *Amarellla* to be prepared with enormous freeing ports.

The foremast has an old-fashioned crow's nest at the top—because when tiptoeing through the entrance in a coral reef, not even the best electronics are a match for a good pair of eyes on high.

These are just the outward signs that this is an unusual yacht. Pull out the blueprints, and you'll discover that *Amarellla* has no fewer than eight watertight compartments, with a collision bulkhead forward and a watertight engine-room. There is a double bottom in the most vulnerable area amidships, and the keel is a box structure that is not integral to the hull. So, if you happen to suffer a navigational memory lapse, the keel can support the vessel and, even if damaged, it won't impact the watertight integrity of the hull.

If there was one guiding factor in the finishing of *Amarellla*, it was to keep things simple and easy to maintain. Throughout the yacht, cherry-stained Brazilian mahogany has been combined with Magilite panels for a pleasant yachty look, and the saloon is as honest as it is square. At the same level as the aft deck (which has a built-in settee and table), the saloon is entered through twin watertight doors, which suggest sea conditions probably best not to think about. There are twin L-shaped settees

Above ★ Heavily built, this 83-footer was made to go places.

Porthole ★ Each of the two twin cabins comes with a private shower.

Opp. bottom ★ Steering from on high.

Below ★ View of the no-nonsense foredeck.

well as direct access to the side deck. The usual appliances are present, plus a Lotus barbecue, an electric oven with steamer feature, and a washer/dryer for clean tea towels.

Forward from the saloon is the foyer from the starboard deck. This entry lobby has a marble-lined day head and stairs both down to the lower cabins and up to the wheelhouse. On *Amarellla*, the wheelhouse is fit for expedition-cruising with a pair of high-backed leather helm chairs, a dedicated chart table to port with chart storage underneath, and an array of electronics in a simple white dash. The big raised settee with granite table converts to a pilot berth when needed, and the visibility is excellent through the reverse angle windows, which create extra space in the pilothouse. The sole is finished in natural Brazilian mahogany and a pair of dogging doors lead to the Portuguese bridge with wing stations for maneuvering.

The remainder of this deck has not the usual sky lounge found on many yachts, but instead, there is an owner's stateroom. Airy and bright, it has a private teak-planked deck aft and large windows on three sides. The king-size berth is set

that serve as a couch (starboard) and as a dining area with table to port. Large windows are framed in solid mahogany, and an entertainment center fills the aft corner.

Forward to port is a mirrored and marble-topped breakfast counter with two stools, and the galley is just forward. The cook is given ample Italian marble counter space as

Main picture ★ Looking forward to the foyer from the mahogany-clad main saloon.

Opp. bottom ★ The wheelhouse is fit for expedition cruising—the settee can be converted to a pilot berth and visibility is excellent through reverse angle windows.

Bottom ★ Looking aft, the saloon is entered through twin, watertight doors.

Below ★ With Italian marble, a Lotus barbecue, and an oven with a steamer, this galley will suit any chef's palette.

athwartships facing a writing desk and office to starboard, and low cabinets line the aft bulkhead. A private head with marble floors and shower is forward, and an entertainment center is also hidden in the forward bulkhead.

Continue up the stairs from the wheelhouse, and you arrive far above the waterline on the flybridge, which sports a second full helm station with bench seat, along with a sunpad, wet bar, and barbecue. Aft of the funnel is a pleasant inlaid dining table, and tucked under the electronics arch is a spa pool and freshwater shower.

The stairs down from the entry foyer on the main deck lead to a lower passage with four more cabins. Two VIP staterooms are forward with raised queen berths and drawers below. The cabins feature mahogany joinerwork, planked floors, and raised panel doors on the lockers and cupboards. Each have a head with Italian marble and a shower. Just aft (with a watertight door in the passage) are a pair of cabins with twin beds, and each also has a head with shower. The forecastle holds the two crew cabins, one with a double and the other with bunks, and each has its own head with shower.

The well deck holds a tender and two watercraft launched with an Italian Mor Saverio hydraulic crane. Aft, a Mor Saverio passerelle extends 16ft in three extensions.

SPECIFICATIONS

LOA:	83ft (25.29m)
LWL:	79ft (24.07m)
Beam:	22ft (6.7m)
Draft:	7ft (2.13m)
Displacement (light ship):	120 tons
Engines:	2 x Caterpillar 3406 DITA 440HP
Speed (power):	10 knots
Fuel capacity:	7,000 gallons
Range at 12 knots (power):	3,000nm
Electricity generation:	Kilopak 2 x 33kW with sound enclosure
Bow thruster:	American Bowthruster
Watermakers:	High pressure
Sanitation:	Headhunter
Security systems:	Ademco
Paint/painters:	International
Air-conditioning:	Aqua-air
Communications:	Furuno
Hull construction:	Steel
Owner and guests:	1 master/4 guest staterooms
Crew:	2
Classification:	Giordano Institute
Project management:	Fernando Jr.
Naval architecture:	Marcio Igreja
Exterior styling:	Inace
Interior design:	Michael Kirchstein/Mavignier Lima
Builder/Year:	Inace Shipyard/2002

Power for the *Amarellla* is a pair of 440hp Cat 3406 diesels and, as you'd expect from a little ship, the engine-room is spacious and organized with a centerline workbench. A pair of Kilopak 31kW generators (one with power take-off) provide electrical power, and other equipment includes Rodriquez stabilizers, Aqua Air air-conditioning, and an 800gpd watermaker.

Because bad fuel is a way of life in exotic ports, *Amarellla* has a fuel system designed so that the Aqua Laval fuel cleaners can run continually, pulling fuel from the two main tanks then filling the day tank. When the day tank overflows, it dumps back into the mains, resulting in both clean and cool fuel.

Two sea chests are designed so one can run all the systems even when partially clogged, and *Amarellla* has sufficient battery power to run all the electrical systems including refrigeration through a Dakar inverter for up to eight hours.

With a range of 4,000nm, *Amarellla* is an ocean wanderer built for simplicity—but her redundancy gives her self-reliance. There is a lot of yacht built into these 83 feet—in fact, she is really more ship than yacht. If you hunger for the horizon, *Amarellla* awaits.

Opp. top ★ Casual dining alfresco.

Opp. bottom ★ When tiptoeing through a coral reef, not even the best equipment is a match for 'eyes on high,' so *Amarellla* has a crow's nest.

Top ★ The master suite is located on the upper deck allowing spectacular views.

Andiamo

140-FOOT FEADSHIP EXPLORATION VESSEL

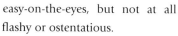

The 140ft motoryacht *Andiamo* is not only a strikingly good-looking vessel with a great deal of character, she is a departure for Feadship, being the first expedition yacht from this company—and she is attracting a great deal of attention as a result. *Andiamo* is a very personal yacht that incorporates an enormous amount of original thinking by the owner, who is one of the few women to own a yacht of this size.

An experienced yachtswoman and long-standing member of the Saint Francis Yacht Club, Nancy Mueller began developing plans for *Andiamo* when she sold her business and had the time to turn her dream into reality. She knew what she wanted: a seaworthy hull that looked good, had a hint of a working boat, and steered away from the rather boxy or wedding-cake models that are all too familiar today. Intrigued with the expedition yacht concept (as the yard sees this as a strong trend), Royal Van Lent Shipyard of Feadship sought out and won the bid. The concept for *Andiamo* required the same highly detailed and finished product characteristic of Feadship's fine yacht-building. Glade Johnson was commissioned to design the interior, which was to be modern, practical, comfortable,

easy-on-the-eyes, but not at all flashy or ostentatious.

The first step was for Feadship's in-house naval architects—De Voogt—to turn Doug Sharp's concept into a fully engineered design that met all the regulatory requirements. The draftsmen were delighted to work on a design with a traditional sweeping sheerline, long foredeck, and compact superstructure of modest height. *Andiamo* has full walk-around decks at both main and upper levels with the superstructure set well aft. An argument against this is that in order to provide a roomy and private owner's suite forward on the main deck, it makes sense to take the superstructure out to the hull sides. The design of *Andiamo* gets over this very simply: there is no owner's suite on the main deck.

Instead, a large and sociable galley occupies the forward end of the superstructure, which is one of the keystones to the layout. Stretching across the superstructure with big windows on both sides and forward, this galley is to be used by both the owner and crew. There is a comfortable dinette on the port side where friends can socialize while the chef whips up some culinary extravaganza. To say this galley is well-equipped would be an understatement—it

Porthole ★ Many areas were designd to specifically display the owner's artwork.

Left ★ The sun deck sports a significant galley with a large bar and a comfortable table arrangement that seats 14.

Opp. top ★ The 140ft *Andiamo* is dedicated to active enjoyment of life.

Opp. bottom ★ The aft bridge deck is organized for grand meal preparation—as one would expect from a professional in the food business.

has been meticulously designed and superbly equipped by a catering professional—Nancy.

It's not often we begin a description of a yacht with the galley, but having done so, let's move aft one step to the dining room, which is also unusual in having the table placed fore-and-aft rather than athwartships. The thinking is that diners on one side of the table can enjoy the view through large picture windows, while those on the other side can see the same scene reflected via large mirrors on the inboard wall.

Still in the dining room, we get a feel for Glade Johnson's relaxed contemporary design that features flat cherry wood-work divided into panels by recessed lines. The large areas of cherry have been brushed crosswise to give a raised grain effect that stands out from the background. The creamy wool carpet is plain, while granite countertops throughout the yacht are of various shades. No marble! No gold!

Moving aft again, the main saloon is the largest open space aboard—and it looks even bigger because a roll-up screen allows guests to look into the dining room. The hallway, with its spiral staircase made from a stainless-steel tube, is also part of this open area. 'Flow' and 'natural' describe the saloon, which has comfortable modern sofas and armchairs grouped around a low table with four ottomans tucked under. All the countertops are in chunky black granite, which speaks of contemporary Zen rather than palaces. A games table is inset with smooth, curved pieces of abalone shell. Here, and throughout the yacht, there are outstanding modern paintings and sculptures from the owner's collection. The big-screen television is concealed behind a panel, while drawers below it pull out to reveal the keyboard of an electric piano and a sound-mixing board, and a guitar stands nearby.

The bridge deck saloon is truly multi-purpose with a workout area/library/office/TV den/coffee lounge. Following

Left ★ With an electric piano, a guitar, and a sound-mixing board, the main saloon is the place to make beautiful music.

Opp. top ★ The saloon arrangement has a wonderful *feng shui* flow.

Opp. bottom ★ The 'gyroscope' sculpture is one of the many pieces of contemporary art displayedaboard *Andiamo*.

Below ★ Flat cherry woodwork, cream colored wool carpet, and the lack of gold and glitz make the dining room conducive to a pleasant, relaxing meal.

the blond maple-and-teak planking forward through the upper lobby (highlighted by an arresting 'gyroscope' sculpture) leads to the pilothouse, which, like the galley, is designed for owner-participation. Two skipper's chairs offer a perfect view, plus there is a comfortable U-shaped settee and coffee table upholstered in deep sea-green leather.

The owner was instrumental in selecting the navigational equipment, which includes an integrated electronics suite that displays charts, radar, autopilot, and systems monitoring information. One of the newer systems is a night-vision monitor that could be exceptionally useful for negotiating harbors or anchorages in the dark. The Geochron shows the time profile anywhere in the world.

Andiamo has a very robust and straightforward engine installation with a pair of Caterpillar 3412 diesels rated at a conservative 720hp each at 1,800rpm. With her easy lines, this will be plenty of power for a cruising speed of 11 knots, which gives a range of

around 4,700 nautical miles with full tanks at 15,712 gallons (and one generator running).

The lower-deck layout places the engines aft, the crew forward, and the guest accommodations in the center. Some owners want their cabin to have the best view, others the most room, but Nancy Mueller chose the position with the least motion at sea: two-thirds aft on the lower deck. This is not a charter yacht, so there was no inclination to cram in twelve guest berths. Instead there are just three large and comfortable guest cabins in addition to the owner's suite, which uses the full-width of the hull.

Being in the widest part of the hull makes it possible for the owner's suite to have a bedroom on one side and a spacious sitting room on the other. Although it is below deck, this suite has a nice, open feel. With soft golden silks, sea-green upholstery, granite and a plain, cream carpet, this is a relaxed but elegant living space. Two of the guest cabins are queen-size and the

other is a 'family' room with a double and twin berths, plus an extra Pullman. A doorway from the cabin lobby to the crew quarters allows easy access when servicing the staterooms.

There is plenty of deck space on *Andiamo*. The sun deck is a complete outdoor living area with spa pool, sunpads for four, game table for dominoes, dining for 12 to 16 and

dancing for 20! Two large "tents" of heavy, white spinnaker fabric protect dining and sunning areas from extreme sun and heat. *Andiamo* also has a fully equipped galley with table service, refrigerators, warming oven, and cooking hobs. Child gates throughout were planned with foresight at the start of the project—and upon completion, grandchildren appeared!

The aft bridge deck houses two Lasers and two sailboards that are neatly stowed along with eight kayaks. This is also the location of the aft drive station. A large barbecue assembly with rotisserie, two burners, and a sink allow casual grilling for large groups.

On the main deck aft, there is the slightly more formal outdoor dining table, which comfortably seats two to 12 people. Music is independently controlled here, as it is throughout all the other spaces on the yacht. The adjacent service bar supplies beverages and ice along with needed supplies. The overhead supplies protection and wing doors shelter from the wind. On the foredeck are the tenders—and these are aluminum-hulled RIBS (built by Northwind of Seattle) with inboard diesels and Hamilton waterjets. Thanks to the Yanmar diesels, there is no requirement to carry gasoline aboard. And no, there are no jet-skis!

This is a yacht planned for active leisure rather than lazing about, for in addition to sailing equipment, there are several full sets of SCUBA gear and an air compressor in

Above ★ Granite and cherrywood add natural elegance to the bath.

Top ★ The master suite, along with all the staterooms, is situated two-thirds aft on the lower deck for the least motion at sea.

Opp. top ★ Two of the guest cabins are queen-size and the third is a family room with two berths and an extra Pullman.

Opp. bottom ★ A cozy spot for reading or writing.

Left ★ A graceful staircase connects the decks.

the lazarette, which is immediately accessible from the aft boarding platform. The jet boats will be equally perfect as dive-tenders or for gunk holing.

The overall feel that *Andiamo* radiates is one of an outdoor enthusiast's superyacht—a four-wheel drive with a woman's touch. It is particularly nice to see a yacht that has sacrificed a little interior space to make it look so nice, both from the inside and outside. Without doubt, she is a real yachtswoman's yacht.

Above ★ The owner was instrumental in selecting the navigational equipment.

Opp. top ★ This bridge deck saloon is a true multi-tasker with a library, office, workout area, coffee lounge, and television den.

Opp. bottom ★ The perfect place to take in a sunset.

Below ★ If the kitchen is the heart of the home, the galley is the heart of *Andiamo*.

Above ★ There are a plethora of places to enjoy a meal or a view aboard *Andiamo*.

Left ★ A wrap-around walkway off the main deck.

LOA:	139ft 4in (42.6m)
LWL:	125ft (38.1m)
Beam:	29ft 2in (8.9m)
Draft:	8ft 10in (2.7m)
Displacement:	443 tons
Main engines:	2 x Caterpillar 3412 DI-TA 720hp @ 1,800rpm
Speed (max):	13 knots
Fuel capacity:	15,712 gallons
Range @ 11 knots:	4,700 nautical miles with one generator
Electrical:	Atlas 100kW Frequency Converter with Atlas Smart Box
Electrical generation:	3 x Caterpillar 3304 105kW
Bow thruster:	Jastram 65kW
Watermakers:	2 x Sea Recovery 2,200gpd
Sanitation:	Evac
Paint:	Awlgrip
Air-conditioning:	Heinen & Hopman
Entertainment systems:	Intelect
Owner and guests:	1 double master; 2 queen state-rooms; 1 family room for 4
Crew:	8
Construction:	Steel hull, aluminum alloy
Classification:	Lloyds +100A1, SSC Yacht (P) LMC/MCA/GMDSS
Naval architecture:	Doug Sharp/De Voogt
Interior design:	Glade Johnson
Builder/Year:	Feadship-Royal Van Lent/2003

Anjilis

124-FOOT TRINITY MOTORYACHT

For the owners of this new 124ft Trinity, *Anjilis* is the visual culmination of two love affairs. Foremost is the couple's love for each other, and secondary is a passion for art deco, the 1940s, and everything that connotes. "We wanted *Anjilis* to be a romantic little cruise ship," said the wife, who worked with designer Dee Robinson to create a look that is charming and functional.

Large yachts are too often impersonal, marked only by the occasional memento or photo in an otherwise beautiful but sterile interior. *Anjilis*, on the other hand, is a warm floating tribute to the owners and their penchant for a world of white top hats, Ella Fitzgerald, and old-fashioned romance. From the concealed martini bar in the saloon to the checkerboard black-and-white marble flooring to the twin Seadoos named Fred and Ginger, *Anjilis* exudes the aura of a bygone era.

For Trinity, the term "little cruise ship" is more than just a catch phrase, since *Anjilis* is literally a small ship. Trinity, of course, has a heritage drawn from military and rugged offshore commercial boats. Trinity VP William "Billy" Smith, calls *Anjilis* a "small big yacht." Unlike many builders that build "big small boats" using the same systems as 70-80 footers, *Anjilis* is downsized from previous Trinity builds such as the 177ft *Katharine* (ex-*Seahawk*). Her sophisticated systems range from cupronickel water piping to oversized sea chests to watertight doors and bulkheads. Both *Anjilis* and her big sister prototype have advanced noise treatments. "*Anjilis* is a pocket megayacht," said Smith, "built to full ABS class and easily capable of transoceanic crossings on her own bottom."

For the owners—who are involved in the construction business—*Anjilis* was a private and delightful project. Said

the husband, "We used a scorched earth approach, leaving nothing undone. Trinity would offer us four ways of installing a bilge pump, for example, so we were aware of all the alternatives and the costs. There were no surprises with any of the 125 owner-initiated change orders." Smith interrupts with a smile, "And when we asked them for a decision, they always chose the best way. The result is that *Anjilis* is a no-compromise yacht."

Needs of potential charterers were taken into consideration, so there are both formal indoor and alfresco dining. For charterers who want solitude, there are private areas in

the saloon, flybridge, aft deck, and office, as well as riding seats on the bow.

"We're outdoor people," said the owners, and *Anjilis* is designed with that in mind. The aft deck is huge, with a teak table that can seat ten for formal dining (it slides out for ease of entry) and the deck has teak planks, which reflect the curve of the table. But the teak-capped bar forward is a favorite, as the couple loves to sit on the aft deck in the morning, enjoying a quiet moment and a breakfast buffet while watching the morning news on the flat-screen television. The aft deck can be fully enclosed

Porthole ★ Guests can sit in comfort at a settee and table in the pilothouse.

Opp. bottom ★ A full bar with permanent stools and barbecue enhance the sun deck.

Top ★ *Anjilis*, anchored off of Sint Maarten, draws just six feet.

Right ★ The raised spa pool on the sun deck.

with isinglass for an all-weather sunroom with both air-conditioning and heating.

The flybridge is just as important to the owners and is one of the reasons they chose a raised pilothouse design rather than a tri-deck. Arranged with entertaining in mind, guests can sit facing forward behind the venturi wind-screen, and wing controls give the captain a good view while maneuvering. The full bar has four permanent stools opposite a settee and table, and a raised spa with three built-in sun lounges separates the boat deck. A built-in Sterling gas barbecue is in a console to starboard, while a 3,500lb Nautical Structure davit launches the tender, the twin Seadoos, and a pair of Vespa motorscooters to either port or starboard. To provide sun protection, a retractable Pipewelders bimini top extends from the electronics arch over the guest area, complete with a removable panel for viewing the stars at night.

The aft deck and bridge are clearly modern, while step-ping through the automatic saloon doors takes you back into another era. From the Royal Oyster inlaid marble entry to the matte-finish American cherrywood paneling that is accented with maple burls and crotch mahogany trim, *Anjilis* is more Orient Express than Florida Moderne. The color scheme used by Dee Robinson and the owner's wife is from a chocolate-and-mocha palette. There are twin velour chairs and wrap-around loose couches, a horn game table with black-and-white chairs is aft to port, and the wool carpet is custom-dyed. The martini bar is concealed to starboard, along with a pop-up 42in plasma television. Flawless joinerwork has art deco styling, and period wall sconces accent the intricately detailed window pillars.

The formal dining area is separated from the saloon by a low buffet between two large black columns with bronze deco designs. Dee Robinson finished the columns with hidden doors that serve as spacious storage compartments. Under an alabaster chandelier, the dining table of goatskin under resin seats ten.

The raised pilothouse fills the center of the deckhouse, and the galley is past the day head and has a portside deck access door. This galley has an unusual L-shaped layout that seems impractical but is extremely workable, thanks to the design of the chef—who doubles as the captain's wife. With granite counters and maple floors, it features three ovens, twin dishwashers, and a big SubZero refrigerator/freezer, a five-burner cooktop, plus an oversized pantry with an additional built-in refrigerator. Arranged to face out through big

Above ★ The bright and cheerful galley has access both to the crew quarters and to the pilothouse.

Main picture ★ In the main saloon, the color scheme used by Dee Robinson and the owner's wife is from a chocolate-and-mocha palette.

Below ★ The dining table is made of goat skin under resin and seats ten comfortably.

windows, the galley is bright and cheerful, with a food prep area closer to the dining area so several crew can prepare and serve meals without crowding. The galley has stairs down to the crew quarters forward and steep non-guest steps into the pilothouse. As a result, the crew can move around and operate the yacht without intruding on the guest areas, and the full walk-around side decks are essential to this end.

An unusual starboard cabin dictates an unusual galley arrangement. While many yachts have a country galley or an on-deck master suite filling the forward superstructure, *Anjilis* has a multi-purpose fifth stateroom forward past a

black-and-white checkerboard entry foyer to starboard. In the absence of a sky lounge, this cabin serves as a pleasant reading area with an ornate brocade couch and a built-in writing desk. When needed, it converts easily to a queen-size stateroom with a private head and shower forward, or it can serve as an office. This gives *Anjilis* a five-stateroom arrangement without sacrificing space in the four staterooms below.

Curving stairs from the entry area lead to a lower foyer that is accented by inlaid marble and a morning buffet counter. The foyer also has a hidden laundry room, as well as concealed SubZero refrigerator drawers to provide refreshments for the guests.

Sized to rival those on 150-footers, the full-beam master suite is breathtaking with a king-size berth beneath a mirrored headboard with a framed painting. Twin burled pillars with gold-and-nickel finials add to the art deco theme, as do the wall sconce reading lights and marble-topped night stands. The port side has a vanity between

Above ★ A love seat, flanked by bookshelves, is to starboard in the master bedroom.

Top right ★ Betty Boop adds a touch of whimsy.

Opp. top ★ The full-beam master suite on this yacht rivals those aboard 150-footers.

Opp. middle ★ The vanity sits between twin deco-faced bureaus.

Bottom left ★ The shower features etched doors, multiple shower jets, and steam.

Bottom right ★ Custom nickel-and-gold sinks are embedded in marble.

sinks with gold and nickel, Royal Oyster marble on the bulkheads, and a spacious shower with etched deco doors, multiple shower jets, and steam.

Forward, a pair of cabins have queen-size berths, art deco window panels, and ensuite heads with Sahara Gold marble counters, Crema Marfil flooring, and large showers. A twin cabin is amidships with a Pullman third berth, brass-railed bookshelves, and a private head with travertine counter and marble flooring.

A custom-designed Van Cappellen sound package was used on *Anjilis* because the owners wanted a quiet yacht. With the saloon sound level below 55dB(A) at the 18-knot cruising speed, they achieved their goal. With floating bulkheads and extensive efforts in the engine-room and machinery spaces (which includes Poseiden flexible shaft couplings that isolate and insulate anything that could either cause vibration or transfer sound), the master stateroom barely registers 40 decibels when the engines or generators are running.

Drawing six feet three inches, *Anjilis* is an unusual combination of a bluewater oceanic yacht with shallow water capabilities, which allows her full access to marinas and harbors in the Bahamas.

The owners may never don white top hats, but the painting in the day head succinctly sums up their life aboard *Anjilis*. It shows an elegant couple dancing on a beach, while a butler holds an umbrella for shade. Truly a small romantic cruise ship with exceptional systems and construction, *Anjilis* clearly reflects her owners' desires.

twin bureaus with deco-faced cabinets, a love seat is to starboard between bureaus, and a large walk-in closet is cedar-lined. The superlative joinery and millwork is particularly evident in the master suite with burled mahogany double entry doors, inlaid burl on the bureau drawers, and fluted deco accents. The his-and-hers head is notable for custom

LOA:	124ft (37.8m)
Beam:	26ft (7.9m)
Draft:	6.3ft (2.1m)
Displacement:	130 tons light
Engines:	2 x MTU/DDEC 16V2000 (1,850hp)
Speed:	21 knots
Fuel capacity:	10,500 gallons
Electrical Generation:	2 x 55kW Northern Lights
Bow thruster:	Quantum 80hp
Stabilizers:	Quantum
Watermaker:	Sea Recovery 2,500gpd
Sanitation:	Headhunter
Paint:	Awlgrip
Air-conditioning:	Marine Air 24 ton
Construction:	Aluminum
Owner and guests:	11 guests/5 cabins
Crew:	6 crew/3 cabins
Classification:	ABS Maltese Cross A-1 Yachting Service AMS
Naval architecture:	Trinity Yachts LLC
Interior design:	Dee Robinson Interiors
Builder/Year:	Trinity Yachts LLC/2002

Above ★ Sweeping staircase to the top deck.

Top ★ The sun deck bar is actually sheltered from the sun.

Opp. top ★ One of the queen-size guest staterooms with its art deco window panels.

Opp. left ★ The head that goes with the library cum spare guest stateroom.

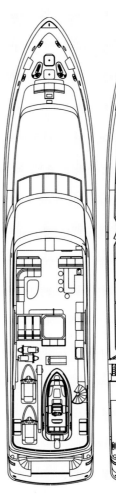

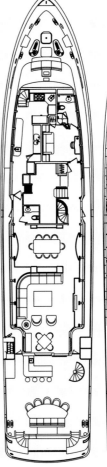

Blue Belle

132-FOOT MONDOMARINE MOTORYACHT

lue Belle, the 43rd motoryacht built by Mondomarine, represents a new direction for the yard—largely due to the exterior styling by Cor D. Rover, a talented young naval architect based in Holland. The project had its inception at the Monaco Yacht Show in September 1999 when Walter Goldstein stopped by Cor's booth. He liked what he saw and decided to give him a stipend for a preliminary design for a 121ft-to-125ft boat (which later became 132ft). With drawings in hand, Walter shopped around for bids. He seriously entertained a bid from a Dutch builder whom he knew and respected. However, he ultimately decided to award the contract to Mondomarine, a subsidiary of Mondo SpA that was established about 50 years ago in Alba.

Walter already owned *New York Lady,* a 96ft fiberglass yacht built in 1995 by Mondomarine. He had had a good experience with them, so he went to Elio Stroppiana, co-owner of the yard (with his brother Ferruccio) and explained that he wanted to build a new all-aluminum, semi-displacement motoryacht. He added, "You know Elio, when you build a boat in Italy, you eat better, and when you build a boat in Holland, you sleep better." Elio grabbed his hand and said, "Walter, I will build you a boat, and you will eat better and sleep better." Goldstein honored their history together, and began his new building project.

As fate would have it, Walter's company and Mondo SpA had some connection. Walter's business supplied the concrete work for the superstructure of the twin towers at the World Trade Center and Mondo supplied a good deal of the rubber flooring for those same two buildings.

The contract was signed in December 1999, and the dream team quickly assembled: Cor D. Rover, as designer of the

external lines, and Genoan consultants SYDAC worked on hull design and engineering. For the interior décor Walter Goldstein's wife Doris worked with Isabelle Blanchère, the same French designer who was responsible for *New York Lady*.

The yard began construction early in 2000, with Walter Goldstein visiting the yard every three weeks to meet with Mondo director Diego Deprati and second in command, Angelo Giaccone. In December 2002, two years to the day after the signing of the contract, *Blue Belle* was launched. It is obvious that the yacht is the fruit of many years' experience, and that great care has been taken to ensure the comfort of the guests down to the finest detail. *Blue Belle* combines sophistication with apparent simplicity. Every aspect of the yacht exudes harmony, from the very flowing,

unaggressive external lines and dark blue hull to the interior fitted out in a single type of wood.

The yacht's bulbous hull and light aluminum superstructure were built at the Savona yard. The stretched, slightly curved bow is fine enough to allow her to cut through the sea easily. Juan Clark-Stukeley, the skipper who has worked on *Savarona* and some other very fine yachts, says, "Everything is so well laid out! The hull is very seaworthy and *Blue Belle* is swift and responsive. From the bridge, maneuvering is easy and, of course, the external wing controls are handy in port or among crowded moorings. The MTU engine system is the best in the world—reliable and economical. *Blue Belle* has a range of 3,500 nautical miles at 12 knots and our maximum speed is 21

Porthole ★ The proportion of the twin beds and the high ceilings gives this cabin a luxurious feel.

Top ★ A light aluminum superstructure gives *Blue Belle* speed—she reaches 21 knots at half-load.

Right ★ At the helm of *Blue Belle* are two Boeing pilot-style chairs, two radars, two DGPS, and a DGPS chart plotter.

Opp. bottom ★ With four deep armchairs, a large settee, and bar seats, the sun deck has plenty of vantage points from which to watch the world go by.

knots at half load, which is remarkable for a yacht of this size. But then we only displace 225 tons unladen and 375 gross tonnage. That is the great advantage of aluminum: a heavy displacement hull can barely make 17 knots."

Blue Belle was built to conform to the US Coast Guard regulations. In the engine-room there is a Hamann sewage treatment system for the black and gray water, as well as a bilge water separator. The vessel is well-equipped for cruising in restricted areas regarding Marpol regulations. Remco Koote, the build engineer, was responsible for creating systems that would allow the Goldsteins to be able to use their boat for extensive cruising in and out of restricted areas—all the while maintaining their share of pollution control for cleaner cruising grounds. Another nice touch is a water softener and conditioner integrated in the fresh water system that then passes through a UV sterilizer, making all water onboard drinkable.

Blue Belle is well conceived in every aspect. The decks, handrails, and external stairways are all lined with teak, and below, the floors are all wide prefinished teak boards, with no carpets anywhere.

Access when moored stern-to is via the port side passarelle that turns 90 degrees and folds down into steps. The transom opens and flips down with the central section of the passarelle to form a large swimming platform. Inside the transom, lockers stow all the equipment needed for water activities, and there are two hot showers. When you have changed, you can mosey up to the sun deck (which is well-sheltered by the overhang of the upper deck) and stretch out on the large settee or relax in one of the four deep armchairs

and watch the world go by, glass in hand. This area is also perfect for breakfast and watching the port wake up.

The mooring cleats and winches on either side of the decks are raised up on platforms (which save you from stubbing your bare toes) and painted ivory like the rest of the superstructure. The magnificently shaped stainless-steel hawse holes hold the internal warps stopping the boat from swinging about when there's a swell. The two side decks are well-protected by high bulwarks and sheltered by the upper deck. Doors on either side and in the transom give access to the engine-room, which takes up the full-beam of the yacht. The side decks end level with the saloon bulkhead; the port door opens into the pantry between the saloon and galley, while the door to starboard takes you into the main entrance hall, which has a double door to the exterior. A stairway leads to the four guest cabins, the owners' suite forward, and the dining area of the saloon aft.

You enter the main saloon via curved doors with four smoked glass panels and stainless-steel frames. They have electric controls and open automatically to let the Goldsteins' dog through. The saloon is divided into three separate areas that flow into one another. First you have the bar, with its half-moon shaped counter topped with blue granite on the starboard side, while to port a table and four armchairs await card players or inveterate night owls who may wish to linger there for a nightcap. The treatment of the bulkheads is dazzling, entrusted to Gianni Celano Giannici, a very well-known local ceramicist and painter. Not many people know that Albisola is one of Italy's main ceramics and artistic centers, enjoying a reputation equal to that of Vallauris in the fifties and seventies. Giannici has created a dream-like scene made of multi-colored pieces of molten glass that evoke the sky and sea with stars, crescent moons, fish—one sporting a cameo profile of the artist. All of the furniture, the tables, and the columns are made of pale maple, worked with the direction of the grain forming a checkered pattern. The same effect is seen in the owners' suite, guest cabins, and throughout the boat.

Two large, striking sofas, upholstered in cheerful blue monochrome-striped canvas, invite idlers to linger and chat. The décor is reminiscent of forties American comedy film sets. Designer Isabelle Blanchère explains, "The owners wanted an interior that was easy to live in—light, elegant, and evocative of the marine world, so lots of blues. They wanted pale wood—hence the choice of maple—and removable washable covers on all the seats, and no carpets or rugs, just teak floors. White Carerra marble, alabaster, and blue marble have also been used. The free-standing pieces are of course solid, but where you see them on flat surfaces such as in the floors or on some of the bathroom countertops, thin sheets were used to save weight." All the cabinetry was done by a company in Bergamo; the small gilded knobs on the furniture doors, shaped like horizontal droplets of water, were selected by Isabelle.

The whole forward section of the saloon is devoted to a round dining table surrounded by ten chairs covered in blue canvas with yellow ties—Provence-style. The bulkhead

Opp. top ★ Two unpainted Picasso ceramic vases flank the sideboard in the dining area.

Bottom ★ These large, comfortable sofas are found in the saloon, which is divided into three sections: the bar, the sitting area, and the dining area.

Below ★ On a cloudy day, the sky lounge—with its sunshine yellows and indigos of Provence—is a cheerful place to enjoy drinks at the bar.

Above ★ The master suite spans the full-beam and is designed with no sharp angles.

Left ★ This is the "hers" of the his-and-hers bathrooms. Hers is equipped with a hydromassage tub and a dressing table; his has a simple bath and shaving table.

Opp. top and bottom ★ There are two VIP suites, each with queen-size beds, Venetian blinds in natural maple, and bathrooms with tubs and double sinks.

Below ★ A light and pleasant office area is an anteroom to the master suite.

above the large sideboard is decorated with a fresco by Parisian artist Véronique Charpy showing gilded, interlacing seaweed—very art deco—representing the bottom of the sea, while on the surface two mermaids frolic with fish and a dolphin. On the sideboard two round unpainted ceramic vases by Picasso fit perfectly into this scene.

The galley, fitted out partially in stainless steel, has a stove with eight induction rings, two Miele ovens, two plate warmers, a grill, microwave, dry steam oven, and dishwasher, along with six refrigerators and five freezers. A stairway leads either down to the crew mess or up to the pilothouse for ease of service.

A door to starboard in the saloon opens forward into the passageway which has an open feel due to the vast mirror above a delightful onyx console table that sits on gold ball feet.

To port in the utility area, aft of the two stairways, you find the laundry and a serving entrance from the galley. To starboard is a day head and the door to the owners' suite forward. You first enter the office, illuminated by two large portholes like the ones in the saloon and the cabin itself. The pale wood and blue-checked sofa coverings make it a cheerful room. Mrs. Goldstein has a computer and printer here, while another communal printer serves the five terminals of the ship's computer. There are a few souvenirs from their villa on the Cap Ferrat: a crayon drawing in color by Cocteau and a lithograph of Parthenia—a tribute to the jewels of the Mediterranean—signed by Braque. The anteroom with its very ornate wood and marble parquet floor that matches the gold marquetry sun motif on the ceiling is in fact the dressing room, while a sliding door concealed in the bulkhead opens into the cabin itself. The king-size bed

is covered in blue-and-white cotton fabric. Also in the room are two dressing tables, a sofa, and two oval bedside tables in the same style as the sideboards in the saloon. Perched behind the sofa is an exquisite Picasso ceramic in the shape of an owl with colors that are harmonious with the setting. This cabin, extending across the full-beam of the yacht, is vast, light, and airy. The television descends from the ceiling when required. Again, there are no sharp angles creating a great impression of space. "Her" bathroom has a hydromassage bath and dressing table, while "his" has a simple bath and shaving table. Like the cabin itself, the bathrooms on either side let in daylight through large portholes with rounded corners in the same shape as those in the saloon.

The lower deck is divided into four very separate areas. Aft is the technical space, then there is the engine-room and

Above ★ Bring toothbrushes for two.

Top ★ The second of the VIP suites.

forward are the crew quarters which have direct access to the wheelhouse. Amidships, the four guest cabins, which open off a large hall reached via a spiral wooden staircase, are thoughtfully fitted with non-slip treads. You are immediately struck by the exceptional headroom and proportions of the twin beds and the depth of the mattresses. When I remarked on this to Walter, he replied that yacht cabins always seem too small when you come in from outside, and he didn't want his guests to feel claustrophobic. Fore and aft are two vast VIP cabins with double beds, one is predominately yellow and the other is blue; each extend across the full-beam of the yacht and have dressing tables, several cupboards, bathrooms with baths and double washbasins and—an important detail—separate WCs in the aft cabin. The opening oval portholes are dressed with Venetian blinds in natural maple. Between the two VIP cabins the other two guest cabins, one in red, the other in blue, have twin beds linked by a single headboard in the shape of a wave, and bathrooms with large enclosed showers.

A second stairway beside the one down to the guest cabins leads up to the upper deck. Forward is the wheelhouse, where two Boeing pilot-style chairs in blue leather dominate the instrument console and controls. Here alongside the two radars, two DGPS connected to an electronic DGPS chartplotter, and the instrument controls, you also find the touch screens for the safety and alarm systems. The skipper's cabin, illuminated by a porthole, is a few paces away.

Outside near the bow is a settee set into the coach roof where you can enjoy the sailing or find a little peace and quiet. The foredeck offers seating and is occupied by one of the two tenders and its hydraulic crane.

The vast sky lounge is the perfect spot to seek refuge from the sun outside or have a little siesta on the settees upholstered in the sunshine yellows and indigos of Provence. It is also the ideal spot for parties with an outside table seating twelve. Also available are drinks at the bar, or games of chess or backgammon at a table especially designed for this purpose. Here, there are three ceramic plaques commissioned by local artist, Serge Vandercam. Aft you find the low profile main tender, accessible to the water by a hydraulic crane.

Forward on the sun deck, bathed in sunshine, is the spa pool and sun beds, along with two vast sofas, low tables, an American-style galley with barbecue, and in the stern, three separate alcoves, each with a sofa, ideal for successive breakfasts or for a little something after a swim. A great feeling of individual freedom emanates from *Blue Belle*, showing the care the owners have taken to ensure their guests' well-being. This yacht leaves you with the impression of happy, carefree cruising marked with that touch of class. And after having achieved perfection, what else is there? Walter Goldstein mentions that he is thinking about his next yacht, then he adds with a smile, "What else would you expect an 80-year-old man to say?"

LOA:	132ft (40.5m)
LWL:	113ft (30.4m)
Beam:	28ft 3in (8.6m)
Draft:	7ft 10in (2.2m)
Displacement (light ship):	225 tons
Engines:	MTU 12V396TE94 2 x 2,285 hp
Speed (max/cruise):	21 knots/19 knots
Fuel capacity:	13,200 gallons
Range @ 12 knots:	3,500nm
Electrical generation:	Northern lights 2x80kw
Water pressure system:	2,640 gallons
Air-conditioning:	Frigorifero-Frigit 24
Construction:	Light alloy
Owner & guests:	2 twins, 3 doubles
Crew:	4 doubles
Classification:	Maltese Cross A1
	"Yachting Service" AMS
Project management:	Juan Clark-Stukeley/Remco Koote
Naval architecture:	Sydac/Cor D. Rover Design
Exterior styling:	Cor D. Rover Design
Interior design:	Isabelle Blanchère
Builder/Year:	Mondomarine/2003

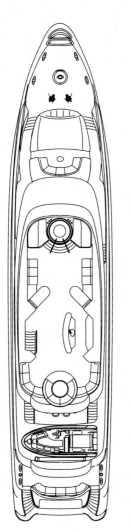
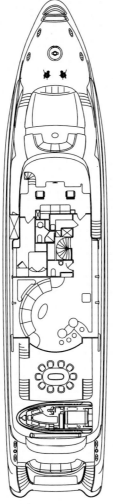
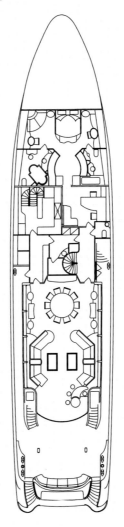
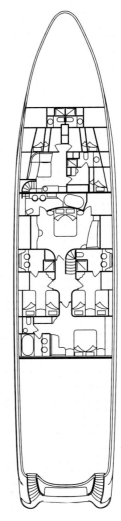

Crescent Lady

121-FOOT CRESCENT CUSTOM MOTORYACHT

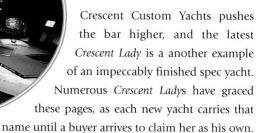

*S*pec yachts have become a dominant force in the megayacht market in recent years, as more and more builders find that it is easier (and certainly more profitable) to offer fully completed yachts to buyers rather than embarking on long custom-build projects. Not only do the buyers have the satisfaction of immediate turnkey access without waiting years for their new toy, but also the builders don't have to put up with endless change orders as the owners nitpick every facet of the project.

Crescent Custom Yachts is at the forefront of the spec market—and has almost single-handedly refined the spec yacht genre from plain vanilla offerings into gracious and luxurious megayacht desgins. Gone are the ho-hum, offend-no-one colors and décor used by many spec builders to reach the widest number of owners. Each new launch from

Crescent Custom Yachts pushes the bar higher, and the latest *Crescent Lady* is a another example of an impeccably finished spec yacht. Numerous *Crescent Lady*s have graced these pages, as each new yacht carries that name until a buyer arrives to claim her as his own.

Not only is she the most opulent *Crescent Lady* yet offered, she also marks a change in design for Crescent Custom as the first 26ft-beam, Jack Sarin-designed yacht. Crescent previously used narrower Westport hulls, but now the hulls are constructed in-house with a mold design that allows the beams to range from 26ft to 28ft and lengths that span 110ft to 135ft. Thoroughly tank tested at the University of British Columbia, the new hull is a sea-kindly and fuel-efficient design that takes full advantage of the wider beam.

That stout beam is first noticeable in the saloon, which is

Porthole ★ The pilothouse includes a settee with granite table for observation and entertainment.

Left ★ On the flying bridge, the spa pool is tucked to starboard for wind protection.

Opp. top ★ On her maiden voyage, *Crescent Lady* topped out at 22.3 knots with a full load!

Opp. bottom ★ A stopover in Mexico before heading for the east coast provided some beautiful scenery.

expansive yet allows room for full walk-around side decks that simplify life for the crew. The interior design team at Crescent chose a theme that blends tropical touches such as the palm leaf carpeting pattern with a muted Oriental décor. However, the owner who does not have the yen for Oriental design can easily create a new interior by changing the carpet, the accent pieces, and some of the gold wall coverings. The sapele and ebony accents work well with a multitude of styles—this look makes a statement, but is a versatile backdrop for any number of concepts.

A pop-up 42in plasma television is aft to starboard, where it can be enjoyed from the wide couch with rounded end and exposed legs, which add a touch of Art Deco. Loose chairs are to starboard, and an overstuffed chair with ottoman is aft as a lounge. Twin stainless-steel sliding doors open to the teak-planked aft deck with the usual curved settee and dining table. Of note in the saloon

are the large windows that provide an unobstructed view, even while seated. The ebony coffee table, built by Crescent, is a good example of this builder's superlative in-house-woodworking skills.

What separates the formal dining area from the saloon are twin buffet counters with ebony columns. A round table sits beneath a ceiling that is more than nine feet high and enhanced by a waterfall effect of mirrored and intricate millwork, plus crown moldings. If fine dining is a religion, this is its chapel.

Another buffet, with a black granite counter, is against the forward bulkhead, and a curved ebony cabinet to starboard conceals a wet bar with sink. Once again, the craftsmanship of the woodwork is superlative, having taken more than 144,000 hours to complete.

The port passageway hides the day head, with an intricately wicker-framed mirror and luxurious bronze wall coverings. With

doors to the side deck and boarding stairs, the starboard passage is the formal entryway, where Crescent created the illusion of a much larger space by curving the inboard wall. This wall presented a challenge to the woodworking team, who fitted a curved cabinet with a black granite top, which acts as a base for the sculptures that match the Oriental wall covering. Two large glass doors and recessed lighting make this entryway spectacular at night.

Forward on the main deck is the country galley, which is as efficient as it is casual. The galley proper has a swoopy center island with a powerful Miele overhead vent to quickly suck up cooking odors and small dogs. The island is curved on the forward side to create a breakfast counter for several guests on bamboo chairs, and it also accommodates the five-burner stovetop. All stainless-steel appliances (including a double-door SubZero fridge) are set in raised-panel sapele cabinets, and the same large windows as the saloon provide a view on both sides. For easy cleaning, the floor is an unusual ostrich-look vinyl that matches the ostrich Magilite overhead. The forward half of the country

galley is devoted to a curved and comfortable settee and dining table with stainless-steel half-columns that match the trim on the center island.

The lower foyer sets the stage for luxury with a compass rose inlaid in the teak-and-holly sole and a breakfast buffet counter. Forward and down from the galley, past a large storage cabinet accented by stained glass doors, is the VIP suite. Double doors give the feel of a completely private master suite, and light comes from the curtained ports. Bureaus are built into each side, and a spacious walk-in closet creates liveaboard storage. The ensuite head is equally well-appointed, and the large marble shower, with a curved glass enclosure and seat, doubles as a steam room.

Off the conventional lower foyer, reached via stairs from the starboard entry passageway, are the owner's suite and two guest cabins. The stairwell is notable for the detailed planking on the curved wall, as well as the leather-laced handrails. Finished in a leather-like wall covering, the lower foyer features a black inlaid marble floor, a breakfast nook cum sculpture niche, and a remarkably spacious walk-in laundry room.

Forward is the master suite, which has a king-size berth on an ornate raised-panel base with drawers. The semi-circular ceiling treatment above the berth showcases Crescent's woodworking abilities, and there is a mirrored panel above the padded headboard and double columns on each marble nightstand. The aft bulkhead has a 42in flat-screen television set apart by an ornate rope column of sapele and, although flat panels would have been the norm, *Crescent Lady* has intricately curved doors with burled inlays in the marble-topped buffet below the television. The

Oriental theme continues with bamboo-design wall coverings. An eight-drawer bureau is to starboard, while the port side has a comfortable desk and drawers below the large opening ports.

A thoughtful choice was to create a single ensuite head to port rather than the usual his-and-hers bath—this leaves the starboard side for a walk-in, cedar-lined closet. The head has ropework columns, marble counters, and a sliding *shoji* screen for the toilet, while the marble shower is equipped with steam.

Opp. page ★ The beamy main saloon and dining area evokes a slightly Oriental feel with ebony and sapele wood accents.

Right ★ Galley gourmet!

Below ★ Looking aft, the swoop of the buffet and the curves of the overheads and moldings present a pleasing effect.

The two guest cabins are aft of the foyer and essentially the same size with twin berths to starboard (with a Pullman berth) and a double to port. As in all the guest areas, the doors are arched and solid with raised-panel treatments, and each have marble nightstands and curved-front drawers.

The pilothouse is simple and efficient, and skippers who believe in paper charts will appreciate the full-size chart table (to port) with six large chart drawers below. A leather Stidd helm seat has a good view through the large windows and, with just two posts dividing the windshield, there are no blind spots. A ship's office is to starboard and raised so that the skipper can work and still keep an eye on the autopilot and the instruments while underway. To port, a settee with a granite table provides comfortable seating. It's worth noting that the raised pilothouse allows for an immense compartment underneath for electronics equipment, complete with air-conditioning and carpet.

The flybridge helm is equally efficient, with repeater electronics in a fiberglass pod and three Stidd chairs raised for a view above the tinted windscreen. Two settees with tables are also located on the raised-helm level, and steps lead down to the boat deck.

Above ★ The double guest cabin is luxuriously appointed.

Below ★ The master suite features a plasma-screen entertainment unit, walk-in closet, and king-size berth.

Above ★ Sunpads conveniently placed for lounging on the foredeck.

SPECIFICATIONS

LOA:	121ft (36.9m)
Beam:	26ft (7.9m)
Draft:	6ft 4in (1.9m)
Displacement (light ship):	347,000 lbs
Propulsion:	2 x 16V 2000 MTU @ 1800 bhp
Speed (max/cruise):	23k/18k
Fuel capacity:	7,800 USG
Range @ 12 knots:	3,650nm
Electrical generation:	2 x 55 kw Gen with A-SEA 70 kva
Bow thruster:	ABT
Stabilizers:	ABT
Watermaker:	Village @2000 gpd
Paint:	Awlgrip
Air-conditioning:	Marine Air
Tenders:	Novurania
Construction:	FRP
Naval architecture:	Crescent/Marshall
Exterior styling:	Crescent/Marshall
Interior design:	Robin Rose and Associates
Builder/Year:	Crescent Custom Yachts/2003

A spa pool is tucked to starboard for wind protection, while a wet bar with Corian counters and an Ultraline barbecue are to port. Two large sunpads (with adjustable backs) are on each side. Aft, a 17ft Novurania tender is launched with a Marquipt 2,500lb crane.

Whoever arranged the crew quarters was obviously once a crew, because this space is not just comfortable, it's comfortably efficient. With access from the transom platform as well as from the aft deck when running, three cabins can handle up to six crew. To port are a pair of cabins with upper/lower bunks, separated by a shared Jack-and-Jill head, while an large captain's cabin is to starboard with a private head and double berth. The midships area is devoted to a crew lounge with a Corian-topped full galley and a settee with table and television.

The engine-room is equally thoughtful, with good access to the twin DDC/MTU 16V2000 diesels, as well as the twin Northern Lights 55kW gensets. With a total of 3,600 hp and slippery hull lines, *Crescent Lady* is no slouch. On her maiden voyage, she topped out at 22.3 knots in spite of full fuel and water—plus 28 guests aboard.

At first glance, you'd never guess that *Crescent Lady* was a spec yacht. Her interior is stylish and luxurious, yet she can easily be changed to fit the tastes of a future owner. Benefiting from more beam and with an intelligent layout, she won't be called *Crescent Lady* for long.

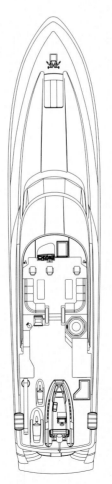
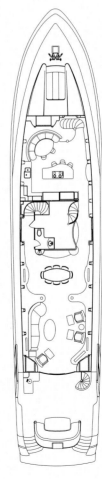

Defiant

124-FOOT DELTA TRI-DECK MOTORYACHT

Viewing her in the finishing stages, Delta's 124-foot *Defiant* shines resplendent despite the inclement weather at this Seattle Shipyard. Her distinctive 'stars-and-stripes' blue hull is a definite bright spot on the gray seascape. *Defiant* is docked alongside a Seiner 58, one of the most popular fishing boats to come out of the shipyard during the 70s and 80s. While Delta has its roots in commercial fishing vessels, what is obvious now at this vast and immaculate facility is that this is where megayachts are built.

As a repeat Delta customer, the owner of this 124ft semi-displacement tri-deck knew what to expect when commissioning the yard for his second motoryacht. His previous Delta, the 117ft *Rainbow*, served him well—but in the world of yachting, upgrading is inevitable. The inspiration for his yachts' names indicates a respect and reverence for historical yachting: *Rainbow* was named after the J-class America's Cup boat popular in the 1930s, and the name *Defiant* is derived from the tall ship *H.M.S. Defiant*.

The owner, an avid sailor, seems to keep tradition at the

forefront, as is evident in the interior and exterior styling of *Defiant*. Her lines are stately and elegant, a marriage of class and quality, while her blue hull, with its high-gloss teak rail, joins the white superstructure in a union of nautical excellence. The 'stars-and-stripes' blue hull, too, has a story: it is the exact same color as Dennis Connor's America's Cup defender *Stars and Stripes*, and it is the color of the owner's 30ft Hinckley sailboat.

Defiant will spend her summers in New England and winters in Palm Beach and the Caribbean. Built as a semi-displacement vessel, she draws only six feet, making her ideal for cruising shallow waters. Added features such as a dive compressor, flybridge spa pool, and copious outdoor entertaining areas make her especially ideal for tropical cruising.

On the main deck, guests can enjoy the outdoors either on the aft deck for dining and entertaining, or on the foredeck in a comfortable riding seat on the bow—a terrific perch when underway. Access to the boat deck is either via a curving stairway aft or through the main saloon to the midships starboard foyer. Upon entering the saloon itself you have the feeling of a true gentleman's yacht, a place where bow ties and Burberrys might abound. The bulkheads are elegantly finished in cherry solids and veneers. The sumptuous woodwork is offset by ivory-colored

Above ★ *Defiant* sits distinctively above the water with her 'stars and stripes' blue hull.

Porthole ★ The master stateroom occupies the full 26ft beam.

Opp. bottom ★ Breakfast on the aft main deck

Below ★ The flybridge is outfitted with matching Stidd chairs and a spa pool.

carpeting. A comfy couch and overstuffed armchairs in blues and whites are subtly arranged to face a hidden 50in plasma-screen television. Next to the aft entry doors to starboard is a standup granite-topped service bar. Moving forward to the dining area, a granite-topped low buffet with twin cherry columns provides visual separation from it and the main saloon. The focal point of the dining saloon is the antique table positioned under a recessed headliner with an alabaster and gold-leaf chandelier. Once again, naval history is omnipresent with several of the owner's detailed ship models accenting the area.

From the dining area forward is the hub of circulation throughout the interior. To port is the galley entrance, which is cleverly concealed by a sliding door activated by a foot switch for ease of serving. The bright and spacious galley is well-designed with multiple work stations. An expansive granite countertop/buffet is situated to starboard. Equipment includes SubZero refrigeration, stacked ovens, and a five-burner halogen stove. A walkway forward through the galley with two large windows leads to the completely comfortable crew and captain's quarters.

The foyer forward of the dining area has maple flooring trimmed in cherry and wenge woods. To starboard and forward leading past a day head is the VIP stateroom. The day head repeats the granite and cherry themes visible in the main saloon and also features gold and brass fixtures from the Seattle boutique, Waterworks—these fixtures can be found throughout the yacht. The VIP stateroom reflects the décor of the main saloon in that it too has ivory carpeting and cherrywood. The bed is accented by a head-board upholstered in crisp blue and white. Opposite the berth, a 42in flat-screen television is mounted on a cherry backboard and twin fluted columns frame the screen. Other amenities include a writing desk to port, an ensuite head, and a cedar-lined, walk-in closet. As this stateroom is located on the main deck, the need for decorative art is at a minimum, because there are spectacular views from four picture windows.

Walking back to the central foyer, there is an elegant stair-case with a cherry banister that leads both up to the sky lounge and pilothouse and down to the guest and master staterooms. Descending to the lower deck, the guest cabins and master stateroom are easily accessed via a shared vestibule. In this area, concealed behind two cherry and upholstered panels, are twin washer/dryer units (for a total of three aboard). Aft are the guest cabins, both with flat-screen televisions and ensuite heads finished in granite. The port cabin is arranged with twin beds and a Pullman berth,

Above ★ An elegant staircase leads to the sky lounge and the master and guest staterooms.

Opp. top ★ The dining area is separated from the main saloon by a granite-topped buffet.

Opp. bottom ★ Clean surfaces and professional equipment comprise this no-nonsense galley.

Below ★ A convivial furniture grouping in the cherry-paneled main saloon makes for easy conversation.

with ample space for storage beneath the elevated bunks. This cabin was most likely designed with grandchildren in mind. The starboard cabin provides a queen-size bed athwartships that is flanked by meticulously crafted cherry nightstands. While the cabin to port was designed with a larger head for multiple users at the same time (i.e. children) by adding a door between the sink and toilet compartments, the starboard stateroom uses this space as a walk-in closet.

The master stateroom, which occupies the full 26ft beam, lies forward of the guest foyer. The king-size bed, berthed in deep cherry with matching night tables, faces aft. To port is a large desk that spans the length of the cabin, answered to starboard by a full-length settee. A 37in plasma-screen television is hidden to starboard behind a heavy burled panel that, when closed, displays a painting. On either side of the cabin, walk-in cedar closets face equally spacious his-and-hers bathroom. A shower steam room, enclosed in glass and stone, joins the two heads. As with the rest of the interior, the simple palate of the master stateroom has an understated elegance.

Journeying to the top of the stairwell reveals the sky lounge cum media room, with its purely patriotic, blue-and-white star pattern carpet. Several large windows provide panoramic views, while cherrywood bookshelves and nautical flair give this space the feel of a race committee room or yacht club library. The second plasma-screen television hides here, along with a host of other audio/visual devices. The pilothouse lies forward, and to starboard is an airy day head with a picture window and light-wood flooring. Aft lies the boat deck entrance. For additional outdoor entertaining, this teak-decked area is fully equipped with a large dining settee, refrigerator, and barbecue. Further aft is a 19ft Nautica tender and 4,000lb telescoping crane to lift her. On the starboard side are stairs to the flybridge.

The open pilothouse is finished in a pearlescent gray hammertone urethane, a material that complements the hi-tech nature of the space. Equipment includes a fully adaptive AC plath, self-tuning autopilot, and several Big Bay premium composite video flat-screens—displaying everything from closed-circuit TV to a Transas chart plotter. A settee to port allows guests to be part of the action when cruising, and to starboard is a command station for the captain. Above on the flybridge is another helm and

Above ★ A vestibule on the lower deck accesses the two guest cabins as well as the master stateroom.

Opp. top ★ Enveloped in cherry, the king-size master bed faces a 37in plasma-screen television that is cleverly concealed behind a painting.

Opp. bottom ★ Multi spray faucets enhance the master shower.

Below ★ On the main deck level, this VIP cabin carries forth the star-themed carpet also found in the sky lounge.

docking station with matching Stidd chairs for guests. In addition to the helm, the flybridge is outfitted with a spa pool and wet bar.

Powered by twin Caterpillar 3412E diesels at 1,400hp each, *Defiant* reaches a maximum speed of 16.5 knots with a cruising speed of 15.5 knots. Her range is 2,500 nautical miles at 12 knots.

Interior and exterior design were at the hands of the in-house Delta Design Group. *Defiant* is the tenth yacht from Delta's 110ft to 124ft semi-displacement range. She is virtually silent when underway, as was evidenced during the sea trials when moving from the engine-room to the quiet solitude of the main saloon. This quietude is a signature that Delta is perfecting, with each subsequent build reaching higher noise reduction levels. But the quality emphasized by the Delta shipyard is apparent in every nook of this yacht. From the stainless-steel deck drains impressed with the Delta logo to the custom-seamed teak decking on the main and boat decks, *Defiant* takes her place as this year's most stately megayacht.

Opp. top ★ Stars and stripes spiff up the sky lounge.

Opp. bottom ★ Hammertone urethane complements the hi- tech nature of the pilothouse.

LOA:	124ft (37.8m)
Beam:	25ft (33.8m)
Draft:	6ft 2in (1.9m)
Displacement:	175 long tons (half load)
Engines:	2 x CAT 3412 E 1,400hp @ 2,300rpm
Speed (max/cruise):	16.5k/15.5k
Fuel capacity:	9,600 USG
Range @ 15 knots:	2,000nm
Electrical generation:	2 x Northern Lights 65kW @ 1,800rpm
Bow thruster:	American 85 HP
Stabilizers:	Naiad 410
Water capacity:	1,000gal
Watermaker:	2 x Matrix S1500 GPD
Entertainment systems:	AV Concepts and Design
Security systems:	Elbex
Paint:	US Paint/Awlgrip
Air-conditioning:	Marine Air Systems 24 Ton
Communications:	Harris Electric
Owner & guests:	8
Crew:	5
Naval architecture:	Delta Design Group
Exterior styling:	Delta Design Group
Interior design:	Delta Design Group
Builder/Year:	Delta/2003

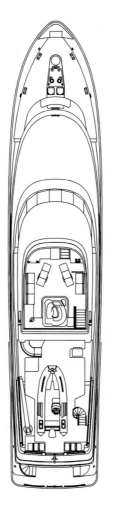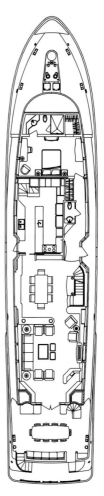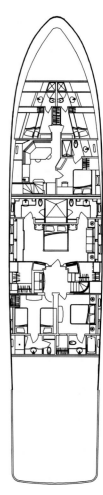

SS Delphine

258-FOOT 1921 GREAT LAKES STEAM YACHT

Like many other extraordinary yachts, *Delphine*, a steam yacht originally built for American car magnate Horace Dodge, has led a tempestuous existence. She was launched at River Rouge on Lake Michigan on Saturday April 2, 1921, just over four months after Horace's death. His widow, Anna, who oversaw the completion of the work, and their son Horace Dodge Junior, who inherited the yacht, wished the launch ceremony to be a quiet affair attended only by family and a few close friends. But the fame of the yacht was already such that nothing could prevent a curious crowd over a thousand strong from flooding into the yard.

Delphine was not Horace Dodge Sr.'s first yacht. From the beginning of the 20th century he and his brother/business partner John had been passionate devotees of steam yacht racing—regarded as the most expensive hobby of its time. In 1903 Dodge became the owner of a 40ft dayboat, *Lotus*, which was superceded by a number of other racing yachts.

He was also a member of several large yacht clubs. In 1914 when he launched the first car bearing his name, a 180ft motor cruiser, *Nokomis*, commissioned by his father, was also launched in New York. In 1917 *Nokomis* was replaced by *Nokomis II*, a 243ft yacht with a clipper bow. In the same year both yachts were requisitioned by the US Navy and, before commissioning a new yacht, Dodge purchased *Caroline*, a 187ft motoryacht built in 1914. He rechristened the yacht *SS Delphine* and in June 1920 his daughter Delphine and new son-in-law James Cromwell set off on a honeymoon voyage around the world.

At the end of 1918, Dodge asked architect, HJ Gielow, to draw up plans for the second *Delphine*, a splendid 258-footer, much larger than Henry Ford's 210ft *Sialia*. She was to be the most extraordinary steam yacht in the Great Lakes in terms of size, propulsion and interior decoration. Construction of *SS Delphine* began a year later, at an estimated cost of

$2 million. Dodge designed her quadruple expansion engines himself as he wanted a fast yacht with a good reserve of power. Sadly he did not live to see her sea trials in May 1921. In June *Delphine* came to berth alongside the private jetty at the Dodges' home, connected to Lake Michigan by a 3,000ft canal, remaining there for the winter.

In 1922 Anna Dodge and friends set off on a cruise from Detroit to New York via Lake Ontario and Saint Lawrence, but during the voyage the yacht ran aground off Toronto—luckily it did not sustain any damage. Tragedy was to strike in 1926 on the evening of September 21st, after a party on board and while Anna Dodge and friends attended a performance of *La Traviata*. Around 10:45pm, fire broke out on board. The crew tried to extinguish the blaze while the captain raised the anchor in an attempt to reach the New York shore. The

captain, unable to reach the quay, asked to be taken in tow, but at 1:00am the dense smoke forced him and the crew to abandon ship. *Delphine* dug her bows in and sank shortly afterwards. Anna Dodge's maid did however have time to go back into her mistress's cabin and fetch her jewelry case containing around $250,000 worth of jewels.

Initially *Delphine* was declared completely lost, but experts revised their opinion and three months later she emerged from the mud of the Hudson River. The task of refitting her was entrusted to the Brooklyn yard James Shewan & Sons and by May 1927 she was fully restored to her former glory. When the US entered the Second World War in 1942, *Delphine* was requisitioned by the US Navy. Renamed *USS Dauntless* and fitted with anti-aircraft guns, she was converted into a patrol boat and assigned escort duties for

Porthole ⋆ Bunk beds make a fun alternative for children.

Opp. bottom left ⋆ *Delphine* has a concave stem partly to allow her to sqeeze into tight areas, and partly to prevent the Navy from chopping off her bow if ever requisitioned.

Opp. bottom right ⋆ The impressive *al fresco* dining area with seating for 28 guests.

Top ⋆ *Delphine* emerged from the bottom of the Hudson River to be restored to her original grandeur.

Right ⋆ Over 12,000 square feet of teak were laid on the extensive deck area.

Above ★ Nearly all of the public areas onboard are the work of one man, aided only by his wife.

Main picture ★ The music room has an air of formality, complete with a Steinway grand piano and a piano bar.

Opp. bottom ★ The elegant dining room.

the US Atlantic fleet. Thereafter *Delphine* entered the annals of history. President Franklin D Roosevelt allegedly spent weekends aboard the yacht on the Potomac preparing for the Teheran and Yalta conferences, accompanied at various times by Harry S Truman, Winston Churchill and other international politicians including Molotov, Russian Minister of Foreign Affairs. This was a well kept secret, however, and is not officially acknowledged even now.

In 1946 *Delphine*, still named *Dauntless*, was repurchased from the US Navy by the Dodge family. From 1967 onwards she passed into the hands of several different owners including the Naval School at Piney Point, Maryland, and several cruising societies, the last of which brought her to Malta where she was sadly neglected. After being up for sale for some time she was bought by an industrialist and yachtsman who read a report about her in our French sister publication *Mer & Bateaux* and acquired her through Antoine and Eric Althaus, Monegasque-based brokers for Fraser Yachts. *Delphine* left Marseilles in May 1997 to be towed to Bruges in Belgium and taken into dock. Her second life was about to start.

At the beginning of Monaco Classic Week 2003, the 258ft steam yacht *Delphine* made a grand entry to the harbor, led by the restored Fife cutter *Moonbeam* and saluted by the sirens of

the tightly-packed fleet and a fountain of spray from the fire-boat, she was escorted to her berth in the place of honor on the Quai des Etats Unis. On the following day 300 guests attended a reception on board and applauded as Princess Stéphanie formally relaunched *Delphine* and accepted the invitation to be her 'godmother'. This was a fitting tribute to the five years of unremitting effort by the Bruynooghe family from Belgium to rescue this famous vessel from the scrapyard and return her to something close to her original 1921 condition.

The history of automobile-maker Horace Dodge's yacht *Delphine* is recounted much more fully in an impressive book written by Ineke Bruynooghe in the small amount of time she could spare from acting as project manager for this dauntingly complex project. Soon after she found out that her father had bought *Delphine*—almost on a whim after seeing her in a very neglected condition in Marseilles during 1997—she began an extensive research effort that was to prove richly fruitful. The State University of Ohio held a large archive of engineering drawings from the defunct Great Lakes Engineering Works that built *Delphine*, while the Mystic Seaport Museum yielded a priceless portfolio of joinery drawings from the original designers, Tiffany's of New York. In addition to a collection of photos that came with the yacht, many more were garnered from members of the Dodge family, relatives of crew members and contemporary newspapers and magazines.

As a result of this research, *Delphine* is well documented and this made it possible to contemplate a full restoration to something close to her original 1921 condition. What

Main photo ★ The palatial owner's stateroom is boldly decorated with paneling in high gloss flame mahogany set off by French Empire style furniture.

Opp. middle ★ All of the guest cabins include spacious ensuite bathrooms.

Opp bottom ★ Stark white walls are set off by the striking use of color on the floor and the furnishings in this stateroom on the accomodations deck.

Below ★ The VIP bathroom has an onyx floor and white marble counters.

the Bruynooghes could not have foreseen was the size of the task that lay ahead. They already knew that *Delphine* had been the largest private yacht in the United States when she was launched, but when they received an offer from a museum to acquire the steam engines for almost the price they had paid for the yacht, they found they had a big dilemma on their hands.

Horace Dodge was a steam enthusiast who had previously owned a 99ft launch that reached a speed of 41 knots using triple expansion steam engines designed by himself. Although 'up-and-down' steam engines were already outdated by 1920, Dodge decided on an 'ultimate' steam plant for *Delphine* and adapted a successful naval design from triple to quadruple steam expansion with one high pressure cylinder, two intermediates and a low pressure cylinder to produce engines of outstanding efficiency and power. Not only are these engines unique, *Delphine* is believed to be the last large seagoing yacht in existence with reciprocating steam engines. To strip the engine-room and install a couple of diesels would have been easy but would have destroyed the character of the vessel. To restore steam power would be immensely difficult and expensive.

Careful inspection revealed that the engines themselves were in fair condition and certainly capable of being repaired

for SOLAS registration as a passenger ship permitted to carry less than 36 passengers. The requirements are much stricter than the MCA code for yachts, especially regarding fire precautions, so *Delphine* had to be fitted with a full list of watertight and fireproof doors, steel decks, fire detectors, Ultra-fog suppressors and numerous alarms and warning signs that you don't find on yachts, plus lifeboats on davits just like a modern passenger ship. There is certain irony in this bearing in mind that *Delphine* caught fire and sank in New York Harbor. Some of the SOLAS rules, for instance those involving fire-resistant stairways, could have been written with this accident in mind. It was a great help that Antoine Wille had worked extensively with passenger ships including the 'Star Clippers' and was well versed in the endless rules to be followed.

The hull was not in bad condition and only four hull plates had to be replaced in the fore part of the hull where leaks from the crew bathrooms had caused corrosion on the inside. *Delphine* had been plated with rivets, but the new steel was welded into place. The inside of the hull was completely cleared, including removal of the three Babcock & Wilcox boilers, but not the engines which were overhauled in situ. As the funnel had been condemned, it was removed and most engine-room equipment could be hoisted out through the resulting large hole in the upper deck. Much of the superstructure was in extremely poor condition with wholesale replacement of steelwork being called for. In addi-

but the boilers were completely shot, having been filled with seawater during the vessel's one and only Atlantic crossing in 1990 during which the feed-water supply failed. The entire electrical system, which had been supplied by steam-driven DC generators was also fit only for the scrap-heap and in any case could never have supplied enough power for modern equipment such as air-conditioning. In one of the small number of compromises made during the restoration, a completely modern electrical system was installed, with diesel generators, so avoiding the need to keep at least one boiler constantly in steam just to generate electricity. Another compromise was to install a bow thruster and an azimuthing (rotatable) stern thruster which together can be used to maneuvre the yacht in harbor. In spite of this, her chief engineer Chris Wiley says she handles extremely well under steam alone and can be placed with complete precision provided the captain is familiar with this form of power.

The new owners wanted to carry out the restoration near their home in Belgium so *Delphine* was towed to a shipyard at Bruges which began the work of stripping out the hull and repairing the steelwork, under the direction of naval architect Antoine Wille. An early decision was to certify the restored *Delphine* for commercial use and, as she is far too big to be restricted to the 12 passengers permitted on a yacht, this called

Opp. top ★ Accented by rich leather, this used to be the smoking room to which the men retired for cigars and brandy.

Opp. middle ★ Stairs from the main entrance lead up to the *Delphine* Lounge and upper deck bar.

Bottom ★ This emergency wheel will steer *Delphine*...if used by someone with strong arms!

Below ★ During WWII, *Delphine* was a patrol boat for the US Navy.

tion, the original deck construction in which wooden planks were laid directly onto steel beams was no longer acceptable and had to be changed to steel decks on which first plywood and then teak planking was laid.

The basic hull and steelwork repairs were made by the Bruges shipyard but afterwards the owners decided to have the vessel restored under their own direction, using a mixture of contractors and their own employees. A small village of shipping containers which could be used as workshops or stores, sprang up alongside the moored *Delphine* as the tempo of work increased. Unfortunately the Belgian authorities proved to be extremely unhelpful and there seemed to be entire government departments devoted to placing obstacles in the way of the work, an example being the occasion on which the vessel was seized and all work ordered to be stopped because the wrong type of temporary toilets had been provided for the workers. Partly as a result, *Delphine* is now registered in Madeira and has been classified by the Portuguese authorities who applied SOLAS rules in a strict but sensible way, making allowances where it was clearly impossible to follow the rules to the letter.

Having made the decision to keep the steam engines, work went ahead steadily with the installation of two new boilers

and auxiliary equipment of every kind including complete rewiring and re-plumbing. Room had to be found for equipment such as air-conditioning and black water treatment that had never been fitted previously but fortunately the original arrangement included a good deal of storage and unused space that could be given a new use. A much greater difficulty now arose regarding the interior decoration. The new owners hoped to copy, as far as possible, the 1921 Tiffany's design which was so well documented, but this had been done in a 'New York baronial' style—heavy with rich, dark timber including wall paneling plus beamed or coffered ceilings. If this were built using solid wood like the original, it would far exceed what SOLAS allows, as the rules strictly limit the amount of combustible material per square meter of surface. The only way around this problem was to make all the timber areas from thin veneer, bonded to an aluminum honeycomb base. This is often done on high-performance yachts for lightness but in *Delphine*'s case it is purely to satisfy the SOLAS fire regulations.

Almost unbelievably, nearly all of the 'public areas' are the work of one man, Georges Marinus whose small company, B&M contracted to build the saloons and dining room. To begin with he had a small team working for him but the difficulty of building paneling and furniture on sheered and cambered decks, with walls that follow the curve of the hull, wore them down until one by one they gave up, leaving Georges, who developed his own unique system for bonding veneers to the aluminum, to work on alone, helped only by his wife. He worked on *Delphine* non-stop for two years and was still aboard, doing final jobs, when she arrived at Monaco.

As you would expect with such a large vessel, the interior space is impressive and there is also much more deck area than a modern yacht; the ratio of interior to exterior space being 50:50. 12,000sqft of teak deck have been laid on three levels and her 'promenade deck' truly deserves the name. This puts her in a different market from even the largest 12-passenger yacht as she can easily host large receptions, fashion shows, trade exhibitions and the like, thanks to this extensive deck area. She can accommodate 28 guests in comfort, opening up the possibility of corporate or special-interest groups.

There are full walk-round decks on both the main and promenade deck level but the superstructure is still wide

enough to provide large interior rooms. The first one you discover after boarding aft on the main deck is the 'music room' where there used to be an Aeolian pipe organ that was thrown out by the US Navy when they requisitioned the yacht during WWII. In its place is a pleasant bar paneled in Padouk (Burmese rosewood) backed by a grille like the one that used to hide the organ pipes, with the Dodge family crest at its center. In addition to several groups of comfortable seats, there is still room for a Steinway grand piano, maintaining the tradition of the music room.

This saloon has a doorway into the main entrance lobby where there are stairs down to the guest accommodation or up to the '*Delphine* Lounge'. Divided into two sections by a pillared portico and paneled throughout with bubinga, the

forward section is a very comfortable lounge that can be used as a cinema with a large television screen appearing from behind an oil painting showing *Delphine* and one of the many speedboats that Horace Dodge Junior raced during the 1920s and 30s. The other half of the room is a piano bar with one of those neat Yamaha pianos that plays itself if there are no pianists available. The bar has an outdoor section that serves the promenade deck.

Returning temporarily to the maindeck, you need to walk forward past the engine-room casing (one of the disadvantages of steam) to reach the main dining room which is perhaps the most richly decorated room aboard being paneled with cherry and with an amazing dome-like feature in the center of the ceiling, exactly as designed by Tiffany's. Apparently the Dodge family did not host large dinners aboard so there is no giant table but instead three large round tables and two smaller ones provide enough space for a full quota of today's guests. In 1920s society, the ladies 'retired' after dinner leaving the men to talk business or politics. From the dining room they went upstairs to the 'smoking room' for cigars and brandy and this clubby, masculine room has been faithfully reproduced, complete with overstuffed leather armchairs. In today's circumstances it is a very nice place to hide away with a good book, watch TV, or enjoy the excellent views overboard.

The two VIP guest cabins are on the main deck, forward of the lobby. The owner's is palatial in size and paneled in high-gloss 'flame' mahogany with French Empire style furniture including rather spectacular winged chairs and an *escritoire* containing headed notepaper suitable for passionate love letters. The ensuite bathroom has a floor of onyx contrasting with white marble counters and offers the choice of a full-size bath or shower. Next to this, and reached by a separate door from the deck, is a somewhat smaller suite, decorated in the same style.

The remainder of the guest accommodation is downstairs from the hallway and consists of nine cabins with a mixture of arrangements opening off a central corridor. This reminds

Above ★ The vast promenade deck is perfect for enjoying afternoon tea.

Top ★ Delphine's splendid profile is recognizable in any port.

one of a hotel and the cabins are very much what you would expect from a good hotel room with a very nice ensuite bathroom, a television and music center, refrigerator, air-conditioning, plenty of storage, etc. Cabins 1 & 2 are a bit larger and grander as they are in a wider part of the hull. At the end of the corridor is a cabin with four bunks that would be suitable for children or perhaps for personal staff.

In a good hotel, you expect more than bedrooms and so you do aboard *Delphine*. One deck below the staterooms, at the forward end, there is a really big and well-equipped gym with a selection of exercise machines and weight-lifting rigs. After 'working out' you can relax in a spa-bath, a sauna or a Turkish bath and after that, take advantage of

the fully-equipped hair and beauty salon, all of these facilities being on the same deck as the gym.

Modern yachts often boast a 'lido deck' but *Delphine*'s top deck surpasses most, having a real swimming pool containing five tons of water with an artificial current to swim against. There's also a welcoming bar, a sunpad area and plenty of comfortable deck chairs. On the same level you can stroll foward to visit the pilothouse with its interesting mix of original and modern features. The engine-room telegraphs are the real thing—there is no other way to control the engines, so it's 'Ding-ding! Full ahead both!'

The next level down, the promenade deck, contains the largest outdoor table I have yet seen, with space for 28 people to sit down together. There is also a smaller, round table for a more intimate group. Along the sides of the superstructure runs the wonderful promenade deck which really deserves the name as it is easily wide enough for two people to stroll arm in arm. *Delphine* has three original boats as tenders including a 35ft 6in cabin launch. These can be hoisted to the promenade deck by traditional davits.

The maindeck is pleasant and interesting as well as being a means of arrival and a working deck. Right aft is a 'real' emergency steering wheel with which you could steer *Delphine* by hand, if you have very strong arms. Or, if you walk right forward, you can find a small steam engine that drives the unusual horizontal anchor capstan on the deck above. "Does it really work?" I asked. "I sure hope so" replied the engineer, "We don't have any other way of hoisting the anchor!"

Delphine is special from all angles. Her profile with the concave stem makes her recognizable in any port. Restoring her has been an enormous effort and a tremendous act of faith by the Bruynooghe family that richly deserves to succeed

LOA: 257.8ft (78.6m)

Beam: 35.5ft (10.82m)

Draft: 14.6ft (4.6m)

Propulsion: 2 x quadruple expansion steam engines, 1,500hp each, built by Great Lakes Engineering Works

Speed (max): 12 knots

Fuel capacity: 55,000 gallons

Range @ 9 knots: 2,500 miles

Generators: 2 x MTU diesel, 470kW

Boilers: 2 x 18 bar water tube boilers, 1 x 14 tons/hour, 1 x 4 tons/hour

Construction: Steel, with aluminum pilot house

Guests and crew: 28/30

Classification: RINA V Class R2 + Hull + Mach, passenger ship, less than 36 passengers, unrestricted navigation.

Naval architecture: Gielow and Orr, New York, (for refit) Antoine Wille

Design: Tiffany's, New York

Builder/Year: Great Lakes Engineering Works, Michigan/1921

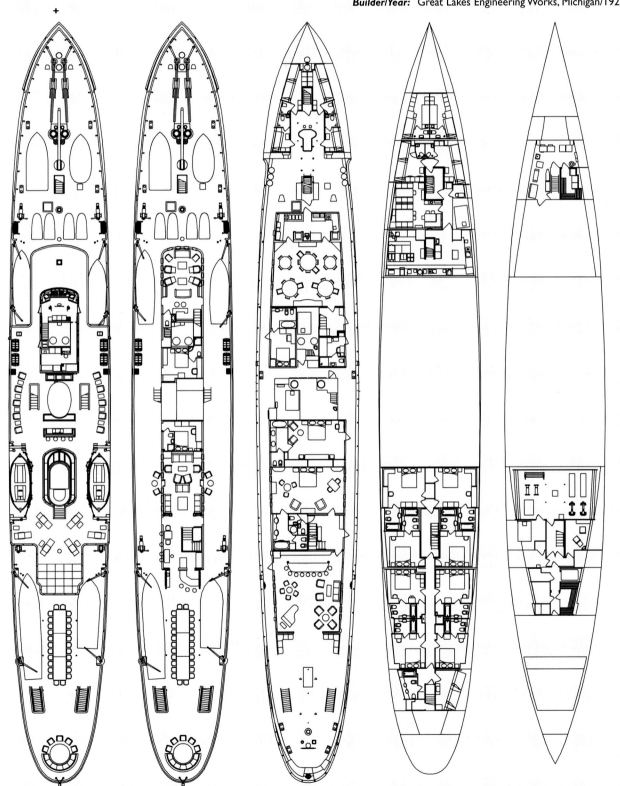

Felicitá west

210-FOOT PERINI NAVI KETCH

*S*tanding at the helm, Ron Holland has a broad, satisfied grin on his face. The designer of her hull and sail plan is trying out 210ft *Felicitá west* for the first time and is astonished to discover just how easy this great ketch is to handle. He says, "She responds like a real sailing yacht and is much more sensitive than I expected. It's a real pleasure to helm with such fine control—you really don't feel as though you have a yacht weighing over 716 tons in your hands."

It is early June and the largest yacht from Perini Navi is in full sail on an oily sea off Cala di Volpe, near Porto Cervo in Sardinia, en route to the island of Tavolara. She is carrying a mainsail and mizzen plus a reacher and self-tacking fore staysail—some 19,368sqft of canvas that give her plenty of power in the light 6.4 knot airs. Her well-balanced hull glides through the water with ease. Arriving in the lee of the island, the wind freshens to over 10 knots and *Felicitá west* instantly gains speed, settling at a heel of 8 degrees, 40 degrees off the wind. The GPS registers 9.8 knots and she responds well to the wind's veering and backing, providing the helmsman with a free hand to trim the sails using any of the 22 joysticks that control the captive electric winches.

At the helm on the flying bridge, controlling this huge yacht single-handed, trimming and handling sails at the touch of a button, it all seems so simple that you can easily forget that you are in fact reliant upon extremely sophisticated technology. No other yacht of this size in the world has such a panoply of instruments. Advanced software analyzes data from more than 500 sensors, allowing the yacht to sail almost completely automatically. Ship engineer Jairo Martins is on watch to make diagnoses when necessary, while we sail along easily in total silence. Even tacking requires no rushing about and we watch as the reacher furls away and the yankee unfurls on the other tack in less than two minutes. A slight problem with the sheet pre-tensioner on the starboard captive winch serves as a reminder that you still have to keep an eye on what is happening. The displays of the electronic sail controls indicate the opposing forces. In 20 knots of wind these can reach 19.8 tons on the main halyard, 15.4 tons on the mizzen halyard and a staggering 22 tons on the sheet of the yankee.

Porthole ★ Food preparation will be no problem in this functional space.

Left ★ The flying bridge is a favorite space to be when the yacht is under sail.

Opp. top ★ A true Perini Navi with all the benefits of a Ron Holland hull and sail plan.

Opp. bottom ★ Foredeck furlers.

Frank Renoux, second in command, is very pleased with *Felicitá west*. He remarked, "You have to learn how to manage all these maneuvers with the furlers and captive winches. To our astonishment we have not encountered a single problem, right from the first trials. The owner asked us to push the boat to her limits in more than 25 knots of wind. We averaged over 17 knots on a close reach 80 degrees off-wind, and she handled extremely well. Now it just remains to be seen how the hydraulic furling booms will perform in bad weather."

The three splendid electric Harken winches —two 1140s and one self-tailing 1110—allow you to hoist light sails, such as the asymmetric spinnaker, and to intervene if there is a problem with any of the 13 Perini Navi captive winches.

Handling the yacht single-handedly, captain Scott Ledbetter steers us into the anchorage in the bay of Spamaltore di Terra, south of Tavolara. The 13ft swinging keel with its 44 tons of lead ballast is lifted, the two foresails are furled, the fully battened mainsail is lowered into the carbon boom with hydraulic furler, and likewise the mizzen. The whole operation takes just two minutes. We enter the bay slowly under engine and Renoux lowers the anchor.

When it is time to leave, it takes only four minutes and 30 seconds before the sails are set again. However, the fickleness of the breeze forces us to give up tacking home.

Under her two Deutz 8 cylinder, 1,220hp engines, *Felicitá*

west has a top speed of 16 knots, a cruising speed of 13.5 knots and a range of 4,000 nautical miles at 12.5 knots. The two variable four-blade propellers are servo-controlled by computer software that automatically adjusts the pitch according to the boat's speed. This very versatile transmission allows you to bring the yacht from full speed to a standstill in less than two-and-a-half times her own length. The rotation test, performed at over 16 knots in a calm sea, is spectacular. The hull, although not fitted with an anti-roll system, does not heel at all as it turns on a circle measuring around 820ft in diameter. Under power, *Felicitá west* beats all records for quietness, the average noise level inside being a barely audible 50 decibels. This has been achieved by building in some 77 tons of sound and thermic insulating materials and using anti-vibration materials in the soles and the linings.

With her classic appearance, emphasized by the counter stern that makes for a very extended deck-line, *Felicitá west* is a true Perini Navi yacht, built in the tradition of her predecessors that made the name of the Viareggio-based yard. However, she is also the incarnation of a new generation of

Main picture and opp. bottom ★ The main saloon has the feel of a classic English yacht with cherrywood and walnut trim joinery and plenty of cozy areas for relaxing.

Top right ★ Forward on the main deck is the formal dining room where you can also enjoy a drink at the bar.

Middle right ★ A magnificent staircase leading to the guest accommodations and owner's suite.

aluminum sailing yachts, none of which have ever before exceeded 550 tons. This achievement is owed to a collaboration with Ron Holland, as Perini's managing director Giancarlo Ragnetti is keen to explain. "We have indeed built a real Perini Navi, with all the benefits of Ron Holland's experience for the hull and sail plan. This project began in July 1999, and construction has taken two-and-a-half years."

For Venetian designer Carlo Nuvolari, working with partner Dan Lenard, the ketch's vast size was a major concern. He says, "The most important thing, in my view, was to make the sheer of the hull work in harmony with the superstructure so that the yacht is pleasing to the eye. I believe we have been successful in this respect, and this is why I wanted her to be finished entirely in white."

The Nuvolari & Lenard studio designed a very uncluttered deck plan, with wide side decks that allow you to move around two abreast. It is clear that much thought has been put into the yacht's ergonomics. For example, all the cables and returns between the sails and the captive winches are concealed in channels in the bulwarks and

Opp. page and above ★ The owner's suite is vast, with a sitting room, bedroom, bathroom, dressing room with separate heads and a running machine which is hidden away in a large closet.

Below ★ The ensuite guest cabins are decorated in the same classic style which runs throughout the yacht.

coamings beneath the deck and in the uprights of the coachroof. Access to the aft deck saloon, fully protected by the overhang of the flying bridge, is on the same level, making it easy to be sociable while underway. Also, a section of the aft deck and a vast door in the transom hinges down to form a boarding and bathing platform with wide steps.

In order to keep the aft deck clear of obstacles, the majority of the deck area forward of the mast is taken up by the two semi-rigid 19ft Zodiac tenders carried in cradles set into the deck. A telescopic crane stows away in a locker between them. The tenders can be lowered and recovered fairly rapidly—it takes about 10 minutes to board both— and in an emergency one can be launched in less than three minutes.

The living space in the aft deck saloon has a central section furnished with three wicker settees and two long banquettes with two separate tables. Twelve people can sit here in

comfort. It is very easy to move about the practically flush stern deck. Those aboard can lounge here undisturbed and enjoy perfect peace, whether the yacht is under sail or moored.

The portside companionway leads up from the deck saloon onto the remarkably large flying bridge. Here you catch shadowy glimpses of the sails through the open-weave bimini overhead. The helm position forward with four separate seats takes up the full width of the flying bridge, while two banquette seats behind offer unrestricted views of the entire 210ft of deck. Aft of these is a bar/food preparation area to port and dining area to starboard. A sun terrace around the mizzen mast overhangs the stern deck. The flying bridge is everyone's favorite place when *Felicitá west* is under sail—a dozen people can move about up here without bumping into one another.

The bridge communicates directly with the external helming position via a companionway to starboard. It is a proper navigation station, as you would expect from a modern automated vessel, and it is large enough to allow six passengers to help sail the yacht or admire the view from a comfortable teak seating area with navy blue leather upholstery. To port is the captain's office. The bridge is undoubt-

edly a part of the interior, yet it allows the owner and guests to experience the pace and feel of the yacht at sea.

Steps lead from the bridge to starboard and curve down to meet a passageway that opens forward into the dining area and bar and aft into the main saloon. Aft of the saloon, on the starboard side, is a day head and to port a servery which is ideal for alfresco catering.

The main saloon does not have wide doors opening out onto the aft deck saloon, because Nuvolari & Lenard wished to keep it as a very tranquil and intimate space. It is adorned with matte-varnished cherrywood bordered with stained walnut, lending it the feel of a classic English yacht. The paintings, of 1920s beach scenes, are in perfect harmony with the wide expanse of sea beyond the expanse of windows. The large, elegant and deeply comfortable settees and wide chairs are upholstered in shades of green, ochre and beige. They are arranged in several seating groups in which people can read, converse, play cards or catch a film on the vast plasma television screen.

The dining area forward is decorated in the same style, with a chess table from the owner's personal possessions. Six stools around the bar counter to starboard have

panoramic views out over the bow of the yacht. The seating area to port with a long banquette seat transforms into a formal dining area when a large tabletop is set upon the two low cylinder-mounted tables.

A stairway amidships descends straight aft from the dining area to a galleried landing, where it then splits and leads both starboard and port into a lobby. From here one can access the four guest cabins and the owner's suite, all well positioned amidships beneath the main deck. Going aft through a heavy fire door, which almost needs a doorman, you enter the owner's suite—a small apartment of perfect proportions. There is a sitting room to port and a good-sized bedroom to starboard. A plasma-screen television is recessed in a handsome chest at the foot of the over-sized double bed. Aft and to port is a spacious dressing room that leads to a separate heads, while in the starboard corner is the monumental bathroom with separate bath tub and shower compartment. This is decorated with marble leaves on a honeycomb background. The owner's foldaway treadmill is hidden in a central cupboard, with a small plasma screen in its line of sight.

Main picture ★ *Felicitá west* is a yacht that will turn heads along any coast.

Right ★ Recessed storage for tenders on the foredeck ensure that the lines of the boat are not marred.

The four guest cabins consist of two doubles and two twins, each with an extra Pullman berth and ensuite shower room. The two forward twins are slightly larger and have dressing rooms. These cabins, like the owner's, are decorated in the same style as the rest of the living space, and all have wide horizontal portholes that look out over the sea.

With this layout, the access ways between the owner's and guest accommodation are separate from those of the dozen crew members. They have their own companionway, aft of the main mast, with a half-landing forward in the deckhouse opening into the captain's double cabin to starboard and the galley to port. The latter has been fitted out very thoughtfully with a central unit, providing excellent working conditions for the professional chef. He also has the use of a cold storage room and large capacity freezer on the lower deck just below the galley, opposite a laundry with washer/dryer and clothes press. In the bow are the teak-lined crew's quarters, with a mess to port, dining area to starboard and four cabins forward with ensuite shower rooms.

Much in-depth research went into *Felicitá west*'s on-board technology to ensure that she would meet the rigorous safety standards imposed by Lloyd's and MCA. Advised by the two classification bodies, Perini Navi's research department and Ron Holland's design office had to specially design the engineering of the first ever aluminum sailing yacht weighing over 716 tons. The results are apparent as soon as you enter the engine compartment, which is laid out excellently. From the control position you have a very clear view of how the equipment is functioning thanks to the computer software that analyzes all the data and indicates any action required.

To conclude, it is hard to fault any aspect of the design or manufacture of this magnificent ketch. Built for sailing with her owner and also for charter with her very professional crew, she is sure to turn heads wherever she goes.

Above ★ The aft deck saloon is fully protected by the overhang of the flying bridge.

Below ★ A bird's eye view is possible from the crow's nest.

LOA: 210ft (64m)

LWL: 167ft 5in (51.1m)

Beam: 40ft (12.7m)

Draft: 13ft 2in/29ft 11in (4.1m/9.4m)

Displacement: 716 tons

Sail area: Doyle Sails – total 19,368sqft

(main) 5,713sqft

(mizzen) 3,368sqft

(staysail) 1,947sqft

(reacher) 8,382sqft

(genoa) 4,917sqft

Engine: 2 x Deutz MWM 1,220hp,

8 cylinder 1,800rpm

Speed (max/cruise): 16 knots/13.5 knots

Fuel capacity: 15,708gal

Range @ 12.5 knots: 4,000nm

Electrical generation: 2 x 125 kW and 1 x 80kW

Bow thruster: 150hp

Water capacity: 3,806gal (fresh)

2,068gal (black and grey)

Desalinator: 2 x Hydromar x 147 gallons

Air-conditioning: Condaria reverse cycle water system

Tenders: 2 x Zodiac semi-rigid 630 230HP hydrojet

Navigation equipment: 2 x Furuno FR21115BB radar,

72 miles with Jotron transponder

Construction: Aluminum 5083

Classification: Lloyd's @ A1 SSC yacht G6 LMC, MCA

Naval architecture: Ron Holland

Interior/Exterior design: Nuvolari & Lenard

Builder/Year: Perini Navi/2003

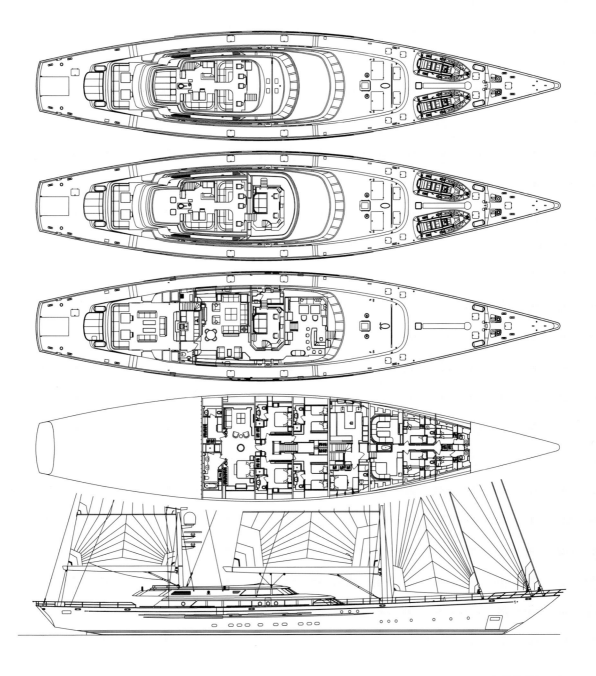

Forty Love

138-FOOT WEST COAST CUSTOM MOTORYACHT

Even though the majority of yachts over 120ft in length are custom built to suit the needs of their owners, it is surprising how similar many are in looks and internal layout. Perhaps this is just a consequence of people wanting much the same thing, or perhaps there is a sense of security when making an investment in a proven product. But every now and then someone builds a real ground breaker that makes the rest of us sit up and ask why we didn't think of that. *Forty Love* is such a yacht.

Forty Love's owners chartered yachts for many years, but they were never satisfied with the way that the boats blended with the family's outgoing, sporty lifestyle. They decided to purchase their own yacht. After a lengthy search for the ideal vessel, the couple concluded that they would either have to build from scratch or modify an existing yacht. To avoid the risk of an expensive new build, they chose the latter course and bought a nearly completed self-build project based on a cored composite Westport 112ft semi-displacement hull.

Today, they are happy with the prize—a well-built vessel that exactly suits the family's needs—but looking back on the seven years that it took to finish *Forty Love*, they admit that with prior knowledge of the task that lay ahead, they might have chosen the easier route.

The original plan was straightforward. With a custom yacht, holidays would be enhanced and some of the running expenses could be defrayed by offering it for charter. Rather than compete with the charter fleet that operates in the Mediterranean and the Caribbean, this yacht would migrate between the idyllic Turkish cruising grounds and the relatively undiscovered waters of the Red Sea, where the winter weather is perfect and there's a host of attractions, including some of the world's best diving grounds, and easy access from Europe. Back in 1994, the political situation in the Middle East looked highly promising, and a twice-annual Suez Canal transit was far less expensive and taxing on a yacht than two Atlantic crossings. The plan seemed eminently workable.

The project was approached in the true spirit of yacht customization—built to suit both the needs of the owners and their chosen cruising grounds. The Red Sea climate is very hot and there are no maintenance facilities for yachts, so huge air-conditioning systems and a very high level of equipment

Porthole ★ The pilohouse includes a full complement of navigational equipment with vital items being duplicated.

Left ★ This *al fresco* eating area is aft on the main deck.

Opp. top ★ A new superstructure was built to create a tri-deck yacht that has an enclosed bridge deck with an open aft area, a spacious sun deck and a flying bridge.

Opp. bottom ★ From the bow pulpit, the wraparound walkway.

redundancy was to be incorporated into the machinery. The owner wanted to carry a good range of watersports equipment and have ample deck space for entertainment. Good exterior lighting was also a necessity because the cool evening is one of the best times to be outside. They asked that the saloons have the greatest exterior visibility possible in order to take advantage of the amazing panoramas in both of the planned cruising areas, and while the cabins should be comfortable, they said they need not be overly large.

An unusual requirement was that the owners wanted the yacht to be able to provide other vessels with essentials. They foresaw that their friends, whose smaller yachts might not have the range or endurance for a lengthy cruise, might need to be supplied with fuel, water, and possibly even power. Large tankage (both diesel and gasoline) and fuel transfer pumps were needed, as was the ability to supply electrical 'shore power' in the same way as a marina. This latter service could also come in handy if their island home in the Red Sea would suffer a power breakdown. A new twist for shore power!

Another unique request was made to accommodate the owners' dogs—labradors and setters (breeds known for their affinity with water). In the fear that they would enter the water but not be able to climb back out onto a regular

Above ★ The forward half of the saloon is furnished with settees, arm chairs, and a television built into the African cherry cabinetry.

Opp. top ★ Sharing the main deck with the saloon is the formal dining area, which is able to seat ten.

Below ★ The wet bar is coupled with a galley that is especially for owner and guest use.

swim platform, the stern of the yacht would be built with wide steps that descended below water level. And all stairs in the yacht would also have to be dog friendly.

With the yacht's particulars settled, the owners took a completely open-minded view at how she could be laid out and began with a few major alterations. Most of the existing interior on the main and lower decks was stripped and rearranged. The Westport GRP hull was lengthened by adding a huge beach-style swim platform to the stern that stepped down into the water, extending the Westport's

112ft hull to 125ft. This added interior volume providing extra space for fuel tanks, storage freezers, and garbage lockers, which give the yacht two months' autonomy.

A fresh look was also given to the layout of the exterior decks. Decks are expensive real estate, and there just was not enough square footage to meet the owners' needs, so they took a cue from city developers and went up. Instead of a two-deck-plus-sun-deck raised pilothouse configuration, a new superstructure was made from aluminum to create a three-deck yacht with a brand new enclosed bridge deck with a huge open area aft, a spacious sun deck, and a flying bridge on top. With such extensive alterations, there was a good chance that everything could go horribly wrong, but with the help of Westport's original naval architect Jack Sarin and his assistant, Michael Schutte (who later set up his own practice and finished the project) the external appearance of *Forty Love* remains highly attractive.

The rebuild—to all intents and purposes a new build by the time it was completed—took place in Long Beach, CA where there was a good pool of experienced marine artisans. And if a certain specialist was not available, one was hired from an established yacht yard such as Palmer Johnson, and flown to the task. The interior decoration

and final cosmetic touches were carried out in Fort Lauderdale, where there was a finer appreciation of the high level of finish required.

The difference between *Forty Love* and the average superyacht is obvious as soon as one enters the saloon: it occupies the entire main deck accommodations. No master suite, no enclosed galley—just an incredible exterior panorama seen through 360° of windows. The forward half of the saloon is comfortably furnished with settees and arm chairs, and a television is built into the African cherry cabinetry. Internal stairs to port lead to the guest accommodations and to the sky lounge. Aft and to starboard is a formal dining table for ten that is overlooked by another television. Built against the aft bulkhead is a combination wet bar and galley (the latter reserved for the use of owner and guests to make snacks or to cook when the chef takes a night off) that opens to a similar wet bar on the aft deck through a sliding glass window. Amidships on the main deck, port and starboard, doors lead from the saloon to the side decks. All decks are accessible by external stairs starboard aft.

Out through the sliding door, the large aft deck feels good to bare feet—not too hard and not too hot in the full sun.

Above ★ Behind the king-size bed in the master stateroom is a steam/shower room.

Left ★ The dressing area of the master bedroom.

Bottom left ★ The navigation station includes a cozy upper saloon cum sky lounge with a writing desk and television.

Opp. top ★ Working out never looked so good.

Opp. bottom ★ This aft seating area overlooks the exercise area.

Below ★ One of the guest cabins.

In fact, it takes a moment to realize that this is not teak, but Marine Deck 2000, a cork composite material made in Holland. Pleasantly shaded by the bridge deck overhang, it offers alfresco dining on a three-function table (that lowers to coffee-table height and slides aft to convert the settee into a day bed) set against a settee built into the original aft bulwark. Stairs to port and starboard once led down to the Westport's relatively small swim platform, but the hull extension has changed the lower area into a huge 'beach.' This fantastic watersports deck has acres of room to assemble diving gear, rig a windsurfer, or just relax on a pair of double steamer chairs. From here, a wide opening in the aft bulwark leads down to a swim platform with a U-shaped cut-out, which has steps right down into the water—this access is easier than on most other yachts of this size. A hydraulic boarding platform on the port quarter can swivel and raise for easy access to dock or quay, alongside or aft, and this also makes a great diving board. When stowed, it rotates to lie across the stern, and this still leaves room beneath it for swimming dogs to mount the steps to the aft deck. This is a great area by day, but at night it shines the brightest with underwater lighting that creates a fluorescent fish-filled pool. Powerful metal-halide floodlights (set on the bridge deck) illuminate the whole the surrounding area. Anyone for night-time water-skiing? It's quite possible!

Forty Love's foredeck has some surprises, too. Considered too valuable to be just a working area (especially as it is visible through the saloon's forward-facing windows), the owners positioned a spa pool at the foredeck's center and added a 13ft bowsprit with a stable walkway to the bow. The spa pool is covered by a solid lid that seals in its water, but then rises on airlifts to form a shady top when in use. The anchor windlass is covered by a box that creates steps up to the bow walkway. Easily negotiable and underlit by night, this is a great diving board and an even better viewing point when under way—especially when accompanied by an escort of dolphins gamboling around the bow. Then there is another surprise—*Forty Love*'s bow sections are not devoted to the usual crew accommodations, but instead house a full Finnish sauna accessed by a flight of stairs aft of the spa pool. As this is a rather uncomfortable section of a boat, this twist from the standard makes sense—during transits in rough weather, the crew are better off further aft. And who would want to sauna in a storm?

Up one level, forward of the pilothouse, a huge sunpad was built into the forward slope, while the boat deck stores an impressive arsenal of tenders and toys, as well as a good selection of gym equipment. With the boats launched, the deck's wide expanse of cork makes a great dance floor for the party deck above, which is a fantastic area offering a

Above ★ With a canopied cover, this is a hot tub for all weather.

combination of bar, dining, lounging, and sunbathing on the forward 'balcony'. Add to it, of course, a music system, barbecue, and incredible panoramic views—and there is yet more. Up another stairway, shaded by a solid bimini, is the flying bridge—as high aloft as a tuna tower. Here there are full controls for the yacht, a great asset when navigating shallow water littered with uncharted coral heads. This is not just a pilotage area but, with swiveling leather seats, it is also a great spot for guests.

With saloon and deck facilities like these, one is happy to accept slightly smaller guest cabins than usually found on a yacht of this size. The master cabin is very spacious with the shower/steam room positioned behind the king-size bed. In an attractive twist, the sink and vanity are open to the bedroom. Forward are two cabins similar in style with the double bed positioned beneath a single bunk bed. There is also a twin cabin and a double cabin. All cabins have ensuite shower rooms. With all beds occupied, *Forty Love* will sleep 12, but this number would most comfortably be reached with at least two children in the mix.

Always an area of interest for guests, the pilothouse was made large enough to include a cozy saloon with a handy writing desk and television in the sizeable area aft of the control desk. The navigation equipment is high quality with vital items being duplicated—and sometimes triplicated—to give bulletproof back-ups. A yacht with two autopilots is quite a rarity!

The captain's cabin (a double with shower) is located to port of this area, while two crew cabins, another double and one with twin bunks, are accessed from the boat deck—much better positioning than in the forepeak. The final two crew cabins—both with double bunks—open from the galley, whose positioning is so unusual that one would be forgiven for wondering where it is. A galley beneath the aft deck with an entry from the beach deck (beside a built-in bait tank continuously flushed with sea water and a centrifuge for the swift drying of bathing suits) is certainly unconventional. The benefit is that it is absolutely huge—with a full complement of professional equipment that can cater up to 100—and it has easy access to the main deck. The downside is serving food across the open deck to the formal dining saloon in a rainstorm, but in that case, there is always the galley in the saloon.

The engine-room, entered from the galley, is a clean, impressive space where the degree of equipment redundancy is obvious. Two 105kW gensets are in this compartment, a third is located further aft in the pump room. Air-conditioning capacity is at 24 tons (rather than the normal 15-18 tons) and utilizes two compressors with two back-ups. The twin 1,350hp Caterpillar engines give *Forty Love* a top speed of 18 knots and a continuous cruise of 15 knots, while an economical 12 knots will squeeze a range of 2,500nm from her 9,600-gallon tanks.

Given her lengthening, additional decks and her bowsprit, it is natural that interested observers ask how *Forty Love* handles at sea. Built to ABS and MCA standards, construction and passenger safety have both been officially approved, while the captain spoke highly of her performance in some rough weather encountered off Panama. He said that in 12ft to 15ft seas, the stabilizers kept roll to a minimum. While the bowsprit occasionally punched through the waves, as it was designed to do, there were no ill effects. From time to time, waves rolled up the stern steps, but the open nature of the transom meant that the deck shed its water easily.

There is no doubt that *Forty Love* exactly meets the owner's original dreams. However, as he wants to move on to other projects, his yacht is now for sale. In the meantime, *Forty Love* is available for charter in Caribbean and in Europe. With its innovative layout, optimum use of deck space, and its huge range of toys, she is certainly a yacht that will provide pleasure to plenty.

LOA:	138ft (42m)	**Air-conditioning:**	4 x CruiseAir SMXII, 24 ton
Beam (max):	25ft (7.6m)	**Search Lights:**	x 15 million CP Carlisle & Finch
Draft:	6ft 4in (2m)	**Communications:**	SEA SSB radio, KW 50 Tracphone satellite, ICOM & Shipmate VHFs
Propulsion:	2 x 1,350hp Caterpillar 3412 diesels	**Passerelle:**	Cramm
Gearboxes:	ZF Marine twin disc MG 5050 2.45:1	**Navigation:**	Leica DGPS and MX480 chart plotter, Furuno radars, Furuno forward facing sonar, depth and weatherfax, B&G Hydra instruments, Leica
Propellers:	5-blade, nibral		
Steering system:	Kobelt		
Speed (max/cruise):	18 knots/15 knots	**Autopilots:**	Robertson AP45/Robertson AP9 Mk3
Fuel capacity:	9,600 gallons diesel, 500 gallons gas	**Gyrocompasses:**	KW Gyrotrac/Robertson RGC-10
Fuel pumps:	Oberdorfer 20gpm	**Laundry equipment:**	Miele
Range at 12 knots:	2,500nm	**Horn:**	Kahlenburg
Electrical generation:	3 x 105kW Caterpillar 3304 gensets	**Owner and guests:**	10 in 5 staterooms, 12 using 2 pullman berths
Bow thruster:	Tork Master 80hp		
Stabilizers:	Naiad 404 with 19sqft fins	**Crew:**	9 in 5 cabins
Watermaker:	2 x 2,000gpd Universal Aqua PF2000	**Construction:**	GRP hull and aluminum superstructure
Water capacity:	2,000 gallons	**Classification:**	Built to ABS, MCA compliant
Sanitation:	Headhunter	**Naval architects:**	Jack W Sarin, WA
Shore Power:	Atlas 50kW	**Finished project:**	Michael Schutte/Brilliant Boats
Monitoring system:	DMP, 155 point	**Interior designer:**	Pavlik Design
Windlass:	Tork Master	**Builder/Year:**	West Coast Custom Yachts/2002
Capstans:	Muir		
Davits/cranes:	Knukel Palfinger PK 9001, 6,500lbs		

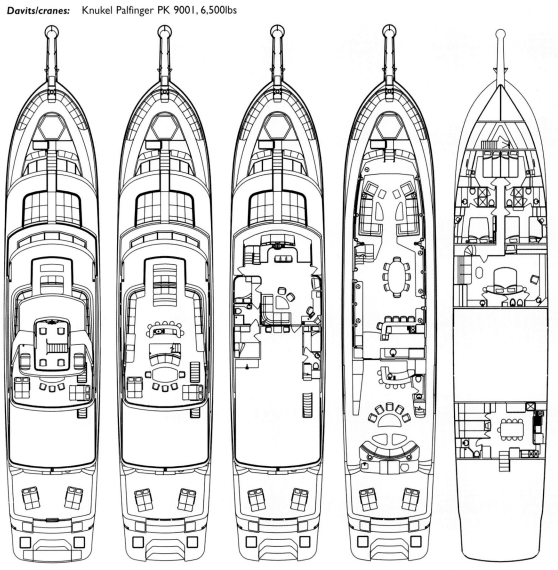

Lady Aleida

107-FOOT WEST BAY RAISED PILOTHOUSE MOTORYACHT

Lady Aleida, named after the lady of the house, is the baptismal name of Leidy Vermeulen, who, with husband Ben, founded West Bay SonShip Yachts 37 years ago. At 107 feet, this yacht is the latest and largest vessel constructed by their Vancouver-based company and was designed especially for the couple.

Lady Aleida is not the Vermeulens' first personal yacht. For several years, Ben—now West Bay's chairman of the board—and Leidy have cruised in SonShip #1, a 78-footer and one of a series of successful, sleek but sea-hardy motoryachts the company has built since 1991. Before that, the yard built all manner of vessels, beginning with an Ed Monk, Sr. classic wooden design in the late 1960s, then branching out into wood, steel and fiberglass workboats, patrol boats, gillnetters and some pleasure craft. In lean times, the boatyard maintained its viability by providing excellent boat repairs. The company's signature yacht, which propelled West Bay into international prominence and made it Canada's largest boatyard (producing about 18 vessels a year) is the SonShip 58. A well-performing Mediterranean-style yacht, more than eighty 58s have been sold. Subsequent West Bays have leapt ahead 10 feet at a time, stimulated in part by the fact that one-third of SonShip 58 owners wanted to move up to a larger yacht. Along with the 64ft yachtfisher, production now includes 68, 78, 87 and 107ft vessels.

The 107-footer, whose hull formed the basis for *Lady Aleida*, was designed by renowned northwest naval architect Jack Sarin. "In 1986 Westport Shipyard asked me to design a new hull mold capable of producing variable beam and length," Sarin explained. "Their clients wanted something in the 85-110ft range." The design has worked admirably and has yielded more than 60 hulls, especially as Westport sold them to such yards as Crescent, Sovereign, McQueen and West Bay. "I guess this has to be the longest running

Above ★ This elegant *Lady*, built for and named after the company's founders, is the largest West Bay yet.

Porthole ★ A lovely oil painting, one of many original art pieces on board, adds subtle color to the dining area.

Opp. bottom left ★ Sunbathing in style on the foredeck.

Opp. bottom right ★ The Cal deck is an inviting area to dine or relax.

show for fiberglass hulls in this size range anywhere, even including pure production builders," Sarin concludes.

Ben and Leidy emigrated to Canada from the Netherlands more than four decades ago and have combined the arts they studied in their native country—Ben was a silversmith/tool-and-die maker and Leidy specialized in fashion design—with the quality and common sense learned from centuries' worth of Dutch boatbuilding expertise. The Dutch, after all, launched their first yacht in 1660. The Vermeulens' proficiency has been handed down to another generation who grew up around the yard: son Wes is now the company's president, his brother Bas heads Design and Operations and sister Rochelle designs boat interiors. In fact, concern for a third generation of Vermeulens accounts for *Lady Aleida*'s being the largest West Bay ever. The 103s built previously terminated in a swim platform with removable, open gates. Afraid that a toddler could easily slip through them, Bas Vermeulen redrew the plans incorporating the platform and transforming the space into a bulwarked fishing cockpit (with a single locking transom gate), complete with bait tank and rod holders. To ensure the now enclosed cockpit drains quickly if the yacht takes water over the bow in heavy seas, hinged freeing ports have been installed to act as giant scuppers. For further safety, docking controls were added to the aft deck wings. Finally, Ben Vermeulen wanted the freedom to walk around the entire vessel so the yacht's main deck was redesigned to include covered weatherdecks.

Ben himself shows off the airy living area which includes a saloon, dining room and extensive bar. Access is from the California deck, or via the Marquipt boarding stair through the port or starboard doors. The floor is covered with a warm sandalwood carpet which is complemented by a

Main photo ★ Owners and their guests can relax on the luxurious fawn sofa or watch the game at the black granite bar in the airy living area.

Left ★ Innovative pop-up outlets provide an added convenience in the U-shaped galley.

luxurious fawn, U-shaped sofa inviting leisurely conversations or relaxed viewing of a movie on the pop-up 42in Panasonic plasma screen. Satin-smooth, rift-cut American cherry, inlaid seamlessly with Carpathian elm burl veneers —a rich combination of wood recurring throughout the vessel—makes up the coffee table. Wide cherry crown moldings provide a transition between the wall panels and the ceiling and hide the rope lighting that contributes to the room's welcoming character. These moldings and all the cabinetry, furniture, wainscoting, newel posts and banisters are built and buffed by an outstanding team of joiners working on the West Bay premises. Ben takes pride in the quality of West Bay's in-house manufacturing. "We build as much of our yachts as we can in our plant," he explains. "It gives us complete quality control."

Across from the sofa, four burgundy-leather Pinson chairs flank a two-tier, black-on-black granite bar, a friendly hub to quaff a beer while watching the ballgame or the scenery through the large windows. It can also double as an eating place if the adjacent eight-person dining table is oversubscribed. Forward of the dining table, a built-in buffet not only stores dishes and stemware in their custom-made slots, but houses two supplemental freezer drawers, a wine cooler, and an electrical panel. Above the lower cabinets, a lovely oil painting of a British Columbia landscape imparts subtle color to the room. A corridor paved with almond travertine highlighted with espresso inlays leads to the galley and also accesses a mirrored day head with its black granite counter. The U-shaped galley has gold-toned granite countertops and a breakfast bar. To plug in appliances away from the

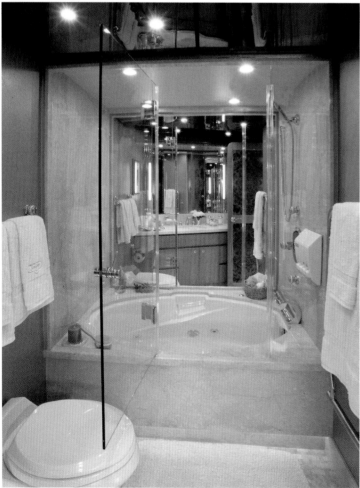

walls, several innovative pop-up outlets have been installed in the granite. The cherry-covered doors of the Subzero refrigerator blend in beautifully with the rest of the woodwork. Karndean strip flooring with an inlaid compass rose makes galley maintenance a breeze. The stainless-steel appliances, including a warming drawer, invite cooking for the whole family, as does the chocolate suede settee surrounding the custom-made oval table.

Lady Aleida offers five staterooms—almost enough to house the entire Vermeulen clan—all of them located on the lower deck. Two are separated from the others and are accessed by a staircase from the galley. The larger port cabin with its modified queen-size bed is decorated with cheerful red, white, and blue fabrics and has a private head with a Corian countertop and mirrored headliner. Twin bunks covered with nautical white sailboats on navy textile are built into the fo'c'sle. The cabin's full head is located in the hallway next to a stacked washer/dryer and linen closet. Both staterooms have a built-in television and the privacy of the area is highly suitable for a couple and two children.

From the dining area, a staircase on port leads to the three other staterooms via a stylish foyer with a travertine floor. A curved, marble-topped cupboard displays an alabaster sculpture with a strongly-tinted watercolor of a windswept British Columbian beach hanging above it. These, along with a myriad of other paintings, are other examples of the original art found on *Lady Aleida*. Buying primarily from regional artists, the Vermeulens have adorned the vessel with refined yet colorful art. "We like the boat dressed up," Ben says with a grin.

Ben sweeps through the master stateroom's double doors and points out a raft of carefully built-in cabinetry. Here as elsewhere, framed family portraits are profuse. The walls next to the king-size bed again display the seamless marquetry of elm burl on cherry and are complemented by sumptuous gold and crimson bed covers. Like all the other rooms in *Lady Aleida*, crown moldings impart a finished, elegant look. A cedar-lined walk-in closet offers ample hanging space as well as a Chubb safe. Sliding shutters matching the wall color provide privacy, while a corner

Right ★ The bridge includes built-in flat screens for displaying charts, radar, sonar, security and the ship's monitoring systems.

Opp. top ★ The spacious queen-size stateroom shimmers with gold and red fabric accents.

Opp. bottom ★ A bone spa tub and shower divides the his-and-hers bathrooms, each complete with granite vanities and towel warmers.

Below ★ A circular companionway accesses the pilothouse with its velour rounded settee and inlaid-cherry table.

Lady Aleida has completely separated crew quarters and the engine-room from the rest of the yacht's living and navigation spaces. Crew quarters are reached from the cockpit and include a double-bed cabin with private head for the captain and twin bunks for two more crew. An additional head has been installed for them, along with a simple galley. The engine room provides easy access to the dual MTU-DDC 16V2000 engines, which can propel the vessel to 24 knots. Northern Light 32kW and 40kW generators supply the ship's load, while the Cruisair 15-ton chilled-water air-conditioning will keep passengers cool even in the tropics. Through the ship's automatic converter, *Lady Aleida* can hook up to 50 or 60 cycles, one or three phase, from 200 to 450 volts.

A circular companionway guides us to the pilothouse with its navy-blue leather helm seat, velour rounded settee, and triangular inlaid-cherry table. Next to the bridge, a space ample enough for several paper charts is made of composite material. "Too much use and too many spilled coffees ruin this area so we substituted a scrubbable surface," explains an ever-practical Ben. The bridge includes built-in flat screens for displaying Nobeltec electronic charts, radar, sonar, security and ship's monitoring system. Simrad manufactured the radar and other navigational instruments, Icom provided the communications equipment, while C-Nav fabricated the computers and displays. Bridge controls also include the

cabinet with retractable doors hides a Sony 27in flat-screen television. An oak writing table in the room's corner is at odds with the rest of the furnishings: its turned legs and accompanying round piano stool recall the furniture style of Holland's Golden Age, when the country ruled the waves. His-and-hers bathrooms with granite vanities and towel warmers are divided by a bone spa tub and shower.

Shimmering gold and red fabrics cover the queen-size bed in the port guest stateroom. The mirrors over the bed make the room look even more spacious. Again, storage has been maximized—even the built-in nightstands contain drawers. A full head with oatmeal granite counters and light columns alongside the vanity mirror make guests feel welcome. The starboard guest room offers twin beds with plush slate-blue covers and handy reading lights. It has a full private head with the same oatmeal granite counters and other amenities.

nine square feet Wesmar RS 900 stabilizers, windlasses, and lights.

Two areas invite *Lady Aleida*'s guests to dine al fresco. The California deck just above the cockpit is furnished with an oval Corian table, brightly-striped Sunbrella-covered settee, and coffee-colored rattan basket chairs. The command bridge, whose aft portion is home to the Rendova and Boston Whaler, supports another Corian table, Sunbrella-covered settee and stainless barbecue. Steak and roasted vegetables, anyone? A six-person hot tub reposes under the mast which carries the usual communication devices and antennae.

When the boatyard's chairman of the board builds a yacht for himself and his family, it must be first class. But is it better than his production vessels? As Ben leans against one of the command bridge's captain's chairs behind the navigation instruments, he rebuffs that idea. "*Lady Aleida* is a supremely comfortable and elegant yacht," he says with fervor. "She runs smoothly and quietly. But, except for some personal details we added, she doesn't differ from our other vessels. Quality is the first concern for all our yachts. As far as I'm concerned, every West Bay customer is chairman of the board."

Opp. top left ★ Supremely comfortable and elegant, *Lady Aleida* is no exception to the quality of any West Bay vessel.

Opp. bottom right ★ A six-person spa tub overlooks the Rendova and Boston Whaler on the command bridge.

SPECIFICATIONS

LOA:	106ft 8in (32.6m)
Beam:	24ft (7.3m)
Draft:	5ft 6in (1.7m)
Displacement (light ship):	195,000 lbs
Propulsion:	2 X DDC-MTU 16V2000 1,800hp
Speed (max/cruise):	24 kts / 20 kts
Fuel capacity:	5,000 USG
Range @ 12 knots:	2,000 nm
Electrical generation:	2 x Northern Lights 32kW, 40kW
Bow thruster:	Wesmar 16in dual prop 50hp
Stabilizers:	Wesmar RS900
Watermaker:	Sealand SRC 1,200 GPD
Water:	800 USG
Entertainment systems:	Panasonic, Sony, Denon, Toshiba, Alpine, Niles
Paint:	Micron/Awlgrip Hull/West Bay
Air-conditioning:	Cruisair, 15-ton chilled water
Navigation and Communications:	Simrad, Panasonic, Icom, Nobeltec
Tenders:	16ft Boston Whaler and 14ft Rendova RIB
Construction:	Composite fiberglass
Classification:	Designed and engineered to ABYC and ABS standards
Project management:	West Bay Group
Naval architecture:	Jack W. Sarin and West Bay Group
Exterior styling:	West Bay Group and Bas Vermeulen
Interior design:	West Bay Group and Ben and Leidy Vermeulen
Builder/Year:	West Bay SonShip Yachts Ltd. /2003

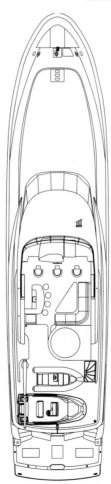
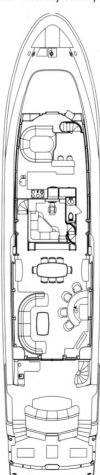
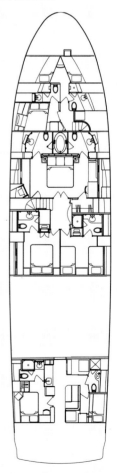

98 Leonardo

98-FOOT AZIMUT MOTORYACHT

With its superb aerodynamic profile designed by Stefano Righini, the first Azimut 98 Leonardo, named in tribute to the Renaissance master Da Vinci, makes a striking impression when you set eyes on her in the port of Viareggio. Boarding the yacht via the portside telescopic gangway, you immediately notice the circular dining area framed by tinted glass doors. This feature separates the 98 Leonardo from other models of a similar size by creating a vast space of 1,272sqft extending from aft deck through to the navigation station.

The aft deck is a classic layout in teak, but with its unusual dining area, it takes a while to get used to the presence of the circular glass structure. When closed, the doors provide sheltered dining around the extendable circular glass table, which seats eight to twelve people. Built in two halves, the doors can be opened electronically, retracting into the uprights of the coachroof. The four central sections slide away manually to allow for dining al fresco. The enclosed space then disappears and the central deck pillar is removed, leaving a cockpit of spectacular dimensions. From the aft deck, the view looking through the dining area to the saloon beyond is striking. The saloon has a bar to port and large settees that adjust to seat between four and eight people. Large, curved side windows are set low and add to the impression of space. To the fore of the saloon, a large plasma television screen is mounted on the bulkhead separating the saloon from the navigation station.

The décor is resolutely fresh and modern looking, with wood trim in satin-varnished oak, a beige woven fitted carpet, burnt orange leather upholstery, bulkheads framed by bars of brushed steel, and Philippe Starck-designed three-legged chairs around the dining table. Wooden slatted blinds filter soft light into this 530sqft saloon where 20 people can relax in comfort. The stairs up to flybridge blend into the décor with wide glass steps and steel frame, as does the bar. A service door behind the bar opens to stairs that lead to the central section of the accommodations deck. Here, forward of the engine compartment, you find two crew cabins, the galley, and the laundry with washer/dryer, which are completely separate from the guest accommodations. With the galley not being on the main deck, a dumbwaiter aids the crew in serving dishes up to the bar, which doubles as a buffet. While this layout offers privacy for the owner and

Above ★ Built for speed, the 98 Leonardo tops out at 32 knots.

Porthole ★ A computer program designed for Azimut by Cantalupi controls the Leonardo via a touch screen.

Opp. bottom ★ Steering on the fly.....bridge.

Right and bottom ★ Copious bow storage can hold anything from tenders to fenders.

guests, the crew can find compensation in the very high-quality finish in the crew quarters. Satin-varnished oak is found in the galley, the skipper's cabin, and crew cabin (for two people). Also, the 96sqft galley is very well laid out, with a three-seater dinette, long work surface that houses a double sink and four-ring ceramic hob, two refrigerators, two freezers, and an oven and microwave in the extension.

This first Azimut 98 Leonardo has three guest cabins forward of the crew quarters. Halfway down a wide stair-well starboard of the navigation station is a landing with heads. Vertical mirrors brighten the stairs. A door opens into the owner's cabin (to midships), which extends across the full-beam of the yacht. This is furnished with a desk to starboard and settee to port, a dressing room and generous ensuite shower room with marble floor and his-and-hers

Above and right ★ In European style, the galley is completely separate from the guest spaces.

Top ★ The circular dining area converts from indoor to al fresco for dining.

sinks set into a dark green glass surface. All the cabins are adorned with the same leather trim as the saloon. This stateroom is intimate and unfussy as natural light filters in through the side portholes and shows the furnishings to their best advantage. The functional port side cabin features twin beds and an extra bunk that folds away into the bulkhead, while the large cabin forward has attractive curved oak furniture.

With the 98, the yard also offers a four-cabin option. In this layout, two side cabins each have an area of 70sqft and their own shower rooms, which slightly reduces the size of the port shower room adjoining the forward cabin.

Ascending the glass stairway to the flybridge one enters a sheltered area with a banquette seating three in the central steering position, a sofa seating eight around an oval table to port, and an impressive bar with refrigerator, icemaker, sink and grill. Most striking is the vast aft sun deck with room for eight to ten people to relax around a spa pool.

The internal stairway provides access to the main deck, where one can walk out through the dining area and along the well-protected teak side decks with the utmost of ease. A sunbathing area lies forward of the coachroof. Here, four sunpads fit on top of each of the four panels, which open to reveal the lazarette containing the tender and a telescopic crane to lower it into the water.

Back on the aft deck, two side stairwells lead to the swim platform. Controls that are cleverly positioned in the handrail operate the folding gangway, the two side lockers containing the jet skis, and the stern counter that lowers to become a mooring platform.

Above ★ Wide glass steps on a steel frame lead up to the flybridge.

Below ★ The saloon provides a stylish area in which to relax.

Naval architect Silvia Fogliuzzi, head of the Azimut design studio in Viareggio, designed the planing hull with a shallow vee, a deadrise of 13.5 degrees and a weight-bearing, curved bow. "This boat was built for speed," he said, "and we have given her a sporty look. We are very satisfied with her, as she cruises at 28 knots and can reach 32 knots, which is very good for this type of motoryacht. On autopilot in a Force 3 we managed to maintain an average of 25 knots between Monaco and Viareggio. The hull rides the sea very comfortably. For the first time we have used the Centek exhaust silencer from the US with a water-gas tank and a conduit of pressure-injected elastomer for the suspended propeller shafts, and we have had very good results in terms of sound insulation and vibration elimination."

For stability, the boat is equipped with the new Intruder system, the dynamic version which is supposed to do away with the need for flaps and anti-roll fins. It consists of metal plates attached to the stern of the hull. Some of these are fixed, and some are mobile and controlled by a computer that regulates trim and stability simultaneously. In regards to propulsion, the angle of thrust of the two five-bladed propellers is reduced to 8.5 degrees, which Fogliuzzi says has made for excellent performance.

Much attention was paid to fore-and-aft trim and the hull was designed with the center of gravity as low as possible. The hard work paid off during the sea trials. The two synchronized 2,000hp MTU engines cause the hull (displacing 92 tons) to start to lift out of the water at 12.5 knots at 1,300rpm with no flaps, but with the fixed planes

LOA:	98ft (29.8m)
LWL:	80ft (24.4m)
Beam:	23.3ft (7.1m)
Draft:	6.8ft (2.1m)
Displacement:	92 tons
Engines:	2 x MTU 16 V M91 2,000hp
Electrical generation:	2 x Kholer 33kW
Propeller:	Rolla 5-blade prop
Speed (max/cruise):	32 knots/28 knots
Fuel capacity:	2,250 gallons
Bow thruster:	38hp hydraulic
Water capacity:	440 gallons
Air-conditioning:	Cruisair 174000 btu
Galley/laundry equipment:	Miele
Navigation equipment:	Raytheon radar, GPS, pilot, VHF, depth sounder, Raytheon
Technology/computing:	Cantalupi/Azimut
Construction:	Laminate/sandwich/GRP
Naval architecture:	Azimut Technical Department
Exterior concept and style:	Stefano Righini
Interior designer:	Carlo Galeazzi
Builder/Year:	Azimut-Viareggio/2002

Above ⋆ An elegant vestibule accessesing the cabins.

Opposite page ⋆ The master suite with full-beam owner's cabin, walk-in closet, and large ensuite shower room with his-and-hers sinks sct into a dark green glass surface.

of the Intruder, it stays upright with the yacht accelerating to 32 knots at 2,370rpm.

The engine compartment—accessible via the passageway from the crew mess or through a door in the stern counter—is laid out thoughtfully, making it very easy to reach all the maintenance positions.

The 98 Leonardo is controlled electronically by means of a touch screen and a computer specifically designed for the yard by Cantalupi. Operating the yacht from the inside navigation station (with a retractable roof), controls have been reduced to a minimum, with two LCD screens for the navigation instrument displays, a touch screen, and a video screen. Sitting on one of the three leather seats at the steering position, there is a good view forward. Otherwise it is obstructed, but there is a multi-directional video camera to see sideways and astern.

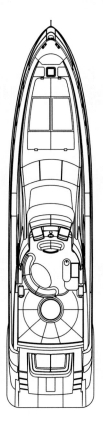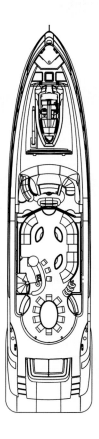

Mystic

150-FOOT TRI-DECK CHRISTENSEN

Megayacht design poses a challenge of balancing unbridled luxury with grace and good taste underpinned by rugged functionality and security. It's a challenge, quite evidently, for which the craftsmen at Christensen Yachts were more than ready, considering the unveiling of *Mystic*.

This latest launch traces an evolution that started with *Silver Lining* and *Liquidity*. *Mystic*, however, is graced by a subtle refinement of lines, highlighted by book matched oval end windows carried through with arched stanchions. To her builder she represents yet one more step in the now definitive Christensen form, nurtured over several years to establish a harmonious melding of the classic with the contemporary.

In executing the 150ft tri-deck, it was important to achieve the clients' principal concern that every room, despite being individually distinctive, should meld well, with a consistency of flow throughout the vessel. This goal was achieved via the generous use of cherrywood throughout. Aesthetic enhancements include etched glass by Portland's Savoy Studios and some equally creative stonework from Jeff Homchick in Seattle. The ample use of the wood along with cautious detail also provides an ideal backdrop that does not compete with several glass sculptures and other artwork chosen by the owners.

Most striking about this vessel is the sense of understated elegance that first greets the visitor on entering its spacious saloon through generous wall to wall, smoked double doors aft. At the instant they close, the silence is readily noticeable—even when *Mystic*'s twin MTUs are fired up—testament to the density of the Airex-cored fiberglass composite superstructure and hull.

The only interruption to such tranquility comes from the gentle gurgling whisper of what is the vessel's most unique feature, a stunningly beautiful aquarium that holds an ecosystem of multicolored Pacific coral, starfish, sea anemones and an ever shifting kaleidoscope of tropical fish.

Porthole ★ One of the guest staterooms.

Left ★ Clean lines all the way to the tip of the bow.

Opp. top ★ The oval windows distinguish the profile of this latest work of art from Christensen.

Opp. bottom ★ Outdoor dining in the shade and lounging in the sun!

The eye is drawn immediately to the glass, framed in cherry and balanced on either side by cabinets with glass panels etched in a contemporary buttress theme that appears throughout, commencing with the light fixtures in the entrance foyer. Contained within are a series of striking glass sculptures by Portland's Elements Glass. Truly a triumph, the installation (which divides the formal living and dining areas) posed its own unique challenges.

The live coral tank maintains a constant temperature of 76 degrees, achieved by the use of a heat exchanger. Spaghetti leather, branching anchor coral and pom pom xenia hammer coral were all sourced specially from the South Pacific and, along with carefully attached rock material, took almost 200 hours to assemble. By the use of two concealed buffer tanks, the surface is never broken (even when the vessel is listing) and the system pumps through 1700 gallons an hour. The one-inch-thick laminated Starfire glass (flat on the saloon side, bowed on the dining room side) is crystal clear, allowing for examination of even the smallest cleaner shrimp or coco worm. The pedestal conceals mechanical components.

Professional aquarist David Morgavi suggests this was one of the most demanding and satisfying projects he's undertaken to date and the Christensen crew still chuckle at the unusual complexities that the 2,200 pound installation posed.

Barely a minute passes when somebody isn't entranced by this fascinating glimpse of aquatic life, testament to the fact that, most of the time, the flat panel TV stored below is no match for entertainment value.

With its bowed half table and elegant *fior de pesco* marble floor bordered in a tri-color rope pattern that is carried throughout the vessel in various schemes—the entrance foyer creates a sense of space. There's also an instant feeling that, despite the main room's obvious formality, here is a sense of ease and comfortable belonging, of 'home'. Grouped around the Sapele coffee table (by Doug Chamblin), for ease of conversation, are a pair of Baker armchairs in gray paisley and twin, three-seat overstuffed couches in a solid charcoal chenille that complements perfectly the conservative, gently masculine feel of the wood. Natural light is plentiful, thanks to the expansive window treatments, bordered by fluted pillar designs that have fully remote controlled blinds. This is a vessel that combines elegance with function, in a layout that—while offering distinctive living areas—also allows thoughtful ease of access for the eight person crew.

Forward of the aquarium, the custom dining table of quarter-sawn sycamore can accommodate up to twelve. Behind is an impressive, dark cherrywood buffet with glass panels detailed in the now familiar etched buttress pattern.

Above ★ The starboard foyer amidships clad with marble flooring and inlaid with a compass rose.

Opp. top ★ The dining table that seats 12 is custom-crafted of rich sycamore.

Below ★ The fabulous live reef aquarium is the focal point of the comfortable main saloon.

The ceiling centerpiece features a pair of matching opaque glass orbs which play off the buffet's etched designs.

Service access to the spacious galley is on the port side. The generous and well-lit working space has the feel of a correctly-designed commercial kitchen that would make any professional chef happy. Aside from the usual necessities, this serious kitchen boasts upper and lower Thermidor ovens, a steamer that can double as a sterilizer, a separate dishwashing station, and a considerable walk-in pantry with full-size wine cooler, beside a concealed utility closet and spice racks. (Principal cold storage takes the form of a walk-in cooler in crew's quarters on the lower deck.)

A central Azularan granite-topped island provides extra work space but also permits the chef some separation from the hustle and bustle of service. The vessel's state-of-the-art communications system is also hard at work here. A flat-panel TV to one side of the oven taps into the Panasonic security system, allowing the chef to keep an eye on all entertainment areas without moving or interrupting guests—including the next-door dining lounge.

The midships starboard foyer is home to a well-concealed elevator that serves all four decks. Here again, Christensen's attention to detail has left no stone unturned. The elevator was tested during rigorous sea trials, with crew making the trip between decks to ensure minimum play on its tracks and ensure absolute safety regardless of weather conditions.

Just forward of the elevator, a rich symphony of cherry-wood and crystal bright LED lit glass with etched details wrap a graciously curved stairwell, while the marble flooring is highlighted by an inlaid compass rose detail in solodite and lapis marble. Completing the foyer's conveniences is a day head with mirrored ceiling and fiber-optic-lit sink.

The entrance to the owners' office denotes a more private feel of the forward main deck. Complementing the large semi-gloss cherrywood desk and credenza, unique to this room, is a beamed ceiling in matching wood. The master suite is bathed in light from three vertical oval ports on both sides, adding height to already spacious quarters. The change in style from the public areas is manifested by the use of padded fabric on the walls and above the king-size headboard. Flanking the bed are bow-fronted, three drawer, portoro granite-topped nightstands.

Making the most of the full-beamed room, and offering a private reading space, a pair of armchairs with matching ottomans graces the starboard side, balanced by a six-

drawer, low-profile, granite-topped bureau on the other. The aft wall is dominated by another bureau with central cabinets that open to reveal a full entertainment center, topped by a flat-screen television concealed behind a pair of bi-panel folding doors, all in matching cherrywood with beveled Regency detail. A midships port escape door doubles as a convenient service access to the galley area and crew stairwell that connects all three decks. Beside it, a paneled door leads into the generous walk-in closet that features a separate, lockable compartment which enables the owners to leave items aboard and undisturbed if the vessel is under charter.

Doors forward on either side lead to spacious his-and-hers baths, which receive plentiful light from frosted skylights. The port side bath, finished in cashew perloto marble, features a deep, full-size soaker tub and *jacuzzi*, bordered by mirror glass etched in an underwater motif. Polished stainless steel fixtures are by Dornbracht, in polished stainless steel while the marble floor replays the inlaid twined rope theme, evident elsewhere, in Emperodor light and dark marble. The smaller starboard head (without bath) is connected by a shared double shower clad in marble with etched glass doors and polished stainless hardware.

Below, varying configurations of five well-appointed guest staterooms, (all with ensuite bath or shower), are joined by a common foyer (with elevator access, luggage storage and a linen closet) and a corridor that also connects to the forward crew quarters, crew galley, day area and laundry. Detail here includes a half table with a curved candelabra pedestal design that matches similar tables elsewhere aboard.

Although the pilothouse represents the working heart of this vessel, it too glows in luxurious wood with Sapele flooring with inlaid rope design, and cherry surrounding seven expansive window panels that give excellent visibility. Working surfaces include a chart desk and six drawer storage starboard.

From the single Recaro chair or standing at the wheel rest beside it, the skipper enjoys access to a wealth of information from five interchangeable displays relayed to four flat screen monitors that includes a satellite compass as opposed to the traditional gyro. At sea, the vessel's quiet ride is further enhanced by rock-solid stability (aided by the 510 Naiad Marine stabilizers with 30sqft fins), with a maximum speed of 19 knots, fast cruising of 16 knots or

Opp. page ★ The master cabin features a king-size bed and comfy armchair lounge area. The master bath is finished in cashew perloto marble with etched mirrored glass.

This page ★ Each of the five guest staterooms all with ensuite bath or shower are enjoined by a common foyer with access to the elevator, luggage storage, linen closet and the crew quarters for service.

long range capability (of 4000 nautical miles) at 10 knots.

Behind the control deck a raised slate-leather booth and marble table with stainless-steel inlay offers comfortable accommodation for guests while leaving plenty of room for the business at hand. Proof that this is indeed a serious cruising vessel is evident from the location and sensible proportions of the captain's quarters, a full suite with double bed, full head and desk, reached by a door on the port side aft wall.

A starboard passageway leads past a day head, stairwell, elevator access and a service area with wet bar, dishwasher and icemaker.

The sky lounge is more a family room than formal area, utilizing rich cherrywood paneling. The space is bathed in natural light with three large windows on either side and full width glass aft. The venetian blinds are made of wood slats that match the paneling and, when closed, contribute a seamless sense of warmth and richness.

Here, the owners have dispensed with the usual bar configuration in favor of more seating to offer flexibility and different conversation areas able to accommodate up to 12 people. A large, sectional sofa in charcoal chenille and a glass-topped coffee table almost fills the starboard side, balanced by twin armchairs aft and a small round table forward with four seats for relaxed meals. For movies or watching the Sea Tel satellite television system, a flat screen concealed behind a corniced wood panel hinges down from the ceiling while artfully concealed speakers complete the deluxe home entertainment system.

There's no shortage of sociable gathering places on *Mystic*. The spacious, covered, aft boat deck boasts a large

round table on four stainless-steel pedestals, which with stackable chairs provides seating for 12. (Further aft is stored a 22ft Nautica tender.)

Perfect for a casual dinner, most of the outside action will no doubt happen on the expansive flybridge. On the forward ledge, instead of the usual upper deck control panel, a full-size hot tub and pads are a magnet for sunseekers, while amidships (just aft of the elevator), a spacious entertainment area boasts a full bar with fridge and icemaker, with six stools faced by a wrap-around taupe and black trimmed banquette and low table on the port side, as well as a Linx gas barbecue. The entire deck offers a delightfully private escape from the rest of the vessel.

When at anchor, guests on *Mystic* have no shortage of

toys of every kind from which to choose. Stowed aft is a small fleet of craft ranging from three waverunners and a sailboat to two sea kayaks. Another fleet of four Vespa scooters provides nimble shore transportation.

Mystic is truly an impressive sum of many parts. The owners' involvement in the project, along with the builder's passion for detail and ability to execute some more unique attributes, have combined to produce a vessel that is quite seamless, a harmonious blending of art and technology that marks a new level in megayacht design.

Above and opp. bottom ★ The sky lounge, more family than formal, has several congenial seating arrangements and a round table and chairs.

Opp. top ★ Outside dining aft of the sky lounge.

Below ★ In the pilothouse, from a single Recaro helm chair, the skipper enjoys access to the five interchangeable displays relayed to four flat screen monitors. Behind is a raised slate-leather booth and marble table.

This page ★ With so many social areas to choose from, the sun deck is sure to be a favorite.

LOA: 150ft (45.7m)

LWL: 135ft 7in (41.4m)

Beam: 28ft (8.5m)

Draft: 6ft 11in (1.86m)

Displacement (light ship): 450,000lbs

Engines: 2 x MTU 8V 4000M90 w/DDEC Control System, 1826 bhp @ 2,100 rpm

Speed: 19 knots

Fuel capacity: 10,500 gallons

Range @ 10 knots: 4,000 nautical miles

Electrical generation: 2 x Northern Lights M668T, 1,800 rpm 99 kW

Bow thruster: 24ft TRAC, Dual props American Bow Thruster 100 hp Electric

Watermakers: Village Marine x 2 @ 1,500gpd

Sanitation systems: Fast Sewage Treatment

Entertainment systems: Interior Audio

Security systems: Panasonic/Christensen

Air-conditioning: AQUA Air 30 Ton

Communications: Sea Tel MS-2x12 Multi Switch

Hull construction: Christensen Cored Fiberglass Composite

Owner and guests: 1 owner stateoom/5 guest cabins

Crew: 1 captain, 4 crew

Classification: The first ever Commercial Yachting Service issued by ABS for pleasure yachts, ABS, Maltese-cross A1 Commercial Yachting Service, AMS & MCA Code of Practice Compliance & Certification

Project management: John Cochran

Naval architecture: Christensen Shipyards Ltd.

Exterior styling: Christensen Shipyards Ltd.

Interior design: Christensen Shipyards Ltd. & Williamson & McCarter, Portland, OR

Builder/Year: Christensen Shipyards Ltd./2003

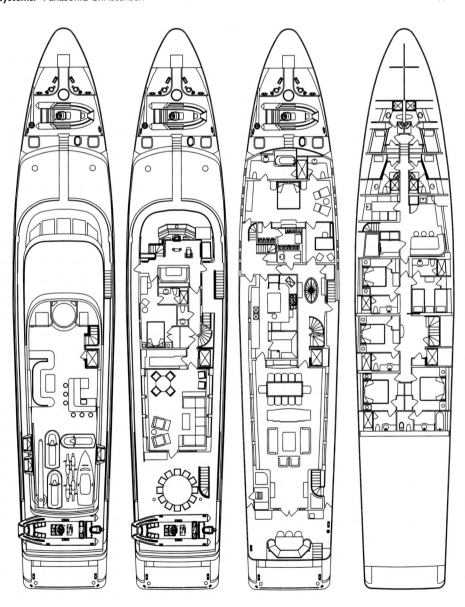

Navetta 30

102-FOOT CUSTOM LINE MOTORYACHT

*I*f the primary attributes of a five-star resort are outstanding accommodations, a superb bar and restaurant, luxurious spa facilities, and a private beach, then Navetta is a name you'd expect to find in a Michelin guide.

However, listing an address in the guide book would pose a challenge, as the Navetta 30 is the flagship of the Custom Line series from the Ferretti Superyachts Division. This floating resort is more likely to be found cruising the world than bound to the land.

Just as with a good hotel, there are a number of choices when it comes to accommodations, and this particular Navetta 30, the first designed specifically for the American market, has a spacious master suite plus a VIP and two twin cabins. You'll find the spa facilities in the master suite (including a spa pool for two), and there is a protected sunning area above the pilothouse. There are two bars—in the saloon and outside the sky lounge—and, with a gourmet galley, the dining is as good as your chef.

But where's the private beach, you ask? The entire transom of the Navetta folds out to create a private swimming beach that accesses the tender and water toys. This could also be an exercise area if desired.

Designed by Gianni Zuccon, the Navetta 30 fulfills two requirements of Italy-based Ferretti: to have classic lines that will always be in style and to have all the comforts of a "villa on the sea." To that end, Zuccon created a multitude of interior options framed within an exterior styling that is clean and fresh. For example, the American market

is addressed with an informal country galley rather than the master suite on the main deck, and clients can add or subtract guest cabins to meet their needs.

Introduced in 2001, the Navetta 30 (we're talking meters here) originally had a smaller sister, the Navetta 27, but it quickly became clear that the larger yacht—with its greater flexibility of layouts (up to five cabins) and better performance—was the more popular. Several 30s were delivered in 2003 and many more are on order for this coming year. In contrast to earlier Navettas, this particular 30 has a lengthened superstructure for sleek lines and increased space on the main deck. The teak-planked aft

deck has the usual dining table and settee, but the main saloon, entered via a full-width stainless-steel sliding door, is a surprise. Unlike some Navettas designed for European clients, this yacht is open, bright, and welcoming with large square windows and unbroken space that stretches far forward.

Aft to starboard is a full wet bar that is located to be convenient both to the aft deck and the saloon. By placing it aft, Zuccon also kept it from becoming a visual distraction in the saloon. A game table is to port, and one of the two fixed cabinets separates the more formal entertaining area with a flexible layout of three couches and chairs.

Porthole ★ Each of the two single-berthed cabins has a private head with shower.

Top ★ The Navetta 30 originally had a smaller sister, but the larger size—with its greater flexibility in layout and better performance—proved to be the more popular model.

Right ★ The pilothouse was spared no luxury: teak-and-holly flooring and a pair of opulent Berenzoni electric helm seats with buttery upholstery will seat any captain in comfort.

Opp. bottom ★ A party-size aft deck with built-in bar.

The saloon is finished in mahogany that is stained a warm reddish color with raised panels and mahogany overhead accents that create a coffered effect. Another surprise is the absence of carpets: this model features easily maintained faux wood flooring throughout the saloon. The seating arrangement provides visual separation from the dining area, plus affords a good view of the plasma-screen television that pops up from the starboard cabinetry.

An oval table seats eight with lighting from wall sconces and concealed overhead lights, and a compact day head is tucked under the stairs to starboard.

Just forward of the dining area bulkhead is the galley (finished in mahogany), which has granite counters and louvered cupboard doors. An interesting touch is the separate granite counter area to starboard with a second refrigerator and wine storage, which allows the chef to work unimpeded while various courses are served and prepped out of the way. In the U-shaped galley area, granite backsplashes extend between the wide windows. An L-shaped settee with a large table is forward for casual dining.

Catering to the desire for spacious cabins, this Navetta 30 has four staterooms on the lower deck with stairs leading to a long fore-and-aft mahogany-paneled passageway reminiscent of luxury liners. The master suite is aft to make use of the full-beam, and it has a centerline king-size berth beneath a padded headboard and bamboo-framed beveled mirror. A desk/vanity area is to starboard with a chair, and live-aboard needs have been considered with a full bureau to port as well as a walk-in closet with more Lucite-faced bureau drawers.

Above ★ With its granite counters and louvered cupboard doors, the galley also features a separate counter area with a second refrigerator that allows the chef to work unimpeded.

Opp. top ★ The more formal of the entertaining areas has a flexible layout with three couches and loose chairs. Warm red mahogany adds a ship-like feel.

Opp. bottom ★ Large windows that frame the sky lounge lower out of sight creating an alfresco lounge in pleasant weather.

Below ★ This table, which seats eight, is beautifully illuminated by wall sconces and concealed overhead lights.

Those put off by the trend of shared his-and-hers heads will appreciate the two private bathrooms on this Navetta. The port head has a shower, the starboard has a spa tub, and both have green marble counters.

Detailing in the master stateroom is notable for the air handlers hidden by waterfall moldings, and the Ralph Lauren look of palm trees and tropical fabrics is set off by nautical touches such as brass sea rails on the bookshelves. Also unique are the unusual ports, which are ellipses with fixed center sections and opening round ports at each end, thus combining ample light with fresh air.

The VIP cabin is all the way forward with a low berth and vertical bulkheads rather than the usual slope to conform to the flaring bow. The queen-size berth has a padded headboard and matching white leather panels inset into the mahogany bulkheads to both lighten the area and set off the artwork. It also has a private head with shower.

On each side of the passageway is a pair of cabins with two single berths, plus Pullmans, and each has a private head with shower. Crew quarters are forward and down from the galley with a single-bunked crew cabin, a laundry with two sets of stacked washer/dryers, and a double captain's cabin.

Stairs from the saloon lead to the pilothouse, which is marked by teak-and-holly flooring and a pair of opulent Berenzoni electric helm seats with buttery leather upholstery. The pilothouse is clearly designed for guests as well as crew, with a comfortable wrap-around settee to port that provides a good view. One particularly nice touch is the mini-office with computer/phone plugs and a fold-out desk. Pantograph doors on each side lead to the Portuguese bridge with wing controls for maneuvering.

Above ★ White panels inset into the mahogany bulkheads set off the artwork that flanks the queen-size berth.

Bottom left ★ Ralph Lauren fabrics enhance the guest staterooms.

Below ★ Rather than the shared his-and-hers style bathrooms found on many ships, this Navetta has two private master baths, one with a shower and one with a spa tub.

Just aft and open to the pilothouse is the sky lounge with teak-and-holly, mahogany paneling, a couch to port, and twin chairs to starboard that are set neatly into the cabinetry. As with the saloon, waist-high dividers separate the area with a pop-up JVC flat-screen television forward, while an area rug continues the motif of palms. The large square windows on both sides and aft lower out of sight, creating an alfresco sky lounge in pleasant weather.

The aft deck is immense, with a built-in bar and four stools tucked under the overhang for sun protection. Twin Alpes-Inox barbecue grills are to port and starboard under flip-up counters that conceal sinks. This particular yacht has sitting and dining areas on the teak-planked deck, and because the tender is tucked into the transom, the deck can be utilized for a spa or water toys. A 1,300lb Berenzoni crane is to port for use when launching the tender or toys.

The Navetta also holds another surprise for visitors: a stairway, almost hidden on the bridge walkaround, that leads up to the sun deck. Fully padded, the area is surrounded by a tall coaming that provides protection not just from the breeze, but from prying eyes in case a guest wants to work on an overall tan.

There are a host of other thoughtful touches on the Navetta 30, such as the concealed stairwell leading from the Portuguese bridge down to the main deck—this allows the crew to work the yacht without intruding on guest spaces. Hidden controls are located aft to starboard on the main deck for backing into quays, and the warping winches are under hinged panels that conceal the dock lines as well.

The fold-out transom is a work of mechanical genius, combining a hinged fold-out panel (the stainless steel rail doubles as a full-width cleat) with a section of the aft deck that accordions out of the way. You can reach the 'beach' either from a spiral stairway from the aft deck or, once open, from the twin boarding stairs on each side of the transom. Either way, there is a teak-planked platform, and the 14ft RIB tender launches with the crane, leaving space for more water toys or scuba gear. A Berenzoni passerelle is hidden to starboard.

Standard power on the Navetta 30 is a pair of 1,300hp MAN diesels that give this yacht a top speed of 19 knots and a comfortable cruise of 16.5 knots. At 12 knots, the range is more than 1000nm.

Designed and executed with the timeless appeal of a small ship, the Navetta 30 can be tailored to the taste of each owner. With a host of pleasantries, not the least of which is the spacious interior, it's no surprise that the Navetta 30 has quickly proven to be a favorite.

LOA:	101ft 7in (30m)
LWL:	88ft 4in (27m)
Beam:	23ft (7m)
Draft:	7ft 5in (2.3m)
Displacement (full):	238.100lbs
Engines:	2 x MAN 12v 2842 LE-404
Power:	2 x 956kW @ 2,300 rpm (2 x 1,300hp)
Speed (max/cruise):	19 knots/16.5 knots
Fuel capacity:	3,963 gallons
Range @ 16.5 knots:	550nm
Electrical generation:	2 x Kohler 27 kW (32 kW for US)
Water:	660 gallons
Security systems:	CCT
Communications:	SSB Furuno
Hull construction:	Composite
Owner and guests:	8/10
Crew:	4
Classification:	Rina Maltese 100-A-1.1 Y
Naval architecture:	CRN Engineering
Interior Design:	Zuccon International Project
Builder/Year:	Ferretti Custom Line/2003

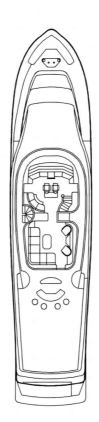
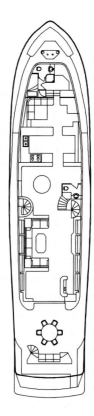

Newcastle 125

125-FOOT NEWCASTLE MARINE EXPEDITION VESSEL

When Newcastle Marine debuted their 102ft expedition yacht two years ago, it was considered exceptional by any measure. That it was the very first design to be built by Newcastle placed the 102 in the range of extraordinary—and the yachting community took notice.

But this crackerjack effort had some naysayers—as do many of man's endeavors. 'Beginner's luck,' said some as they looked at the lines of boat show visitors waiting to get aboard the 102. 'A fluke,' said some builders, like children whistling in a dark forest.

At the launch of Newcastle's second yacht, the 125ft Newcastle Voyager, there was floating proof of two things: the first being that the success of the 102 was no fluke and

it was not luck—it was simply the opening salvo from a very talented team. The second thing apparent was that with their new build, Newcastle Marine raised their already high standards to a new level.

The reason for building a 125-footer was simple: more staterooms. Kevin Keith, Newcastle president, said, "The 102ft expedition yacht had three staterooms plus one convertible area. With this 125-footer, we have five staterooms, plus a convertible, so it's much more appealing to an owner who wants to bring family and friends along on a cruise."

A key reason for the quality of the Voyager is Kevin Keith. Though Newcastle Marine is a new company, Keith

is no stranger to boatbuilding—he grew up alongside his family's commercial boatyard. With 24 years of experience building tough boats, he saw there was a need for equally tough yachts.

On Florida's Palm Coast, he created the setting in which to build his vision: the newly built Newcastle Marine yard, which features a six-story construction building with an overhead crane, a 1,000-ton marine railway, and a capacity for yachts up to 200ft (perhaps foretelling of future projects).

The Voyager was built on spec to showcase the Newcastle Marine concept: a take-no-prisoners-shoot-the-wounded philosophy of going offshore. With a steel hull, aluminum superstructure, and impeccably high construction standards, this is one tough yacht. Dejong and Lebet, who have nearly four decades of experience with offshore commercial hulls, did the naval architecture. The interior is from Luiz de Basto, whom Keith first encountered on another project. Luiz de Basto took the basic concept and, according to Keith, "came back with incredible drawings."

While the talented, 30-man crew of welders and shipwrights were building the hull and superstructure, de Basto's concepts and the detailed Newcastle computer plans were delivered to Wind Dancer International, which created all the joinerwork in prefabricated form and shipped it from their facility in Sarasota.

Above ★ The Newcastle 125 has a rugged profile that towers four stories high.

Porthole ★ The pilothouse with a center helm console has a walkaround in front.

Below and opp. bottom ★ On the sun deck, the faux funnel blends into a shaded seven-seat, fully-equipped bar with a large Dynasty barbecue grill. Add a spa pool and who would want to be anywhere else?

The interior is as stunning and luxurious as the exterior of the Voyager is tough. Mahogany has fallen out of favor as builders outdo each other with ever more exotic woods, but there is a real beauty to it aboard the 125—the warm yacht-like glow it exudes. In this case, the raised-panel styling resembles the fashion of a 1920s classic yacht. With recessed lighting to cast subtle emphasis and shadow, the main saloon seems to stretch endlessly from the rugged entry door off the aft deck. Adding to that effect is the head-room of seven feet, which carries throughout the yacht.

Comfortable couches are to port, and to starboard is a curved bar with a polished Absolute Black granite counter and four stools. Separating the dining area is a credenza with fluted columns and a pop-up 42in plasma television that rotates to face either the bar and sitting area or the dining table. The large rectangular dining table easily seats ten beneath a recessed and mirrored overhead that, like the crown molding encircling the saloon, was cleverly slotted to become the air-conditioning outlets. A sculpture nook on the forward bulkhead belies the rough-and-tumble nature of the Voyager.

A day head is located forward, and the galley is a truly commercial design from the six-burner stove to the wall of refrigerators and freezers. Arranged for efficiency and convenience to the dining area, it has granite counters, stainless steel appliances, and direct access to the side deck.

The master suite fills the forward end of the deckhouse with an unusual arrangement that places the his-and-hers heads along the starboard side. This frees up space for the offset king-size bed facing a 42in plasma-screen television in the forward bulkhead. Large windows are to port, and a desk/vanity area is opposite, along with a walk-in closet. The millwork is exceptional, and the detailing of the night-stands is intricate. The heads are divided by a spa tub, and the area is finished in honey onyx.

Stairs from the saloon lead to a hallway on the lower deck, where guests can find a buffet and refrigerator for snacks—and their rooms. Three queen staterooms and one twin, each with an ensuite marble-tiled bathroom, have writing desks, underberth drawers, cedar-lined closets, and padded silk headboards.

At the forward end of the ship-like passageway, a water-tight bulkhead (which allows for safe access in bad weather) leads to the crew quarters forward. The crew of six has a two-level living area in the forecastle with three two-bunk cabins (each with its own head and shower) on the lower level, and a spacious crew lounge on the main-deck level. The lounge not only has a fully equipped galley and settee, but a dedicated office area complete with computer, printer, and fax.

This section forward has an immense laundry area that is conveniently close to the guest cabins, and at the aft end of the passage is a spacious walk-in cooler/freezer to handle cold stores for long cruises.

On the upper deck is the sky lounge, a pleasant retreat with twin couches, a writing desk, and entertainment center. With one of the couches convertible to a queen-bed, the area can also serve as a sixth stateroom since the head is equipped with a shower. Twin stainless-steel and glass doors open onto the teak-planked aft deck with a full buffet and wet bar, as well as a seven-foot teak-and-holly table with a lazy-Susan center. Protected by the overhang of the sun deck above, the aft deck combines with the sky lounge to become a pleasant all-weather area.

Just forward, along the starboard passage from the sky lounge to the pilothouse, is a dedicated ship's office with

Above ★ From the entry door on the aft deck, the mahogany-paneled main saloon appears to stretch forever, and with a seven-foot headroom, the space appears vast.

Opp. bottom ★ The gorgeous dining area is separated from the saloon by a credenza with fluted columns.

Below ★ The curved bar in the main saloon with polished Absolute Granite counter.

bookshelves, computer, and radio facilities. Opposite the office is an exceptional master electrical panel that not only shows the quality of the systems on the Voyager, but the built-in redundancy.

With a center helm console and a walk-around in front of the helm (for a better view through the outward-slanting windows of half-inch tempered glass), the pilothouse is appropriate to a small ship. The mahogany-and-blue leather instrument panel houses a full array of engine monitors and navigation electronics, and there is a matching Tracy helm chair in front of the raised settee against the aft bulkhead. Twin chart tables are to port and starboard, as are doors leading to the Portuguese bridge with Kobelt wing controls. Just aft of the pilothouse, the captain has a private cabin that is finished like the guest cabins with raised panel mahogany bulkheads and marble tile in the head.

The sun deck comes as a surprise to many visitors, and it is likely to be a much-used area by the owner and guests. The faux funnel blends into a shaded seven-seat, fully equipped bar with a large Dynasty barbecue grill and, while there are two built-in settees with tables aft, guests

are probably going to head for the teak lounge chairs scattered about this spacious area. Concealed in the funnel are a day head on the port side, and a sauna on the starboard side. Forward, and raised for viewing, is a spa pool between twin sunpads.

The boat deck amidships is large enough to easily handle the 19ft and 11ft Nautica tenders as well as two WaveRunners, all of which are launched with the Marquipt 5,000lb crane on centerline. This deck is a good example of the quality built into the Voyager: the frames are exposed above deck level. Because this is a high-wear area, each frame has a stainless-steel half-round bar on the edge, and if the paint is worn away by lines or chafe, the frame won't show rust marks. The same stainless-steel protection has been used in the freeing ports and other wear areas.

Reached via stairs from the aft deck (or directly from the transom platform), the spacious lazarette has an office for the engineer to port, plus a spacious workshop with full tool storage. There is an additional washer and dryer, and more than ample storage for an array of water toys.

The engine-room on the 125 is likely to make an engineer weep with joy because it's been sensibly laid out with ample space for easy servicing of all the systems. The twin 600hp Cat 3406e diesels seem dwarfed in this immense area of diamond-plate flooring and neatly arranged

Above ★ The sky lounge on the upper deck is a pleasant retreat and an entertainment center.

Opp. top ★ The his-and-hers heads are placed along the starboard side of the master cabin.

Opp. bottom ★ The sumptuous master suite fills the forward end of the deckhouse.

Below ★ One of the three queen staterooms— all fit for a king!

Above ★ With a capacity for 14,300 gallons of fuel, the 125 has a transatlantic range at a cruising speed of ten knots, while top speed is 13.5 knots.

Bottom right ★ Convenient walk-around side decks.

Below ★ The teak planked aft deck sports a seven-foot teak-and-holly table with a lazy Susan.

systems. Twin Northern Lights 80kW gensets are aft and, even in their sound shields, they barely dent the walk-around areas. With a capacity for 14,300 gallons of fuel, the 125 has transatlantic range at a cruising speed of ten knots, while the top speed is 13.5 knots.

With a rugged profile that towers four stories high, the Newcastle Voyager meets the highest standards of yachting luxury. Both tough and comfortable, this is a yacht that can carry her owners and guests worldwide on amazing adventures.

LOA: 125ft (38.1m)

Beam: 28ft (8.5m)

Draft: 7ft 11in (2.2m)

Displacement (light ship): 300 LT

Propulsion: Caterpillar 3406E 600HP x 2

Speed (max/cruise): 13.5 knots/10 knots

Fuel capacity: 14,300 USG

Range @ 10kts: 4,500nm

Electrical generation: Northern Lights 80 KW x 2

Bow thruster: American Watermaker

Stabilizers: American Watermaker

Water pressure system: Headhunter

Sanitation: Headhunter

Entertainment systems: Bose

Paint: Marine Custom Paint

Air-conditioning: Cruise Air

Tenders: Nautica R11D and a Nautica R19D

Communications: mini-M

Construction: Steel Hull/Aluminum Superstructure

Naval architecture: DeJong and Lebet

Exterior styling/ Interior design: Luiz de Basto

Builder/Year: Newcastle Marine/2002

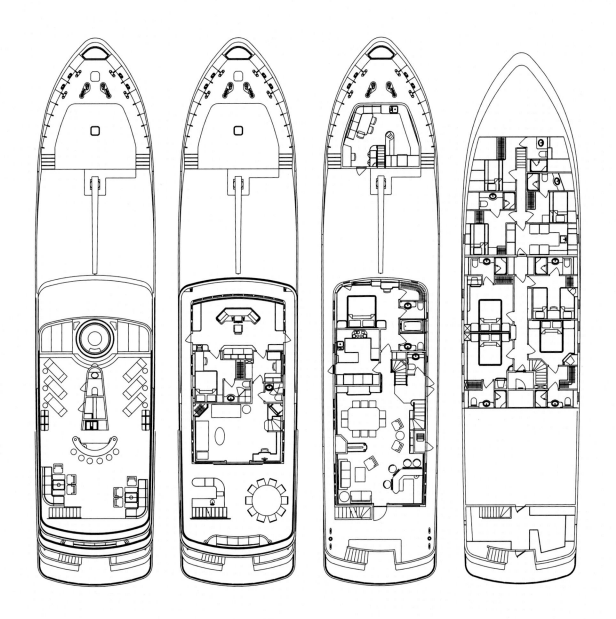

Rivolta 90

90-FOOT RIVOLTA SAILING SLOOP

n the 1960s and 1970s, the name Rivolta was revered by connoisseurs of fine cars who were drawn not just to the sleek, sensuous lines of these grand touring automobiles, but to the practicality under the skin. This was an era when the names Ferrari and Maserati were synonymous with luxury GT cars, but they also had a reputation for being temperamental and expensive to maintain.

The father and son team of Renzo and Piero Rivolta solved such problems by creating the Iso Rivolta GT, with styling as Italian as the Ferrari and Maserati and interiors of fine wood and supple leather. However, where the other Italian cars relied on homegrown V-12 engines that were often unpredictable, the Rivoltas solved the problem by installing the V-8 engine from the Chevrolet Corvette.

This gave the Iso Rivolta the lines of an exotic car with the absolute simplicity and thunderous torque of a powerful American engine. The result did not exactly take the world by storm (these were expensive cars, after all), but they did set a new standard for the automotive world. The philosophy of the Rivoltas—combining good looks with reliability—is one that is carried on today by European boatbuilders who use American-made engines and systems in their yachts.

Piero Rivolta was always fascinated by boats, initially speedboats, on the Italian lakes. Now settled in Florida, he continues the Rivolta tradition of forward-thinking design with his Rivolta 90. This remarkable cruising sloop

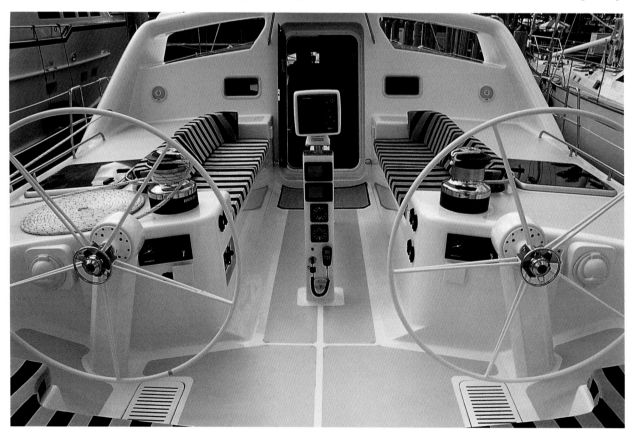

combines a light displacement and an efficient hull with full cruising amenities to create a waterborne, grand touring yacht.

Piero readily admits that, when drawing the lines of the hull, he and naval architect Hakan Sodergren used modern America's Cup and round-the-world racing yachts as their inspiration, and there is no question that this 90ft vessel is truly a modern performance cruiser. "I could see no reason," he says with Italianate passion, "why a cruising yacht had to be slow."

The Rivolta 90 is more than just a swanky interior slapped into a high performance hull—it is the result of

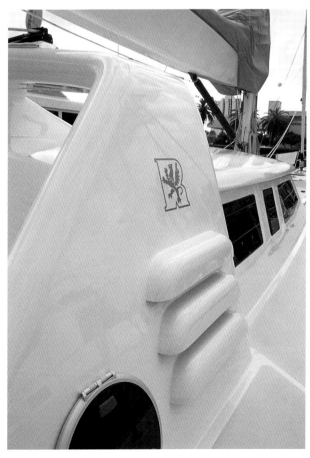

Porthole ★ The saloon steering station forward and to starboard.

Top ★ The Rivolta 90 combines light displacement with an efficient hull design.

Right ★ Modern Italian styling prevails.

Opp. bottom ★ Twin helms for port and starboard maneuvering.

careful planning in order to solve many of the problems of large sailing yachts. Piero wanted to fill a void in the maxi-sailing market and he believed that the most important ingredient, just as with the Rivolta cars, was simplicity. "We concentrated on eight aspects of simplicity—simplicity in design, sailing, maneuvering, access for the owner and crew, cleaning and maintenance, motoring, interior functions and engineering."

Facing a blank sheet of paper, Piero's quest was to create a fast boat, yet one that was easy for a couple or family to handle. Twin outward-angled rudders like those on long distance racers give fingertip control and, combined with twin MaxProp propellers in front of each rudder, make the yacht easy to handle under both power and sail. The 14-ton keel has a sturdy and reliable retracting mechanism that allows the Rivolta 90 access to shallow waters and marinas with depths of just six feet. Fully extended to a draft of nearly 13ft, the keel provides a high level of stability and, when retracted, still provides several centimeters of protection deeper than the tips of the rudders.

If the helm is the heart of a sailing yacht, then the Rivolta 90 has two hearts—with steering positions both on deck and in the saloon. The cockpit is large and comfortable, with twin Whitlock wheels and a full-width bench seat for the skipper. A pair of immense Harken 1120 electric winches are in the aft corners for trimming the bowsprit-

tacked genacker and engine controls are both port and starboard for maneuvering. Just forward of the wheels are twin settees, set well inboard for wind protection behind the doghouse, and separated by a sturdy folding table that doubles as a hand grip. A pair of Harken 980 electric winches handle the mainsheet and self-tacking jib, buttons control the electric roller furling genoa and the Harken mainsheet traveller spans the raised pilothouse aft.

An important benefit of the forward mainsheet is the ability to cover the cockpit with a Bimini top even while sailing and, with the cockpit separated from the saloon by just three steps, there is safe and simple access.

The raised saloon is open and airy with large windows, matching L-shaped settees and American cherrywood tables to port and starboard. The finish is pale birch on the bulkheads with cherrywood soles. The helmstation fills the forward starboard corner with a full electronics panel and a padded bolster with a seat that hinges up electrically to allow either standing or sitting. This helm is intended for powering, since it has a limited view of the sails and no way to trim them. To port is a companion seat and chart table, as well as the AC/DC electrical distribution panels. Just inside the companionway door are foul weather gear lockers.

Three steps down from the saloon is the galley to port, tucked behind a pair of stainless steel-topped counters that

create a leaning brace for the cook at sea. Finished in bright white with woven stainless-steel doors on the lockers, the galley is cheerful and compact. Just forward is a small banquette and burled table that provides a private dining nook for the owners.

The centerline keel well provides a natural bulkhead between the galley and the owner's cabin to starboard, and it has been disguised with a tropical, hand-painted mural. The cabin is entered from forward of the keel well via a separate dressing room with a vanity unit and hanging lockers which have intricately woven leather doors. The

Opp. top ★ The main saloon encompasses an indoor helm station forward.

Left ★ The centerline keel has been masked by a tropical hand-painted mural on the bulkhead.

Below ★ The galley is a few steps down from the main saloon on the port side.

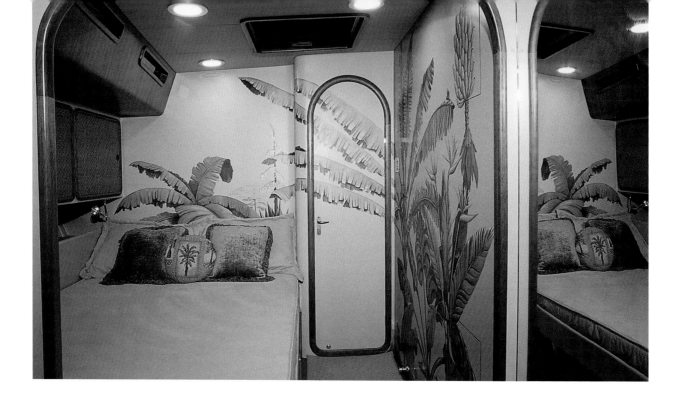

bedroom is aft with a double bed to starboard and additional leather-faced lockers. A painting of palm trees gracing the bulkhead aft separates the bedroom from the head and shower room.

Forward of the owner's cabin is the crew quarters, with a stacked double and single berth to starboard, a lounge area with settee to port, and heads forward. Stairs forward of this provide the crew with separate access to the foredeck so they do not have to pass through the guest areas.

Aft of the saloon are two additional cabins, with a VIP to

Above ★ The owner's suite with a palm tree mural.

Opp. top ★ A private dining area for the master.

Below ★ The master bathroom.

Bottom right ★ VIP guest cabin aft.

LOA (with bowsprit):	93.2ft (28.4m)
LOA (hull):	89.8ft (27.3m)
LWL:	21.3ft (24.3m)
Beam:	21.3ft (6.5m)
Draft (keel up/down):	12.9ft/5.8ft (3.9m/1.7m)
Displacement:	103,617lbs
Sail area:	3,987.7sqft (370.4m2)
Engine:	2 x Yanmar 315hp diesel
Speed (max/cruise):	12.8/8.5knots
Fuel capacity:	823gal
Electrical generation:	2 x Onan – 20kW & 8kW
Ballast:	30,870lbs
Water ballast:	8,800lbs
Water capacity:	1428gal
Construction:	E-glass reinforced with carbon fiber, Kevlar and PVC
Conceptual design:	Rivolta Design
Structural design:	SP Systems
Naval architecture:	Hakan Sodergren
Builder:	Rivolta Marine

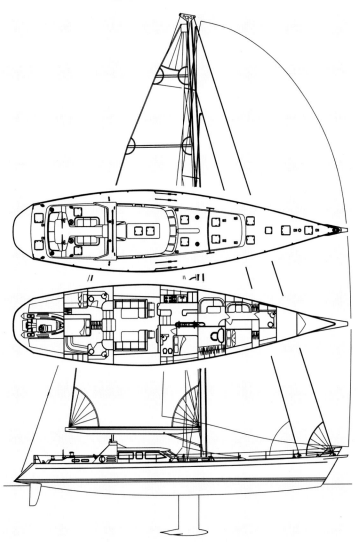

starboard with a large double bed tucked under the cockpit, a wrap-around settee outboard and an en suite shower room with circular shower. The smaller port side cabin has twin bunks but, surprisingly, still has an ensuite shower room.

Rivolta has used every nook and cranny for storage, including the wide transom which hinges out to reveal the 13ft tender with 25hp outboard power. With the tender in the water, the storage space turns into a spacious bathing platform.

She is built with an E-glass hull, reinforced with carbon fiber, Kevlar and PVC coring. The deck is lightweight carbon fiber which has been finished with a non-slip Awlgrip surface rather than heavy teak planking. The keel is a foil-shaped stainless steel strut with a lead bulb, while a carbon fiber and Kevlar reinforced structure provides exceptional strength in the area around the mast step, Kevlar chainplates and keel.

Standard power is a pair of Yanmar 315hp diesels which give the Rivolta a top speed of 12.8 knots or, with one engine, a cruising speed of 8.5 knots at an economical five gallons per hour and 1,300 nautical mile range. Two Onan generators of 20kW and 8kW allow both full power and night-time use.

The four-spreader carbon fiber mast is no less sophisticated, with swept-back spreaders, Ocean Yacht Systems rod rigging and Navtec vang. The wide Park Avenue-style boom allows the full-battened mainsail to stow neatly and electric Harken two-speed winches hoist the main and the asymmetrical headsail.

Adding to her sailing ability are water ballast tanks capable of carrying more than four tons of water which can be added or quickly dumped at the touch of a switch.

The result is a yacht that brings the Rivolta tradition of styling excellence and practicality to the water. Designed for short-handed fast cruising, either worldwide or for weekends, the Rivolta 90 offers speed, strength and luxury in a package that does not disappoint.

Sis W

127-FOOT BURGER MOTORYACHT

The launch of *Sis W* was classic Americana in the best sense possible. The importance of the event became clear to me when I picked up my rental car at the Green Bay, Wisconsin, airport. "Going to the launching?" asked the Hertz agent. "Here for the launching?" asked the hotel clerk when I checked in. And, indeed, at the launching itself it was obvious that the entire town was participating. Families arrived with coolers and folding chairs, endless group photos were taken with *Sis W* as background, the oompah band played on…

Driving into the Burger Boat Company yard, the first thing you feel is a sense of disconnect, almost a time warp. After all, this is an American yacht yard with a sterling reputation for building state-of-the-art motoryachts of excellent quality and craftsmanship. My first impression, when I arrived to witness the launching of the 127ft *Sis W*—the largest motoryacht in the company's history—was that I was right back in a typical Downeast boatyard, a large wooden shed that had obviously seen better days, the odd bit of plywood covering gaps in the clapboards, a couple of trailers, and a shingle cottage which clearly was meant to be the main office. On the stocks nearby, a pair of brand new red 250-ton Manitowoc cranes at the ready to lift her, was *Sis W*, a shining white modern creation, the latest in the impressive series of flawless motoryachts for which Burger is justly famous.

Then again, upon further reflection, the disconnect, the time warp, is appropriate. What becomes very quickly obvious is that this is a yacht builder that has its priorities well defined—the essential element is the boat, and if the old shed serves, and the designers can apply their talent to the task at hand in a trailer serving as a design office, why change it? If you want proof, consider *Sis W*. Her owners commissioned their first Burger in 1956, a 65-foot steel motoryacht. No doubt her keel was laid in that same shed. Two more Burgers followed, with this *Sis W* completing the roster as their fourth commission for Burger. Owner satisfaction? Charles R. Walgreen, Jr. (son of the founder of the pharmacy chain) is 97, Mrs. Walgreen is 96. They intend to keep on cruising.

Burger Boat Company's reputation has been built not only upon their meticulous attention to detail but their contin-

uing insistence on building motoryachts of a somewhat more traditional design while employing the most modern technology available. *Sis W* is the fifth Burger I have had the good fortune to write about in recent years, and it is evident to me that her creators have carefully incorporated the successes of previous boats, designed a completely handicap-accessible yacht from the inception, while steadily developing the areas they feel showed room for further refinement.

The most apparent example of this continuous evolutionary process is an aesthetic one, and *Sis W* exemplifies it perfectly. A few years back, there was a period when Burger produced a series of yachts whose lines, I felt, were perhaps a bit too angular. *Sis W* is the antithesis of that style, with her rounded corners and edges giving her a more graceful and softer profile. She is, indeed, easy on the eye. Seen from any perspective, her lines remain harmonious. And it is apparent that the Burger Design Team understands visual effects—her main saloon deadlights, which might initially seem overlarge and too square, read black to the eye, and in fact relieve what would otherwise be an excessive expanse of white. If I may be allowed to cavil, the only minor discordant note I could find is in the corner detail of her triangular bridge deck deadlights; which have sharp corners in contrast to the softer rounded corners of all the other deadlights. As I said, a small detail.

Above ⋆ Rounded corners and edges give *Sis W* a graceful and harmonious profile.

Porthole ⋆ The sizeable captain's cabin is a stately stateroom indeed.

Opp. bottom ⋆ The boat deck includes the amenities of a lounge space with grill, refrigerator, wet bar, and spa pool.

Below ⋆ A Portuguese bridge with hand rails leads to the bow.

Boarding *Sis W* immediately offers a sense, to anyone conversant with Burger yachts, of familiarity. Eschewing stylistic excesses, the excitement is in the execution. And, as can be expected in a yacht intended strictly for family use, the extended Walgreen family had significant input in her development. Jim Bean, the captain of their past yacht, worked closely with Burger engineers and designers throughout the building process, and the interior décor reflects the work of granddaughter Joanne Walgreen, owner of her own interior design company in Chicago.

The overall tone is one of understated elegance. Douglas Richey, Burger's in-house interior designer, created a cohesive design motif employing the same makoré wood (African cherry) throughout, with exquisitely executed details such as carved rope moldings and raised paneling. The panels use the wood's burl grain for contrast; it was described to me as 'mottled makoré', an apt enough portrayal of the effect. Dark marble is used for the sole in all passageways, with the rest of the living spaces carpeted.

On the main deck one enters the saloon through two large electric sliding doors from the open area aft deck, a comfortable and sheltered outdoor lounging space. Immediately the quality of both materials and workmanship becomes evident, as does the informal atmosphere befitting a yacht intended for extended family cruising. Comfortable furniture in muted colors and a marble-topped wet bar provide the amenities here; just forward, sharing the same open space, is the dining area, with seating for ten people. Port forward from here is the access to the galley and crew mess, and companionway to the crew's quarters on the lower deck. The galley is fully equipped with commercial grade equipment, finished in stainless steel for practicality; the sole here is varnished cork, my favorite for comfort over long periods of time standing up. Just forward and outboard is the crew mess.

Forward and to starboard of the dining area is the passage to the owners' suite. A day head is included here. Just before entering the owners' stateroom is a small but comfortable cabin with ensuite head for a two nurses. The owners' stateroom takes up the full beam of the boat. While this arrangement forces the crew to employ a more circuitous route to reach the foredeck, it does provide complete privacy for the occupants. As befits the age of the Walgreens, two fixed hospital-style beds are installed here. Ample counter/desk space and stowage lockers are of course evident. The ensuite heads, with large central shower, are works of art, a light

Above ★ The galley is fully equipped with commercial grade stainless-steel equipment and a varnished cork sole for comfort.

Opp. top ★ The dining area shares the same open space as the main saloon.

Opp. bottom ★ An electric fireplace and bookshelves add warmth to the main saloon.

Below ★ African makoré paneling and muted colors lend the main saloon an understated elegance.

green striped finish on the lower panels culminating in gorgeous, pale jade green onyx countertops.

A set of stairs just forward of the dining area leads up to the bridge deck. The boat deck aft is shared by the ship's tender and a comfortable lounge space. A grill, refrigerator, and wet bar offer welcome amenity here. Forward of this is the traditional sky lounge, an intimate living area complete with theater quality entertainment center. Incidentally, an unusual feature on *Sis W* is her hydraulic elevator, which spans three deck levels including the topmost sun deck. Centrally located is the captain's suite, with the control

bridge forward. As is becoming increasingly common, the main feature are the four LCD monitor screens forming the 'glass bridge', which can be used interchangeably to monitor all navigating and operating functions: engine performance, radar, chart plotter, even entertainment. The usual 'spectator bleachers' are tastefully executed just aft of the helm station; the one unusual feature here, in deference to her owners, is the ability to lock in a wheelchair which can rise hydraulically to provide a clear view over the vessel's bow. Wing controls are installed port and starboard just outside the side doors. They protrude somewhat into the width of the side deck, a minor annoyance given the relatively light traffic along here.

A curved stair from the aft open deck leads up to the flybridge, an al fresco relaxing space complete with a wet bar and Jacuzzi. An auxiliary steering station is at the forward end.

The lower deck forward is reached by stairs located forward of the galley. The crew quarters consist of four staterooms with a variety of berth combinations. All have ensuite heads, a thoughtful touch. While the flared hull shape restricts the volume of the two forward spaces somewhat, the privacy afforded will surely be appreciated by the crew. A washer/dryer is included here.

Engine-room access is through a watertight door at the stern platform. The main engines are a straight installation. This was made possible by setting the propellers in tunnels, thus avoiding excessive shaft angle and, incidentally, reducing the vessel's draft. The two generators are set on the centerline in soundproof boxes. I should note here, having been an admirer of Burger engine rooms for years, that all engine rooms look good on new boats. But I have visited older Burger yachts whose engine rooms were still in pristine condition, with none of the modifications and 'customizing' so frequently seen. This is the heart of the ship after all (although on *Sis W* her galley runs a very close second!) and it is reassuring to find such quality and thoughtful attention to ease of operation.

And, while complimenting the builders, I would add

Opp. top ★ Guests are well taken care of aboard *Sis W*, witness to this luxurious queen-size cabin.

Bottom ★ The bridge deck or sky lounge is an intimate gathering place with a theater quality entertainment center.

Below ★ A spacious bath graced with jade green onyx countertops ajoins the master stateroom.

subject of thoroughness, a couple of other details are noticeable on deck. All deadlights have a built-in provision for fastening storm port covers, as befits a yacht intended for extended cruising. And, providing beneficial access, a ten-inch wide ledge at main deck level runs forward outside the owners' stateroom ports. A handrail set above the ports makes the crew's work of keeping the boat clean easy. A minor detail perhaps, but so many large yachts send their crews out hanging in bosun's chairs to wash windows.

Promptly at one o'clock, the yard whistle blew; the two giant cranes lifted *Sis W* and gently lowered her into the water. As soon as the applause had finished and the crowd started to disperse, it was business as usual at Burger Boat Company. A crane lifted the radar arch and lowered it onto the boat. Meanwhile the cleanup crew had removed all evidence of the launching, while finish carpenters and electricians swarmed aboard for the final details. The old buildings and rusting railroad bridge continued to provide the contrasting background for *Sis W*, herself a tribute to her owners' and builders' repeated quest for the ideal yacht.

that a visual inspection of the more remote bilge spaces reveals their customary thoroughness: all welds are smooth, corners rounded, edges radiused. While on the

LOA:	126ft 8in (38.7m)
LWL:	111ft 7in (34.1m)
Beam:	26ft 6in (8.1m)
Draft:	6ft (1.8m)
Displacement (light ship):	180
Engines:	2 x Caterpillar 3508B-DITA
Speed:	1,300 bhp @ 1,835 RPM
Fuel capacity:	14,300 USG
Water Capacity:	2,500 U.S. Gallons
Range @ cruising speed:	2,500 nm
Electrical generation:	2 x Northern Lights 65 kW
Bow thruster:	Quantum QT 120
Stabilizers:	Quantum Controls QC 1000/1 Zero Speed
Watermakers:	Watermakers, Inc.
Sanitation:	Matrix Desalination
Entertainment systems:	Team Electronics
Paint:	Awlgrip II
Air Conditioning:	Marine Air
Communications:	Yachtronics
Tender:	Northwind Custom 21ft 7in
Davit/Crane:	Nautical Structures EZ-4000-KB
Hull Construction:	Aluminum
Owner and guests/Crew:	5/6
Project management:	Captain Jim Bean/Burger Boat Company
Naval architecture/Exterior styling:	Burger Design Team
Interior design:	Belden Interiors/Burger Design Team
Builder / Year:	Burger Boat Company/2003

Above ★ A twin guest cabin furnished in the Walgreen's favorite color; yellow.

Top ★ Handicap access to all three decks is possible via the internal elevator.

Opp. top ★ Aft main deck dining.

Opp. bottom ★ Four LCD monitor screens form the 'glass bridge' in the pilothouse.

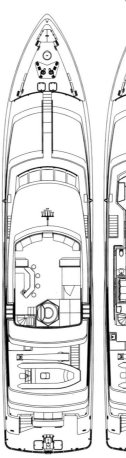
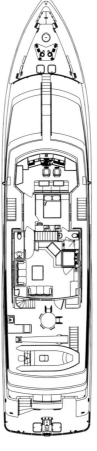
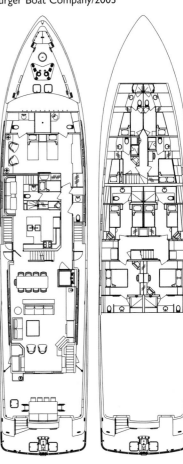

Sovereign Lady

135-FOOT SOVEREIGN YACHTS TRI-DECK

nyone who followed the television coverage of the last America's Cup series between defenders *Team New Zealand* and their Swiss challengers, *Alinghi*, most likely noticed one motoryacht that, unlike most other spectator craft, remained in close contact with the two competitors throughout every race. The yacht in this privileged position was the Royal New Zealand Yacht Squadron's spectator boat, *Sovereign Lady*, a Sovereign Yachts 135ft tri-deck launched just ten days before the Cup races began.

Bill Lloyd, a native New Zealander and owner of the composite motoryacht builder Sovereign Yachts, dreamed up this *Lady* at the last New Zealand defense of the America's Cup. His vision was to build a competitively priced semi-custom 135ft tri-deck motoryacht for series production, a style of yacht that he believed was increasingly fashionable. Now, just a few years later, his dream had been realized—and she is a real head-turner. The naval architect, Ward Setzer, and Sovereign's in-house designers in Canada created a fresh, new design that was laid up in Sovereign's British Columbia yard until the bare hull and superstructure were shipped to the new Sovereign (NZ) yard, where it was completed by Sovereign's locally recruited workforce.

This new build received generous praise at the Cup races as her exterior and interior finishes are of exceptional quality, plus she ran noiselessly and comfortably through the chop kicked up by the thousands of spectator craft.

In her looks, *Sovereign Lady* is a high bowed, modern classic with a gracefully rounded superstructure and three tiers of fully teaked decks (four, if one counts the fishing cockpit), which provide for a good range of outdoor activities. The hull, impeccably molded from cored GRP, is encircled by just one ring of decks that run from the main deck aft to the master stateroom, and then reunite forward of the pilothouse, where a Portuguese bridge running down the forward slope of the superstructure gives access to the foredeck. This layout, which is ideal for yachts of this size, maximizes the interior volume by allowing a full-beam sun lounge aft on the upper deck and a wide owner's suite forward on the main deck. At the same time, it permits easy routes for the crew and gives privacy to guests on the upper two decks (which can only be accessed from the yacht's interior or up a set of stairs from the main deck aft).

Where to stow the tenders and larger water toys is always a difficult decision on yachts of this size, and as *Sovereign Lady*

Porthole ★ The pilothouse has a a half oval leather-covered guest seating area behind the helm.

Left and opp. bottom ★ A Portuguese bridge makes for easy access to the bow.

Opp. top ★ *Sovereign Lady* can max out at a speed of 21.7 knots when lightly laden.

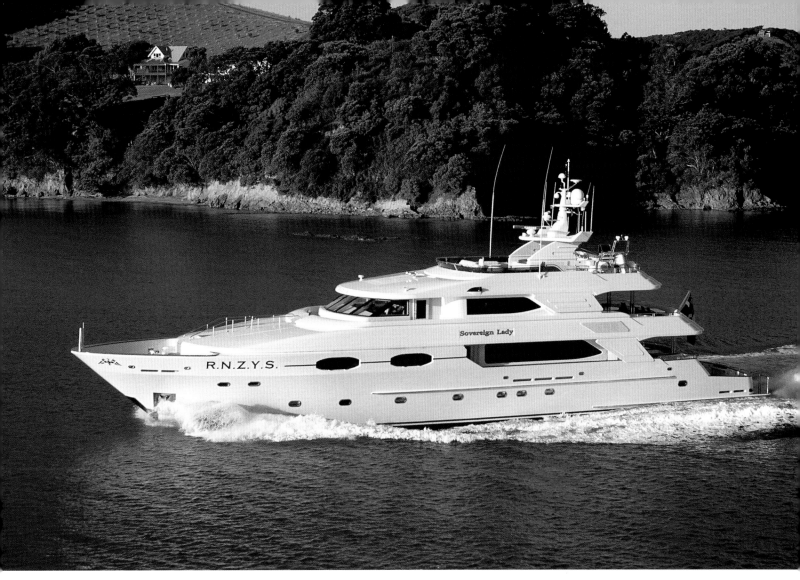

was designed with a fishing cockpit, a stern garage was out of the question. So, the designers sensibly chose to divide the fleet. *Sovereign Lady*'s exceptional hull stability allowed the large tender (and its launching crane) to be positioned aloft on the aft part of the sun deck—even though this area also carries the weight of a spa pool and its teak decking—while the rest of the fleet is stowed in a huge clam-shell locker in the forward part of the main deck superstructure. In this way, all four craft get a good degree of protection from the elements, and because it is the large tender that is usually launched first, it also means that its position on the sun deck is normally available as a sunning area when the yacht is at rest.

The sun deck is primarily a play area. At its forward end, two settees face the bow on either side of an open air helm station, while two other L-shaped settees face aft and inwards towards the spa pool and close to the bar.

Alfresco dining is the main function aft of the bridge deck, where a long settee set against the aft rail is an ideal meeting place for sunset, followed by dinner served directly from the barbecue to the adjacent ten-seat, circular dining table. After dinner? Just forward through the wide sliding doors is the upper deck saloon, with its bar, audio-visual entertainment center based on a 42in flat-screen television, and a games table—this is surely the perfect formula for an evening's entertainment.

Daytime fun is the preserve of the main deck aft, where a curve of seating against the aft rail enfolds a split-center dining table. This is the place to be while the sportier guests use the fishing cockpit just below as a base for a variety of watersports. The main intent of the cockpit is fishing, of course, so there are two bait tanks, one of which is an aquarium that constantly circulates sea water to keep the bait in good health. The day's catch can be stored in two long freezers beneath the cockpit sole. If it's not a good day for fishing, then this is the place to prepare your dive gear or rig the windsurfer. Those guests who wish for solitude can retreat to the foredeck, where another seating area is built into the forward part of the superstructure.

Restrictions that were inherent with the hull's configuration dictated that the interior space be laid out with a master suite on the main deck and four guest cabins amidships on the lower deck, and the crew forward. The main deck carries a saloon and a dining area, while the master suite fills the superstructure forward of the midships galley and the starboard side foyer.

Sovereign Lady's highly detailed interior was designed in-house and magnificently built by the Sovereign (NZ) craftsmen. The main saloon and dining area have curved surfaces, raised-and-fielded paneling, fluted columns, arched door heads, and intricate moldings within the interior woodwork, which combines sapele and pomele with ebony inlays and occasional marble surfaces. But dark woods do not make this a gloomy interior, being balanced by a white, simulated-leather deck head, pale carpets and off-white upholstery that all reflect the daylight pouring through large windows to port and starboard, as well as through the large doors aft. Comforts abound with a pair of soft sofas and two easy chairs; wine coolers are hidden within the cabinets; and a 42in flat-screen television, which can be swiveled to face into the dining area, forms the heart of the entertainment system.

Beyond the marble-floored foyer, which gives access to the

starboard side deck, is the master suite. A glazed door leads to the owner's office, and beyond that is the bedroom. In this grand room, the bed faces a huge television that, when not in use, is concealed by a painting rising from the counter-top. His-and-hers walk-in closets, lined with cedar, fill the aft corners of the room, while a built-in chest of drawers to starboard give ample storage for clothes. So that the owners have

a private place to relax, to port is a settee. Doors on either side of the bed access the two bathrooms, each identical in its layout and elegantly adorned with granite and marble, which are separated by a huge, shared shower.

Guests are treated to equal standards of luxury, albeit on a smaller scale. The four guest cabins open off a comfortably sized, marble-paved foyer at the foot of the main

Right ★ Granite countertops grace the galley.

Opp. top ★ The main saloon and dining area designed in-house have curved surfaces, raised-and fielded-paneling, fluted columns, and more...

Below ★ Dining for eight beneath an oval overhead that mirrors the oval dining table.

stairway. Not only does the foyer have a storage for guests' suitcases—a necessary and often overlooked amenity—but there is also a washer and dryer (located beneath a granite counter) for guests' personal use. Aft, sharing the yacht's beam, are two mirror-image double cabins with inboard-facing beds, their interiors dappled with daylight from a pair of portlights. The lady's closest provides long hanging space for dresses—another feature often neglected by male interior designers. The adjoining bathrooms feature a single sink, head, and shower, as do the slightly smaller ones within the two double and twin-bedded cabins forward of the foyer. All the rooms have 21in flat-screen televisions and DVD players.

The crew is also well looked after. Without some of the restraints seen in red-flagged charter vessels resulting from MCA regulations, the crew have a two-ring burner with adjacent dishwasher, refrigerator, and freezer drawers and, opposite, a pleasant mess area in which a settee wraps around an oval table. A two-washer/dryer laundry has granite work surfaces, and a folding ironing board is opposite, while a large double/single engineer's cabin and two good-size, twin bunk cabins, all with good shower rooms, complete the area.

At the head of the crew stairs, the guest galley has décor to please the owner's wife, and equipment—such as granite worktops and Kitchenmaid appliances—to please the chef.

To its aft side, adjacent to the dining room, the crew have their own servery with sink, coffee-making machine, and two dishwashers.

Sovereign Lady's technical areas are well-conceived and well-built. The pilothouse, incorporating a half-oval of leather-covered guest seating, is one of the six control stations aboard—the others are the two wing stations, the flybridge, and two aft stations used when docking and fishing. It is comprehensibly equipped with the new NAVnet system from Furuno that includes radar, sounder, plotter, and weatherfax in one package, a Robertson autopilot, Furuno SSB and VHF DSC radios, and a second stand-alone Furuno 64-mile radar. Aft of the pilothouse, the captain's cabin is to port—its huge windows make it a highly enviable resting place—while to starboard is the ship's office and radio room that connects aft to the yacht's stairwell and sky lounge.

The engine-room can be reached via the fishing cockpit through an area that is an electrical room cum water-toy storage. This space is home to the air-conditioning plant, electricity converters, and the AC/DC switchboards.

Edged by immaculately laid out pipework, the main elements of the engine-room are the twin DDC/MTU 12-cylinder 4000-series diesels, each of which develop some 2,750hp at 2,100rpm, driving the yacht at a maximum speed

Above ★ In this grand master stateroom, the bed faces a huge television concealed by a painting when not in use.

Right ★ The two bathrooms in the master suite, separated by a shared shower, are elegantly adorned with granite and marble.

Opp. bottom ★ One of the four guest cabins, each of which have 21in flat screen televisions and DVD players.

of 21.7 knots when lightly laden, and at a comfortable extended cruising speed 15 to 16 knots. Underway at this speed, *Sovereign Lady* is particularly quiet, while her TRAC active-fin stabilization keeps the yacht steady, both at sea and in a rolly anchorage. And she was tested—in a beam sea off the east coast of North Island, New Zealand with the wind gusting to 40 knots and the confused seas approaching some 20ft in height. *Sovereign Lady* coped easily with the stabilizers, never failing to hold the yacht upright.

Sovereign Lady has just been sold to an undisclosed buyer, but a second similar yacht will soon be available. This will be a 138-footer from the same mold, this time with its fishing cockpit exchanged for a larger saloon. She will be available in 2004 and is priced at around $15 million.

By the end of what was the longest America's Cup series to date, Bill Lloyd was pleased with his new *Lady*. She had carried, entertained, and fed a full load of guests on every race day and, despite the fact that she had only just been launched, she performed flawlessly. There was just one thing that bothered both Lloyd and his guests from the Royal New Zealand Yacht Squadron—*Team New Zealand* was thoroughly thrashed by the Swiss-based *Alinghi* team. Ah well, you can't have everything.

Top left ★ The pilothouse is one of six control stations aboard.

Top right ★ Protected dining al fresco is an option aft of the bridge deck.

Left ★ The yacht has a gracefully rounded superstructure and three tiers of fully teaked decks.

LOA: 135ft (41.2m)

LWL: 118ft 9in (36.3m)

Beam (max): 28ft (8.5m)

Draft: 6ft 10in (1.9m)

Displacement (half-load): 400,000lbs

Propulsion: 2 x 2,750hp DDEC/MTU 12V-4000 series diesels

Gearbox: 3: 1 reduction

Propellers: Osbourne 52 x44 pitch

Shafts: Aquamet 22 HS, 4-1/2in dia

Speed (max/cruise): 21 knots/16 knots

Fuel capacity: 10,000 gallons

Range @ 12 knots: 3,000 miles

Electrical generation: 2 x 80kW Northern Lights

Power converter: Vectek, 100 amp input

Monitoring system: Cervina Multi Page

Bow thruster: TRAC, 80 hp 20in dia

Stabilizers: American Bow Thruster 3 Axis

Watermaker: 2 x Filter Concepts, 1,600gpd

Windlass: 2 x Maxwell 6000

Cranes: Circa Marine

Fire control system: Wormalds Monitor, Chubb FM200 gas

Entertainment systems: Sony TVs, DVD, amplifier

Paint: Awlgrip, Matterhorn white

Air-conditioning: Clima 390,000 BTUs

Communications: Furuno FS2570C SSB DSC/GMDSS; Furuno FM-8500 VHF DSC/GMDSS; 2 x ICOM IC-M127 VHF

Autopilot: Robertson AP45

Navigation: Furuno NAVnet system incorporating: Furuno 1933C Radar, Furuno ETR-6/10N Network Sounder, Furuno GD-1900C Color Video Plotter, Furuno FZX-30 Weather Facsimile Receiver

GPS: 2 x Furuno GP-31

Wind instruments: B&G

Galley equipment: SubZero fridges, Miele Range and Kitchenaid Oven, Franke sinks, F&P dishdrawer

Construction: Composite hull & superstructure

Owner and guests: 10 guests in 4 x double & 1 x twin staterooms

Crew: 8 crew in 1 double, 3 twin bunk cabins

Tank testing: BC Research, Vancouver, Canada

Naval architect: Ward Setzer

Exterior styling: Sovereign Yachts (NZ) Ltd/Ward Setzer

Interior design: Sovereign Yachts (NZ) Ltd

Builder/Year: Sovereign Yachts (NZ) Ltd/2003

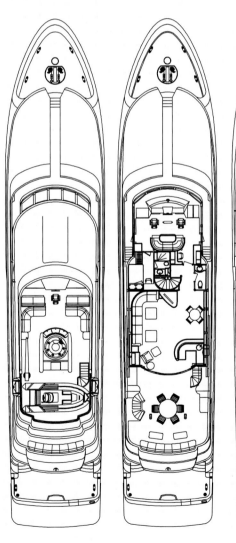
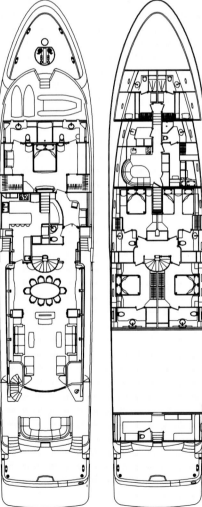

Susanna Bella

106-FOOT LAZZARA MOTORYACHT

*I*t has been said that a company must be judged not just by how well it builds a product, but by the innovations and fresh ideas that it brings to its industry. If that is the case, then Lazzara Yachts should be held in the highest esteem because the company has consistently been one to think 'out of the box'; a builder which always seems to start with a blank sheet of paper.

Some of the concepts have been used before, but Lazzara brought these ideas to fruition, improving upon them until they become a signature for each new Lazzara. For example, the transom garage is hardly a new idea, yet Lazzara split the garages to create twin compartments that leave room for a conventional transom platform. Lazzara also took the conventional sky lounge and created an entertainment area for all conditions, with electrically opening windows and a layout that blended with the aft deck.

The new Lazzara 106 carries on this tradition with a spacious and liveable yacht that has the space of much larger yachts, yet remains easy to handle. It combines the high-quality finish of a custom yacht with the practicality of a production yacht.

For the owner of hull number three, the appeal of the Lazzara 106 was that he could get the fit and finish of a true custom yacht without having to start from a blank sheet of paper. In the process, he took the basic 106 concept and created a custom yacht that fit his lifestyle.

Certainly the most obvious change aboard *Susanna Bella* is the absence of the flybridge hardtop, which is intended to provide sun and weather protection for guests in both warm and cold climates. Instead, a venturi windscreen wraps around the forward bridge which doesn't even have a bimini top.

One invisible feature of the Lazzara 106 is that it doesn't rely on a single hull mold. Instead, designer Dick Lazzara created interlocking molds that can be used to modify anything from the bow flare to the deadrise. In the case of the 106, more than 60 molds are joined to produce the hulls, which can be rescaled from 90ft to 130ft.

Aside from the overall length, clients most often want changes to details such as the transom shape or, in this case, the flybridge. But without the patented Lazzara modular mold system, the cost could be prohibitively expensive.

Porthole ★ The dining area is set off by an inlaid cappuccino marble floor and an overhead treatment that mimics the oval table for six.

Opp. top ★ More than 60 interlocking molds are joined to produce the hull of this 106.

Opp. bottom ★ An ISIS system provides a wealth of information in the efficiently-designed pilothouse.

Left ★ *Susanna Bella* features a sleek venturi windscreen around the forward bridge in place of a flybridge hardtop.

The 106 has widebody styling, leaving just an outside ledge around the superstructure and starting the side decks amidships, which creates a striking saloon that stretches more than 30ft in length and 20ft in width.

The standard saloon arrangement places the sitting area near the sliding stainless-steel doors to the teak-planked aft deck with its alfresco dining table and, through the large teardrop windows, guests have a superb view outside. Helping to separate the entertaining and television area from the formal dining saloon forward is a full bar to starboard and a game table to port, along with a low buffet with full height column to port.

The saloon is finished in high-gloss cherrywood with black granite on the Art Deco-shaped bar counter. But it is the huge windows that are the most striking features, although the intricately detailed woodwork, such as fluted window pillars and the starburst bar facia, are certainly compelling.

The dining area is also delineated by an inlaid cappuccino marble floor and an overhead treatment that mimics the oval table for six. Buffet counters are on each side, and the forward bulkhead features twin beveled-glass china cabinets. The day head is to starboard, with beautiful hand-painted wallpaper, the same spectacularly patterned marble as the dining area, and 24k gold fixtures.

Taking the portside passage from the dining area leads— via a curving stairwell—to a stylish lower foyer with dark marble inlaid with cappuccino. An ornate mirror presides over a breakfast buffet, with twin vial-shaped sconces on each side. Double doors open to the master suite, which spans the full-beam with three lozenge-shaped windows on each side that can be hidden behind sliding *shoji* screens.

The king-size berth is centered between cherrywood panels with intricate sconces, a large sofa is to port and an equally large desk/vanity is to starboard. Completing the

Main picture ★ Strikingly large windows surround the saloon giving guests a superb view.

Left ★ An ornate recessed overhead treatment marks the walk-around granite island in the country galley.

suite are built-in bureaus topped with beveled glass curio cabinets that match those in the dining saloon.

The his-and-hers head is aft, with cherrywood paneling, a marble-lined shower and hand-painted wallpaper. Just forward of the stateroom is an expansive walk-in closet with a wall of shelves.

Twin VIP cabins just forward of the foyer are the usual arrangement, but the owner of *Susanna Bella* chose to create only a double cabin to starboard with ensuite head and shower. In the usual VIP cabin to port, he fitted an office with a built-in desk, loose chair, and beveled glass book cabinets. With a day bed for occasional guest use, the office still has the full head with shower, giving it dual usage.

The 106 features a country galley that fills the forward main deck past the pilothouse. The galley features a walk-around granite island with sinks, while the aft bulkhead is a tribute to SubZero, with a double-door refrigerator/freezer above

four pull-out refrigerator drawers and, with long cruises in mind, two more freezers are tucked under the pilothouse.

High marble backsplashes accentuate the large windows and, once again, the 106 provides guests and crew with superb views. A curved settee is forward and, unlike the often workman-like galleys in some yachts, this one is marked by an ornate recessed overhead treatment similar to that in the dining area.

Stairs from the galley lead to a private VIP forward, which is surprisingly spacious in spite of the tapering hull sides. The double berth is raised on a cherrywood platform with rope millwork trim, a hanging locker is to starboard, and the all-marble head with shower is aft.

The pilothouse is both seaman-like and comfortable, with a Stidd pedestal chair and a raised settee so guests can look forward through the steeply slanted windshield. A model of efficiency, five monitors are set into the dash-

Above ★ An office with a daybed and full shower replaces the portside VIP cabin on *Susanna Bella*.

Top ★ The expansive master suite.

Opp. top ★ Hand-painted wallpaper and cherrywood paneling graces the his-and-hers head.

Opp. bottom ★ Cherrywood panels with intricate sconces flank the master suite's king-size berth.

board, with navigation and communications electronics on a second panel, and a large chart table/office area to port.

Lazzara Yachts has always been data-oriented, and the ISIS (Integrated Ships Information System) monitors 64 different shipboard functions, storing all the data from the launch date. The system not only provides the skipper and owner with a wealth of useful information, but it also becomes a valuable tool at resale as well.

In addition to the ISIS system, Lazzara also has a pro-active maintenance and customer support program, SeaCheck, which provides for a comprehensive annual assessment, with SeaCheck technicians downloading the ISIS information, checking for corrosion, testing fluids, and performing a sea trial. The result, after careful analysis against existing parameters, is then presented to the owner in a hardcover book that becomes a part of the yacht record. Even better for Lazzara yachts insured with Chubb Insurance, the cost of SeaCheck is paid by the insurance company.

Accessible from the pilothouse or the aft deck, the flybridge is a party waiting to happen. Keeping the standard layout but without the hardtop, the bridge has a plethora of Stidd chairs forward, with singles behind the helm and to port, and a double to starboard. The fiberglass instrument pod has repeaters for most of the electronics and monitors, as well as hidden wing controls on each side.

Just aft is a compact dinette with facing bench seats, while a large teak-and-mahogany-topped bar is to port with four permanent stools. Further aft are curving lounges with cocktail tables, and a Jacuzzi spa is on the centerline aft. The boatdeck is more than ample for the Nautical Structures crane and a 15ft Novurania RIB tender, while one of the transom garages holds a SeaDoo (the other is dedicated to water toys and storage).

Lazzara also excels at the various systems, and the engine-room is a model of efficiency, with a workshop to port and power takeoffs on both main engines. With twin DDC Series 2000 16-cylinder electronic engines, the 106 is surprisingly fast, which probably accounts for the fact that NASCAR driver Jeff Gordon owns the second 106. With a top speed of 27 knots, the 106 can cruise comfortably at 10 knots while consuming just 25 gph.

Just aft of the engine-room are the crew quarters, with a double cabin to starboard for the captain and bunks to port, both with private heads with showers. A lounge area between the cabins has a mini-galley, settee, and direct access to the transom platform.

All of the electronic equipment is neatly installed in an air-conditioned and carpeted 'attic' just aft of the pilot-

house, which makes maintenance a pleasure. The 106 also has a crawl space that runs fore and aft above the saloon to provide full access to electrical and air-conditioning systems, so no woodwork has to be removed for service. Perhaps because the Lazzara family started in sailboats, every possible cranny has been utilized for storage, whether it be dedicated glassware drawers in the galley or an immense 'basement' under the lower sole.

Cleverly designed and thoughtfully equipped, the Lazzara 106 will be a surprise to potential buyers who think of her as a production yacht, only to discover that she is the equal of many custom yachts but without the headaches.

This page ★ Guest staterooms are fitted with the same attention to detail as the master.

LOA:	105ft 8in (32.3m)
LWL:	84ft 8in (25.9m)
Beam:	23ft 1in (7.0m)
Draft:	5ft 6in (1.7m)
Displacement (light ship):	190,000lbs
Engines:	2 x DDC 2000 series 16 cylinder @ 1,800hp
Speed:	27kts
Fuel capacity:	4,300gal
Electrical generation:	2 x 45Kw Onan
Bow thruster:	American Bow Thruster
Watermaker:	Sea Recovery1,500gpd
Entertainment systems:	AMX Control, plasma or LCD TVs throughout
Stabilizers:	American
Security systems:	ISIS
Technical equipment:	Lutron Lighting System
Paint:	Interspray
Hull construction:	Fiberglass
Air-conditioning:	Cruise Air
Communications:	KVH sat phone, ICOM SSB, ICOM VHF, cell phone
Owner and guests:	4 plus owner's office
Crew:	2
Construction:	Fiberglass
Project management:	Lazzara Yachts
Naval architecture:	Lazzara Yachts
Exterior styling:	Dick Lazzara
Interior Design:	Lazzara Design Studio
Builder/Year:	Lazzara Yachts/2003

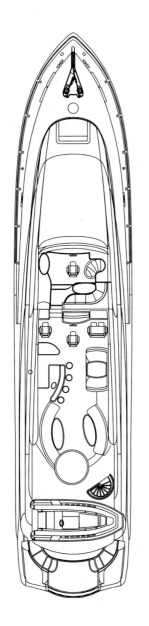
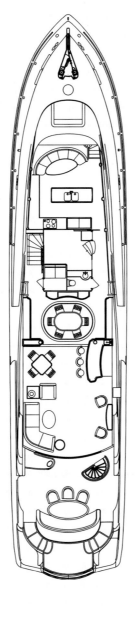
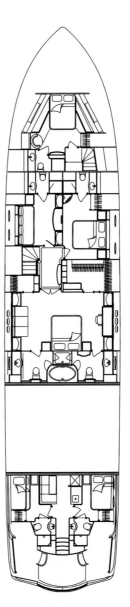

Unforgettable

137-FOOT ROYAL DENSHIP MOTORYACHT

It may be a somewhat vague connection, but in retrospect it seems only appropriate that in Denmark, a country where electricity-generating windmills dot the countryside, *Unforgettable*, the 137ft Royal Denship motoryacht, has twice the usual number of propellers.

This unusual adaptation of a commercial propulsion system is not her only noteworthy feature, however. From a technological standpoint, she is a thoroughly modern and innovative yacht, while in design, comfort, and finish she is a showcase of her builders' craftsmanship. As befits a yacht built on speculation, her interior is elegant yet unostentatious, maintaining a neutrality appropriate to the likelihood that her future owner would almost certainly modify many of her features to suit his or her taste.

But neutrality does not mean lack of quality, and in the execution of all her design details and amenities she is indeed remarkable. The first impression upon stepping aboard is of expanses of high gloss white paint and flawlessly laid teak decks. Boarding at main deck level from the starboard side, massive sliding doors lead into a foyer with a contiguous day head. While the distribution of spaces follows a relatively conventional practice, their proportion is somewhat unusual, and reflects the practical thinking of her designers. All the living and sleeping quarters are finished in contrasting American cherry joiner work, using bird's-eye grain panels with straight-grain moldings and trim pieces at wainscoting

height, and muted off-white fabric panels above. While spaces such as the heads and foyer have a marble sole, the remaining areas use a rich beige wool carpet underfoot.

Forward on the starboard side is the access to the commodious owner's suite. The first space entered is a large office, providing a privacy buffer between living areas and the sleeping quarters. The size of the office would allow it to be used also as a private sitting room or library. The owner's stateroom takes up the full beam of the yacht, with a king-size berth on the centerline. A vanity, coffee table, easy chairs, and settee enhance the space. An unusual, and visually ingenious feature is the hanging and clothes stowage lockers; partial height partitions accommodate these necessary amenities, creating semi-private dressing areas behind them. By keeping the tops of the partitions approximately two feet shy of the overhead, an illusion of open space is created, making the stateroom appear larger than it actually is. Still forward is the master bathroom, featuring a large spa tub, shower stall, double wash basins, and a separate toilet compartment. All are finished in marble with gorgeous contrasting honey-colored marble trim.

To port of the owner's office and the foyer are the galley and pantry. As can be expected on a yacht of this caliber, the galley is fully equipped with commercial grade appliances, granite countertops, and—in the interest of safety and practicality—a marble-finish linoleum sole. The galley's location allows easy access to both the dining area aft and the crew mess on the lower deck. The pantry separates the galley from the dining area, a practical way of containing noise and odor away from the guests. The dining area itself shows

Above ★ Large square ports visually break up the *Unforgettable*'s massive appearance.

Porthole ★ To starboard is a twin guest room.

Opp. bottom ★ A swooping settee adds grace to the main aft deck and extends the living area of the main saloon.

Below ★ A Portuguese bridge allows for easy access to the bow.

Above ★ Granite countertops and commercial-grade equipment make for an efficient galley.

Opp. top ★ A credenza separates the saloon from the dining area.

Opp. middle ★ Blue suede upholstery lends a very lush inviting feel to the sky lounge.

Opp. bottom ★ Five mulit-purpose video screens dominate the bridge.

Below ★ The 12-person dining table is laid out fore and aft creating more space.

some original thought processes on the part of the designers, as it is laid out on a fore-and-aft axis, and occupies only half the width of the deckhouse; there is nonetheless ample space for twelve people. A credenza separates the dining area from the main saloon. While the saloon is on the small side, more space has been allotted to the aft deck which results in a grand inside-outside living area for lounging and entertaining. When the saloon sliding doors are open, the deck becomes an extension of the saloon. On the bridge deck, the sky lounge is actually larger than the main saloon, not a bad idea considering its higher location. All in all, *Unforgettable* ends up with significant and comfortable living space.

Interesting technical details are the Maxwell mooring line winches, an unusual design clearly intended purely for handling dock lines, not merely an adaptation of sailboat winches. Large pods, for lack of a better word, are located port and starboard. To port are stowage space and ventilation ducts for the engine-room. To starboard are access stairs to the aft bridge deck.

The guest accommodations consist of four staterooms located on the lower deck. Curved stairs from the main deck foyer lead down to a central vestibule; two staterooms

aft each have a queen-size berth and a settee with coffee table. A small office/study space to port adds a welcome facility and could easily be converted to a dressing room if desired. The two forward guest staterooms have twin berths, and are slightly smaller in size. All have ensuite heads. At the forward end of the passageway is a large linen storage space. A discreet door allows access from the crew's quarters, located forward on this same level. All crew cabins have ensuite heads, a thoughtful detail. These and the crew mess are finished in off-white with cherry trim. All the way forward is a laundry room with two washer/dryers and additional refrigerator and freezer capacity.

It should be noted that all living and sleeping spaces are equipped with flat-screen monitors: all purpose screens that can be programmed for video, television, ship's radar, engine monitoring—in short—all the options available on the actual bridge deck. In the interest of safety, access codes are needed to, for instance, actually change radar settings or shut down a generator. Multi-purpose light switches are another example of clever thinking. These are essentially small video screens which control all lights, both on/off and dimmer options, also, temperature, music, entertainment, as well as receiving messages and wake up calls. For anyone finding themselves mystified by the range of options, there is a further thoughtful feature: a button to call the stewardess, who can remotely access your panel and program it for you.

The entire aft part of the lower deck consists of the engine-room. While at first glance one might question the wisdom of locating guest quarters adjacent to the machinery space, it becomes immediately obvious that the Royal Denship engineers have addressed the issue. A rather unusual feature here is the fact that the main engines are completely enclosed in sound-proof cases. Two generator sets on the centerline are also soundproofed. This practice obviates the need of a soundproof engineer's booth, as the noise level with motors running is amazingly well contained. What is immediately noticeable is the lack of transmissions or clutches attached to the engines. The engine shafts turn 90 degrees into the rotating propeller pods—more on this unusual feature later. From the engine room one descends into a passage running the full length of the boat, providing access to wiring, plumbing, tanks, watermakers, and similar equipment.

To the bridge deck now, for an explanation of the vessel's propulsion system. Access to this level is via the central circular stairs, or the stairs set into the aft starboard pod. As mentioned before, the lounge is amply proportioned, and equipped with a wet bar and a truly state-of-the art entertainment center. The blue suede upholstery on the furniture is simply gorgeous, giving this area an intimate yet luxurious atmosphere. To starboard, just off the foyer, is a day head, while to port are the captain's quarters.

The bridge itself is dominated by five multi-purpose video screens, as is increasingly the practice. An interesting detail is the heavy, large (four-inch diameter) trackball set into the flat surface just before the screens—much easier and steadier to operate than the typical small trackball—controlling a cursor which moves across continuously from screen to screen, enabling the operator to operate all functions from a single control.

Personally, I always find it unnerving to be on a boat that has no steering wheel (although my sense of tradition was somewhat appeased here by the presence of a magnetic compass). But here, for once, a steering wheel is completely unnecessary, since *Unforgettable* has no rudders. As I mentioned earlier, rotating vertical shafts terminate in a

Opp. top and opp. bottom ★ The owner's suite has an office as a buffer between the sleeping quarters and the living quarters.

Opp. middle ★ A Jacuzzi tub, stall shower, and double sinks are all trimmed in honey-colored marble in the master suite.

Top right ★ Marble enhances the head in the twin guest rooms.

Right and below ★ Portside aft, this queen-size guest stateroom, similar to the sister cabin to starboard, has a settee and coffee table.

hub from which two propellers are driven, one forward and one aft. One of the advantages of using four propellers instead of the usual two is that they are of a smaller diameter, thus reducing the vessel's draft. Steering is accomplished by rotating the vertical shafts and thus aiming the propellers in the desired direction. Fly-by-wire controls on the bridge house the throttles on rotating mountings. Rotating the shafts 180 degrees puts the boat in reverse, and neutral is achieved by aiming the propellers at each other, thus neutralizing their thrust. Needless to say, a benefit derived from this system is the ability to 'walk' a 137ft motoryacht sideways into a berth, using the bow thruster of course.

Walking away from this new motoryacht, I conducted my usual dockside aesthetic survey. I have to confess that I miss varnished cap rails, as they provide horizontal accents for the eye to follow. However, *Unforgettable* has a noticeably sculpted look, the deck overhangs and resulting shadows relieving what would otherwise be a somewhat massive appearance. The large square ports are paired, a good design feature which breaks up the otherwise disproportionately large expanses of glass. Overall she has a purposeful stance, in keeping with her no-nonsense engineering.

My first ever experience with a rudderless motoryacht in the end only served to confirm the impressions I had been gathering as I visited the various shipyards which comprise Royal Denship—impressions of an ongoing and systematic effort to constantly achieve new levels of innovation while maintaining their tradition of quality. If *Unforgettable* is any indication, they are succeeding on all fronts.

Top ★ A spa pool and bar on the top deck.

Left ★ The aft sky lounge deck sports a table for entertaining and dining.

LOA: 137ft (41.8m)

Beam: 26ft 7in (8.1m)

Draft: 7ft 6in (2.3m)

Displacement (light ship): 205 tons

Propulsion: 2 x Caterpillar 3406E Dita 600hp
Diesel with Schottel Drives

Speed (max/cruise): 13.6 knots/11 knots

Fuel capacity: 36 tons

Range @ 11 knots: 3,500nm

Electrical generation: 2 x Stanford 86 Kw/208V
3phase 60Hz

Bow thruster: American Bow Thruster 75 Kw

Stabilizers: American Bow Thruster

Watermaker: Hydromar 2 x 5,000 ltr p/d

Water pressure system: Grunfos

Sanitation: Hamman

Entertainment systems: Lantic

Paint: AwlGrip

Air-conditioning: Servex

Communications: Kelvin Hughes

Tenders: Royal Denship people mover +
Zodiac Rescue boat

Construction: Composite/GRP

Classification: DNV/MCA

Project management: Royal Denship

Naval architecture: Danyard

Exterior styling: Danyard

Interior design: Francois Zuretti

Builder/Year: Royal Denship/2003

HEIRLOOMS

Since 1984

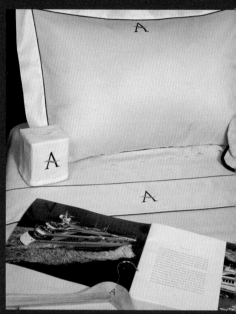

The finest bed, bath and table linens for Superyachts, Aircraft and great voyages

MANUFACTURERS OF THE WORLD'S FINEST BED, BATH AND TABLE LINENS.

RENOWNED FOR AN UNPARALLELED SERVICE TO THE SUPERYACHT INDUSTRY.

Prêt a Porter & Bespoke Linens,
Accessories, Clothing & Embroidery.
Shipped Worldwide.
Serving Owners, Designers, Project Managers,
Captains & Stewardesses.

HEIRLOOMS Ltd
UNIT 2 ARUN BUSINESS PARK
BOGNOR REGIS
WEST SUSSEX, PO22 9SX
GREAT BRITAIN
0044 (0)1243 820252 phone
0044 (0)1243 821174 fax
sales@heirlooms.fsnet.co.uk

You *deserve* a luxury charter vacation...

LOOK NO FURTHER THAN RICHLEIGH YACHTS

With over 500 luxury crewed motor yacht, sailboat or catamaran charters in the most fun and exotic of destinations to choose from, we cater to the most discerning of tastes and personal preferences.

Look forward to this: Your chef aboard will tantalize you with culinary delights, there will be luxury accommodation and equal space for all guests, your Captain and crew will be friendly, professional, experienced and - yes, you will be dealing with a charter company with a proven track record and solid reputation.

We love what we do! Let us show you why.

You deserve it ... remember?

RICHLEIGH *yachts* SALES CHARTERS MANAGEMENT

Destinations

A Golfing Charter

In the Spanish Virgin Islands

CYNTHIA KAUL AND DANA JINKINS

Sunshine, magnificent flora, golf, and Latin rhythms...idyllic cruising and diving in tropical seas...an ease with customs, communication, and currency—what could be better? The Spanish Virgin Islands have long been stepping stones for migrating tribes of Caribbean peoples, so it seemed a fitting locale for a rendezvous of a group of erstwhile yachting nomads, some of whom have lately gone over to golf. Fragrant warm breezes blessed our winter weary souls as we embarked on a yacht charter from San Juan.

Reconnaissance led us to the *MJ*, a newly refitted 90ft Posillipo raised-pilothouse motoryacht. She's a handsome vessel that was enlarged and greatly improved in a total refit in 2003. Among many innovations is a remarkable underwater exhaust system by Eco Sound, which not only significantly reduced noise, vibration, and fumes, it also gave lift and an additional few knots to the vessel's speed. And speed was a consideration, as we intended to maximize our time on both the links and the cruise.

MJ's captain Mark met us at the San Juan airport and drove us to the vessel's home port of Palmas del Mar, on the east coast of Puerto Rico, which faces the tradewinds. As we entered the main gates, we caught a glimpse of bougainvillea-flanked fairways before winding downhill through a Mediterranean-style village around a private cove. We found the yacht moored at a palm-fringed slip near the harbor's entrance. Welcomed by the boat's owners and crew, we settled into the comfortable cabins, then went topsides to savor a cool drink and the view from the expansive covered top deck.

Long-time residents of Palmas, the owners squired us around their community. Originally developed in 1973 by the late Charles Fraser, and modeled on Sea Pines at Hilton Head, this residential complex has two championship golf courses and two grand resorts set along the beautiful Candelero Beach. Palmas has received awards for its environmentally progressive design in light and water use. The colonial architecture is appealing with ochre and terra cotta walls adorned by fronds of hibiscus and bougainvillea. From the heights, we viewed a canalized inlet enclosed by a modest breakwater that was used not so long ago, we were told, by pirates and rum runners. Then we descended to a fine French restaurant, Chez Daniel, on the pier where we enjoyed a superb seafood lunch.

Toward evening we boarded golf carts to preview the courses and the many offerings of Palmas del Mar. Guests of the yacht marina are entitled to utilize the considerable facilities of the complex—pools, spa, casino, equestrian connections, and a world-class tennis club. Dusk was warm and fragrant as we followed the paths through a discreet shopping district and past distinctive villas that line the fairways of the Palms course, designed by South African Gary Player. Raucous parrots and a brilliant macaw squawked at us from the handsome tiled terrozza of the Candelero Beach Hotel and Casino. Our twilight tour then wound past the surf's edge green of Palms Hole Number Three to the Flamboyan course, between blossoms, ponds, and the pounding waves, up climbing cart paths, to the splendor of sunset. Impressed, ravenous, and content, we returned to a feast prepared by Tracy, *MJ*'s magnificent chef.

A brief squall freshened the world early the next morning as we set off to golf, and the sun soon emerged amidst towering clouds. The Palmas Club House is reminiscent of an albergo or museum in Spain, and endowed with a gracious and informed staff. It features Moorish architecture with three dining rooms serving cuisine that we later verified to be excellent.

Soon after teeing off on the Flamboyan course, we encountered the daunting bunkers, heavy tropical rough, and water hazards that make this one of the toughest challenges on the island. One can play any length of course by following the red, blue, black, or white-painted coconut markers at the tee boxes. Noteworthy on the Rees Jones-designed course is Hole Number Three, a par five 'cape,' across an immense elbow lake to a green on a peninsula. Many holes are uphill, upwind, or both. On the back nine, the Palms course offers a different challenge, with generally shorter holes that require more curved shots and finesse. Panoramic Hole Number 14 has breathtaking prospects of nearby islands and El Yunque rainforest peak.

Above ★ Looking out to Culebrita, a pristine islet west of Culebra.

Opp. middle ★ The Flamboyan course at Palmas del Mar uses painted coconut markers at the tee boxes.

Inset ★ This score card is a keepsake regardless of who won.

Below ★ At anchor in Vieques, a back flip off the bow of *MJ* gets a round of applause.

Above ★ A beautiful house overlooks the breakwater and some fishing boats.

Main picture ★ The *MJ* moored at the Palmas del Mar Yacht Club.

Opp. bottom left ★ La Mina Falls at El Yunque, Puerto Rico's renowned rainforest.

Opp. bottom right ★ Old San Juan retains its distinctive Spanish roots.

Below ★ Teeing off at the Flamboyan course.

Meanwhile, some of our company went to tour Old San Juan, the island's Spanish soul, where stone walls, arches, and forts recall its colonial roots. Having been claimed for Spain by Columbus on his second voyage in 1493, the port of San Juan Bautista soon became Spain's gateway to the treasures of the New World. It was the first Caribbean port of call for two fleets of galleons dispatched each year by the King of Spain to retrieve gold and plunder from the Americas. One fleet sailed south to Cartagena and Portobello to load up with pearls, silver, and the wealth of the Incan empire, while the other sailed west to Veracruz to claim silver and gold from Mexico. Spanish conquistador Ponce de Leon became its first governor, and in defense against English and Dutch challengers, mandated the massive defenses around the port that we strolled and

marveled at today, as well as his ancestral home, La Casa Blanca, where the governor still lives.

The Puerto Rican people radiate an easy charm in a culture that reflects a lively fusion of native, Caribbean, and African influences. Walking cobblestone streets among Caribbean pastels, there is art, anthropology, and high fashion to savor in San Juan galleries and boutiques. Cathedrals, shrines, and ubiquitous offerings to the saints attest to the predominant Catholic faith. For refreshments, we stopped at El Convento, a beautiful Carmelite convent that has been transformed into a luxury hotel.

We all reassembled back on board the *MJ* in the afternoon for a pleasant hour's cruise to Vieques. White sands beckoned and we went overboard to kayak ashore, swim, and waterski. Between golf, culture, and watersports, we had worked up quite an appetite, and another spectacular meal was served alfresco in a glorious sunset.

Prior to the Colonial era, Vieques and Culebra had long been visited by migrations of Central American tribes. The museum of art and history in the main town of Isabel Segunda exhibits relics from this chronological parade, as well as natural attractions like the semi-wild pasofino horses abandoned here by the conquistadors.

More recently, these Spanish Virgins have been in the news as the controversial bombing targets of the US Navy, which acquired two-thirds of the island during WWII for military purposes. After considerable controversy, the use of the island as an artillery range is now history. As one

Above ★ The location of this idyllic pool is a secret...you have to book a trip aboard *MJ*.

Left ★ Relaxing on the foredeck.

Opp. middle ★ Easy access to the swim platform.

Opp. bottom left ★ Culebra-style business hours.

Opp. bottom right ★ *MJ* speeds towards Luis Pena, Culebra.

Viequesne said, the island is 22 miles long, and the periodic bombing was like heat lightning and thunder in the distance, barely perceptible in the civilian zone. Ironically, it seems that naval control has spared these islands from high-volume resort tourism.

A good example is the fishing village of Esperanza, which is a rare vestige of a natural Caribbean unspoiled by development. Located on the south coast, this village has a *malecon* (seaside promenade) that strolls between houses, small inns, and simple fishing craft.

Not far from Esperanza is a most spectacular local attraction, the Bioluminescent Bay, which we visited the next evening at dusk with BioBay Ecotours. During the course of a bumpy ride in a rustic bus, our tour guide shed light on local natural history, with occasional stops to view fireflies or sample night-blooming fragrances. In the light of a quarter moon, we arrived at BioBay, a sizable estuary whose entrance from the sea is nearly blocked by reefs. This enclosure, combined with a lack of development and the rich saline biology of the surrounding mangroves, produces an unusually high density of pyrodinium bahamenses, the fluorescent plankton found in traces in most ocean waters. We boarded an electric boat and cruised out into the bay, where spooked tarpon and turtles darted off in cloaks of light. Soon we dove in and joined the magic, making light angels and diamond shawls in the

darkness. Looking skyward as we floated on our backs we listened to a brilliant discourse on astronomy and mythology. It was a truly memorable event.

Culebrita was our next port of call, a pristine islet west of Culebra. One of the Caribbean's oldest lighthouses crowns the hill, a destination for a pleasant hike. We made use of the 22ft Caribe, *MJ*'s fast, comfortable tender equipped with a full center console, depth sounder, fishing gear, rinse shower, and ice chest. The real attraction here, though, is submarine—snorkeling in the magical rapture of coral reefs with rays and sea turtles and a panoply of colorful sea

Above ★ The lovely marina at El Conquistador.

Opp. far right ★ *MJ* on the horizon, as seen from under the shade of a palm on Vieques.

Opp middle ★ Swan dive and somersault—someone either won or lost a bet... or was it a dare?

Opp. bottom ★ The yachting golfers turned into lobstermen, par excellence.

Bottom left ★ I-guana play at Rio Mar Country Club.

Below ★ Slaying a shot at El Conquistador.

life. These—and the sizable lobster that were snared for dinner—served as pretty good evidence that the reef is alive and well.

Proximity to the Puerto Rico Trench offers serious potential for scuba diving, which *MJ*'s crew can help arrange from either Vieques or Culebra. Situated on the crest of an underwater range where the Atlantic meets the Caribbean, these islands are not far from the deepest spot in the Atlantic—the Milwaukee Depth—at 27,493ft.

Culebra, another island gem, has a quiet and snug harbor and fabulous beaches. A quaint little canal and lift bridge cut through the town to the other coast. Culebra and the surrounding islets form part of a marine preserve that effectively protects the outstanding marine life. Once again, we enjoyed the baptism of tropical seas when we stopped to picnic and snorkel at Luis Penã, one of these lovely cays. This charter cruise was hassle free, as the crew operated the vessel with proficiency and assurance.

The golfers among us were restless, so later that afternoon we hauled anchor and cruised back. On the main island of Puerto Rico we moored at Cayo Largo (Marina del Rey), which accesses two remarkable golf resort complexes. The enormous complex at El Conquistador crowns a peninsula on a point of land where the Caribbean meets the Atlantic. It features a palatial Grand Hotel, inns, and

the Golden Door Spa with surrounding pools, plazas, and galleries. A novel and functional touch is the funicular that accesses a cluster of lodgings midway down a forested hillside, with terminus in a Mediterranean-style marina encircled by more villas and shopping.

This golf course was the most dramatic yet. Arthur Hills designed it with an elevation change of more than 200ft. We were awed by the spectacular scenery, challenged by continual play between precipice and valleys, and pleasantly distracted by flocks of egrets, pelicans, the occasional iguana, and the magnificent flowers everywhere. The Eagle's Nest, Hole Number 15, features an extreme vertical drop and a grand view of El Yunque. Among other hazards are rocks with petroglyphs from the Taino Indians.

The next stop was Rio Mar Country Club, which is only 19 miles from San Juan and popular with the locals. The Ocean Course, designed by Tom and George Fazio, is

Above ★ A pot of gold was found at the end of this rainbow.

Opp. top ★ One of the specialties of the house is alfresco dining at sunset.

Opp. middle right ★ Fare of the sea, like this shrimp and mango salad, was both plentiful and pleasing to the palate.

beachfront golf at its finest. Large iguanas prowl both courses. Greg Norman designed the scenic River course with spectacular challenges, like Hole Number 12, which requires a 150-yard carry over marshland into the wind. This newly finished complex has a large hotel and condos, plus GPS-equipped golf carts.

Towering behind the River Course is the peak of El Yunque, the only tropical rainforest in the US National

CHARTER & GOLF GUIDE

MJ, **Raised Pilothouse Motoryacht**
LOA: 90ft
Beam: 21ft
Hull construction: GRP
Capacity: 4-8 guests in two queen
and two twin staterooms
Speed (max/cruise): 26 knots/21 knots
Builder/Year: Posillipo/1986, refit 2003

Contact:

Richleigh Yacht Charters
Fort Lauderdale, FL
leigh@richleighyachts.com
Tel: (800) 578-4348, (954) 236-8800
Fax: (954) 236-8822

Golf courses:

Palmas del Mar, Humacao, PR
Tel: (787) 285-2256, Fax: (787) 285-2275
Westin Rio Mar, Fajardo, PR
Tel: (787) 888-6000, Fax: (787) 888-6600
Wyndham El Conquistador, Las Croabas, PR
Tel: (787) 863-6784, Fax: (787) 860-1144

Restaurants:

Chez Daniel, Anchor Village Palmas del Mar,
Tel: (787) 850-3838
Palmas del Mar Country Club
Tel: (787) 285-2256
Copamarina Beach Resort, Guanica, PR
Tel: (787) 821-0505

Park system. It shelters many endangered species in 28,000 acres of misty highlands, and offers many accessible hiking trails amidst magnificent flora and waterfalls. Though we could only spare a few hours, we hiked to La Mina waterfall, seeing several kinds of orchids, parrots, and other birds, and marveled at the exotic sounds and gorgeous abundance of tropical nature. Fortunately, we did not encounter the Puerto Rican Boa, but I am quite sure we were serenaded by the coqui, the celebrated singing tree frog that is unique to Puerto Rico.

There remain a dozen more courses to play, a mountain cordillera to explore, and distinct ports of call to visit. We were particularly intrigued by the tremendous birdwatching and wildlife in the Bosque Seco (Dry Forest) near the unique Guanica Resort on the south coast. Our days on the good ship *MJ* were about to end, but Golf/Cruise Puerto Rico is not done in just one week. The wise vacationing golfer is advised to relax, enjoy, and know he will have to save some of Puerto Rico for the next trip.

Long Island & New England

From Port Washington, LI to Nantucket
aboard M/Y MITseaAH

TEXT BY JILL BOBROW, PHOTOGRAPHY BY DANA JINKINS

lappers, fly-by-nights, spies, whalers and what not. Our five-day excursion aboard the 114ft high speed motoryacht *MITseaAh* took us from Manhasset Bay, New York to the island of Nantucket off the coast of Massachusetts—a voyage replete with American history and local color. Long Island, our point of departure, conjures a variety of connotations: 'lawn-GUY-land' pronounced the wrong way is an anathema, yet for those weekend warriors braving the summer traffic to the Hamptons, this island east of Manhattan is more of a Mecca. The North Fork of LI is not the Hamptons, it is the other Long Island—a Long Island that has history and full time residents. Enroute to meet *MITseaAh* at the Capri West Marina in Port Washington, we popped into an exhibition at the LI Museum in Stony Brook portraying the infamous

flapper age with a commemoration of Zelda Fitzgerald, legendary (and allegedly crazy) wife of American writer F. Scott Fitzgerald. No doubt this 'other' Long Island was the setting for the Fitzgerald classic, *The Great Gatsby*.

That accounts for the flappers, now, the fly-by-nights, spies and whalers: This shore of Long Island has years of American history hidden in places such as Cold Spring Harbor and Oyster Bay. From 1836-1860, Cold Spring Harbor, bordered by 180ft cliffs and named for icy fresh waters, was Long Island's leading whaling port. The main street, rife with an eclectic mix of nationalities, was called Bedlam Street. A whaling museum with old prints, scrimshaw, and a genuine whaleboat is located in the center of the town. Blubber aside, other local folklore revolves around numerous episodes of

espionage during the Revolutionary War. Spies proliferated in this area. We saw a sign marking a waterfront park site as home to a spy who tried to assassinate our first president, while George Washington's top spy, Robert Townsend, hailed from next door in Oyster Bay. A few miles away, in Huntington Bay, is Halesite, a monument to Nathan Hale, noted American spy who, when captured by the British, uttered shortly before his death, "I only regret I have but one life to give to my country."

The next morning *MITseaAh* weighed anchor and departed from Capri West. Manhassett Bay is dotted with Greek revival mansions and other large historical houses. The first day of our cruise was perfect weather for cloaks, daggers, and spies; that is, foggy and on the verge of drizzling. The large shoreside estates appeared ethereal in the mist until they disappeared altogether as we powered down Long Island Sound. We were headed north east across the Sound to the town of Essex, CT. As our trip would take four hours, we had plenty of time to orient ourselves to our comfortable cabins and with the affable crew. Despite the drab weather, the seas were even and our ride was smooth. The weather miraculously cleared as we approached the mouth of the Connecticut River at Old Saybrook in the early afternoon. A satisfyingly typical lighthouse has marked the entrance of this magnificent river since the early 1800s. Having summered on the CT shore since I was an infant, the landscape is familiar territory to me. As we passed Fenwick Point next to Old Saybrook, I directed the others' attention to the late, great Katherine Hepburn's house.

The sun shone on us as we headed up the river. While there are several marinas hugging the river, we chugged past them, heading for Essex, six miles north of the mouth. Close to our destination, we passed the historic Steamboat Dock, which now houses the CT River Museum. During the eighteenth century more than 500 large commercial ships were built in this location and in the last century, the present dock was used as a port of call for steamboat passen-

Above ★ Alongside the dock in Mystic, *MITseaAh's* sleek profile dominates the harbor.

Opp. middle ★ Everywhere you turn in Nantucket is a scene worthy of a painting.

Opp. bottom ★ Nantucket's boat basin is replete with boats of every description.

Below ★ A rocky shoreline on the North Fork of Long Island.

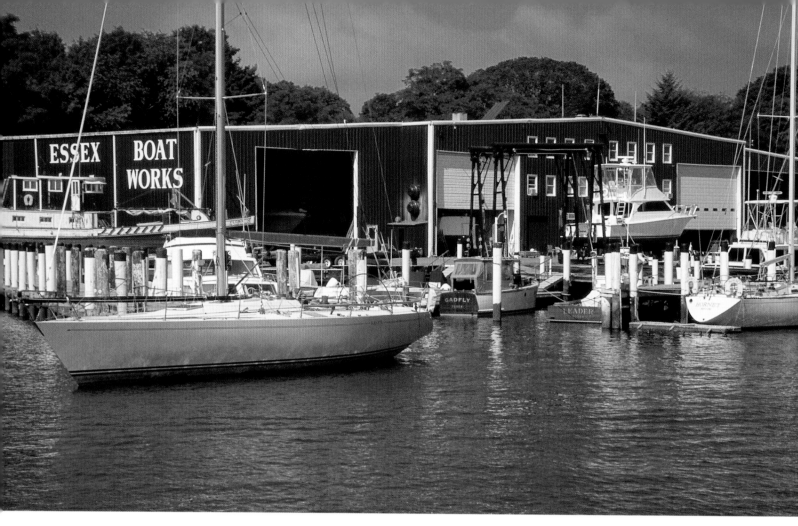

gers from New York to Hartford. We docked at Essex Island Marina, a colonial-style complex sporting a pool and game room, as well as the usual practical facilities. There is a small ferry which shuttles yachtsmen across the 150ft channel to the quaint town of Essex.

The weather turned glorious and after a luncheon of seafood *en croute*, our daughters, Sabrina, 10, and Quincy, 12 were anxious to explore the river by tender. Our Captain, Johannes Buys, broke out the charter toys for sea tubing and water-skiing. Up river from Essex with reedy saltmarshes on either side, are Hamburg Cove and Selden Creek where American boats hid from British raiders during the Revolutionary War. Here the salt water turns to fresh. The girls had a fabulous time in the tepid, flat, calm water, being pulled helter skelter by the high speed tender— like bumper cars in an amusement park, they slammed into each other and squealed with delight.

We enjoyed dinner in the sun-dappled light on the spacious and beautiful flybridge, followed by an evening stroll through the postcard-perfect town of Essex with clapboard shops and vintage houses. The historic Griswold Inn has long been a watering hole for sailors. Sea shanties and an ever-popping old-fashioned popcorn machine keep revelers in the vaulted-ceiling bar for hours. The restaurant itself is bedecked with hundreds of antique paintings of marine art. On a plaque verifying the date—1776— are written tavern rules which read, "bed and supper may be obtained for sixpence, but, no more than five to a bed, boots may not be worn in bed, organ grinders must sleep in the washhouse, razor grinders and tinkers are not welcome at all."

While Essex was not a whaling station, it was a major ship-building center. Large sailing vessels were constructed there in 1700s. Uriah Hayden built the warship, *The Oliver Cromwell*—the first warship for the Continental Army in 1775—a 300-ton battle-

Opp. top ★ MITseaAh was docked at Essex Island Marina opposite the Dauntless Shipyard.

Opp. bottom left ★ The historic Griswold Inn in Essex has been doing business since 1776.

Opp. middle ★ Tubing behind the tender on the CT River.

Middle left ★ Captain Johannes expertly guides the lovely *MITseaAh* through her paces.

Bottom ★ The steward sets up for dinner on the flybridge.

Below ★ Seafood *en croute*...a divine repast.

ship carrying 20 guns and 125 crew. Over the years, many famous yachts like the 120ft *Dauntless* owned by arms maker Samuel Colt, found their way to Essex. She was purchased by NYYC Commodore James Bennett, and raced in 1870 in the America's Cup placing 4th. *Dauntless* was built in nearby Mystic, CT, our next port of call.

Motoring back to the entrance of the CT River and heading east down the LI Sound, Mystic would be a scant hour and forty-five minutes away. A digression is in order to describe our yacht, *MITseaAh* is a sleek high-performance custom-built motoryacht with interior and exterior architecture by Richard Liebowitz and naval engineering by Sparkman & Stephens. She is extremely fast with cruising speed at 25 knots (Of course if you want a range of 2000nm, you better stick to 12 knots). I was unaware of what we were clocking on our way to Mystic, but all of a sudden the distinctive US Coast Guard vessel was on our tail with sirens blaring. I've never seen a cooler, more collected captain. It turned out we were not being busted for speeding, but merely spot-checked for the ship's papers, now a common, random procedure in Northeast waters. As all was in order, the Coast Guard tipped their hats and carried on their way—homeland security in

Above ★ Sitting pretty on the foredeck.

Below and bottom right ★ Sailing dinghies and lighthouses are but an element of Mystic's nautical charm.

action. Minutes later we were passing the Noank Peninsula at the mouth of the Mystic River. Greater Mystic Harbor has about 20 marinas. The region is most famous for the Mystic Seaport Museum and the Mystic Aquarium.

As our captain had the perspicacity to call ahead for reservations, we knew we would have prime dockage at the Mystic Seaport Museum. The Amtrac swing bridge is usually open unless a train is coming. However, heading north, the Bascule drawbridge in the center of Mystic opens 15 minutes after each hour from 8:15 AM to 7:15 PM, (no 12:15 opening on weekends). We had a half hour wait, so *MITseaAh* pulled alongside a dock and we disembarked to wander around town. The captain pointed in the distance to the east side of the river above the swing bridge where looming large was the rigging of a topsail gaff-rigged schooner, at the Mystic Seaport— indicating where we could find the *MITseaAh* later on.

Town has its charm despite the throngs of tourists eating ice cream and shopping for T-shirts. Sabrina was drawn to a sign bearing her name touting palm-readings and psychic powers. There was a special that day @$5.00 a palm. I decided to indulge the girls. Smack in the middle of Main Street, above the galleries and boutiques, we tread a long staircase and tiptoed down a dubious

Above ★ The 1841 whaleship, *Charles W. Morgan* at Mystic Seaport Museum.

Below ★ The window and door behind the saloon bar can open entirely to become a part of the aft deck.

hallway leading to private residences. We knocked and entered (how bad could it be right in the middle of cheery downtown Mystic?). A woman with copious children in every direction led us to her inner sanctum adorned with religiosity, crystal balls, and what not. She sanctimoniously read the girl's palms. Entertained by the ritual, we all left giggling with spirits soaring, and anxious to rejoin *MITseaAh* at the Seaport for our next adventure.

Mystic Seaport occupies 17 acres and is definitely one of the premiere maritime museums in the world. Not only can you view history, you can experience it. Aboard the 1841 whaleship the *Charles W. Morgan*, you witness real sails being furled by real people high up in the rigging. This vessel sailed for 80 years as a profitable

whaling boat. Whale blubber was rendered into oil in the furnace on the deck of the ship. You can also cruise aboard the coal-powered steam engine driven boat, *Sabino*, built in 1908 in East Boothbay, Maine. Other famous vessels are the *Joseph Conrad*, a sail training ship that has its roots dating back to 1882, and the 1921 Gloucester fishing schooner *L.A. Dunton*. Besides the boats, you can take a glimpse into 19th century New England village life. Informed Seaport workers draw you into the cooperage and show you how to make barrels and buckets from wood, or into the printing shop to demonstrate setting type. Blacksmiths, boatbuilders, and sailmakers all are on the scene to demonstrate their trades, not to mention ice cream being hand cranked, and lemonade being squeezed. In the

midst of the antiquity and wholesomeness, we witnessed a fashion photographer from New York shooting a catalog with models, stylists, makeup artists, and a myriad others, taking advantage of the too-good-to-be true ambience of the Seaport. Being docked at the Seaport allowed us the privilege of infiltrating the museum by night. It was a treat to be able to walk around without any other tourists.

Imbued with new historical anecdotes, visuals, and rock candy, we were ready to leave the next morning to explore Narragansett Bay and Newport, RI. There are three important passages running up the Bay; a west passage, an east passage and the Sakonnet River. Newport is the yachting hub for cruising in this area. The east passage leads to the 108-year old Rose Island Lighthouse just below the Newport Suspension Bridge. We motored up close, but did not go ashore to tour it. The lighthouse is restored and open to the public. It even has several turn-of-the-century guestrooms available.

The town of Newport on Aquidnick Island is one of the busiest summer yachting centers on the East Coast. While it has always been a sailing yacht capital and 12-meter racing center, Newport has now become a summer version of Ft. Lauderdale in terms of the number and quality of megayachts. There are two harbors; the inner and the outer divided by Goat Island, both fairly well protected. There are numerous piers along the historic waterfront and there is the Newport Shipyard for dockage and repair that sports Belle's Café and an awesome facility for crew. Bannister's Wharf for years has been 'the place to be' with the famous Clark Cooke House / Candy Store restaurant, multiple bars, and disco scene. Next door, The Black Pearl is the spot for clam chowder. The Moorings, Christies, and The Pier are all landmark restaurants. The Armchair Sailor is the most complete nautical shop in the greater area. Also of note are the Museum of Yachting at Fort Adams, the International Yacht Restoration School (IYRS), and the Tennis Hall

Above ⋆ Clam chowder is king at The Black Pearl restaurant.

Main picture and top right ⋆ *MITseaAh* in front of the Newport Bridge and Rose Island Lighthouse.

Opp. top ⋆ Newport has long been the sailing capital of the East Coast.

Middle ⋆ Newport's inner harbor from above.

of Fame. Beyond the shops and boutiques, it is an architectural adventure walking up and down the side streets that run perpendicular to Thames, Spring, and Bellevue. Church Street has a magnificent, quintessential white steepled church and just up the road is Touro Synagogue, America's oldest synagogue, where once a year, a letter written to the congregation by George Washington is read. History abounds on Bellevue Avenue, the street of mansions: chateaux and villas built from 1870–1915. These homes (humbly referred to as cottages) from the gilded age belonged to a handful of men who made their fortunes during the Industrial Revolution: Astor, Vanderbilt, Goelet, Lorillard, Belmont…our pseudo royalty. You can walk

the Cliff Walk along the ocean and view the mansions from the outside or take tours to see Louis the XIV furniture and other extravaganzas. Here we have come full circle to *The Great Gatsby*, which had its origins in Long Island. Well, at least in Hollywood terms, as the Robert Redford version of the film depicting the decadence of the era was actually filmed at Rosecliff in Newport.

While we were passing through, Northrop and Johnson was hosting a Brokerage Show at Goat Island. *MITseaAh* was participating as she is actively for charter and for sale since her owners are building a new, high-performance 156ft sailing yacht due to launch at the Pendennis Yard in late 2003. We guests opted to get off for the afternoon for exploration. It's always hard to merely drop in on Newport, there is much to see and do. We caught a Wednesday night outdoor music concert at the Art Museum on Bellevue. A lawn affair, with picnics and lots of kids.

The next morning we were underway again, this time to Nantucket, 68 nm from Newport and about 30 miles off of Cape Cod. It is far enough offshore to have a distinctive feel all its own. Unlike Martha's Vineyard, which is a very large island, when you are on Nantucket you know at all times you are on an island with the sea just over the next hill. Nantucket's history actually dates back to the Vikings, but is more known for its whaling during the Civil War time. In its heyday, Nantucket was known to seafaring folk all over the world (again whaling is a theme that has followed us from Long Island to CT to Mass). It is said that many sailors from the South Seas knew about Nantucket before they ever heard of Boston, New York or London. We entered Nantucket Sound from the west heading down the shipping lane directly to the Boat Basin, where again we had advance reservations. The waterfront is filled with weathered-shingled adorable shacks, all entwined with roses and hydrangea. Even the A&P supermarket follows the aesthetic code. Main Street is cobbled and the sidewalks are uneven bricks, so leave your high heels in the shoe basket aboard the boat.

Here again our youthful crew and captain were accommodating to the young ones and we went out in the tender to explore sand spits and to go wake boarding, skiing and tubing. Coming back aboard, there is a hot shower hose on the swim platform, just perfect to wash off the salt and the chill.

Nantucket has something for everyone, from Nantucket light baskets and Sailor's Valentines, to 'Nantucket reds', Lilly Pulitzer, and Cartier. If you want to stay away from the shops, visit the terrific Whaling Museum, or attend one of the many lectures in

FOR SALE & CHARTER GUIDE

M/Y MITSEAAH

LOA: 114ft (34.7m)

BEAM: 24ft (7m)

DRAFT: 6ft 5in (2m)

CRUISING SPEED: 25/26 knots

HULL CONSTRUCTION: Aluminum

EXTRAS: Sat Com, tel/fax, tenders, waterskiing, wakeboarding, tubing

GUESTS: 12 in 5 ensuite cabins (each with television, VCR, and CD stereo system SurroundSound)

BUILDER: Derecktor Shipyard

NAVAL ENGINEERING: Sparkman & Stephens

INTERIOR / EXTERIOR ARCHITECTURE: Richard Liebowitz

CONTACT FOR SALE / FOR CHARTER:

Northrop and Johnson Yachts-Ships, Inc

1901 SE 4th Ave., Fort Lauderdale, FL 33316

TEL: (954) 522-3344

FAX: (954) 522-9500

EMAIL: njyachts@aol.com

FOR CHARTER:

Northrop and Johnson Charters

26 Coddington Wharf, Newport, RI 02840

TEL: (401) 848-5540

TOLL FREE: (800) 868-5913

Camper & Nicholson

Tel: (954) 524-4250

Email: info@pal.cnyachts.com

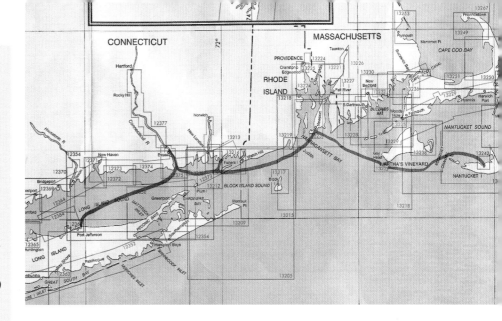

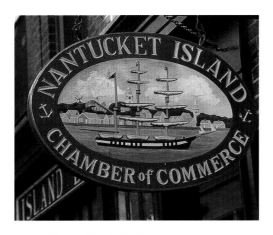

Above ★ Hospitable Nantucket.

Middle ★ MITseaAH alongside the dock at Nantucket Boat Basin.

Opp. page ★ Weathered shingles and white trim are pretty much the uniform in Nantucket.

Top ★ MITseaAH's route from Long Island Sound to Nantucket.

town – the night we arrived Dr. Marsha Green, founder of the Ocean Mammal Institute, was giving a lecture on the impact of acoustics on marine mammals at the church at the head of Main Street (call 800-226-8216 for more info on a fascinating topic).

Similar to Newport, Nantucket is an amazing architectural feast. While every house seems to have weathered clapboards and cedar shake shingle roofs, there is a slight variation and the window boxes and front yard gardens are magical. For out of town enjoyment, it's a great idea to rent bicycles, perhaps go out to the village of Siasconset, or hire a four wheel drive vehicle to tear around the beaches at Great Point where there are sand dunes, bayberry, beach plums, and fishermen surf casting.

Our full Nantucket day ended up with an enjoyable dinner on the aft deck. We had invited an artist friend and her husband from Nantucket to join us and they were overwhelmed by the hospitality of the crew of *MITseaAH* and delighted by the Art Deco interior and pristine condition of the yacht. One of the best parts of the yacht's interior design is the aft corner of saloon where the bar's glass partition and door can be electronically lowered to bring the outdoors in or vice versa. Our last dinner on the aft deck in the intimate setting of a balmy Nantucket evening was a superb finale to a delightful trip. We thoroughly enjoyed being immersed in American history; flappers, fly-by-nights, spies, whalers, and what not…at the same time enjoying the privilege of cruising in the lap of luxury.

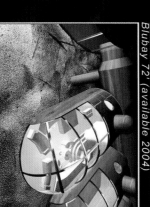

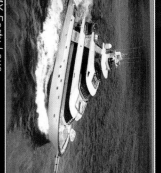

The 100 Largest North American-Built Yachts

elcome to the *The Megayachts USA*'s listing of the 100 Largest North American-Built Yachts. The health of the industry is evidenced by the fact that ever since the last publication of this listing in the June 2003 issue of *Boat International USA*, 12 new yachts have either been, or will be launched. With the new launchings, Trinity Yachts has catapulted into the position of the most prolific builder. Our list is laid out in order of length. Length is a quantitative description, certainly not qualitative. Also, perhaps a better representation of physical size should include internal volume encompassing the length, beam and draft of the vessel. Unfortunately, this is not easy to calculate with any reliability so, in reality, length is the only basis that is both readily available and easily understandable. When making size comparisons based on this list, however, one should be aware that sailing yachts and most of the older motor vessels are probably given higher positions than is warranted as, generally speaking, their beam tends to be much narrower and the height of their superstructures much less than those found on modern motoryachts. This, naturally, results in much smaller internal volume. In order to keep comparisons as fair as possible, you will notice

that we have ruled that bowsprits are spars, and are therefore not included in a yacht's overall length.

A second point that should be mentioned is that where yachts have the same overall length, we list them alphabetically. This fact is most apparent at the lower end of the size scale where, for instance, no less than 12 yachts are listed at 130ft overall length, while two more of this size are omitted altogether because the initial letter of their name is just too far down the alphabet. We do apologize to the owners of the 130-footers, *Skyetyme*, and *Sojourn* who have been left out of the list in such arbitrary fashion.

Lastly, a plea for help. Keeping such a list as this accurate is a difficult and unending task, and despite our efforts we are aware of its shortcomings. If readers have knowledge of yachts missing from this list, with changed names or any other inaccuracy, we would be delighted to hear from you. By the way, we define a 'yacht' as a privately owned pleasure vessel which, if offered for charter, is available together with its crew as a complete vessel—thus excluding vessels used for vacationer's day-excursions. We hope that you enjoy this condensed history of American yachtbuilding.

CHRISTINA O

1. CHRISTINA O

ex-Argo, ex-Christina, ex-HMCS Stormont
325ft 3in; Twin screw motoryacht; Steel; 1943
Canadian Vickers, Montreal, Canada. Rebuilt
Howaldt Werke 1954 to design of Prof. Pinnau;
2 x 2775hp MAN Diesels; Greek owner
Christina O is the largest North American-
built yacht in existence today, although she is
a conversion having been originally built in
Canada as *HMCS Argo*, an Escort Frigate for
N. Atlantic convoys during WWII. She was
purchased post-war by the Greek shipping
tycoon Aristotle Onassis who, in 1954, converted her into a the most spectacular yacht of
the era. Onassis used *Christina* to entertain
many of the world's rich and famous including his mistress, the opera diva Maria Callas,
and the British war-time leader Sir Winston
Churchill. *Christina O* is now owned by a con-
sortium. She was comprehensively rebuilt in
Croatia in 2001 and is available for charter.
She is featured in *The Superyachts*, Volume 15
and in *The Megayachts USA*, Volume 3.

2. BART ROBERTS

(ex-Narwhal)
265ft; Twin-screw exploration vessel; Steel;
1963; Canadian Vickers, Montreal, Canada.
Rebuilt by Tradepower International 2002 to
the design of Lennart Edstrom; 2 x 2,000hp
Ruston 6RKC diesels; Owned by American,
Arnie Gemino
Built in 1963 as a Canadian Coastguard ice-
class vessel the *Narwhal* was put up for sale by
closed bid by the Canadian authorities in
2002. There were only two bidders; the
Russian Government and Arnie Gemino, a
Floridian with business interests in the avia-
tion industry. To his surprise, Gemino won
the auction and his company, Tradepower
International, managed the conversion of the
vessel into a luxury charter yacht with a flam-

boyant pirate theme, renaming her *Bart
Roberts* after the notorious pirate of that name.
The vessel is featured in *The Superyachts*,
Volume 16.

3. DELPHINE

(ex-Dauntless, ex-USS Dauntless, ex-Delphines)
257ft 9in; Twin screw steam yacht; Steel; 1921;
Great Lakes Engineering Works, Ecorse,
Michigan, USA; Henry J. Gielow; Steel; 2 x 4-
cylinder Great Lakes Engineering quadruple
steam expansion engines; Belgian owner
Built for the car manufacturing mogul Horace
Dodge, *Delphine* (named after his daughter)
was a familiar sight around Detroit and
Chicago in the 1920s. She was equipped with
an unusual quadruple steam expansion engine
designed by her owner which gave her an
impressive top speed of 15 knots. During
WWII she served as the flagship of Admiral
King, who was C-in-C of the US Fleet. Finally
laid up in 1962, she was bought by the
Seafarers International Union for use as a
headquarters ship but fell into disrepair in the
early 1990s. She was acquired by a Singapore
company to be converted for use as a mini-
cruise liner in Asian waters, but this sale fell
through after she had traveled halfway to the
Far East. She has now been bought by a
Belgian and has been thoroughly converted
and restored in Belgium. It is understood that
she will, in due course, be available for charter.
(Featured in *The Megayachts USA*, Volume 5)

4. GOLDEN SHADOW

219ft; Twin screw motoryacht; Steel; 1994;
Campbell Shipyard, San Diego, USA; Francis &
Francis; 2 x 2,665hp Deutz-MWM SBV 9M 628
diesels; Saudi Arabian owner
This vessel is certainly a yacht, but one with a
difference, being the support vessel for *Golden
Odyssey*, the 264ft German-built superyacht
that has the same owner. Together, they travel
the world's oceans in tandem, *Golden Odyssey*
carrying the owner and his family, and *Golden
Shadow* carrying supplies, provisions and extra
staff for the oceanographic research work that
fascinates her owner. Built by San Diego
builder Campbell Industries to the design of
Francis & Francis, *Golden Shadow* carries an
amphibious aircraft as well as many special-
purpose tenders.

5. FREQUENCY

(ex-La Baronessa)
195ft; Twin screw motoryacht; Aluminum;
1997; Palmer Johnson Inc., Sturgeon Bay,
Wisconsin, USA; Sparkman &
Stephens/Nuvolari & Lenard; 2 x 1,950hp
Caterpillar 3512 diesels; Turkish owner
This vessel remains the largest purpose-built
yacht to have been constructed in America
since 1930. She was launched as *La Baronessa*
for a Singaporean owner and was recently
renamed *Frequency* when acquired by a Turk.
Frequency is the largest aluminum yacht on
this list and is, so far, the largest yacht to
emerge from the yard of Palmer Johnson.
Naval architecture is by Sparkman & Stephens
of New York and styling and interior design
by Nuvolari & Lenard of Italy. She is featured
in *The Superyachts*, Volume 13 and in *The
Megayachts USA*, Volume 1 as *La Baronessa*.

6. ULYSSES

192ft; Twin screw motoryacht; Steel; 2002;
Trinity Yachts, New Orleans, Louisiana, USA;
Trinity Yachts/Ricky Smith; 2 x 1,500hp
Caterpillar 3512B diesels; New Zealand owner
Ulysses is a heavily constructed explorer-type
yacht capable of traversing the world's oceans
with ease and in the greatest of comfort. She
can accommodate 14 guests and is alleged to
have a range of some 8,000nm. Don't get confused—her New Zealand owner previously had
a 160ft Feadship of the same name that is now
called *Teleost* (See *The Superyachts*, Volume 16).

7. HENRIETTE

(ex-Henrietta II, ex-Argo, ex-Danginn)
191ft 3in; Twin screw motoryacht; Steel; 1950
Welding Shipyards Inc., Norfolk, Virginia, USA;
John H Wells; Steel; 2 x 663hp Sulzer-Busch
diesels; Greek owner
Henriette is unusual in that she was built in
1950, a time when very few large yachts
were constructed following the post-war economic slump. Originally built as *Danginn*
for the Texan oil millionaire Daniel K.
Ludwig, she was acquired by the renowned
Greek shipowner John Latsis for use by his
daughter. *Henriette* is currently based near
Athens in Greece.

FREQUENCY

8. TACANUYA

(ex-Defiance, ex-Swiftship, ex-Intrepid)
187ft; Twin screw motoryacht; Aluminum; 1992; Swiftships Inc., Morgan City, Louisiana, USA; Grant Robinson/Susan Puleo; 2 x 2,800hp Caterpillar 3561DI-TA diesels; Saudi Arabian owner

This impressive yacht was completed as *Intrepid* for a casino owner in 1992. In 1997, she was acquired by an Arab buyer and was placed under management of the Greek Latsis fleet. *Tacanuya* was lengthened 29ft 6in during a complete refit at Lusben Shipyard, Italy in 1997 to the designs of Studio Scanu. She is now used privately for Mediterranean cruising.

9. LADY J

(ex-Quest)
185ft; Twin screw motor yacht; Steel; 1976; Halter Marine, New Orleans, Louisiana, USA; Quest Inc • 2 x Wärtsilä Nohab G-28V-D825 diesels; American owner

Quest is a converted oil rig supply ship that was recently used as an exploration and research yacht in Caribbean waters. She was chartered to the Discovery Channel for the making of a series of feature films on new animal and plant species.

10. PANGAEA

(ex-Dream, ex-Samantha Lin)
185ft; Twin screw motoryacht; Steel; 1999; Halter Marine, New Orleans, Louisiana, USA; Halter/Puglia Marine; 2 x 2,100hp Caterpillar 3508B diesels; American owner

Pangaea is another expedition yacht. She was originally built as *Samantha Lin* for an experienced US owner who has recently taken delivery of another large expedition yacht built in Denmark. Sold soon afterwards to another American who kept her in charter, she was recently resold to yet another American with baseball interests who renamed her *Pangaea*—the name of the primordial super-continent that split apart to create America, Africa and Europe. She was featured in *The Megayachts USA*, Volume 2 as *Samantha Lin*. She remains available for charter.

11. REVELATION

(ex-Patagonia, ex-Robur IV, ex-Southern Breeze)
178ft 1in; Twin screw motoryacht; Steel; 1964; Zigler Shipyard, Louisiana, USA; GB Zigler/Jon Bannenberg; 2 x 1,800hp Fairbanks-Morse diesels; American owner

Originally constructed as *Southern Breeze* for an American, this yacht had a string of distinguished owners prior to being acquired by Henry Ford II in the 1980s. Modernized and refitted to the design of Jon Bannenberg at Palmer Johnson in 1994, a subsequent French owner changed her name to *Robur IV* and she was later renamed *Patagonia* following her purchase by a Chilean. She has recently changed hands once again, and is now owned by Dan and Cheryl Stabbert, who lengthened her by 10ft and renamed her *Revelation*. She is available for charter in Alaska in summer and Costa Rica in winter. Contact (206) 547-6161. She is featured in the Supercharter section of *The Superyachts* Volume 4.

12. KATHARINE

177ft; Twin screw motoryacht; Aluminum; 2001; Trinity Yachts, New Orleans, Louisiana, USA; Trinity Yachts/Claudette Bonville; 2 x 2,735hp MTU/DDEC 12V4000 diesels; American owner

Katharine is one of the finest yachts to emerge from a US yard in recent years. Built to high standards by Trinity Yachts, her owner spared no expense in ensuring that *Katharine* compares favorably in terms of style, quality & engineering to Northern European-built vessels. Her palatial interior, which boasts a particularly high volume, was designed by Claudette Bonville and incorporates intricately cut marble, gold chandeliers and silk upholstery. Having recently cruised in SW Mexico, *Katharine* was seen in Mediterranean during summer, 2003. She is featured in *The Megayachts USA*, Volume 4.

13. BEAUPORT

167ft 6in; Twin screw motoryacht; Steel; 1960 Davie Shipbuilding, Beauport, Quebec, Canada; Canadian Ministry of Transport; 2 x Fairbanks-Morse diesels; Canadian owner

Originally a buoy tender and research vessel for the Canadian Coast Guard, *Beauport* was converted to a yacht in 1995. Her Canadian owner has recently put her through a major refit prior to putting her up for sale through Fraser Yachts with an asking price of $2,400,000. She has an ice-reinforced hull, a helicopter landing pad, and carries a pair of 30ft fishing tenders. Powered by economical 640hp diesels, she has a top speed of 14 knots.

PANGAEA

14. HAIDA

(ex-Ashtoreth, ex-Astarte, ex-Elda, ex-Haida)
167ft 6in; Twin screw motoryacht; Steel; 1947 Bath Iron Works, Bath, Maine, USA.; John H. Wells; 2 x 1,100hp Enterprise diesels; American owner

Built in 1947 for Maj. Max C. Fleishman as hull number 277 at the Bath Iron Works, *Haida* is one of the finest yachts of the immediate post WWII period and is an excellent example of US yachtbuilding skills. Sold to a fellow New Yorker, Arthur V. Davis, she was renamed *Elda* and following a resale spent many years in Greece as *Astarte*, always maintained in first class condition. *Haida* recently changed hands and is now undergoing a major refit in Dubai for her present US owner.

15. YANBU

(ex-Pollyanna, ex-Aleta II, ex-Corfu, ex-Calypso, ex-Yankee, ex-Seapine,)
164ft 11in; Twin screw motoryacht; Steel; 1931; Bath Iron Works, Bath, Maine, USA; Henry J. Gielow; 2 x 800hp GM diesels; Greek owner

This elderly yacht was built as *Seapine* for Theodore C. Hollander at the time of the Wall Street Crash. She has since had many owners and has been altered in appearance several times since WWII. *Yanbu* is now based in Greece.

16. OSPREY

163ft; Twin screw motoryacht; Advanced Composite; 2003; Delta Marine, Seattle, Washington, USA; Delta Design Team; 2 x Caterpillar 3508 diesels; American owner

Due for delivery in June 2004, *Osprey* is a true world-roaming expedition yacht with a 6,000nm range and built to the highest structural and safety standards. Her full-displacement, advanced composite hull, designed in-house by the Delta Design Team with the aid of finite element analysis, has a 31ft 6in beam and 9ft draft and is carbon fiber reinforced for ultimate strength. Superstructure styling and interior design are also by the Delta Design Team. *Osprey* boasts a helipad, crow's nest observation platform and two elevators, and carries advanced sonar mapping equipment to support her well equipped diving capabilities which include Nitrox and Trimix compressors. An extensive audio visual system includes a bow-mounted 'dolphincam' and a full video editing suite. Her colors—a gray hull, with a red boot-top and white superstructure—are sure to make her a very distinguished vessel.

KATHARINE

AQUARIUS W

GALLANT LADY

ANSON BELL

EVVIVA

17. HOLO-KAI

(ex-French Look II)
162ft 7in; Twin screw motoryacht; Steel; 1976; Rysco Shipbuilding; United States; Rodney E. Lay/Thierry d'Andon; 2 x 368kW GM diesels; French owner

This is an interesting vessel that was built as an oil rig supply ship and later converted to a sportsfishing mothership by a French owner, traveling across many oceans to all the world's sportfishing sites. Recently refitted and renamed *Holo-Kai*, she is now used as a research platform for universities and organizations that need access to ocean waters. *Holo-Kai* carries the 41ft G&S sport fishing/diving/research vessel, *Holo-Ke* on her purpose-built aft deck.

18. AQUARIUS W

(ex-Black Douglas, ex-Te Quest)
162ft 1in (174ft 10in incl. bowsprit); Auxiliary Three Mast Schooner; 1930; Bath Iron Works, Bath, Maine, USA; Henry J. Gielow/John Munford; Steel; 2 x 350hp Volvo Penta diesels; German owner

The largest sailing yacht in this list and yet another survivor from the famous Bath Iron Works yard in Maine, *Aquarius W* is a three-masted schooner that is currently based on the French Côte d'Azur. She was launched as *Black Douglas* for an American owner and underwent an extensive rebuild by Abeking & Rasmussen in Germany in 1983. She is featured in *The Superyachts*, Volume 2.

19. EVVIVA

161ft 10in; Twin screw motoryacht; GRP Composite; 1993; Admiral Marine Construction, Port Townsend, Washington, USA; William Garden/Donald Starkey; 2 x 3,460 MTU 396TB94 diesels; American owner

Evviva was the largest US-built GRP composite-hulled yacht when she was launched eight years ago in 1993 and she still holds that title. She remains in the hands of her original owner, the founder of the highly successful Bayliner sports boat company. She is featured in *The Superyachts*, Volume 8.

20. ANSON BELL

161ft; Twin screw motoryacht; Aluminum; 2002; Palmer Johnson Inc., Sturgeon Bay, Wisconsin, USA; Vripack International/Sparkman & Stephens/Ramsay Engler; 2 x 2,000hp Caterpillar 3508B DI-TA diesels; American owner

Launched last year from the Palmer Johnson yard in Sturgeon Bay, *Anson Bell* is named after the bell of the British warship *HMS Anson*, which, salvaged from the vessel after it sank in a 1907 storm, now adorns the yacht's main companionway. *Anson Bell*'s tastefully decorated interior has two saloons, a dining room, and accommodation for 10 in an owner's suite, which includes a study sitting area and walk-in closet, and four guest staterooms. One of the yacht's most stunning features is a dramatic central circular stairwell, rising to the full height of the boat. Recently extended in length to 161ft,

Anson Bell is considered by her builders to be one of their best ever yachts. She is featured in *The Megayachts USA*, Volume 4.

21. GALLANT LADY

160ft 1in; Twin screw motoryacht; Aluminum; 2000; Delta Marine, Seattle, Washington, USA; Doug Sharp/Glade Johnson/Las Olas Design; 2 x 1,100 Caterpillar 3508B diesels; American owner

The latest in a long line of yachts named *Gallant Lady* that have been owned by the American Toyota importer, James Moran. Most of Moran's previous yachts have been built in Holland by Feadship, but his yacht-building loyalties have now been transferred to the USA. Built by composite specialists Delta Marine, *Gallant Lady* is unusual in that she features an aluminum hull and a composite superstructure. She is illustrated in *The Superyachts*, Volume 14 and replaces an earlier 130ft Feadship of the same name which, like this vessel, is kept on Florida's Intra-Coastal Waterway.

22. THEMIS

(ex-Allegra)
156ft; Twin screw motoryacht; Aluminum; 1998; Trinity Yachts, New Orleans, Louisiana, USA; Ward Setzer/Dee Robinson; 2 x 1,191hp Caterpillar 3512B diesels; American owner

Built as *Allegra* in 1998 for a well-known family of US yacht owners, *Themis* remains Trinity's third largest launch, but will change status when the 180ft *Mia Elise* is launched. She is featured in *The Megayachts USA*, Volume 1 as *Allegra*.

THEMIS

23. INSPIRATION

(ex-Bubba Too)

155ft 1in; Twin screw motoryacht; Aluminum ; 1994; Broward Marine, Dania, Florida, USA; Broward Marine/Marc Michaels; 2 x 2400hp Detroit/Allison 16V-149DDEC diesels; American owner

Broward Marine, recognized as the most prolific US builder of aluminum yachts in the region of 100ft to 120ft, launched *Bubba Too* in 1994, and this yacht remains the largest to emerge from the yard so far. Now named *Inspiration* following a change of ownership, the yacht features a luxurious interior by Marc Michaels.

24. LIQUIDITY

155ft; Twin screw motoryacht; GRP Composite; 2001; Christensen Shipyard, Vancouver, Washington, USA; Christensen/Donald Starkey/Doug Sharp; 2 x 1,820hp DDC-MTU diesels; American owner

The second in a line of large composite motoryachts from this Pacific Northwest builder, *Liquidity*'s walnut-lined interior was designed by London-based Donald Starkey Designs, while US West Coast-based designer Doug Sharp worked on the naval architecture in collaboration with the builder. *Liquidity* is featured in *The Megayachts* book, Volume 3.

25. SILVER LINING

155ft; Twin screw motoryacht; GRP Composite; 1997; Christensen Shipyard, Vancouver, Washington, USA; Christensen/Donald Starkey Designs; 2 x 1,948hp Deutz-MWM 604BV12 diesels; Canadian owner

Silver Lining was commissioned by a retired Canadian oil tycoon who has since cruised extensively aboard the yacht with his family. Glade Johnson was responsible for designing the tasteful interior and also carried out some of the exterior styling. *Silver Lining* is featured in *The Superyachts* book, Volume 11.

26. WHEELS

155ft; Twin screw motoryacht; Aluminum; 2004; Trinity Yachts, New Orleans, Louisiana, USA; Trinity/Dee Robinson; 2 x 2,250hp Caterpillar 3512B; American owner

Built to ABS classification and fully compliant with the British MCA safety regulations, *Wheels* is Trinity Yachts' hull number 28 and will be delivered in March 2004 to her owner, a famous personality in the racing world who has won seven championships in the last eight years. Powered by twin 2,250hp Cats, she is forecast to achieve a top speed of 22 knots and will cruise at 18.5 knots. With a draft of just 7ft 1in, she will be able to access areas barred to many yachts of her size. *Wheels* has accommodation for an owner's party of 10, including a master suite on the bridge deck with a marble-lined bathroom offering both a whirlpool tub and shower, while two of the four remaining twin berth staterooms have twin berths that can be rearranged as king-size doubles. Interior design is by Dee Robinson, an American designer who is proving very popular with Trinity clients. Among the accommodation for 12, the engineer has his cabin right next to his workplace aft of the engine room—his consolation is that it's a nice double cabin with an ensuite bath and shower.

27. SCHEHERAZADE

154ft 7in; Auxiliary Ketch; Advanced composite; 2003; Hodgdon Yachts, East Boothbay, Maine, USA; Bruce King/Andrew Winch

Delivered in late 2003, the lovely Bruce King-designed *Scheherazade* is the largest sailboat recently launched in the US and the largest yacht to be launched from the Boothbay, Maine builders, Hodgdon Yachts. Her exquisite contemporary style interior designed by Andrew Winch uses fiddleback sycamore and black walnut for her harlequin bookmatched panels, carved seashell bands and burl walnut furniture tops. Classical in her looks, her hull actually exhibits state-of-the-art construction using cold molded construction and space age composites.

28. ROXANA

154ft; Twin screw motoryacht; GRP composite; 1997; Admiral Marine, Port Townsend, Washington, USA; Donald Starkey Designs/Lou Codega/Glenn Bauer/Mario Buatta; 2 x 1650hp Caterpillar 3512B diesels; American owner

This elegantly-styled yacht was built for a US newspaper publisher from the Midwest and is used by the owner and his growing family for cruising. Her interior, by Donald Starkey Designs,

SILVER LINING

is outstanding, making extensive use of light colors and interesting decorative themes. *Roxana* is featured in Volume 13 of *The Superyachts*.

29. CHEROSA

153ft 6in; Twin screw motoryacht; Steel/Aluminum; 1999; Swiftships Inc., Morgan City, Louisiana, USA; Tim Borland/Franzen & Associates; 2 x 2,250hp MTU 12V396TE94 diesels; American owner

Delivered in 1998 by her Louisiana based builder, *Cherosa* is a private yacht that replaced a smaller Broward that the owners had cruised for 15 years. With her curvaceous superstructure and dark green hull, this good-looking yacht was designed by Tim Borland. She is normally based in West Palm Beach on Florida's eastern seaboard and was featured in *The Superyachts*, Volume 13.

30. CHANTAL MA VIE

(ex-Atlantique, ex-Nordic Prince)

152ft; Twin screw motoryacht; Steel; 1984; Nylen, Fort Lauderdale, Florida, USA; John Nylen/James Krogen/Lou Benskey 2 x 365hp Caterpillar diesels; American owner

Her original owner, John Nylen, built *Chantal Ma Vie* in Fort Lauderdale over a period of six years. A long time you may think, but the end result was a strong and seaworthy yacht comparable to many yachts from established yards. She was lengthened to her present size in 1995 and is currently active on the charter market.

31. D'NATALIN

(ex-Sally Ann)

151ft 8in; Twin screw motoryacht; GRP Composite; 1996; Delta Marine, Seattle, Washington, USA; Delta Design/James Hoeferlin; 2 x 855hp Caterpillar 3508TA diesels; American owner

Exhibiting a superb mix of practicality and elegance, *Sally Ann* was among the largest of yachts to emerge from Delta Marine. *Sally Ann*'s owners commissioned H. James Hoeferlin to design a classical style interior utilizing high quality mahogany paneling. She recently completed a four year long circumnavigation with her owner and his family aboard, during which her 13.5 knot cruising speed and 6,000nm range were highly positive assets. Recently sold, she is now named *D'Natalin* and is available for charter. She was featured in Volume 11 of *The Superyachts* as *Sally Ann*.

LIQUIDITY

AMORAZUR II

TURMOIL

32. TURMOIL

151ft 6in; Twin screw motoryacht; Aluminum;
1996; Palmer Johnson, Sturgeon Bay,
Wisconsin, USA; Dick Boon/Van der
Meulen/Marshall Field; 2 x 820hp Caterpillar
3508DI-TA diesels; American owner
Named for a famous rescue tug, *Turmoil* is an
exploration-type yacht par excellence. She was
designed by Dutchman, Dick Boon of Vripack
Yachting and was built by Palmer Johnson.
Her owner, involved with the mail order
clothing business, has previously owned
yachts from the same yard. *Turmoil* was featured in Volume 10 of *The Superyachts*.

33. AFFINITY

151ft 3in; Twin screw motoryacht; GRP
Composite; 1999; Delta Marine, Seattle,
Washington, USA; Delta Design/Ron
Holland/Ardeo Design; 2 x 1,000hp Caterpillar
3508TA diesels; American owner
Ron Holland is better known as a sailboat
designer but he picked up this commission
because of his past involvement with sailboats for this owner, a leading figure in the
American yacht racing scene. One key aspect
of the build that was successfully accomplished was that the yacht should be completed in time for her to travel to the 2000
America's Cup races in New Zealand, where
her distinctive dark green hull, high foredeck
and spacious fishing cockpit were much
admired. *Affinity* is featured in *The Megayachts
USA*, Volume 2.

34. FORTUNATE SUN

(ex-Dream, ex-Samantha Lin)
151ft; Twin screw motoryacht; Steel; 1992;
Tacoma Shipbuilding Inc/Puglia Marine,
Tacoma, Washington, USA; Gerhard
Gilgenast/Teague Inc/Susan Carson; 2 x 775hp
Caterpillar 3508 diesels; American owner
This attractive yacht, first launched as *Samantha
Lin*, was started by Tacoma Shipbuilding in
Washington State but completed privately by
her owner when the yard went into liquidation
midway through construction. Notwithstanding
this early setback, the resulting yacht, powered
by reliable Caterpillar 3508 diesels that give her
a 12 knot cruising speed, can accommodate up
to 10 guests (all in king-size beds) and a crew of
eight in comfort that is comparable to her
owner's previous Feadship. She was last refitted
in 2000 and is currently available for charter.

35. AMORAZUR II

(ex-La Baroness)
150ft 1in; Twin screw motoryacht; Aluminum;
1994; Palmer Johnson, Sturgeon Bay,
Wisconsin, USA; Palmer Johnson/Tom
Fexas/Robert Knack; 2 x 1,900hp Deutz-MWM
TBD604 diesels; American owner
This modern yacht was originally delivered to
her Singaporean owner as *La Baroness* and was
sold to an American when her original owner
took delivery of his new 195ft yacht *La
Baronessa* (now *Frequency*) from the same
builder. Her new owner commissioned a refit
with design by Terence Disdale and changed
her name to *Amorazur II*. She features an extra
large galley to first class hotel standards.

36. IMAGINE

150ft; Twin screw motoryacht; Aluminum;
2003; Trinity Yachts, New Orleans, Louisiana,
USA; Trinity/Dee Robinson; 2 x Caterpillar
3512B; Canadian owner
Delivered in 2003, *Imagine* was originally
known as *Mia Elise* but, sold by its original
owner before completion, it was never registered as such. Twin 2,250hp Cats drive this
semi-displacement hull to a top speed of 22
knots and will cruise continuously at 18.5
knots. The interior is by Dee Robinson.

37. IONIAN PRINCESS

150ft; Twin screw motoryacht; GRP Composite;
2002; Christensen/Palmer Johnson, Vancouver,
Washington & Savannah, Georgia, USA; Pavlik
Design; 2 x 2,040hp MTU 396TE84 diesels;
American owner
This tri-deck yacht, its hull built by
Christensen (where it was known diversely as
Oriental Honor & *Victor's Choice*) and finished
by Palmer Johnson, delivers a high top speed
of 19 knots and a cruising speed of 17.5 knots
from her twin MTU diesels. *Ionian Princess*
sleeps 12 in her owner & guest quarters and
has accommodation for 9 crew.

38. LADY LINDA

(ex-Bellini)
150ft; Twin screw motoryacht; Aluminum;
1999; Trinity Yachts, New Orleans, Louisiana,
USA; Trinity Yachts/Paragon Design/Dee
Robinson; 2 x 2,250hp Caterpillar 3512 B
diesels; American owner
Lady Linda is an excellent example of just how
far US builders have advanced in large yacht
construction over the last few years. Her dark
blue hull and European lines conceal a magnificent interior by Dee Robinson. She is featured in Volume 14 of *The Superyachts*.

39. LAI FAIL

150ft; Twin screw motoryacht; GRP Composite;
2004; Northern Marine, Anacortes, Washington,
USA; Ward Setzer/Setzer/Setzer; 2 x 1,200hp
Caterpillar 3508 diesels; American owner
Currently under construction at Northern
Marine in Anacortes, Washington and due for
launch in spring 2004, *Lai Fail* is the second
Ward Setzer-designed tri-deck to be built by
this company. An impressive 29ft 6in beam
ensures a high volume interior which is eminently suitable for family or corporate use.
Within the yacht, a spiral staircase unites the
marble tiled foyer with the three decks which
offer two main saloon areas and a dining
room. Accommodation for an owner's party
of 10 includes an elegant full-beam owner's
apartment in the fore part of the main deck,
while four large guest staterooms with marble-
clad bathrooms are located on the lower deck.
Up to ten crew can also be accommodated in
five cabins. *Lai Fail* has a top speed of 16
knots and cruises at 14 knots.

40. MIA ELISE

150ft; Twin screw motoryacht; Aluminum; 2004; Trinity Yachts, New Orleans, Louisiana, USA; Trinity/Dee Robinson; 2 x 2,250hp Caterpillar 3512B; American owner

This latest *Mia Elise* is owned by a loyal client of Trinity Yachts, who currently has a 142ft Trinity of the same name. He has been trying to get the yard to build him a bigger yacht for some time now, but never seems to take delivery because, before his yacht is launched, someone makes him an offer he can't refuse. The latest *Mia Elise* was signed up in May 2002 and, if generous offers aren't forthcoming, this all-aluminum semi-displacement vessel will be delivered in early 2004. Just in case he does get a suitable offer, he has a 180ft *Mia Elise* also under construction at Trinity, which is slated for delivery in late 2004. The interior, by Dee Robinson, features Appalachian cherry accented by Carpathian elm and crotch mahogany inserts.

41. MYSTIC

150ft; Twin screw motoryacht; GRP Composite; 2003 Christensen Shipyards, Vancouver, Washington, USA; 2 x 1,820hp MTU/DDC 8V4000 series diesels; American owner

Built to ABS regulations and to comply with the MCA code, *Mystic* was launched in April 2003. Lavishly decorated with cherrywood and blue marble, with the added attraction of an aquarium in the main saloon, this yacht offers six staterooms including a master, three queens and two with twin-beds. Her twin 1,820hp MTU/DDC diesels will provide a top speed of around 20 knots, a cruising speed of 16 knots and an estimated range of 4,000nm. She is built to ABS classification and complies with MCA rules. *Mystic* appears in this Volume (5) of *The Megayachts USA*.

42. NOBLE HOUSE

(ex-Princess Marla, ex-Victory Lane)
150ft; Twin screw motoryacht; Aluminum; 1998; Trinity Yachts, New Orleans, Louisiana, USA; Trinity Yachts/Paragon Design/Dee Robinson; 2 x 1,800hp DDC/MTU 16V2000 diesels; American owner

Noble House was commissioned by the American yacht entrepreneur, Felix Sabates, who built her as a speculative project. This impressive vessel certainly showcased her builder's entry into serious large yacht construction and, following her display at the Fort Lauderdale Boat Show in 1997, she was quickly sold and re-named *Princess Marla*. She was recently resold to another American and is now named *Noble House*, but a further name change is likely following the delivery of a new *Noble House* from Sensation Yachts in New Zealand later this year. She was featured in *The Superyachts*, Volume 12.

43. NOVA SPIRIT

150ft; Twin screw motoryacht; Aluminum; 1999; Trinity Yachts, New Orleans, Louisiana, USA; Trinity Yachts/Paragon Design/Dee Robinson; 2 x 2,250hp Caterpillar 3508B diesels; Canadian owner

Nova Spirit is yet another large yacht from Trinity, this time for a Canadian owner in the electrical products business. She replaced a smaller Broward that the owner had run for many years. Like *Noble House*, *Nova Spirit* also has a superb interior by Dee Robinson.

44. SEAHAWK

150ft; Twin screw motoryacht; Aluminum; 2003; Trinity Yachts, New Orleans, Louisiana, USA; Trinity/Claudette Bonville; 2 x 2,250hp Caterpillar 3512B; American owner

The latest launch in Trinity's popular 150ft tri-deck 'Victory Lane' series, *Seahawk* boasts a stunning interior from US interior designer Claudette Bonville. Owned by North Carolina businessman Jim Mattei, for whom it is an interim yacht while he carries out preliminary design and specification work on a 194ft vessel that he plans to build, possibly at Trinity Yachts. Powered by Cat 3512B diesels, *Seahawk* has a top speed of 23 knots and cruises effortlessly at 19 knots. At a reduced speed of 12 knots she has transatlantic range. *Seahawk* has accommodation for 10 guests in a main deck master suite plus four guest cabins on the lower deck. She is operated by 10 crew.

45. FULMARA

(ex-Paget, ex-Niki I, ex-Luisa II, ex-Carmac III, ex-Leonore, ex-Janidore)
149ft 11in; Twin screw motoryacht; Steel; 1930 Defoe Boat & Motor Works, Bay City, Louisiana USA; John H. Wells; 2 x 650hp Caterpillar diesels; British owner

Fulmara is a survivor from the post WWI era of large yachts that occurred in the late 1920s and early 1930s. She has been rebuilt, lengthened, renamed and modernized over the years, but retains her classic elegance. Now based in Nice on the Côte d'Azur, she charters in the Mediterranean.

46. ZEUS

147ft 8in; Auxiliary twin screw sloop; Cold-molded wood composite; 1993; Robertson, Fort Lauderdale, Florida, USA; David Pedrick/Jay Benford/Angus Robertson/Christina Thompson; 2 x 680hp MAN D2848LX diesels; Latin American owner

This is a yacht with a difference: a sloop-rigged sailing yacht whose hull (designed by Dave Pedrick) was acquired from an uncompleted earlier project and extended before conversion into a sailing superyacht by her original owner in a private facility in Dania, Florida. She features an avant-garde deck layout developed by her original owner and exotic accommodation designed by Christina Thompson. At the time of her completion, *Zeus* had the tallest mast fitted to any single masted sailing yacht. She was acquired by a Latin American owner a few years ago.

47. MAHA

(ex-Matahari, ex-Maha Al Mojil, ex-Al Mojil 5, ex-Bernadette, ex-Cibeles V, ex-Zimba, ex-Halimede, ex-Mimosan, ex-Paridot, ex-Bymar)
147ft 1in; Twin screw motoryacht; Steel; 1938;

Defoe Boat & Motor Works, Bay City, Michigan, USA; Cox & Stevens; 2 x 500hp Caterpillar diesels; Saudi Arabian owner

A yacht which, in her 65-year lifetime, possibly holds the record for the largest number of names. Originally built as *Bymar* for American Byron D. Miller, this interesting pre-WWII survivor is still giving sterling service to her present Saudi Arabian owner. Based in Dammam, *Maha* occasionally appears in the Western Mediterranean.

48. FORTUNA

(ex-Contico of Cayman, ex-Contico)
147ft; Twin screw motoryacht; Steel; 1992; Keith Marine, Florida, USA; Fryco/Rezende/Nicholson Interiors; 2 x 850hp Caterpillar 3508 diesels; Russian owner

This interesting yacht was built as *Contico* for an American manufacturer of plastic surfaced chipboards and plastic consumer items, who chartered her when not using her himself. She was sold to a Russian in 1997 when she was extensively refitted, and given a new interior the following year. Featured in *The Superyachts*, Volume 7 as *Contico*, she now sports a fashionable dark blue hull.

49. GRAN FINALE

147ft; Twin screw motoryacht; GRP composite; 2002; Delta Marine, Seattle, Washington, USA; Delta Design/Juan-Carlos Espinosa; 2 x 2,400hp Caterpillar 3512 diesels; American owner
The first in Delta's new 147ft series, *Gran Finale* was built by the Delta Marine yard in Seattle,

and delivered to her Californian owner last year. Juan-Carlos Espinosa was responsible for both her much acclaimed styling and interior design, while twin 2,400hp Caterpillars provide a top speed of 21 knots and a comfortable cruising speed of 18 knots. She is featured in *The Superyachts*, Volume 16.

50. TAJIN

(ex-Nassa Too)
147ft; Twin screw motoryacht; GRP composite; Trident Marine, Tampa, Florida, USA; Trident/Serge Cutolo/Juan-Carlos Espinosa; 2000; 2 x 3,000hp MTU diesels; Mexican owner
Tajin is one of the last yachts to emerge from the original Trident shipyard in Tampa, Florida. Twin 3,000hp MTU diesels provide a top speed of 22 knots for this GRP-hulled yacht. Her interior, designed by Juan Carlos Espinosa, offers a showcase of Mexican art set against a rich background of anigré and mahogany. ABS classified and MCA compliant, she is now owned by a Mexican businessman and is available for charter.

51. GRAY MIST III

146ft 2in; Twin screw motoryacht; Aluminum; 1998; Breaux Baycraft, Louisiana, USA; Tim Borland/Paul Marchetti; 2 x 1,540hp Caterpillar 3512 diesels; American owner
Owned by a retired Midwest couple, *Gray Mist III* replaces another yacht from the same yard. This latest yacht is an outstanding example of the work of these Louisiana builders. She is featured in *The Superyachts*, Volume 12 and can be spotted at her berth on Fisher Island, Florida when she is not cruising.

52. LADY M

(ex-Raven)
145ft; Twin screw motoryacht; Composite; 2001; Intermarine (USA), Savannah, Georgia, USA; Hansen/Cross-Buchanan; 2 x 4,500hp Caterpillar 3512 diesels; American owner
Raven was built at the Intermarine yard at Savannah, Georgia. Her accommodation, for ten guests, is the work of British designer Andrew Winch and American Todd Marckese. She is featured in Volume 4 of *The Megayachts USA*.

53. LISERON

145ft; Twin screw motoryacht; Wood; 1954; Tacoma Boat Building, Tacoma, Washington, USA; US Navy; Cleveland diesels; American owner
Liseron started life as a US Naval minehunter and was converted to a yacht in Florida in 1989. Now based in Poulsbo, Washington, this yacht is available for charter in the Pacific Northwest region.

54. SHENANDOAH OF SARK

145ft; Auxiliary Three Masted Gaff Schooner (177ft 2in including bowsprit); Steel/teak; 1902; Townsend & Downey, Shooters Island, USA; Theodore E Ferris/Francis & Francis/Terence Disdale; 2 x Lugger diesels; Italian owner

Now over 100 years old, this beautiful schooner was given a new lease on life when she underwent a painstaking rebuild and restoration at the McMullen & Wing yard in Auckland, New Zealand in 1996. She was originally owned by Gibson Fahnestock, who kept her for ten years prior to selling her to the first of a succession of owners, some good and some less so. Her last two owners have maintained her to the highest standard. She is featured in *The Superyachts*, Volume 7 and *The Megayachts*, Volume 2.

55. PRIMADONNA

145ft; Twin screw motoryacht; GRP composite; 2002; Christensen Shipyards, Vancouver, Washington, USA; Christensen/Christensen/Smith; 2 x 1,820hp DDC/MTU diesels; American owner
Interior designer, Paola D. Smith used madrona wood, animal print upholstery, honey onyx and glass to create a sumptuous interior for this yacht. At the time of its launch, *Primadonna* was reputed to be the most expensive yacht ever to be launched from her builders, Christensen Shipyards. She is featured in *The Superyachts*, Volume 16.

56. FOUR WISHES

144ft; Twin screw motoryacht; Aluminum; 2003; Palmer Johnson, Sturgeon Bay, Wisconsin, USA; Vripack/Palmer Johnson; 2 x Caterpillar 3412 diesels; American owner
Launched in November 2003, *Four Wishes* has a high volume hull with a 28ft beam by Dutch naval architects, Vripack which has been tastefully married to a Palmer Johnson-designed superstructure which gives her more than a passing resemblance to *Inevitable* or *Azure Leisure* (ex-*Paraffin*). She is built to Lloyd's classification and complies with the British MCA safety rules.

57. SEA FALCON B

143ft 1in; Twin screw motoryacht; Aluminum; 1990; Angus Yachts, Bayou la Batrie, Alabama, USA; Angus Edwards; 2 x 1,250hp MTU 331TI diesels; Saudi Arabian owner
Sea Falcon B (the B distinguishes her from other yachts of the same name for registration purposes) was built in 1989 by Angus Yachts utilizing the central section of a commercial hull. She features an innovative stern garage/launch platform for a large tender and is cruised worldwide by her current Middle-Eastern owner.

58. WESTSHIP LADY

143ft; Twin screw motoryacht; GRP composite; 2003; Westship World Yachts, Fort Lauderdale, Florida, USA; Jack Sarin/Westship Design Team; 2 x 2,735hp MTU 12V 4000 series diesels
The latest tri-deck motoryacht from Westship World Yachts and the second largest so far is currently building as a speculative project. Launched in the summer 2003, she features a main deck master suite, plus four guest cabins and a gymnasium on the lower deck. She is built to Lloyd's letter of acceptance standards.

59. AZURE LEISURE

(ex-Paraffin)
142ft; Twin screw motoryacht; Aluminum; 1997; Palmer Johnson, Sturgeon Bay, Wisconsin, USA; Tom Fexas/Terence Disdale; 2 x 1,800hp Detroit 149 DDEC diesels; American owner
Although *Azure Leisure* was built by Palmer Johnson as a speculative project, she did not have to wait long before she was purchased by an owner in the candle manufacturing business, hence her original name. Following the delivery of a larger Feadship to this first owner, she was recently purchased by another American. She is featured in *The Superyachts*, Volume 11 as *Paraffin*.

60. BIG PLAY

(ex-Namoh, ex-Soldier of Fortune)
142ft; Twin-screw motoryacht; GRP composite; 1995; Christensen Yachts, Vancouver, Washington, USA; Christensen/Paragon Design/Dee Robinson; 2 x 1,948hp Deutz-MWM TBD604V diesels; American owner
Big Play was bought midway through her construction when the original buyer (who was going to name her *Soldier of Fortune*) withdrew. Fitted with an ebullient interior that makes great use of black and gold, this yacht is recognized as a masterpiece of contemporary design. Her American owner placed her on the charter market with great success over the past few years a trend that is set to continue following a recent change of ownership. She is now named *Big Play*, a particularly apt name in view of her huge collection of tenders and toys. She was featured in *The Superyachts*, Volume 10 as *Namoh*.

61. BURNA

142ft; Twin screw motoryacht; Aluminum; 2003; Trinity Yachts, New Orleans, Louisiana, USA; Trinity/Dee Robinson; 2 x Caterpillar 3512B; American owner
Trinity Yachts is continuously building its reputation as America's most prolific builder of megayachts and in support of this they have no less than 13 yachts this list—the largest number from any one builder. Following the recent delivery of the 150ft *Seahawk*, *Burna*, launched in the Fall, 2003 was followed by her sistership *Chevy Toy*. *Burna*, luxuriously appointed and well equipped with an on-deck Jacuzzi and a wide array of water toys, is active on the charter market.

62. CHEVY TOY

142ft; Twin screw motoryacht; Aluminum; 2004; Trinity Yachts, New Orleans, Louisiana, USA; Trinity/Dee Robinson; 2 x MTU/DDEC 16V2000 diesels; American owner
The second yacht in the 142ft series from Trinity Yachts, *Chevy Toy* replaces an earlier 118ft Trinity of the same name that is very active on the charter market. This new yacht differs from her sistership *Burna* in that MTU engines have been chosen to power her. She was launched in the Fall 2003 and, like her forerunner, will also be offered for charter in due course.

63. REGENCY

142ft; Twin screw motoryacht; Aluminum; 2003/4; Palmer Johnson, Sturgeon Bay, Wisconsin, USA; Tom Fexas/Claudette Bonville; 2 x Caterpillar 3412 diesels; Owned by Palmer Johnson
Regency remains in the Palmer Johnson Sturgeon Bay yard which was running under the protection of Chapter 11 at press time. The yacht is near completion, and while work on her was halted it is expected to recommence shortly. Her stunning interior design from the drawing board of Claudette Bonville originated from a request by her owner for a yacht that was similar in style to the Trinity-built *Seahawk*, whose interior was also by Bonville. Built to a very high standard and featuring a stunning 'Grand Staircase' the interior has been completed and is in the yard, but is yet to be installed on the yacht. *Regency* is being offered for sale through Palmer Johnson in Fort Lauderdale.

64. COCOA BEAN

141ft 10in; Twin screw motoryacht; Aluminum; 1996; Broward Marine, Dania, Florida, USA; Broward Marine/Robin Rose; 2 x 2,400hp Detroit DDEC diesels; Middle Eastern owner
Launched in 1996, this is the second largest yacht built by Broward Marine and features an interior by American designer Robin Rose. *Cocoa Bean* is a strictly private yacht that spends much time in Mediterranean waters.

65. DOUBLE G

(ex-Mia Elise)
141ft; Twin screw motoryacht; Steel; 2001; Trinity Yachts, New Orleans, Louisiana, USA; Trinity/Dee Robinson; 2 x 1,800hp MTU/DDEC 16V2000 diesels
Another yacht that started life at Trinity Yachts under the name of *Victory Lane*, ordered as a speculative project by entrepreneur Felix Sabates. She was never registered as such, being sold shortly after launching and christened *Mia Elise*. She has a five stateroom layout, with a main deck master suite, while the remaining four staterooms include two VIPs with king-size beds and a spa tub, one queen and a twin. All are lavishly decorated to designs by Dee Robinson who created a classical interior backed by rare quilted makoré and vavona burl. Recently sold and renamed *Double G*, she is available for charter.

66. SAINT JAMES

141ft; Twin screw motoryacht; Aluminum; 1996; Flagship Marine/Huffstutler, Biloxi, Mississippi, USA; Huffstutler; 2 x 750hp Detroit diesels; American owner
Originally this vessel was constructed as a crew boat for use by the offshore oil industry in the Gulf of Mexico. After many years of service it was converted, re-plated and its stern lengthened by 10ft at Flagship Marine, who also re-powered her with Detroit diesels. She was later lengthened once more and converted for Caribbean charter work in 1996. She has accommodation for ten guests.

67. WALKABOUT

(ex-Big Bad John)
141ft; Twin screw motoryacht; GRP composite; 1999; Christensen Yachts, Vancouver, Washington, USA; K C Designs/Sarah Fahey; 2 x 2,000hp DDC-MTU diesels; American owner
Unusual for a yacht of this size *Walkabout* has a raised pilothouse configuration. She was originally built for the singer/songwriter and sausage manufacturer Jimmy Dean, who specified an interior layout for six guests, and a grand piano in the saloon. She was featured in *The Megayachts USA*, Volume 2 as *Big Bad John*.

68. MAGNIFICO

140ft; Twin screw motoryacht; GRP composite; 1991; Christensen Yachts, Vancouver, Washington, USA; Christensen/Apollonio/Robert; 2 x 1,400hp DDEC V92 TI diesels; American owner
Magnifico is available for charter, primarily between Mexico and the Pacific Northwest, where she has operated successfully for the last few years. At the time of her launch in 1991, she was the largest US-built composite yacht.

69. MARTHA ANN

(ex-Westship One)
140ft; Twin screw motoryacht; GRP composite; 2000; Westship World Yachts, Fort Lauderdale, Florida, USA; Jack Sarin/Wesley Carr/Yacht Design Associates; 2 x 2,285hp MTU 12V396TE94 diesels
The first of Westship's new flagship series made her debut at the Miami Boat Show in February 2001. She averaged over 22 knots on her maiden voyage en route from her builder's yard to Miami, and took just 18 hours for the passage. Following their acquisition of the one-time Trident Shipworks yard in Tampa where this yacht was built, Westship is now in a position to challenge the established American builders of large composite yachts. This vessel was featured in *The Megayachts USA*, Volume 3 as *Westship One*.

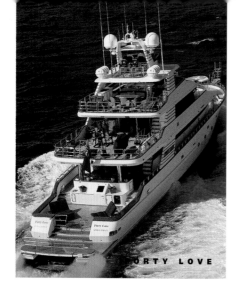

FORTY LOVE

70. ARABELLA

(ex-Centurion)

139ft; Sailing cutter; Aluminum; 1983; Palmer Johnson, Sturgeon Bay, Wisconsin, USA; Maclear & Harris; 1 x 215hp Caterpillar diesel; American owner

This interesting sailing yacht has had a checkered career since she was completed by Palmer Johnson in 1983 as *Centurion* for a British owner. She ran aground near Lisbon in 1985 and had to be extensively rebuilt, then, after she had been sold to a well-known American actress, she suffered fire damage. Eventually acquired by another American, *Arabella* was been rebuilt in an East Coast yard and lengthened for charter work.

71. FORTY LOVE

138ft; Twin screw motoryacht; Aluminum/GRP cored composite; 2002; West Coast Custom Yachts, San Diego, California, USA; Jack Sarin/ Brilliant Yachts - Michael Schutte; 2 x 1,450hp Caterpillar 3412 diesels; Egyptian owner

The Egyptian owner of this yacht purchased a partially-finished, Westport 112ft semi-displacement, raised pilothouse vessel with a cored-composite hull and extended it to 138ft (including a bow platform) to create an amazing 'Party Boat'. The stern features wide steps that descend below water level so that the owner's water-loving dogs can leave and board the yacht at their leisure. Intended for charter, *Forty Love* is currently based between th Caribbean and the Mediterranean. It is ABS classified and complies with the MCA code. She appears in this volume (5) of *The Megayachts USA*.

INVADER

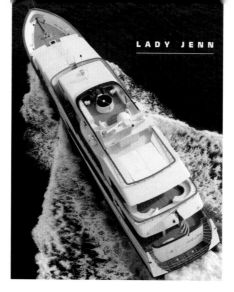

LADY JENN

72. STATUS QUO

138ft; Twin screw motoryacht; Cored GRP composite; 2004; Sovereign Yachts, Richmond, British Columbia, Canada; Setzer Design Group/ Owner/Sovereign Design Team; 2 x 2,250hp Caterpillar 3512 diesels; American owner

Status Quo, a tri-deck motoryacht, was built from GRP composite in the same adjustable mould that created *Sovereign Lady*, the first yacht of this attractive series. While this second yacht has similar interior accommodation, her owner has foregone the fishing cockpit so as to have larger saloons. She is due for delivery in early 2004.

73. HIS GRACE

137ft; Twin screw motoryacht; GRP composite; 1989; Westport Shipyard, Westport, Washington, USA ; Jack Sarin/Paolo Caliari; 2 x 1958hp MWM-Deutz 604B diesels; American owner

Built at Westport Shipyard, Washington, with naval architecture by Jack Sarin, *His Grace* has styling by the Italian designer Paolo Caliari. She is named after her Californian owner's wife and was refitted and extended by 10ft in 1999.

74. STARFJORD

(ex-Americana, ex-Liberty, ex-Campana, ex-Dixonia, ex-Acania)

136ft 10in; Twin screw motoryacht; Steel; 1930; Consolidated Shipbuilding, USA; John H Wells; Steel; 2 x 500hp GM diesels; American owner

This classic yacht was originally launched as *Acania* in 1930 for an American. Since then she has had a variety of US and Canadian owners and is now to be found in New York as the *Starfjord*. Her most recent refit was in 1986.

75. BOSSY BOOTS

(ex-Mia Elise)

136ft; Twin screw motoryacht; GRP composite; 1998; Intermarine Savannah, Savannah, Georgia, USA; Paragon/Luiz de Basto/Marc Michaels; 2 x 2,260hp MTU 12V396TE94 diesels; American owner

Bossy Boots, launched as *Mia Elise*, was the second hull from Intermarine Savannah, a yard that has recently been acquired by the Savannah branch of Palmer Johnson. Richly decorated by Marc Michaels, the accommo-

tion comprises a master stateroom forward on the main deck, and four staterooms on the lower deck—three with queen size beds and the fourth with two singles. She also offers two lounges, a separate dining saloon, a gymnasium and a steam room.

76. INVADER

136ft (160ft including bowsprit); Auxiliary schooner; Steel; 1905; Lawley Shipbuilding, USA; Albert Cheeseborough; GM diesels; Italian owner

This historic old schooner was originally built for the American Roy A. Rainey in 1905. After many different owners, she eventually wound up cruising as a day charter vessel in the 1990s in the Caribbean. She was acquired by a well-known lady owner in 1997 with a view for restoration at Lürssen Shipyard, but she has since been sold to an Italian owner who has taken her to Viareggio, Italy, where her captain is managing a complete refit. She was finished in late 2003.

77. LADY JENN

136ft; Twin screw motoryacht; Aluminum; 1994; Palmer Johnson, Sturgeon Bay, Wisconsin, USA; Tom Fexas/Robert Knack; 2 x 16 cylinder 10,404hp Detroit diesels; French owner

Palmer Johnson delivered this motoryacht in 1993 to a French owner who used her for worldwide cruising. Classic lines from naval architect Tom Fexas complement her luxurious interior by American designer Robert Knack. *Lady Jenn* has recently been put on the market with an asking price of $11,700,000 after serving her first owner for the last eight years. She was featured in Volume 8 of *The Superyachts* book.

78. ATLANTICA

135ft; Twin screw motoryacht; Cored GRP composite; 2000; Christensen Yachts, Vancouver, Washington, USA; Christensen/Donald Starkey; 2 x 1,800hp DDC-MTU 16V2000 diesels; American owner

Another fine example of the work of the Vancouver, Washington-based Christensen Yachts, *Atlantica* features an interior by British designer Donald Starkey. Although not one of her builder's largest vessels, she must be considered one of the best to emerge from this West Coast builder. She is featured in *The Superyachts*, Volume 14.

ATLANTICA

79. SOVEREIGN LADY

135ft; Twin screw motoryacht; Cored GRP composite; 2003; Sovereign Yachts, Richmond, British Columbia, Canada; Setzer Design Group; 2 x 2,750hp DDEC MTU 12V 4000 diesels; Owner nationality unknown
Launched in early 2003, this yacht has an interesting history in that the hull and superstructure was molded in Richmond, British Columbia and shipped by freighter to New Zealand, where it was fitted out with a truly luxurious interior at Sovereign Yachts (NZ)'s new facility at Auckland's old Hobsonville Air Base. Sailing enthusiasts might have seen her while watching the 2003 America's Cup—always at the thick of the action, she was the Royal New Zealand Yacht Squadron member's boat. *Sovereign Lady* was originally built as a speculative project but has recently been sold and is likely to be renamed in the near future. She is featured in this volume (5) of *The Megayachts USA*.

80. CALISTO OF NP

134ft; Twin screw motoryacht; Wood; 1944; Astoria Shipyard, USA; US Navy; 2 x Deutz diesels; French owner
This elderly yacht, built during WWII, is a rare survivor in today's world of modern motoryachts. *Calisto* was originally a mine sweeper and was converted into a yacht in 1951 by Vosper in England for Loel Guinness. She has been based in Antibes for many years.

81. ALLIANCE

133ft; Twin screw motoryacht; Cored GRP composite; 1989; Delta Marine, Seattle, Washington, USA; Delta Design/Gila Lehrer; 2 x 705hp Caterpillar 3508 TA diesels; American owner
Alliance was one of the largest yachts launched by Delta Marine in the 1980s. She was lengthened by her builders in 1994 with the addition of a swim platform and fishing cockpit and was refitted in 1999. Unusually, her crew accommodations are equal in size to the guest cabins. She is the corporate yacht of the Paccar group based in Bellevue WA.

82. UTHINGO

(ex-Candida A, ex-Shogun)
133ft; Twin screw motoryacht; Steel; 1930 Lawley & Son, Massachusetts, USA; Tams & King; 2 x 680hp GM diesels; South African owner
Another elderly survivor from the yacht building period in the late 1920s/early 1930s. This fine yacht was originally built as *Shogun* for A C Murphy and was also owned by Henry Ford in the pre-war years. *Uthingo* is now based in Durban, South Africa. She was featured in Volume 4 of *The Superyachts*.

83. SANDRA LYNN

(ex-Katharine)
132ft; Twin screw motoryacht; GRP composite; 1999; Trident Marine, Tampa, Florida, USA; Trident/Wesley Carr/Serge Cutolo/Elizabeth Dalton; 2 x 1,720hp Caterpillar 3412DI-TA diesels; American owner
Launched as *Katharine*, this yacht was a product of the Tampa, Florida based builder Trident Shipworks in 1999, and replaced her owner's former yacht, a 103ft Cheoy Lee. She is currently active on the charter market and carries eight guests in her luxurious accommodations designed by Elizabeth Dalton.

84. NORWEGIAN QUEEN

132ft • Twin screw motoryacht; GRP composite; 2000; Trident Marine, Tampa, Florida, USA; Trident/Jack Sarin/Wesley Carr/Yacht Design Associates; MTU diesels; American owner
This chic yacht was delivered to her Boca Raton, Florida-based owner in 2000. A pair of MTU diesels power her to a top speed of 24 knots, while her interior, by Yacht Design Associates, incorporates some interesting design features, including the use of stainless steel columns in the main saloon.

85. LIFE'S FINEST II

(ex-Aquasition, ex-Life's Finest, ex-Countach)
131ft 10in; Twin screw motoryacht; Cored GRP composite; Northcoast Yachts, Anacortes, Washington, USA; 1996; Jack Sarin/Tom Henderson/Pokela Design; 2 x 2,400hp Detroit 149TIB diesels; American owner
Northcoast Yachts completed this yacht in their Anacortes shipyard as *Countach* a few years ago and she is the largest to emerge from this builder so far. Her pair of powerful DDC engines, each developing 2,400hp, provide *Life's Finest II* with a top speed of 26 knots.

86. LIFE OF RILEY

(ex-P'Zazz)
131ft 8in; Twin screw motoryacht; GRP composite; 1989; Delta Marine, Seattle, Washington, USA; Delta Design/Schubert & Minor/Glade Johnson; 2 x 705hp Caterpillar 3508TA diesels; American owner
This interesting yacht was delivered to her

Californian owner as *P'Zazz* in 1989 when she was notable for her avant garde interior. She was sold to a new owner last year and has since undergone an extensive refit and lengthening by her original builder. She was featured in *The Superyachts*, Volume 3 as *P'Zazz*.

87. CV-9 OF CAYMAN

131ft 3in; Twin screw motoryacht; GRP composite; 1995; Delta Marine, Seattle, Washington, USA; Delta Design/ Glade Johnson; 2 x 775hp Caterpillar 3508 diesels; Turkish owner
This yacht was delivered in 1995 to her original US owner, a former USAF fighter, who named the yacht after the aircraft carrier on which he once served. Glade Johnson was responsible for the interior on this smart yacht. She was later sold to a Turkish owner who retained her name. She was featured in *The Superyachts*, Volume 9.

88. INEVITABLE

131ft; Twin screw motoryacht; Aluminum; 2000; Palmer Johnson, Sturgeon Bay, Wisconsin, USA; Palmer Johnson/Dick Boon/Patrick Knowles; 2 x 1,700hp Caterpillar 3412 TA diesels; American owner
It may be inevitable that all Palmer Johnson yachts are among the best in US yacht building, and the aptly named *Inevitable* is no exception. Designed by Dick Boon of the Netherlands-based Vripack Yachting, she has a classically styled interior by Patrick Knowles. She is featured in Volume 3 of *The Megayachts*.

89. ALTEZA

130ft; Twin screw motoryacht; GRP composite; 1992; Christensen Yachts, Vancouver, Washington, USA; Christensen/Howard Apollonio/Glade Johnson/Susan Puleo; 2 x 1,400hp Detroit V92TI-DDEC diesels; American owner
Alteza features a particularly striking interior which doubtlessly makes her one of the best looking yachts to have emerged from an American builder in recent times. Perfectly proportioned, this Christensen-built motoryacht was delivered to exacting California-based owners with an eye on the charter market. Sold in 2002 she retains her original name.

INEVITABLE

SACAJAWEA

90. CANGARDA

130ft; Twin screw steam yacht; Steel; 1901
Pusey & Jones, Wilmington, Delaware, USA;
HC Wintringham; 2 x Sullivan steam reciprocating engines; American owner
This veteran steam vessel, one of just a handful
of steam powered yachts still in existence, can be
found in Gloucester, Massachusetts. She was built
at the turn of the century by Pusey & Jones at
Wilmington, Delaware for an American owner.

91. CHARISMA

(ex-Allegra, ex-Victory Lane)
130ft; Twin screw motoryacht; GRP composite;
1995; Hatteras Yachts, New Bern, North
Carolina, USA; Jack Hargrave/Ward Setzer/Dee
Robinson; 2 x 2,500hp Detroit 149DDEC
diesels; American owner
Charisma is the largest yacht built by prolific
US builder Hatteras of New Bern, North
Carolina. She was originally commissioned by
Felix Sabates of Victory Lane Enterprises, and
has recently been completely refitted for serv-
ice as a charter yacht. She is featured in *The
Superyachts*, Volume 9.

92. CRYSTAL SEA

130ft; Twin screw motoryacht; Cored GRP composite; 2001; Westport Shipyard, Westport,
Washington, USA; Garden/Marshall/Pacific
Custom Interiors; 2 x 2,735hp MTU/DDC 4000
diesels; American owner
This, the second yacht in the Westport 130 tri-
deck series was launched in 2001 as *Rejoyce II*,
with accommodation designed by Sheryl &
Peter Guyon of Pacific Custom Interiors. These
yachts are offered for sale at a competitive $13
million price including Baccarat crystal, formal
silver and all one's household needs from
loose furniture to bed linen, so this listing will
in the future be almost certain to see more of
this model. Sold in 2003, she remains in
American ownership but has been renamed
Crystal Sea. The yacht is featured in *The
Megayachts USA*, Volume 4 as *Rejoyce II*.

93. LT SEA

130ft; Twin screw motoryacht; Cored GRP composite; 2000; Westport Shipyard, Westport,
Washington, USA; Greg Marshall/William
Garden/Pacific Custom Interiors; 2 x 2,735hp
MTU/DDC4000 diesels; American owner
This fine yacht is the first example of Westport's
130ft tri-deck series. *LT Sea* was originally built
on speculation but was sold almost immediately after she was completed. The success of

CRYSTAL SEA

Westport's 130ft design is underlined by the
fact that *LT Sea* has three sisterships afloat and
four more under construction.

94. LADY ALICE

(ex-Pegasus)
130ft; Triple screw motoryacht; Aluminum; 1991;
Broward Marine, Dania, Florida, USA;
Broward/Peggy Bey/Jean Hermanson; 3 x 1,450hp
Detroit 92TA DDEC diesels; American owner
One of the finest yachts ever built by Broward
Marine, Florida's prolific builder of aluminum
motoryachts, *Pegasus* was originally built for
an experienced yachtsman in the oil drum
manufacturing business, and is particularly
unusual in that she is fitted with three
engines. Her original owner has taken delivery
of a 194ft Dutch-built yacht of the same name
and her new owner, another American, has
changed her name to *Lady Alice*. She is featured in *The Superyachts*, Volume 5 as *Pegasus*.

95. MAGIC

130ft; Twin screw motoryacht; Cored GRP com-
posite; 2003; Northern Marine, Anacortes,
Washington, USA; Setzer/Ardeo Design/Setzer;
2 x 3,700hp Detroit 2000 DDEC diesels;
American owner
Having sold his previous Hatteras to golfer,
Tiger Woods, this Michigan owner commis-
sioned his dream boat from US naval architect
Ward Setzer. Launched in the summer 2003,
Magic based in Palm Beach is designed to
operate in the shallow waters of the Bahamas
Bank. The Anacortes, Washington-based
Northern Marine has another large motor-
yacht project underway, a 152-footer called
Lai Fail which is due for delivery 2004.

96. VANGO

130ft; Twin screw motoryacht; Cored GRP composite; 2001; Westport Shipyard, Westport,
Washington, USA; Garden/Marshall/Pacific
Custom Interiors; 2 x 2,735hp MTU/DDC 4000
diesels; American owner
This is the fourth yacht in the successful
Westport 130 tri-deck series, with accommodation designed by Sheryl & Peter Guyon of
Pacific Custom Interiors. *Vango* was delivered
to her American owner in May 2003. Two
more sisterships are under construction, one
for delivery by press date and the second in
early 2004. As yet unnamed, these latter
yachts do not feature in this listing.

97. ROYAL OAK

130ft; Twin screw motoryacht; GRP composite;
1989; Christensen Yachts, Vancouver,
Washington, USA; Christensen/Howard
Apollonio/Glade Johnson/Mary Roberts;
Composite; 2 x 1,150hp Mitsubishi diesels;
Japanese owner
This Christensen-built yacht has been based in
Japan since she was delivered 12 years ago.
Her Japanese owner also took simultaneous
delivery of a 115ft Christensen.

98. SACAJAWEA

*(ex-Bellini, ex-Daybreak of Cayman,
ex-Genevian)*
130ft; Twin screw motoryacht; GRP composite;
1994; Hatteras Yachts, New Bern, North Carolina,
USA; Hatteras/Hargrave/Robinson; 2 x 2,400hp
Detroit 149DDEC diesels; American owner
Another of the Hatteras 130ft tri-deck series
that is now available for charter. Originally
delivered as *Genevian*, then sold and renamed
Daybreak of Cayman, this vessel is now the
property of a Californian-based owner.

99. SERENGETI

130ft; Twin screw motoryacht; Cored GRP composite; 2002; Westport Shipyard, Westport,
Washington, USA; Garden/Marshall/Pacific
Custom Interiors; 2 x 2,735hp MTU/DDC 4000
diesels; American owner
The third yacht in Westport's 130 series and
the first with a hard bimini shading the sun
deck, *Serengeti* was launched in 2002. She
offers five staterooms—a master on the main
deck and four on the lower deck.

100. SERENDIPITY

130ft; Twin screw motoryacht; Cored GRP composite; 2002; Westport Shipyard, Westport,
Washington, USA; Garden/Marshall/Pacific
Custom Interiors; 2 x 2,735hp MTU/DDC 4000
diesels; American owner
Serendipity is the fourth launch in Westport's
130ft series. Like her sisterships, she is powered by twin 2,735hp MTU/DDCs which provide a top speed of 28 knots and cruise in the
mid-20s. Of the four yachts in this series currently under construction, two are already
sold and the remaining two are available at
around $14 million.

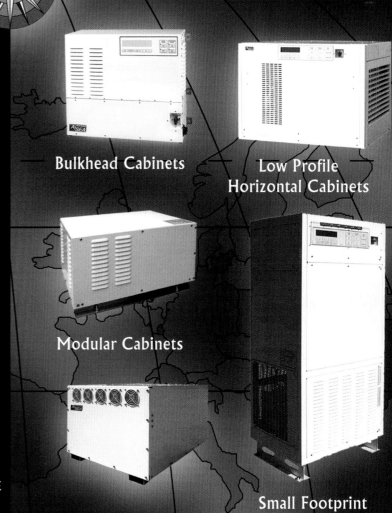

Megayachts Registry

BOAT NAME	VOL.	BUILDER	NAVAL ARCHITECTURE	INTERIOR DESIGN	PAGE
Aerie	1	Nordlund Boat Co.	Edwin Monk & Son	Pokela Design	36
Aerie	3	Delta Marine	Delta Design Group	Jonathan Quinn Barnett Ltd.	88
Affinity	2	Delta Marine	Delta Design Group	Ardeo Design	88
Alegria	5	Hargrave	Hargrave	Shelley Higgins/Owner	106
Alexa C²	5	Nordlund Boat Co.	Edwin Monk/Nolan Marine Design	Pokela Design	112
Alexis	2	Palmer Johnson	Palmer Johnson/Tom Fexas	Owner/Palmer Johnson	96
Allegra	1	Trinity Yachts	Trinity Yachts	Dee Robinson Interiors/Carolyn Sabates	42
Amarellla	5	Inace Shipyard	Marcio Igreja	Michael Kirchstein/Mavignier Lima	120
Andiamo	5	Feadship - Royal Van Lent	Doug Sharp/De Voogt	Glade Johnson Design	126
Andromeda	1	Omega Marine Developers	Omega/Nissan/Sciomachen	Brindan Byrne Design	50
Anjilis	5	Trinity Yachts	Trinity Yachts	Dee Robinson Interiors	136
Anson Bell	4	Palmer Johnson	Vripack Yachting	Ramsey Engler Ltd.	100
Antonisa	2	Hodgdon Yachts	Bruce King Yacht Design	Bruce King Yacht Design	104
Aphrodite	4	West Bay SonShip	West Bay SonShip	Kathy Koutsky/Portobello Design	110
Aria	3	Sensation New Zealand	Ray Harvey	Donald Starkey Designs	96
Bella Dawn	4	Benetti	Benetti	François Zuretti	116
Bendycta	4	CBI Navi	CBI Navi/Luca Dini	Luca Dini	122
Big Bad John	2	Christensen	Christensen	Sarah Fahey (Christensen in-house)	112
Blue Belle	5	Mondomarine	Sydac/Cor D. Rover Design	Isabelle Blanchère	144
Blue Moon	2	Feadship - Royal Van Lent/Zonen	De Voogt	Donald Starkey Designs	118
Carib Queen	2	Inace	John Overing	CAS Design Group	128
Christina O	3	Canadian Vickers/Victor Lenec	Rebuild: Carabelas/Apostolos	Decon	104
Condalora	4	NorthStar Yachts	Jack W. Sarin	Lora Blanchard	128
Continental Drifter	2	Cheoy Lee	Tom Fexas	Savio Interior Design	136
Crescent Lady	5	Crescent Custom Yachts	Crescent/Marshall/Sarin	Robin Rose & Associates	152
Dare to Dream	1	Crescent Custom Yachts	Jack W. Sarin	Knowles Design Group	58
Defiant	5	Delta Marine	Delta Design Group	Delta Design Group	158
Delphine	5	Great Lakes Engineering Works	Gielow & Orr/Refit: Antoine Wille	Tiffany's of New York	166
Destiny One	2	Destiny Yachts	Giovanni Arrabito	Evan K. Marshall	144
Detroit Eagle	3	De Vries	De Voogt	John Munford/Mariecke Siezen	124
Discovery	1	Romsdal/Discovery	Jonathan Quinn Barnett Ltd.	Jonathan Quinn Barnett Ltd./Lucy Design	66
Excellence III	4	Abeking & Rasmussen	Abeking & Rasmussen	Donald Starkey Designs	134
Felicitá west	5	Perini Navi	Ron Holland	Nuvolari & Lenard	178
Forty Love	5	West Coast Custom Yachts	Jack W. Sarin/Michael Schutte	Pavlik Design Team	188
Genesis 153	4	NAYS	Sergio Cutolo	Ralph Lauren Home	144
Georgia	2	Alloy	Paolo Scanu/Butch Dalrymple-Smith	Glade Johnson Design	152
High Cotton	3	Hargrave	Hargrave	Yacht Interiors by Shelley	132
Hound Dog	2	Hargrave	JB Hargrave	Yacht Interiors by Shelley	162
Hyperion	1	Royal Huisman	German Frers	Pieter Beeldsnijder	72
Inevitable	3	Palmer Johnson	Vripack Yachting	Patrick Knowles Design	138
Intermarine 118	3	Intermarine Savannah	Intermarine/Luiz de Basto	Luiz de Basto/Ari-Cross Buchanan	146
Intrinsic	2	Benetti	Benetti	François Zuretti/Marty Lowe Design	168
Janet	1	Cheoy Lee	Tom Fexas	Savio Interior Design	82
Katana	2	Blohm & Voss/Lurssen	Martin Francis/Blohm & Voss	François Zuretti/Seccombe Design	176
Katharine	4	Trinity Yachts	Trinity Yachts	Claudette Bonville	152
Katrion	1	Feadship	De Voogt	John Munford	88
La Baronessa	1	Palmer Johnson	Sparkman & Stephens	Nuvolari & Lenard	94
Lady Aleida	5	West Bay SonShip	Jack W. Sarin/West Bay Group	West Bay Group/Ben & Leidy Vermeulen	196
Lady Breanna	3	Ferretti Custom Line	Ferretti/Zuccon	Stodgell Yacht Interiors	152
Lady Grace Marie	1	Burger Boat Co.	Don O'Keefe	Owner/Douglas Richey/Burger	102

Lady Grace Marie	4	Burger Boat Co.	Don O'Keefe	Owner/Burger Design Team	162
Lady Linda	1	Delta Marine	Delta Design Group	Claudette Bonville	108
Lady M	4	Intermarine	Intermarine	Intermarine/Hansen	168
Legacy	3	Lazzara Yachts	Lazzara Yachts	Lazzara Yachts	158
98 Leonardo	5	Azimut-Viareggio	Azimut Design/Stefano Righini	Carlo Galeazzi	204
Liquidity	3	Christensen	Christensen	Christensen	164
Maiora 102	3	Maiora/FIPA	Robert Del Ray	Pavlik Design Team	172
Marlena	1	Trinity Yachts	Trinity Yachts	Dee Robinson Interiors/Marlena Gershowitz	116
Mia Elise	1	Intermarine Yachting	Intermarine	Marc Michaels	122
Missy B	4	Hargrave	Hargrave	Hargrave	176
Montana	1	Ferretti Custom Line	Ferretti Engineering	Zuccon International	128
Mystic	5	Christensen	Christensen	Christensen/Williamson & McCarter	210
Navetta 30	5	Ferretti Custom Line	CRN Engineering	Zuccon International Project	220
Newcastle 125	5	Newcastle Marine	DeJong and Lebet	Luiz de Basto	226
Newcastle Explorer	4	Newcastle Marine	Murray & Associates LLC	Octavid Rezendes	182
Oregon Mist	2	Queenship	Howard Apollonio	Zoë Luyendijk	186
Pamina	2	Royal Huisman	Ted Hood Design	Pieter Beeldsnijder	194
Paraffin	4	Feadship	De Voogt	Owners/De Voogt	194
Patti Lou	4	Crescent Custom Yachts	Jack W. Sarin	Robin Rose & Associates	188
Perseus	4	Perini Navi	Perini Navi	Perini Navi	204
ReJoyce	4	Westport Shipyard	Bill Garden	Pacific Custom Interiors	212
Rivolta 90	5	Rivolta Marine	Hakan Sodergren	Rivolta Design	234
Samantha Lin	2	Halter Marine	Halter Marine	Owner/Samantha Staats	200
Savannah	1	Concordia Custom Yachts	Pedrick Yacht Designs	John Munford	134
Savannah	2	Intermarine	Intermarine	Luiz de Basto/Sally J. Ferguson	210
Serenity	3	Burger Boat Co.	Don O'Keeffe	Owners/DJ Kennedy, Douglas Richey, ASID Burger	178
Shenandoah	2	McMullen & Wing	Theodore & Ferris	Terence Disdale Design	216
Sheriff	1	Hatteras	Hatteras	Hatteras	142
Sinbad	4	Delta Marine	Delta Design Group	Duet Designs of Singapore	220
Sir Jon	2	Hatteras	Hargrave/Hatteras	Patrick Knowles Designs	226
Sis W	5	Burger Boat Co	Burger Design Team	Belden Interiors/Burger Design Team	240
Soulmate	2	Azimut	Stefano Righini	Marty Lowe Inc. Design	234
Sovereign Lady	2	Sovereign Yachts	Jack W. Sarin	Pacific Custom Interiors	240
Sovereign Lady	5	Sovereign Yachts	Ward Setzer	Sovereign Yachts	248
Stupendous	4	Destiny Yachts	Arrabito	Marshall/Weiner	228
Surprise	4	McMullen & Wing	Setzer Design Group	Setzer Design Group/Ann Motion, Sandra Johnson	234
Susanna Bella	5	Lazzara Yachts	Lazzara Yachts	Lazzara Design Studio	256
Symphony	3	Benetti	Benetti	Marty A. Lowe	186
The Boss	4	Westship	Jack W. Sarin	Westship	240
The Crowned Eagle	3	Destiny Yachts	Giovanni Arrabito	Susan Hellman-Weiner	118
Thunderball	4	Baglietto	Studio Paszkowski	Baglietto	246
Tigress	1	McQueen's Boat Works	Edwin Monk & Son	Pokela Design	148
Timoneer	3	Vitters	Dubois	John Munford	200
Tivoli	3	Proteksan/Turquoise Yachts	Vripack Yachting	Vripack Yachting/Owner	194
Ubiquitous	1	Westport Shipyard	Jack W. Sarin	Pacific Custom Interiors/Sheryl McLaughlin	154
Unforgettable	5	Royal Denship	Danyard	François Zuretti	264
Unfurled	3	Royal Huisman	German Frers	Andrew Winch	208
Valkyrie	3	Crescent Custom Yachts	Jack W. Sarin	Robin Rose & Associates	216
Varsity Jacket	1	Broward	Broward	Merrit-Knowles Design Group	162
Wehr Nuts	1	Christensen	Christensen	Robin Rose & Associates	170
Westship 140	3	Westship	Westship	Yacht Design Associates	222
Whale Song	3	Halter Marine	Halter Marine	Lou Kipp and Andrew Parker & Co	230
Wild Horses	1	Brooklin Btyrd/Rockport Marine	Joel White	Joel White	178

Directory

KEY TO CATEGORY SYMBOLS

B	Builder
BMA	Builder Marketing Agent
NA	Naval Architect
YS	Yacht Services
D	Interior Designer
BR	Yacht Broker
C	Charter Broker
O	Other

TELEPHONE NUMBERS

Please note that telephone numbers are written in International Notation, with the national code number prefixed with a '+'.

To call foreign numbers you must first dial your own country's International Access Code—i.e. 011 if you are in the United States, or 00 if you are in the UK—and omit any number within brackets. If the number is within your own country you should omit the number prefixed with a '+' and include the bracketed numbers.

A

Abeking & Rasmussen
P.O. Box 1160
Lemwerder, D-27805
Germany
Tel: +49 (0) 421 673 3531
Fax: +49 (0) 421 673 3115
info@abeking.com
B

AC.T Studio
Istanbul Mercan
Ihlamur Sok 14
Tuzla 81700, Istanbul
Turkey
Tel: +90 (0) 532 597 6124
Fax: +90 (0) 216 395 4001
actstudio@tnn.net
www.actstudio-design.com
D

Alan Andrews Yacht Design, Inc.
259 Marina Drive
Long Beach, CA 90803
Tel: (562) 594-9189
Fax: (562) 594-1859
alan@andrewsyacht.com
www.andrewsyacht.com
NA

John G. Alden Naval Architects
89 Commercial Wharf
Boston, MA 02110
Tel: (617) 227-9480
Fax: (617) 523-5465
NA

Alliance Marine, Inc.
2608 N. Ocean Blvd.
Pompano Beach, FL 33062-2955
Tel: (954) 941-5000
Fax: (954) 782-4911
BMA, BR, C
A full-service yacht brokerage specializing in large yachts, Alliance Marine, Inc. has extensive knowledge of both international and domestic markets. Alliance is the marketing agent for two European megayacht builders and is especially proud of the Alliance Marine Expedition Series of motoryachts ranging from 80ft to 175ft. They are also the worldwide distributor for the DayTripper Jet Series of high tech composite New England lobster-style boats from 40ft to 60ft.

Alliance Marine Risk Managers, Inc.
1400 Old Country Road
Westbury, NY 11590
Tel: (516) 333-7000
Toll Free: (800) 976-2676
Fax: (516) 333-9529
YS
Consultation and arrangement of insurance for large yachts worldwide.

Allied Marine
401 SW 1st Avenue
Fort Lauderdale, FL 33301
Tel: (954) 462-7424
Fax: (954) 462-0756
BR, C

Allied Richard Bertram Platinum Yacht Collection
801 Sea Breeze Blvd.
Fort Lauderdale, FL 33316
Tel: (954) 467-8405
platinum@alliedrichard
   bertram.com
www.alliedrichardbertram.com
BR

Alloy Yachts International
1 Selwood Road
Henderson
Auckland, New Zealand
Tel: +64 9 838 7350
Fax: +64 9 838 7393
mailbox@alloyyachts.co.nz
www.alloyyachts.com
B
Alloy Yachts International is recognized as one of the world's leading builders of custom-built aluminum superyachts. Alloy

Yachts can build luxury sailing yachts and motoryachts between 100ft and 180ft in length in their 60,000sqft factory.

Amels Holland BV
P.O. Box 1
Makkum, 8754 ZN
The Netherlands
Tel: +31 515 334 334
Fax: +31 515 232 719
info@amels-holland.com
www.amels-holland.com
B
With over 80 years of shipbuilding experience and shipyards in Makkum and Schelde, Amels Holland are world leaders in first-class luxury yacht construction. Makkum offers a covered dry dock of 394ft and Schelde has two dry docks at 476ft and 656ft.

Amels - Nigel Burgess
801 Seabreeze Blvd.
Bahia Mar Yachting Center
Fort Lauderdale, FL 33316
Tel: (954) 525-1090
Fax: (954) 525-0297
ftlaud@amels.nigelburgess.com
www.amels.nigelburgess.com
BMA, BR, C
Marketing arm of the Amels Shipyard in conjunction with Nigel Burgess, also specializing in the sale, purchase and charter of large yachts worldwide.

American Bow Thruster
517-A Martin Avenue
Rohnert Park , CA 94928
Tel: (707) 586-3155
Fax: (707) 586-3159
YS

American Marine Model Gallery
12 Derby Square
Salem, MA 01970
Tel: (978) 745-5777
Fax: (978) 745-5778
wall@shipmodel.com
O
The prestigious American Marine Model Gallery is located in historic Salem, Massachusetts. Here, on view, is an extensive selection of one-of-a-kind ship models built by internationally acclaimed marine model artists. Custom-made models of historic ships, contemporary vessels, and modern yachts are a specialty and may be commissioned.

Anderson Fine Scale Replicas
405 Osage Drive
Derby, KS 67037
Toll Free: (800) 314-7447
Fax: (316) 788-8904
anderent@msn.com
O

Manufacturer of museum-quality custom model replicas. Your favorite yacht, boat, or any marine vessel can be duplicated from photographs. Custom models can be created in any size or paint scheme.

Anita's Interiors, Inc.
3501 Keyser Avenue, #52
Hollywood, FL 33301
Tel: (954) 989-7500
Fax: (954) 989-0070
anitasint@aol.com
www.anitasinteriors.com
D
Specializing in interior design, interior styling, and space planning for yachts.

Antibes Yachtwear
1532 Cordova Blvd.
Fort Lauderdale, FL 33316
Tel: (954) 761-7666
Fax: (954) 779-1144
info@antibesyachtwear.com
O
Antibes Yachtwear is an American corporation that provides uniform and logo apparel to the marine industry. Our offices and warehouse are in Fort Lauderdale, Florida, but our customers are worldwide.

Apollonio Naval Architecture and Marine Engineering
1225 East Sunset Drive
Suite 514
Bellingham, WA 98226-3597
Tel: (360) 733-6859
Fax: (360) 715-9474
napollo@az.com
NA, D
Leading-edge yacht and commercial craft design. Engineering, styling, and space planning for a wide range of unique and advanced craft including catamarans, SWATHs, and hydrofoils. Licensed Professional Engineers. Specialists in hull form, ride comfort, propulsion, structure, and noise control.

Ardell Yacht & Ship Brokers
1550 SE 17th Street
Fort Lauderdale, FL 33316
Tel: (954) 525-7637
Fax: (954) 525-1292
yachts@ardell-fl.com
BR, C
With offices in Fort Lauderdale and Newport Beach, California, Ardell enjoys an excellent reputation of credibility in yacht brokerage. Ardell's first-hand knowledge of both international and domestic markets ensures confidence with a team of brokers who work well together.

Ardell Yacht & Ship Brokers
2101 West Coast Highway
Newport Beach, CA 92663
Tel: (949) 642-5735
Fax: (949) 642-9884
yachts@ardell-ca.com
BR, C

Ardeo Design, Inc.
755 Winslow Way East
Suite 301
Bainbridge Island, WA 98110
Tel: (206) 855-9027
Fax: (206) 855-9028
scott@ardeodesign.com
www.ardeodesign.com
D

Yacht Interior designer Scott Cole chose the firm's name, Ardeo Design, with his customary attention to detail. Ardeo is the Latin word for 'passion,' which describes this design team's commitment to excellence. This extends from the smallest detail to the most important element of a yacht's design: the client.

Joseph Artese Design
16003 34th Avenue NE
Seattle, WA 98155
Tel: (206) 365-4326
Fax: (206) 365-7009
artesedesign@attbi.com
www.artesedesign.com
D

ASEA Power Systems
7392 Vincent Circle
Huntington Beach, CA 92648
Tel: (714) 841-0540
Fax: (714) 841-0560
sales@aseapower.com
www.aseapower.com
O

ASEA Power Systems is a leading manufacturer of compact-lightweight Shore Power Converters, Line Voltage Regulators, Normalizing Transformers, Isolation Transformers and Switch Gear Management Controls. ASEA Power Systems offers products ranging from 8-105kVA (1 Phase) to 25-300kVA (3 Phase).

Atlantic Dry Dock Corp.
8500 Heckscher Drive
Jacksonville, FL 32226-2400
Tel: (904) 251-1507
Fax: (904) 251-3500
kwilson@atlanticmarine.com
YS

Located in Jacksonville, Florida on the St. John's River, our facility is just two miles from the Atlantic Ocean and less than one day's transit from South Florida. Atlantic offers the best-value service, high-quality craftsmanship, fast turnaround, and on-time delivery.

Atlantic Yacht & Ship
Harbour Towne Marina
850 NE 3rd Street
Dania, FL 33004
Tel: (954) 921-1500
Fax: (954) 921-1518
atlantic@bellsouth.net

The Marina at Atlantis
P.O. Box N-4777
Nassau, The Bahamas
Tel: (242) 363-6068
O

The Marina at Atlantis is a centerpiece of Atlantis, Paradise Island, a unique celebration of the legends of the lost continent of Atlantis. The marina has 63 megayacht slips accommodating yachts from 40ft to 220ft. The facilities, services, and attractions of the spectacular Atlantis resort are only steps away and fully available to all marina guests, putting the marina in a class all by itself.

Atlas Energy Systems
5101 NW 21st Avenue, Suite 520
Fort Lauderdale, FL 33309
Tel: (954) 735-6767
Fax: (954) 735-7676
mikep@atlasenergysystems.com
www.atlasenergysystems.com
YS

Atlas Energy Systems manufactures and distributes one of the most complete and extensive lines of energy products worldwide. Atlas' products include the unique ShorPOWER Frequency, Power Conversion systems and the TecPOWER Marine Electrical Switchboards.

Azimut-Benetti S.p.A
Via Martin Luther King, 9-11
10051 Avigliana
Torino, Italy
Tel: +39 (0) 0119 3161
Fax: +39 (0) 0119 367270
B

Also:

Azimut Shipyard
Via Michelle Coppino 441
Viareggio, 55049 Italy
Tel: +39 (0) 0119 3161
Fax: +39 (0) 0119 367270
B

Azimut-Benetti is the leading builder of motoryachts and one of the world's largest megayacht producers.

B

Babcock Yachts
Queens Parade
Private Bag 32902
Devonport
Auckland 9, New Zealand
Tel: +64 (0) 9 446 1999
Fax: +64 (0) 9 446 1740
yacht services@babcock.co.nz
B

Cantieri Navali Baglietto S.p.A
Viale San Bartolomeo, 414
19138, La Spezia Italy
Tel: +39 (0) 187 59831
Fax: +39 (0) 187 564765
baglietto@baglietto.com
www.baglietto.com
B

Arthur M. Barbeito & Associates
4967 SW 74th Court
Miami, FL 33155
Tel: (305) 669-3211
Fax: (305) 669-3228
D

Jonathan Quinn Barnett Ltd.
116 Vine Street
Seattle, WA 98121
Tel: (206) 322-2152
Fax: (206) 322-2153
info@jqbltd.com
www.jqbltd.com
D

Seattle-based design firm specializing in exterior and interior yacht design. The well-staffed studio provides full design services including CAD design, 3D computer modeling, interior specification/purchasing/supply, and project management.

Jon Barrett Associates
36 Green Street
Newport, RI 02840
Tel: (401) 846-8226
Fax: (401) 846-8309
BMA

Bartram & Brakenhoff LLC
2 Marina Plaza
Goat Island
Newport, RI 02840
Tel: (401) 846-7355
Fax: (401) 847-6329
bartbrak@aol.com
BMA, YS, BR, C

Bartram & Brakenhoff LLC specializes in the marketing, sales, charter, and donation of high-quality and high-caliber sailing, power, and luxury yachts (new and used). Bartram and Brakenhoff offers two locations for client convenience: Newport, Rhode Island and Fort Lauderdale, Florida.

Beard Marine Air Conditioning and Refrigeration, Inc.
624 SW 24th Street
Fort Lauderdale, FL 33315
Tel: (954) 463-2288
Fax: (954) 527-0362
info@beardmarine.com
www.beardmarine.com
YS

Beard Marine Air Conditioning and Regfrigeration, Inc. is based in Fort Lauderdale with affiliate offices in Palm Beach and Savannah. We are dedicated to designing and producing high-quality air-conditioning, refrigeration, and watermaker systems for the yachting industry.

Peter Beeldsnijder Design
Voorhaven 20-22
1135 BR
Edam, The Netherlands
Tel: +31 (0) 299 372739
Fax: +31 (0) 299 37159
beeldsnijder@pbdesign-edam.nl
NA, D

Specializing in the design of large power and sail yachts using CAD/CAM, and complete building and rebuilding projects.

Belina Interiors Inc.
4540 South Adams Street
Tacoma, WA 98409
Tel: (253) 474-0276
Fax: (253) 471-2474
info@belinainteriors.com
www.belinainteriors.com
D

Long recognized for the building and installation of yacht interiors, Belina offers diverse services to support every phase of construction. Designers' concepts are developed into approved shop drawings and then executed by craftsmen who are highly skilled in wood, veneer, metal, and upholstery.

Bell Design Group
1301 Northlake Way
Seattle, WA 98103
Tel: (206) 547-6113
Fax: (206) 547-6323
belldesign@msn.com
D

Bell Design Group provides comprehensive, state-of-the-art interior design services using computer images, 3D modeling, composite materials, and high-tech construction techniques. Founder Judy Bell-Davis has 26 years' experience as a design professional.

Benetti Shipyard
Via Michelle Coppino, 104
Viareggio, 55049 Italy
Tel: +39 (0) 0584 3821
Fax: +39 (0) 0584 396232
azimut.benetti@telcen.caen.it
B

Builders of luxury motoryachts from 115ft to 230ft.

Also:

Benetti
Le Panorama, Bloc B
57, Rue Grimaldi
MC 98000, Monaco
Tel: +377 97 77 24 44
Fax: +377 97 77 24 40
info@benettiyacht.it
B

Azimut-Benetti is the leading builder of motoryachts in the world. The Viareggio, Italy based shipyard was founded in 1873 and has been part of Azimut since 1985. The group has recently acquired the Lesben Craft and Moschini shipyards to extend its production capacity. Benetti specializes in semi-custom GRP yachts from 100ft to145ft (Tradition/Classic/Vision lines) and the fully custom steel range from 150ft to over 230ft.

Bennett Brothers Yachts
Cape Fear Marina
1701 J.E.L. Wade Drive
Wilmington, NC 28401
Tel: (910) 772-9277
Fax: (910) 772-1642
bbyachts@bellsouth.net
B, YS, BR

Bennett Brothers Yachts is a full-service repair yard with the same staff of skilled craftsmen who work on our custom-building projects. We offer fine yacht brokerage and specialize in selling world-class cruising boats, both power and sail.

Bloemsma & van Breemen
Stranwei 30
8754 Ha Makkum
The Netherlands
Tel: +31 (0) 515 231 785/9
Fax: +31 (0) 515 231 844
werf@bloemsma-vanbreeman.nl
B

Blohm & Voss GMBH

PO Box 10 0526
Hamburg, D-20004
Germany
Tel: +49 (0) 4031 198 000
Fax: +49 (0) 4031 193 333
info@blohmvoss.com
www.blohmvoss.com

B

Donald L. Blount and Associates, Inc.

1316 Yacht Drive, Suite 305
Chesapeake, VA 23320
Tel: (757) 545-2172 x214
Fax: (757) 545-8227
bblount@dlba-inc.com
www.dlba-inc.com

NA

Donald L. Blount & Associates, naval architects and marine engineers, specialize in the design of high-performance luxury motoryachts. Our services include preliminary design, contract design, and owner's representation services. The firm has continuously produced successful designs that incorporate the owner's specifications and styling requirements, while achieving classification society rules and possessing superior ride qualities.

Blubay Yachts

130 Rue d'Antibes
Cannes, 06400
France
Tel: +33 (0) 4970 62 020
Fax: +33 (0) 4970 65 497
sales@blubay.com
www.blubay.com

B

Bluewater Books & Charts

Southport Center
1481 SE 17th Street
Fort Lauderdale, FL 33316
Tel: (954) 942-2583
Fax: (954) 522-2278

O

Sylvia Bolton Design

1818 Westlake Avenue North
Suite 230
Seattle, WA 98109
Tel: (206) 217-0863
Fax: (206) 286-7633
sylvia@sbd-inc.com
www.sbd-inc.com

D

Involved in interior design and architecture for custom-built yachts, new construction, and refits. The company is based in Seattle with clients throughout the US and Europe.

Bradford Yacht Sales

1800 SE 20th Avenue, Suite 215
Fort Lauderdale, FL 33316
Tel: (954) 791-2600
Fax: (954) 791-2655
yachtinfo@bradfordyachts.com
www.bradfordyachts.com

BMA, BR, C

Our brokers and sales staff specialize in the sales and marketing of brokerage yachts, luxury charter vacations, and new construction with the highest level of professionalism.

Bray Yacht Design And Research, Ltd.

P.O. Box 75175
White Rock, BC V4B 5N4
Canada
Tel: (604) 531-8569
Fax: (604) 531-6333
www.brayyachtdesign.bc.ca

NA

Philippe Briand Yacht Design

26 Rue Saint Sauveur
1700, La Rochelle
France
Tel: +33 (0) 5 46 50 57 44
Fax: +33 (0) 5 46 50 57 94
philippebriand@compuserve.com
www.philippebriand.com

NA

Brilliant Boats

7 Transverse de la Tour
Cannes, France
Tel: +33 680 650 191
brilboats@aol.com

NA

Broward Yachts, Inc.

750 NE 7th Avenue
Dania, FL 33304
Tel: (954) 925-8118
Fax: (954) 927-4200

B

Custom aluminum yacht builder, 85ft to 155ft.

Luke Brown & Associates

1500 Cordova Road # 200
Fort Lauderdale, FL 33316
Tel: (954) 525-6617
Fax: (954) 525-6626
sales@lukebrown.com
www.lukebrown.com

BR, C

Burger Boat Company

1811 Spring Street
Manitowoc, WI 54220
Tel: (920) 686-5100
Fax: (920) 686-5101
www.burgerboat.com

B

Also:

Burger Yacht Sales

17th Street Quay
1535 SE 17th Street, Suite 107
Fort Lauderdale, FL 33316
Tel: (954) 463-1400
Fax: (954) 463-3100
bys@burgerboat.com

BR

Nigel Burgess

Monte-Carlo Sun
74 Blvd. d'Italie
Monte Carlo, 98000
Monaco
Tel: +377 (0) 97 97 81 21
Fax: +377 (0) 97 97 81 25
monaco@nigelburgess.com
www.nigelburgess.com

BR, C

Also:

Nigel Burgess Ltd.

16/17 Pall Mall
London, SW1Y 5LU
United Kingdom
Tel: +44 (0) 20 7766 4300
Fax: +44 (0) 20 7766 4329
london@nigelburgess.com
www.nigelburgess.com

BMA, NA, YS, BR, C

Specialists in the sale, purchase and charter of the world's finest large yachts. Full management, technical services and new construction also a specialty. Marketing agents for the Amels shipyard.

Felix Buytendijk Yacht Design

Uiterdijk 13
4011 ET Zoelen
The Netherlands
Tel: +31 (0) 344 682 596
Fax: +31 (0) 344 682 595
fbdesign@worldonline.nl

D

Interior and exterior styling of sail and motoryachts.

C

C&L Insurance

7301 W. Palmetto Park Road
Suite 101 C
Boca Raton, FL 33433
Tel: (561) 395-3730
Fax: (561) 395-4239
info@clinsurance.com
www.clinsurance.com

YS

Marine insurance including yachts, marinas, boat builders, shipyards, dealers, and marine-related industries.

Camper & Nicholsons International

450 Royal Palm Way
Palm Beach, FL 33480
Tel: (561) 655-2121
Fax: (561) 655-2202
info@pal.cnyachts.com

YS, BR, C

CNI's global office network delivers its clients an unrivaled range of services in the most professional, ethical, and discreet manner possible. CNI is a full-service company with emphasis on larger yachts. CNI's divisions interact to provide complete customer satisfaction.

Also:

Camper & Nicholsons International

The Courts
141 Alton Road
Miami Beach, FL 33139
Tel: (305) 604-9191
Fax: (305) 604-9196
info@mia.cnyachts.com

YS, BR, C

Also:

Camper & Nicholsons International

Les Princes
7 Avenue d'Ostende
Monte Carlo, MC 98000
Monaco
Tel: +377 (0) 97 97 77 00
Fax: +377 (0) 93 50 25 08
info@mon.cnyachts.com

YS, BR, C

Also:

Camper & Nicholsons International

Av. San Jeronimo 273
Local 21
Suite MX 067-382
Tizapan San Angel, CP 10908
Mexico
Tel: +525 (0) 281 4545
Fax: +525 (0) 281 5926
al@mia.cnyachts.com

YS, BR, C

Also:

Camper & Nicholsons International

London, W1J 6QH
United Kingdom
Tel: +44 (0) 20 7491 2950
Fax: +44 (0) 7629 2068
info@loncnyachts.com

YS, BR, C

Cantieri di Pisa SpA

Via Aurelia Sud
Km. 334
Pisa, 56121 Italy
Tel: +39 (0) 50 220 551
Fax: +39 (0) 50 500 799

B

Cantieri di Pisa builds fast motoryachts known with the brand name of AKHIR.

Cape Horn Trawler Corporation

One Port Street East
Port Credit, ON L5G 4N1
Canada
Tel: (905) 274-9999
Fax: (905) 274-9998
psever@thecapehorn.com
www.thecapehorn.com

B

We build the strongest, safest, luxury trans-ocean trawler yachts in the world.

Tony Castro Ltd.

Rio House
76 Satchell Lane
Hamble, Southampton
Hampshire, SO31 4HL
United Kingdom
Tel: +44 (0) 23 8045 4722
Fax: +44 (0) 23 8045 6011
tonycastro@tonycastro.co.uk
www.tonycastro.co.uk

NA

Catepillar Inc. Engine Division

PO Box 610
Mossville, IL 61552-0610
Tel: (309) 578-3106
Fax: (309) 578-2559
cat-power@cat.com

O

Catepillar has been manufacturing marine diesels since 1939.

Cavendish White

Lutidine House
Newark Lane, Ripley
Surrey, GU23 6BS
United Kingdom
Tel: +44 (0) 207 381 7600
Fax: +44 (0) 207 381 7601
mike@cavendishwhite.com
www.cavendishwhite.com

YS, C

C.B.I. Navi SpA
Via Giannessi-Via Pescatori
55049 Viareggio (Lucca), Italy
Tel: +39 (0) 584 388 192
Fax: +39 (0) 584 388 060
info@cbinavi.com
www.cbinavi.com
B
CBI Navi SpA is an Italian shipyard that specializes in the building of displacement motoryachts made of steel and aluminum. The construction is according to the rules of most outstanding registers such as Lloyd's Register of Shipping and Registro Italiano Navale, the compliance to the strict MCA code and the achievement of the R.I.N.A. Comfort Class and reflect the style of C.B.I. Navi aimed at the research of the maximum design and construction quality.

Cheoy Lee Shipyards North America
Bahia Mar Yachting Center
801 Seabreeze Blvd.
Fort Lauderdale, FL 33316
Tel: (954) 527-0999
Fax: (954) 527-2887
info@cheoyleena.com
www.cheoyleena.com
B, BMA, BR
New yacht construction, custom, and production up to 200ft built in FRP, alloy steel, or a combination thereof.

Christensen Shipyards
4400 SE Columbia Way
Vancouver, WA 98661
Tel: (360) 695-3238
Fax: (360) 695-3252
info@christensenyachts.com
www.christensenyachts.com
B
Christensen has established itself as the world leader by building more composite megayachts over 120ft than any other shipyard in the world. All are built onsite and comply with ABS classification, AMS, and European MCS.
Also:
Christensen Shipyards, Ltd.
Fort Lauderdale, FL
Tel: (954) 766-8888
Fax: (954) 766-8889
sales@christensenyachts.com
BR

CNB America, Inc.
2246 SE 17th Street
Fort Lauderdale, FL 33316
Tel: (954) 763-9891
Fax: (954) 763-9851
cnbusa@gate.net
BMA, BR
US representation for the CNB Yard (Construction Navale Bordeaux), builder of aluminum and composite yachts 70ft to 150ft. Specializes in the sale, management, and refit of sailing yachts 60ft+.

Also:
CNB
162 Quai De Brazza
Bordeaux, 33100
France
Tel: +33 (0) 557 80 8550
Fax: +33 (0) 557 80 8551
cnb@cnb.fr
B, D
In 1996, CNB became the custom yachts and work boats division of the Beneteau Group including all custom naval construction such as motor and sailing yachts for 60ft to 150ft, passenger ferries, fishing boats, and catamarans.

Codecasa
Via Amendola
Viareggio, 55049 Italy
Tel: +39 (0) 0584 383 221
Fax: +39 (0) 0584 383 531
info@codecasayachts.com
www.codecasayachts.com
B
Since 1825 the Codecasa Shipyard has grown into a group comprised of Codecasa Ugo SpA, Codecasa Due SpA, and Codecasa Tre SpA. Using the most sophisticated modern technologies available, Codecasa produces luxury motoryachts of the highest quality.

Angela Connery Yacht Charters
P.O. Box 8512
Salem, MA 01971
Tel: (978) 741-4448
Toll Free: (877) 741-4448
Fax: (978) 741-7775
acyc@comcast.net
C

Guy Couach
Gujan Mestras, 33470
France
Tel: +33 (0) 55 622 3550
Fax: +33 (0) 55 666 0820
couach@couach.com
www.couach.com
B
Since 1897, Guy Couach shipyard has been building high-tech custom made yachts from 53ft to 125ft. International reference of French luxury, Guy Couach yachts are considered the haute couture in the yachting world.

Cox Marine
12 Goodwin Street
Newport, RI 02840
Tel: (401) 845-9777
Fax: (401) 845-2666
mj@coxmarine.net
www.coxmarine.net
C
Cox Marine has two main focuses: charter broker for power and sail yachts in cruising destinations worldwide and charter management for a select group of large luxury-crewed charter yachts.

Crescent Custom Yachts, Inc.
11580 Mitchell Road
Richmond, BC V6V 1T7
Canada
Tel: (604) 324-1333
Fax: (604) 323-7427
gtyachts@bellsouth.net
B, BMA, YS
Crescent Custom Yachts is a manufac-

turer of custom fiberglass motoryachts from 95ft to 140ft. As a builder of custom yachts, Crescent has been called upon to build fully classed vessels by both the American Bureau of Shipping and Bureau Veritas.

CRN SpA
Ferretti Group
Via Mattei, n. 26
60125, Ancona Italy
Tel: +39 (0) 071 5011 111
Fax: +39 (0) 071 200 008
info@crn-yacht.com
www.crn-yacht.com
B
With a fleet of 115 megayachts, CRN shipyard (located in Ancona since 1963) has been one of the principal world builders of luxury yachts in steel and aluminum. Recognizable for their characteristic bow, CRN yachts have always been an undisputed symbol of luxury and prestige. Their unmistakable 'family feeling' has fascinated the most famous names among the international industrial community and many royal families.

Crown Ltd.
1001 Staley Avenue
Savannah, GA 31405
Tel: (912) 352-0715
Fax: (912) 352- 0726
malcolm@crownltd.com
www.crownltd.com
O
Since 1981, Crown Ltd. has been the world leader in design and fabrication of helm chairs, stools, table tops, and pedestals for the megayacht industry. Our products are the perfect blend of hand crafted quality and beautiful styling that can be customized.

Custom Boat Blinds, Inc.
3470 WSW 15th Street
Deerfield Beach, FL 33442
Tel: (954) 421-8116
Fax: (954) 421-8117
boatblinds@boatblinds.com
www.boatblinds.com
YS
World leader in custom wood and exotic-wood blinds and plantation shutters for yachts. AC Louvers are in exotic wood with an exclusive patented system. Manufacturer for Palmer Johnson, Bertram, Ronin, Buddy-Davis, Broward, etc. with offices in Sao Paulo, Brazil and Nice, France.

D

Butch Dalrymple-Smith
Chantier Naval
13600 La Ciotat
France
Tel: +33 (0) 442 980 918
Fax: +33 (0) 442 980 919
mail@butchdesign.com
www.butchdesign.com
D
Design and engineering of sailing yachts with special expertise in large sailing yachts and classic replicas. Technical management of refits and classic restorations.

Rikki Davis Inc.
1323 SE 17th Street, Suite 209
Fort Lauderdale, FL 33316
Tel: (954) 761-3237
Fax: (954) 764-0497
charter@rikkidavis.com
www.rikkidavis.com
C

Luiz de Basto Designs, Inc.
444 Brickell Avenue, Suite 928
Miami, FL 33131
Tel: (305) 373-1500
Fax: (305) 377-0900
luizbasto@aol.com
www.luizdebasto.com
NA, D
Luiz de Basto Designs is a full service yacht design firm based in Miami. The company specializes in the design of luxury yachts - custom, production, and commercial boats. From the hull design to the space planning, exterior styling and interior design and décor, creativity and excellency are the main consideration, always with a constant awareness of function.

Guido de Groot Design
Hogewoerd 122
2311 HT Leiden
The Netherlands
Tel: +31 (0) 71 566 3040
Fax: +31 (0) 71 566 3039
info@guidodegroot.com
www.guidodegroot.com
NA, D
Guido de Groot Design specializes in the design of innovative interiors and exteriors for both luxury motoryachts and sailing yachts.

Roel de Groot Design
Vine Cottage, 9 West Street
Titchfield, Hampshire, PO14 4DH
United Kingdom
Tel: +44 13 2984 3201
Fax: +44 13 2984 3203
roel@rdgdesign.co.uk
www.rdgdesign.co.uk
NA

De Voogt Naval Architects
PO Box 5238
2000 GE Haarlem
The Netherlands
Tel: +31 (0) 23 524 7000
Fax: +31 (0) 23 524 8639
NA

DeJong & Lebet, Inc.
1734 Emerson Street
Jacksonville, FL 32207
Tel: (904) 399-3673
Fax: (904) 399-1522
info@dejongandlebet.com
www.dejongandlebet.com
NA
DeJong and Lebet, Inc. is a full-service naval architecture company best known for its passenger vessel designs. The 31-year old company also designs large yachts and yacht conversions. SWATH vessels are a specialty.

Delta Marine

1608 South 96th Street
Seattle, WA 98108
Tel: (206) 763-2383
Fax: (206) 762-2627
mjones@deltamarine.com
www.deltamarine.com

B

As specialists in large yacht (200ft+) fiberglass and metal construction, Delta combines new technologies and creative ideas with proven building techniques. All yachts are custom-designed, engineered, and constructed on-site in full-service facilities including mechanical, electrical, composite, metal, cabinet, and paint workshops.

Also:

Delta Marine International

P.O. Box 22070
Fort Lauderdale, FL 33335
Tel: (954) 791-0909
Fax: (954) 321-8145

B

Derecktor Shipyards, Florida

775 Taylor Lane
Dania, FL 33004
Tel: (954) 920-5756
Fax: (954) 925-1146
pattasloan@aol.com

YS

Also:

Derecktor Shipyards

311 East Boston Post Road
Mamaroneck, NY 10543
Tel: (914) 698-5022
Fax: (914) 698-4641
general@derecktor.com
www.derecktor.com

B

Since 1947, Derecktor has been building yachts of the highest quality. From the America's Cup Racers to today's superyachts, Derecktor-built yachts can be found all over the world.

Design Alliance Ltd.

3911 Southridge
West Vancouver, BC V7V 3H9
Canada
Tel: (604) 926-9408
Fax: (604) 926-9405
designalliance@home.com

D

Design Alliance's activities cover the following areas: interior design, exterior design and styling, construction consultation, concept development, new and refit yachts and charter vessels, and on occasion will take on residential commissions.

Design Q Limited

60 Heming Road
Washford, Redditch, B98 0EA
United Kingdom
Tel: +44 (0) 15 2750 1499
Fax: +44 (0) 15 2751 5314
mail@designq.co.uk
www.designq.co.uk

D

A visionary design consultancy whose pedigree comes from the automotive industry. They offer premium interior design for superyachts and corporate jets.

Design Unlimited

Lakeside Studio
Carron Row Farm
Segensworth Road - Titchfield
Hampshire, PO15 5DZ
United Kingdom
Tel: +44 (0) 13 2984 7712
Fax: +44 (0) 13 2984 1068
info@designunlimited.net
www.designunlimited.net

D

DETCO Marine
(Sterling Coatings)

Box 1246
Newport Beach, CA 92659
Toll Free: (800) 845-0023
Fax: (949) 548-5986
we@detcomarine.com
www.detcomarine.com

YS, O

DETCO/STERLING markets premier linear/polyurethane coatings, crystal varnish, and caulking compounds worldwide for megayacht application. High gloss, gloss retention, and primers for every surface and product highlights.

Detroit Diesel Corporation

13400 Outer Drive West
Detroit, MI 48239-4001
Tel: (313) 592-5000
Fax: (313) 592-5137

O

Detroit Diesel is engaged in the design, manufacture, sale, and service of heavy-duty diesel and alternative fuel engines, automotive diesel engines, and engine-related products. The company offers a complete line of engines from 22 to 13,000 horsepower for the on-highway, off-road, and automotive markets and is a QS-9000 certified company.

Devonport Yachts

Devonport Royal Dockyard
Devonport, Plymouth, PL1 4SG
United Kingdom
Tel: +44 (0) 17 5232 3311
Fax: +44 (0) 17 5232 3247
yachts@devonport.co.uk
www.devonport.co.uk

B

Terence Disdale Design

31 The Green
Richmond, Surrey, TW9 1LX
United Kingdom
Tel: +44 (0) 20 8940 1452
Fax: +44 (0) 20 8940 5964
terencedisdale@terence
disdale.co.uk
www.terencedisdaledesign.co.uk

D

Doyle Superyacht -Division of Doyle Sailmakers

89 Front Street
Marblehead, MA 01945
Tel: (781) 639-1490
Fax: (781) 639-1497
robbie@doylesuperyacht.com
www.doylesuperyacht.com

O

Well-known for its innovative expertise in the design and production of super-yacht sales, Doyle Superyacht Division focuses exclusively on the engineering, design, material, and servicing challenges of yachts 75ft and larger.

Dubois Naval Architects

Beck Farm, Sowely
Lymington, Hampshire, SO41 5SR
United Kingdom
Tel: +44 (0) 15 9062 6666
Fax: +44 (0) 15 9062 6696
design@duboisyachts.com
www.duboisyachts.com

NA

Also:

Dubois Yachts

Beck Farm, Sowely
Lymington, Hampshire, SO41 5SR
United Kingdom
Tel: +44 (0) 15 9062 6688
Fax: +44 (0) 15 9062 6696
yachts@duboisyachts.com
www.duboisyachts.com

BR, C

We specialize in the sales and charter of Dubois-designed yachts, power and sail.

Dahlgren Duck & Associates

2554 Tarpley, Suite 110
Carrollton, TX 75006
Tel: (972) 478-5991
Fax: (972) 478-5996
dda@dahlgrenduck.com
www.dahlgrenduck.com

YS

DD&A specializes in special dinner services for the yachting industry that include china, crystal, flatware, and table, bed and bath linens. Also, custom sun care and bath care amenities. DD&A represents most of the world's finest manufacturers, as well as highly skilled artisans in Europe.

E

Edmiston & Company

62 St. James's Street
London, SW1A 1LY
United Kingdom
Tel: +44 (0) 20 7495 5151
Fax: +44 (0) 20 7495 5150
london@edmistoncompany.com
www.edmistoncompany.com

BR, C

Also:

Edmiston & Company

La Panoramo
57, Rue Grimaldi
MC 9800 Monaco
Tel: +377 93 30 54 44
Fax: +377 93 30 55 33
monaco@edmistoncompany.com
www.edmistoncompany.com

BR, C

Elegant Quarters, Ltd.

5776 Marine Drive
West Vancouver, BC V7W 2S2
Canada
Tel: (604) 921-6796
Fax: (604) 921-8719
elegantquarters@telus.net

D

Established in 1990, the company provides complete interior design for the luxury yacht market. Led by the vision of its founder, Jane Morrison, the company continues to provide its clients with style, service, and value in the completion of yacht interiors whether it be a new build or refit on the West Coast of Canada.

Also:

EQ Audio Video

5740 Telegraph Trail
West Vancouver, BC V7W 1R2
Canada
Tel: (604) 921-1937
Fax: (604) 921-8719
elegantqav@telus.net

O

A division of Elegant Quarters, Ltd., EQ Audio Video designs, supplies, and installs integrated electronic systems for entertainment and security. The company specializes in custom systems for motor vessels in both commercial and luxury yacht markets, combining the latest technology with Old World craftsmanship.

Ivan Erdevicki Naval Architecture & Yacht Design

400–1200 West Pender Street
Vancouver, BC V6E 2S9
Canada
Tel: (604) 879-0363
Fax: (604) 632-0363
ivan@ivanerdevicki.com
www.ivanerdevicki.com

NA

Espinosa, Inc.

1320 South Federal Hwy.
Suite 216
Stuart, FL 34994
Tel: (772) 287-4925
Fax: (772) 287-4858
info@espinosainc.com
www.espinosainc.com

D, O

Espinosa, Inc. is recognized worldwide as one of the leading yacht stylists and interior designers in the megayacht arena. The firm specializes in the styling, interior design, and refurbishing of large yachts as well as the design of production yachts.

F

Falcon Yachts srl

Via Petrarca
55049, Viareggio Italy
Tel: +39 (0) 584 388 027
Fax: +39 (0) 584 383 412
info@falconyachts.com
www.falconyachts.com

B

Farr Design

613 Third Street
Suite 20
P.O. Box 4964
Annapolis, MD 21403-0964
Tel: (410) 267-0780
Fax: (410) 268-0553
info@farrdesign.com
www.farrdesign.com

D

Feadship

P.O. Box 5238
2000 GE
Haarlem
The Netherlands
Tel: +31 (0) 23 5247000
Fax: +31 (0) 23 5248639
info@feadship.nl
www.feadship.nl

B, NA

Designers and builders of the most perfect luxury yachts in the world.

Also:

Feadship America
801 Seabreeze Blvd.
Bahia Mar
Fort Lauderdale, FL 33316
Tel: (954) 761-1830
Fax: (954) 761-3412
feadship@ix.netcom.com
BMA

Ferretti Group USA
1535 SE 17th Street
Fort Lauderdale, FL 33316
Tel: (954) 525-4550
Fax: (954) 525-7451
www.ferrettigroupusa.com
BMA

Also:

Ferretti Custom Line
Via Ansaldo 5
Forli, 47100 Italy
Tel: +39 (0) 543 474 411
Fax: +39 (0) 543 782 410
www.ferretti-yachts.com
B

Tom Fexas Yacht Design, Inc.
1320 South Federal Highway
Suite 104
Stuart, FL 34994
Tel: (772) 287-6558
Fax: (772) 287-6810
D

Filtration Concepts, Inc.
2226 South Fairview
Santa Ana, CA 92704
Tel: (714) 850-0123
Fax: (714) 850-0955
info@filtrationconcepts.com
www.filtrationconcepts.com
O

Superyacht and commercial applications to 26,275gpd. All stainless steel high pressure pumps and fittings - the highest rated pressure vessels in the marine industry.

**Fipa Italiana Yachts/
Maiora Yachts**
Via Sarzanese - Piano
Quercion Massarosa, 55054
Italy
Tel: +39 (0) 0584 93353
Fax: +39 (0) 0584 93118
info@maiora.net
www.maiora.net
B

FIPA Italiana Yachts builds VTR M/Y Maiora from 65ft in length to 121ft in length. The care for detail and the possibility of completely personalizing the inner rooms make these crafts unique with an unmistakable style.

First New England Financial
1600 SE 17th Street
Suite 300
Fort Lauderdale, FL 33316
Tel: (954) 763-1089
Toll Free: (800) 380-6644
Fax: (954) 763-1055
O

First New England Financial is one of the nation's leaders in marine financing. We have been an active participant for over 25 years and have assisted buyers in the purchase of over one billion dollars in pleasure boat transactions.

Flagship Marine
2427 SE Dixie Highway
Stuart, FL 34996
Tel: (561) 283-1609
Fax: (561) 283-4611
email@flagshipmarine.com
www.flagshipmarine.com
YS

Manufacturer of marine air-conditioning, alarm systems, CCTV, and marine pumps. The Flagship Marine air-conditioning systems are the quietest, most efficient, and easiest to start that are available and are standard issue for the US and Canadian Coast Guard survival craft, the 47 MLB.

Fontaine Design Group
92 Maritime Drive
Portsmouth, RI 02871
Tel: (401) 682-9101
Fax: (401) 682-9102
inquiries@fontaine
    designgroup.com
www.fontainedesigngroup.com
NA

Francis Design Ltd.
12 Regents Wharf
All Saints Street
London, N1 9RL
United Kingdom
Tel: +44 (0) 207 923 5360
Fax: +44 (0) 207 923 5361
francis@francisdesign.com
www.francisdesign.com
NA, D

Specializes in naval architecture and styling on high-quality and innovative power and sailing yachts.

Vic Franck's Boat Company
1109 N. Northlake Way
Seattle, WA 98103
Tel: (206) 632-7000
Fax: (206) 632-0627
B, YS

Founded in 1926, the company is now being run by the third generation of the Franck family. Their expertise is building and repairing wood and fiberglass boats.

Fraser Yachts Worldwide
180 SE 10th Avenue Suite 400
Fort Lauderdale, FL 33316
Tel: (954) 463-0600
Fax: (954) 763-1053
info@fraseryachts.com
www.fraseryachts.com
BR, C

Also:

Fraser Yachts Worldwide
3471 Via Lido Suite 200
Newport Beach, CA 92663
Tel: (949) 673-5252
Fax: (949) 673-8795
info@frasernb.com
BR, C, O

Also:

Fraser Yachts Worldwide
320 Harbor Drive
Sausalito, CA 94965
Tel: (415) 332-5311
Fax: (415) 332-7036
info@frasernb.com
BR, C

Also:

Fraser Yachts Worldwide
9, Avenue d'Ostende
Bloc C, 5th Floor
98000 MC
Monaco
Tel: +377 (0) 93 10 0495
Fax: +377 (0) 93 10 0491/97
davidl@fraseryachts.com
www.fraseryachts.com
BR, C

Also:

Fraser Yachts
2353 Shelter Island Drive
San Diego, CA 92106
Tel: (619) 225-0588
Fax: (619) 225-1325
info@frasersd.com
BR, C

Also:

Fraser Yachts Worldwide
1500 Westlake Avenue North
Suite 1300
Seattle, WA 98109
Tel: (206) 382-9494
Fax: (206) 382-9480
BR, C

Fredericks/Power & Sail
16 Rainbow Falls
Irvine, CA 92612
Tel: (949) 854-2696
Fax: (949) 854-4598
fredericks-p-s@att.net
YS, BR

Specialize in brokerage of yachts, both power and sail, as well as project coordination and management for new construction.

**Freeman Marine
Equipment, Inc.**
28336 Hunter Creek Road
Gold Beach, OR 97444
Tel: (541) 247-7078
Fax: (541) 247-2114
info@freemanmarine.com
www.freemanmarine.com
O

Freeman Marine is recognized worldwide as the leader in the design and manufacture of marine closures, supplying premium quick-acting hatches and custom lens hatches, as well as custom and standard portlights, windows, and doors. Freeman's broad product line includes hinged weather-tight and water-tight single, Dutch and French doors, as well as pantograph doors.

Ken Freivokh Design
Ash Studio
Crocker Hill Fareham
Hampshire, PO17 5DP
United Kingdom
Tel: +44 (0) 13 2983 2514
Fax: +44 (0) 13 2983 3326
all@freivokh.com
www.freivokh.com
D

Styling and interior design studio specializing in the highest-quality motor and sailing superyachts.

Carl French Yacht Sales
901 Fairview Avenue North, Suite 150
Seattle, WA 98109
Tel: (206) 223-9993
BR

German Frers
Guido 1926 - 1st Floor
1119, Buenos Aires
Argentina
Tel: +54 (0) 11 4806 4806
Fax: +54 (0) 11 4801 0423
gfrers@germanfrers.net
www.germanfrers.com
NA

Also:

German Frers
Via S Paolo 1
20121, Milan Italy
Tel: +39 (0) 2 8646 5417
Fax: +39 (0) 2 8646 5464
debfrers@compuserve.com
NA

Internationally known naval architectural practice, fast expanding from racing craft into the largest cruising superyachts.

FRY Associates, Inc. (FRYCO)
5420 Waddell Hollow Road
Franklin, TN 37064-9422
Tel: (615) 591-8455
Fax: (615) 591-8485
frycomar@aol.com
NA

FRYCO designs vessels up to 300ft and specializes in megayachts. FRYCO's founder, Ed Fry's building background assures practical, economic designs with emphasis placed on reliability and serviceability for their worldwide clientele.

G

Galaxy
277 Fairfield Road
Fairfield, NJ 07004
Tel: (973) 575-3440
Fax: (973) 575-5253
YS, D

Custom manufacturer and installer of premium quality glass, mirror, metal, and stone products.

Gerard's Service en Mer
The Bahia Mar Yachting Center
801 Seabreeze Blvd.
Fort Lauderdale, FL 33316
Tel: (954) 523-0465
Fax: (954) 523-6156
gerards@mindspring.com
YS

Gerard's Service en Mer is the answer for one-stop shopping when it comes to outfitting a yacht with products such as china, crystal, cutlery, bed, bath and table linens, or a specialty service item. Gerard's has assembled and currently showcases and catalogs the finest products available from over 150 manufacturers worldwide such as Baccarat, Lalique, Christofle, Hermes & Saint Louis, to name a few.

Gilman Yacht Sales, Inc.
1212A US Highway One
North Palm Beach, FL 33408
Tel: (561) 626-1790
Fax: (561) 626-5870
palmbeach@gilmanyachts.com
BMA, BR

We are the exclusive East Coast Distributor for Horizon America.

Also:

Gilman Yachts of Fort Lauderdale, Inc.
The Quay
1535 SE 17th Street Suite 103
Fort Lauderdale, FL 33316
Tel: (954) 525-8112
Fax: (954) 459-9997
lauderdale@gilmanyachts.com
www.gilmanyachts.com
BMA, BR

Also:

Gilman Yacht Sales of Maryland, Inc.
Baltimore Marine Center
2736 Lighthouse Point East
Baltimore, MD 21224
Tel: (410) 276-4803
Fax: (410) 276-4813
baltimore@gilmanyachts.com
www.gilmanyachts.com
BMA, BR

Global Power Systems
801 Hailey Street
Ardmore, OK 73401
Tel: (206) 301-0515
Fax: (206) 301-0660
YS
We manufacture voltage, phase, and frequency converters in sizes for 8-120KVA, single or three-phase AC power.

GMC Marine Ltd.
Seestr.15
Kilchberg-Zurich
CH 8802 Switzerland
Tel: +41 (0) 1715 0400
Fax: +41 (0) 1715 0480
gmc@pop.agri.ch
NA, YS, D, BR, C
Yacht consultants for sale and charter of megayachts worldwide. New building supervision, insurance surveyors. Consultants for yacht designs and interior decoration.

Gobbi Shipyard
29025 Saraino di Gropparello
Piacenza, Italy
Tel: +39 (0) 0523 854711
Fax: +39 (0) 0523 858223
marketing@gobbiboats.com
www.gobbiboats.com
B
Builders of express cruisers since 1968 and recently acquired by Azimut-Benetti.

Gary Grant (AMS) Ltd.
218 Main Street
Suite 302
Kirkland, WA 98033
Tel: (425) 827-2643
Fax: (425) 822-1140
D

Timothy Graul Marine Design
211 North Third Avenue
P.O. Box 290
Sturgeon Bay, WI 54235
Tel: (920) 743-5092
Fax: (920) 743-7936
NA
TGMD serves owners by designing able, no-nonsense yachts with a commercial/workboat heritage. Don't come for swoopy styling, but for yards and owners who demand rugged good looks and dependability.

Greenbay Marine
4, Pioneer Sector 1
628416 Singapore
Tel: +65 (0) 861 4178
Fax: +65 (0) 861 8109
greenbay@singnet.com.sg
B, NA
Quality, uniqueness, value for the money, and innovative solutions are only a small part of the Greenbay total expertise package. Plus, Greenbay Marine now provides the advantages of a dedicated building facility in China.

GTH Design Techniques, Inc.
17791 Fjord Drive, Suite Z
Poulsbo, WA 98370
Tel: (360) 779-1909
Fax: (360) 779-6133
info@gthdesign.com
www.gthdesign.com
D
GTH Design Techniques, Inc. is a full service interior design firm marketing services to the marine industry and owners of fine yachts. GTH Services include interior architecture, space planning, styling, joiner detailing, systems integrations, lighting design, exterior styling and detailing, and supply of finishes, furnishings, materials, and accessories.

H

Hall of Fame Marina
435 Seabreeze Blvd.
Fort Lauderdale, FL 33316
Tel: (954) 764-3975
Fax: (954) 779-3658
hfmarina@bellsouth.net
YS
Open slip dockage for boats from 40ft to 135ft with 50amp, 220v and 100amp 208v single and three-phase electricity. We accommodate up to 9ft depth and are adjacent to the beach and shopping.

Hallberg-Rassy Varvs AB
Hällavägen 6
SE-474 31, Ellös
Sweden
Tel: +46 304 54 800
Fax: +46 304 513 31
www.hallberg-rassy.com
B

Halter Marine Group
13085 Seaway Road
Gulfport, MS 39503
Tel: (252) 638-5550
Fax: (252) 638-6844
B

Harbour Towne Marina
801 NE Third Street
Dania Beach, FL 33004
Tel: (954) 926-0300
Fax: (954) 922-5485
hrbrtowne@aol.com
YS, D, BR
Just south of Port Everglades Inlet in South Florida, Harbour Towne is easily accessible and can accommodate yachts up to 150ft. There are complete marine storage facilities, extending from rack storage for 450 boats, maintenance and repair, to bottom work, rigging, painting, refinishing, custom woodwork, and engine service.

Hargrave Custom Yachts
1887 West State Road 84
Fort Lauderdale, FL 33315
Tel: (954) 463-0555
Fax: (954) 463-8621
info@hargrave-usa.com
www.hargrave-usa.com
B, NA

Hatteras Custom Yacht Sales
350 SW Monterey Road
Stuart, FL 34994
Tel: (561) 220-0707
Fax: (561) 220-3002
C
Sale of new and brokerage Hatteras yachts.

Also:

Hatteras
110 North Glenburnie Road
New Bern, NC 28560
Tel: (252) 633-3101
Fax: (252) 633-2046
B

Headhunter
4100 Ravenswood Road
Fort Lauderdale, FL 33312
Tel: (954) 581-6996
Fax: (954) 587-0403
YS
Manufacturer of Royal Flush™ toilets, Tidal Wave™ sewage treatment systems, and Mach 5™ fluid monitors for fuel and water. Headhunter is the only manufacturer to address the complete sanitation system, offering design and support during new construction and onboard field support after delivery.

Heesen Yachts
P.O. Box 8
5340 AA Oss
The Netherlands
Tel: +31 (0) 412 66 55 44
Fax: +31 (0) 412 66 55 66
info@heesenyachts.nl
www.heesenyachts.nl
B
Builder of durable high-quality yachts with exclusive styling.

Heli d.d.
Sv. Polikarpa 8
HR-52100, Pula
Croatia
Tel: +385 52 37 55 00
Fax: +385 52 37 55 10
info@heliyachts.com
www.heliyachts.com
B
Build and repair motoryachts and sailing yachts in steel and aluminum.

Also:

Heliyachts International SA
Via Motta 34
CH-6900, Lugano
Switzerland
Tel: +41 91 924 99 50
Fax: +41 91 924 99 51
info@heliyachts.com
www.heliyachts.com
B

Hideaway Marina
599 South Federal Highway
Pompano Beach, FL 33062
Tel: (954) 943-3200
Fax: (954) 943-9775
p.gaudreau@hideawayyachts.com
www.hideawayyachts.com
BR
US distributor for Cantieri di Pisa.

Hinckley Company
130 Shore Road
Southwest Harbor, ME 04679
Tel: (207) 244-5531
Fax: (207) 244-9833
marketing@hinckleyyachts.com
www.hinckleyyachts.com
B, YS, BR
Builder of custom and semi-custom power and sailing yachts that marry state-of-the-art boatbuilding techniques with the finest traditional woodworking.

HMY Yacht Sales
817 NE 3rd Street, Suite 1
Dania Beach, FL 33004
Tel: (954) 926-0400
Fax: (954) 921-2543
hmyyachtsales@att.net
BR
HMY has been serving the yachting world from South Florida since 1979. In addition to brokerage sales, HMY is a new boat dealer for Cabo, Post and Viking Yachts, Viking Sports Cruisers, Cigarette by Otam, and San Lorenzo American Series.

Also:

HMY Yacht Sales
24 Patriot Point Road
Mt. Pleasant, SC 29464
Tel: (843) 971-2555
Fax: (843) 971-2508
hmysc@infoave.net
YS, BR

Also:

HMY Yacht Sales
2401 PGA Blvd. Suite 182
Palm Beach Gardens, FL 33410
Tel: (561) 775-6000
Fax: (561) 775-6006
hmypg@hmyyachtsales.com
www.hmyyachtsales.com
BR

Hodgdon Yachts
P.O. Box 505
10 Church Street
East Boothbay, ME 04554
Tel: (207) 633-4194
Fax: (207) 633-3703
info@hodgdonyachts.com
www.hodgdonyachts.com
B

Ron Holland Design
28 Lr. O'Connell Street
Kinsale County Cork,
Ireland
Tel: +353 (0) 21 477 4866
Fax: +353 (0) 21 477 4808
info@ronhollanddesign.com
www.ronhollanddesign.com
NA
Designers of high-performance cruising yachts.

Holland Jachtbouw
Vredweg 32B
150 5HH
Saandam, The Netherlands
Tel: +31 (0) 75 6149 133
Fax: +31 (0) 75 6149 135
B

Jeff Homchick, Inc.
1605 South 93rd
Building-E, Unit P
Seattle, WA 98108
Tel: (206) 762-3933
Fax: (206) 762-3974
YS
Our company specializes in composite stone fabrication for yachts and aircraft including carbon fiber, honeycomb, and fiberglass-backed stone composite.

Huckins Yacht Corporation
3482 Lakeshore Blvd.
Jacksonville, FL 32210
Tel: (904) 389-1125
Fax: (904) 388-2281
info@huckinsyacht.com
www.huckinsyacht.com
B

C. Raymond Hunt Associates
69 Long Wharf
Boston, MA 02110
Tel: (617) 742-5669
Fax: (617) 742-6354
huntyachts@msn.com
NA, D, BR
C. Raymond Hunt Associates continues to advance deep-vee hull design (an innovation of its founder) that makes possible a soft ride at high speed, even in rough water. Custom designs include motoryachts beyond 100ft with 30+ knot performance.

Ideal Windlass Company
5810 Post Road
P.O. Box 430
East Greenwich, RI 02818
Tel: (401) 884-2550
Fax: (401) 884-1260
idlwindlas@aol.com
O
Since 1936, Ideal Windlass has been building rugged, dependable anchor windlasses and accessories for boats up to 200ft. Our Custom Division specializes in planning and manufacturing windlass systems for yachts from 70ft to 200ft. Because Ideal Windlass manufactures gear boxes, the company has the capacity to offer a wide range of customized units.

IK Yacht Design, Inc.
Harbour Towne Marina
809 N.E. 3rd Street
Dania, FL 33004
Tel: (954) 922-9220
Fax: (954) 922-8999
Orn22ik@aol.com
www.ikyacht.com
D

Inace
Av Presidente Kennedy
100 Praia de Iracema
60060-610 Fortaleza Ceara,
Brazil
Tel: +55 (0) 85 231 4287
Fax: +55 (0) 85 251 9110
inace@inace.com.br
www.inace.com.br
B

Injoi
4651 SW 72nd Avenue
Miami, FL 33155
Tel: (305) 667-4656
Fax: (305) 667-4636
injoimiami@aol.com
D, O
Manufacturer of Premium Teak dock, deck, interior and garden furniture. Marine, residential, commercial applications. Miami-based company owner, Synthia David.

Insignia Yachts
Anavryta Building
225-227 Kifissias Av.
145-61 Kifissia, Athens
Greece
Tel: +30 210 612 9932
Fax: +30 210 612 0161
info@insignia-yachts.com
www.insignia-yachts.com
B, NA

Peter Insull's Yacht Marketing
Residences du Port Vauban
19 avenue du 11 Novembre
06600 Antibes, France
Tel: +33 (0) 4 93 34 44 55
Fax: +33 (0) 4 93 34 92 74
info@insull.com
www.insull.com
C

Intelect Integrated Electronics
2500 NW 55th Court Suite 210
Fort Lauderdale, FL 33309
Tel: (954) 739-4449
Fax: (954) 739-4342
enquiries@intelect
    electronics.com
www.intelect-electronics.com
O
Intelect designs and installs integrated electronic systems exclusively for the superyacht market. Our designs include-but are not limited to-distributed audio and video entertainment, home theater, satellite television, touch-screen automation control systems, computer display distribution, security systems, and the integration of any and all of the above.

Interlux Yacht Finishes
2270 Morris Avenue
Union, NJ 07083
Tel: (908) 964-2374
Fax: (908) 686-8545
YS

Intermarine S.p.A.
P.O. Box 185
Via Alta
19038 Sarzana La Spezia, Italy
Tel: +39 (0) 0187 6171
Fax: +39 (0) 0187 674249
marketing@intermarine.it
www.intermarine.it
B

International Yacht Collection
1515 SE 17th Street, Suite 125
Fort Lauderdale, FL 33316
Tel: (954) 522-2323
Fax: (954) 522-2333
info@yachtcollection.com
www.yachtcollection.com
BR, C
IYC is an international yacht brokerage firm specializing in the sale and purchase of new and late-model motor and sportsfishing yachts. IYC was created to address the needs of the experienced and demanding yachtsman. IYC has brought together an experieced, effective, and honest team of brokers that represent the 'Boutique' brokerage organization of the 1990s and beyond.
Also:

International Yacht Collection
Port de Plaisance/Casino & Marina
Union Road Cole Bay
Phillipsburg, Sint Maarten
The Netherlands/Antilles
Toll Free: (888) 213-7577
BR, C
Also:

International Yacht Collection
Casey's Marina, Spring Wharf
Newport, RI 02840
Tel: (401) 849-0834
Fax: (401) 849-0835
BR, C

Interphase Technologies, Inc.
2880 Research Park Drive, Suite 140
Soquel, CA 95073
Tel: (831) 477-4944
Fax: (831) 462-7444
comments@interphase-tech.com
www.interphase-tech.com
YS
Interphase Technologies is the leading supplier of forward-scanning sonar electronics for pleasure boaters, cruisers, and sportsfishermen worldwide, as well as light commercial fleets. First introduced in 1991, the company's patented phased-array technology set the standard for affordable high-performance sonar systems.

Izar
C/Velazquez 132
Ed. II, 4a planta
28006, Madrid Spain
Tel: +34 (9) 1 335 86 18
pdrosario@izar.es
www.izar.es
B

J Class Management
32 Church Street
Newport, RI 02840
Tel: (401) 849-3060
Fax: (401) 849-1642
mjw@jclass.com
www.jclass.com
YS, D, BR, C
Project management, yacht management, crew hire and training, yacht insurance, payroll management, systems interior and deck design, specification, bidding and new build oversight and restoration oversight, yacht brokerage and charter brokerage - all for classic yachts.

Lynn Jachney Charters
P.O. Box 302
Marblehead, MA 01945
Tel: (781) 639-0787
Toll Free: (800) 223-2050
Fax: (781) 639-0216
ljc@boston.sisna.com
C
Lynn Jachney Charters, an independent yacht charter brokerage established in 1968, specializes in private, crewed yacht charters. Our knowledgable, helpful, experienced brokers offer motor and sailing yachts worldwide. The AYCA and CYBA are represented among our staff.

Jackson Marine Center
1915 SW 21st Avenue
Fort Lauderdale, FL 33312
Tel: (954) 792-4900
Fax: (954) 587-8164
info@jacksonmarine.com
www.jacksonmarine.com
YS
Full-service marine/boatyard with a 70 ton marine travelift and 15 specialty marine businesses on-site.

Japan Radio Company, Ltd.
1011 SW Klickitat Way #B-100
Seattle, WA 98134
Tel: (206) 654-5644
Fax: (206) 654-7030
sales@jrcamerica.com
www.jrcamerica.com
YS
Sales and service of marine electronic equipment.

JFA Chantier Naval
Quai des Seychelles
29900 Concarneau, France
Tel: +33 (0) 298 604 948
Fax: +33 (0) 298 604 940
JFA.CN@wanadoo.fr
B

Glade Johnson Design, Inc.
11820 Northup Way Suite 220
Bellevue, WA 98005
Tel: (425) 827-1600
Fax: (425) 827-2147
gjdi@gjdi.net
www.gjdi.net
D, O
Glade Johnson Design, Inc. offers exterior styling and complete interior design and outfitting services for yachts over 100ft. Our experienced team produces artistic conceptual work, as well as highly detailed control drawings that only the latest AutoCAD systems can realize.

Jones Boat Yard, Inc.
3399 NW South River Drive
Miami, FL 33142
Tel: (305) 635-0891
Fax: (305) 633-6758
Victorb@jonesdrydock.com
www.jonesdrydock.com
B

Jongert BV
P.O. Box 116
NL-1670 AC Medemblik
The Netherlands
Tel: +31 (0) 227 54 25 44
Fax: +31 (0) 227 54 12 46
info@jongert.nl
www.jongert.nl
B
Founded in 1953, Jongert has earned an unrivaled reputation for craftsmanship, yachting know-how, and innovation. Specializes in semi-custom (Modern and Traditional Line) and custom-built yachts from 70ft to 200ft in length, mainly built in steel or aluminum.

K

KaiserWerft GmbH
Hafenstrasse 34
D-93342 Saal, Bavaria
Germany
Tel: +49 94 41 17 670
zed@kaiserwerft.de
www.kaiserwerft.de
B
KaiserWerft GmbH is a custom builder of high quality yachts between 98 and 197ft with facilities in Saal, Bavaria. The facility has been building yachts for 11 years and currently employs 80 skilled people.

D.N. Kelley & Son Inc. Shipyard
32 Water Street
Fairhaven, MA 02719
Tel: (508) 999-6266
Fax: (508) 999-2513
andrew@dnkelley.com
www.dnkelley.com
B
D.N. Kelley & Son Inc. Shipyard will celebrate its 140th anniversary next year as the oldest family-owned shipyard in the country.

Bruce King Yacht Design
P.O. Box 599
Newcastle Square
Newcastle, ME 04553
Tel: (207) 563-1186
Fax: (207) 563-1189
NA, D
This is a yacht design firm that is able to provide complete naval architecture and design services for any type of yacht, for both production and custom projects. The firm has become known as a leader in modern retro-style yacht design.

Michael Kirchstein Designs
23 Mill Plat Avenue
Isleworth
London, TW7 6RD
United Kingdom
Tel: +44 (0) 20 8758 1703
Fax: +44 (0) 20 8232 8403
mikekirchstein@cs.com
D
International megayacht designer specializing in interior design, exterior styling, and project coordination of large yacht new constructions and refits combining high-tech CAD design with conventional design methods.

Knight & Carver Yacht Center, Inc.
1313 Bay Marina Drive
National City, CA 91950
Tel: (619) 336-4141
Fax: (619) 336-4050
info@knightandcarver.com
www.knightandcarver.com
B, YS
Knight & Carver is a builder of composite boats, both custom and production, ranging in size from 60ft to 150ft. Knight & Carver also operates a marine repair facility with a 300-ton lifting capacity.

Patrick Knowles Designs
2030 Northeast 18th Street
Fort Lauderdale, FL 33305
Tel: (954) 832-0108
Fax: (954) 537-7766
pk@patrickknowlesdesigns.com
www.patrickknowlesdesigns.com
D
Primarily focused on the designs of custom yacht interiors, other strengths include exterior styling, interior arrangements, technical interior drawings and specifications, as well as complete décor selection and coordination.

Koch, Newton & Partners
1830 SE 4th Avenue
Fort Lauderdale, FL 33316
Tel: (954) 525-7080
Fax: (954) 525-7095
yachts@kochnewton.com
www.kochnewton.com
BR, C

KVH Industries, Inc.
50 Enterprise Center
Middletown, RI 02842
Tel: (401) 847-3327
Fax: (401) 849-0045
info@kvh.com
www.kvh.com
O
KVH Industries utilizes its proprietary fiberoptic, auto-calibration, and sensor technologies to produce navigation and mobile satellite communication systems for commercial, military, and marine applications. KVH is the world leader in providing stabilized satellite TV and communication systems for marine use. KVH also produced the first Inmarsat type-approved, stabilized maritime antenna for Inmarsat-phone mini-M service.

L

Langan Design Associates
17 Goodwin Street
Newport, RI 02840
Tel: (401) 849-2249
Fax: (401) 849-3288
info@langandesign.com
www.langandesign.com
D

Reymond Langton Design, Ltd.
Rayleigh House
2 Richmond Hill, Richmond
Surrey, TW10 6QX
United Kingdom
Tel: +44 (0) 20 8332 7789
Fax: +44 (0) 20 8332 6890
yachtdesigns@aol.com
D

An international design studio focusing on the conception, exterior/interior styling, and decoration of the world's finest sailing and motoryachts.

Lazzara Yachts
5300 West Tyson Avenue
Tampa, FL 33611
Tel: (813) 835-5300
Fax: (813) 835-0964
info@lazzarayachts.com
www.lazzarayachts.com
B, BMA, NA, D, BR
Combining their family legacy of 50 years of master yachtbuilding with the latest advances in computer and marine technology resulted in a new and imaginative company that produces yachts in a class by themselves. The Lazzara motoryacht is the most technically innovative production yacht ever created.

LeClercq Marine Construction
1080 West Ewing
Seattle, WA 98119
Tel: (206) 283-8555
Fax: (206) 286-1726
leclercq@leclercqmarine.com
www.leclercqmarine.com
B
LeClercq Marine Construction specializes in new construction and refit of custom fiberglass composite luxury motoryachts ranging from 60ft to 130ft.

Legendary Yachts, Inc.
P.O. Box 206
2902 Addy Street
Washougal, WA 98671
Tel: (360) 835-0342
Fax: (360) 835-5052
B
Our wooden classics fill a critical void in yachting by offering a unique, high-quality product that is simply not available anywhere else. Like great music, our boats are masterworks, testaments to the creativity, perseverance, and talent of designers such as Herreshoff, Stephens, Alden, Fife and Rhodes, to mention only a few.

Leight-Notika
2019 SW 20th
Suite 243
Fort Lauderdale, FL 33315
Tel: (954) 767-4921
Fax: (954) 767-4922
michael@leightyachts.com
www.leightyachts.com
BR

Liebowitz & Pritchard Architects & Yacht Designers
Penmenna House
Thirteen Erisey Terrace
Falmouth Cornwall, TR11 2AP
United Kingdom
Tel: +44 79 7027 0500
or (212) 240-9000
info@lparch.com
www.lparch.com
D, O
Yacht design and interiors are our specialty.

Linn Products
Floors Road, Waterford
Glascow, G76 0EP
United Kingdom
Tel: +44 (0) 14 1307 7777
Fax: +44 (0) 14 1644 4262
O

Little Harbor Yacht Charters
1 Little Harbor Landing
Portsmouth, RI 02871
Tel: (401) 683-7000
Fax: (401) 683-7029
charters@lhyb.com
www.lhyb.com
B, C

Little Hoquiam Shipyard
Hoquiam, WA
SALES: Fraser Yachts Worldwide
1001 Fairview Avenue North
Suite 1300
Seattle, WA 98109
Tel: (206) 382-9494
Fax: (206) 382-9480
B

Lürssen Yachts
Zum Alten Speicher 11
28759 Bremen
Germany
Tel: +49 (0) 421 6604 166
Fax: +49 (0) 421 6604 170
yachts@luerssen.de
www.luerssen.de
B
Known for their high quality of work, discretion and close interaction with their clients, Lürssen has delivered some of the largest megayachts to date. They also have a repair/refit department with drydocks accommodating vessels up to 490ft.

Lyman-Morse Boatbuilding, Inc.
82 Water Street
Thomaston, ME 04861
Tel: (207) 354-6904
Fax: (207) 354-8176
jb@lymanmorse.com
www.lymanmorse.com
B, YS
Lyman-Morse is a custom boat building yard on the coast of Maine with a distinguished history that specializes in custom projects in power and sail from 30-130ft. The yard has an excellent reputation for having built a variety of exceptional custom sailing yachts and custom motoryachts for world class naval architects and discriminating owners.

M

M. Castedo Architects
307 Seventh Avenue
Suite 2406
New York, NY 10001
Tel: (212) 255-4111
Fax: (212) 929-7350
architecture@mcastedo.com
www.mcastedo.com
D
M. Castedo Architects is a New York City-based architecture and interior design firm involved with high-end residential projects and motoryacht styling/interior design.

MacDougall's Cape Cod Marine Service, Inc.

145 Falmouth Heights Road
Falmouth, MA 02540
Tel: (508) 548-3146
Fax: (508) 548-7262
ccmarine1@capecod.net

YS

Full-service yacht yard with electronics, canvas, 80ton railway, and 50ton travelift. Located halfway between Newport and Nantucket.

MAN B&W Diesels Ltd.

Bramhall Moor Lane
Hazel Grove Stockport
Cheshire, SK7 5AH
United Kingdom
Tel: +44 (0) 16 1483 1000
Fax: +44 (0) 16 1487 1465

O

MAN B&W Diesels is a manufacturer of a range of engines. The VP185 range is compact with excellent fuel economy and long service intervals - ideal for the propulsion of superyachts. The top of the range 18VP185 is rated at 4,000kWb at 1,950r/min.

Mangia Onda Company

401 West A Street, Suite 1650
San Diego, CA 92101
Tel: (619) 232-8937
Fax: (619) 232-8759
info@mangiaonda.com
www.mangiaonda.com

D

Marc-Michaels Interior Design, Inc.

720 W. Morse Blvd.
Winter Park, FL 32789
Tel: (407) 629-2124
Fax: (407) 629-0910

D

Marc-Michaels Interior Design, Inc. has long been regarded as one of the country's most talented interior design firms specializing in architectural interiors for private residences, luxury yachts, as well as commercial and model home projects. Co-CEO's Mark Thee and Michael Abbott lead a staff of 65 with office locations both in Winter Park and Boca Raton, Florida.

Marine Design International

3821 NE 12 Terrace
Pompano Beach, FL 33064
Tel: (954) 785-6893
Fax: (954) 785-0233

D

Marine Medical International

1414 South Andrews Avenue
Fort Lauderdale, FL 33316
Tel: (954) 523-1404
Fax: (954) 523-1403

YS

Maritech Marine Electronics

3 Yacht Haven Marine Center
Stamford, CT 06902
Tel: (203) 323-2900
Fax: (203) 967-9717
info@maritech.com
www.maritech.com

YS

Sales of navigation, communications, computer networking, and entertainment systems for yachts worldwide.

Mars Metal Company

4130 Morris Drive
Burlington, ON L7L 5L6
Canada
Tel: (905) 381-5335
Toll Free: (800) 381-5335
Fax: (905) 637-8841
mars@bserv.com

YS

Produces custom and production keel configurations from 1,000 pounds to over 100,000 pounds. Company's capabilities include pattern-making, mold-making, stainless steel fabrication, and specialized finishing areas. The company also specializes in custom bulb additions for draft reduction and added stability.

Evan K. Marshall

Usonia IV, 4 Coral Row
Plantation Wharf York Road
London, SW11 3UF
United Kingdom
Tel: +44 (0) 20 7801 9244
Fax: +44 (0) 20 7801 9245
ekmu4@aol.com

D

Gregory C. Marshall Naval Architect, Ltd.

1571 West Burnside Road
Victoria BC, V9E 2E2
Canada
Tel: (250) 388-9995
Fax: (250) 388-4260
info@gregmarshalldesign.com
www.gregmarshalldesign.com

NA

Rodger Martin Design

P.O. Box 242
1 Washington Street
Newport, RI 02840
Tel: (401) 849-9850
Fax: (401) 846-7200
info@rodgermartindesign.com
www.rodgermartindesign.com

NA

Maxwell Winches

1606 Babcock Street
Costa Mesa, CA 92627
Tel: (949) 631-2634
Fax: (949) 631-2846

YS

McKinna Yachts

400 Roberts Road
Flagler Beach, FL 32136
Tel: (386) 439-5272
Toll Free: (888) 625-4662
Fax: (386) 439-5254
info@mckinna.com
www.mckinna.com

B

McMullen & Wing Ltd.

21 Gabador Place
Mt. Wellington
P.O. Box 14-218 Panmure
Auckland, 1006
New Zealand
Tel: +64 (0) 9 573 1405
Fax: +64 (0) 9 573 0393
mcwing.boats@xtra.co.nz
www.mcmullenandwing.com

B

Building custom sailing and motor-yachts in steel, aluminum and composite to 130ft. Five dedicated indoor construction areas including a 330ton covered slipway. Comprehensive in-house marine skills from joiner work to electrical. Refit service and painting. Facilities incude a CNC router, 77ton travelift, and private marina with harbor access.

McQueen's Yachts Ltd.

11571 Twigg Place
Richmond, BC V6V 2K7
Canada
Tel: (604) 325-4544
Fax: (604) 325-4516
mcqueens@uniserve.com

B

Doug McQueen followed in his father's footsteps, and twenty years ago took over his father's custom yacht building business and has flourished with it. The Ed Monk Sr./McQueen relationship continues today with Ed Monk Jr./McQueen. Motoryacht and sportfishers are McQueen's forte.

MedLink, Inc.

1301 E. McDowell Road, Suite 204
Phoenix, AZ 85006
Tel: (602) 452-4300
Fax: (602) 252-8404
info@medaire.com
www.medaire.com

YS

MedLink provides Emergency Telemedicine at sea with access to emergency room physicians 24 hours a day, seven days a week, coordination of land-based emergency medical resources, health advisories, and immunization recommendations.

Mega Yachts Ltd.

Suite 20 Block 6
Watergardens, Gilbraltar
Tel: +350 41516
Fax: +350 47998
mega_yachts@yahoo.com

BMA

Exclusive agent for Palladino Yacht Designs.

Merrill-Stevens Dry Dock

1270 NW 11th Street
Miami, FL 33125
Tel: (305) 324-5211
Fax: (305) 326-8911
msddmiami@aol.com

YS

Also:

Merrill-Stevens Yacht Sales

1270 NW 11th Street
Miami, FL 33125
Tel: (305) 547-2650
Fax: (305) 547-2660

BR

Metalnave

Estaleiro Italjai S/A
Rua Mario Trilma 271
Ilha da Conceicao
Nitero, RJ24050-190
Brazil
Tel: +55 (0) 21 620 1414
Fax: +55 (0) 21 620 8017

B

Metaxa Marine S.A.

Metaxa Building
4 Meleagrou Street
Athens, 10674
Greece
Tel: +30 210 729 9161
Fax: +30 210 729 9171
www.metaxamarine.gr

B

Metrica Interior

Bahnhofstrasse 73
D-48308 Senden
Germany
Tel: +49 (0) 253 633 0900
Fax: +49 (0) 253 633 0919
info@metrica.de
www.metrica.de

D

Also:

Metrica Interior AG

Marketing & Sales
Terossenweg 17
CH-Oberaggeri, ZG
Switzerland
Tel: +41 41 750 4475
Fax: +41 41 750 6270
D

Monaco Marine Group

1500 Cordova Road
Suite 214
Fort Lauderdale, FL 33316
Tel: (954) 462-0116
Fax: (954) 462-4665
info@monacomarineusa.com
www.monacomarineusa.com

BMA, BR, C

Yacht sales brokers, charter brokers, exclusive distributor for Kennedy Yacht & Ship and Vicem Yachts in the USA. Home office of Monaco Marine Group in Monaco with additional sales offices, service and repair facilities, and marinas throughout Europe. Assist in an experienced and professional manner with anything relating to yachting.

Mondomarine

Lungomare Matteotti 6
17100 Savona, Italy
Tel: +39 (0) 19 82 8516
Fax: +39 (0) 19 82 3418
campanellspa@
campanellaspa.com
www.mondomarine.it

B

Edwin Monk

P.O. Box 10397
Bainbridge Island, WA 98110
Tel: (206) 842-2167
Fax: (206) 842-3182

D

Monte Fino Custom Yachts

1887 West State Road 84
Fort Lauderdale, FL 33315
Tel: (954) 463-0555
Fax: (954) 463-8621

B, BMA

Mulder Design

Appeldijk 33
4201 AE Gorinchem
Holland
Tel: +31 (0) 183 692001
Fax: +31 (0) 183 692002
info@mulderdesign.nl
www.mulderdesign.nl

NA

Conceptual design, design, naval architecture, and engineering of high-speed, semi-displacement luxury motoryachts and commercial boats.

Naiad Marine Florida, Inc.

Broward Business Park
3700 Hacienda Blvd, Suite 1
Fort Lauderdale, FL 33314
Tel: (954) 797-7566
Fax: (954) 791-0827
nmfl@nmfl.com
www.nmfl.com

YS

Also:

Naiad Marine Systems

50 Parrott Drive
Shelton, CT 06484
Toll Free: (800) 760-naiad
Fax: (203) 929-3594
sales@naiad.com
www.naiad.com

YS

Naiad Marine Systems designs and manufactures Naiad roll stabilization systems, stabilizer controllers, bow thrusters and integrated hydraulic systems for vessels from 35ft to 300ft. Naiad Marine Systems also installs, services, and repairs our systems through our worldwide dealer network.

Nautica International, Inc.

1500 SW 66 Avenue
Pembroke Pines, FL 33023
Tel: (954) 986-1600
Fax: (954) 986-1631

B

Our deluxe rigid inflatable boats are tenders to many exclusive yachts world-wide. Featuring faster, better-planing hulls for optimum performance and luxurious, well-appointed deck plans with emphasis placed on comfort. Each 9ft to 36ft RIB boasts a 10-year warranty.

Nautor AB

P.O. Box 10, FIN-68601
Pietarsaari, Finland
Tel: +358 (0) 6 760 1111
Fax: +358 (0) 6 766 7364
email@nautors-swan.com
www.nautors-swan.com

B

Nautor has been building Swan yachts since 1966. Considered the world's premier production yachts, the current range comprises 11 models including the Swan 80, Swan 82, Swan 100, and Swan 112. The principle for Swan is seaworthiness, built to cross oceans, proving safe, comfortable accommodations with Whitbread race-winning pedigree, performance is as vital as the luxurious interiors.

Navitas Corp.

1041 SE 17th Street, Suite 101
Fort Lauderdale, FL 33316
Tel: (954) 523-3131
Fax: (954) 523-3636
navitas@bellsouth.net
www.posillipo-yachts.com

BMA, O

We are the exclusive dealers and distributors for Posillipo yachts. Our luxurious Italian yachts are custom-built by Rizzardi, a well-known Italian boat manufacturer specialized in designing and building true masterpieces of art and technology. A wide array of sizes and styles can be built to your liking and shipped to the US after completion.

Newcastle Marine

5658 North Oceanshore Blvd.
Palm Coast, FL 32137
Tel: (386) 447-0999
Fax: (386) 447-7810
kkeith@newcastlemarineinc.com
www.newcastlemarineinc.com

YS

Nexus Marine Corporation

3816 Railway Avenue
Everett, WA 98201-3838
Tel: (425) 252-8330
nexus_marine@juno.com

B

Nexus has a custom shop that builds 15ft to 40ft boats.

Nordic Tugs

11367 Higgins Airport Way
Burlington, WA 98233
Toll Free: (800) 388-4517
Fax: (360) 757-8831

B

Nordlund Boat Co.

1626 Marine View Drive
Tacoma, WA 98422
Tel: (253) 627-0605
Fax: (253) 627-0785
info@nordlundboat.com
www.nordlundboat.com

B

Nordlund Boat Company is a custom builder of cored fiberglass boats ranging in size from 63ft to 112ft. Established in 1956, the company has built motoryachts, yacht-fishers, and sportfishers and has established a reputation for high-quality workmanship.

Nortek Group
(Custom Navigation South)

3200 South Andrews Avenue
Fort Lauderdale, FL 33316
Tel: (954) 761-3678
Fax: (954) 522-5526
nortekgrp@nortek.net
www.nortek.com

YS

1. Custom Navigation South, Inc. Communication & navigation systems.
2. Nortek Entertainment, Inc. Audio/Video entertainment systems.
3. Cole Marine Distributing, Inc. Mechanical and finished goods.

North American Yachts & Shipbuilding

515 Seabreeze Blvd., Suite 549
Fort Lauderdale, FL 33316
Tel: (954) 713-8110
Fax: (954) 713-8199
mail@nays.cc
www.nays.cc

B

Also:

North American Yachts & Shipbuilding

c/o Cantieri Naval F. Ili Rossi
Localita Darsena
Pisana Via Della Darsena
56100 Pisa, Italy
Tel: +39 (0) 050 43 263
Fax: +39 (0) 050 220 6603
mail@nays.com

B

North Star Yachts

35 Ironwood Circle
Coto de Caza, CA 92679
Tel: (949) 244-0560
Fax: (949) 589-9616
rmbaker@cox.net

B

Northern Lights/Lugger

P.O. Box 70543
4420 14th Avenue NW
Seattle, WA 98107-0543
Tel: (206) 789-3880
Fax: (206) 782-5455
ade@northern-lights.com
www.northern-lights.com

YS

Northern Marine

3115 V Place
Anacortes, WA 98221
Tel: (360) 299-8400
Fax: (360) 299-2600
sales@northernmarine.com
www.northernmarine.com

B, NA, YS

Located in the heart of the San Juan Islands, Northern Marine is a premier custom yacht and trawler builder. We produce the finest custom boats that are rugged, luxurious, economical, and above all else, seaworthy and safe.

Northrop and Johnson Yachts-Ships, Inc.

1901 SE 4th Avenue
Fort Lauderdale, FL 33316
Tel: (954) 522-3344
Fax: (954) 522-9500
njyachts@aol.com
www.northropandjohnson.com

BR, C

Northrop and Johnson Yacht-Ships, Inc. is committed to providing clients with the best brokerage experience possible, whether listing a yacht, purchasing a yacht, choosing a builder, finding the right crew, or anything in between.

Also:

Northrop and Johnson Yachts-Ships, Inc.

5 Marina Plaza
Newport, RI 02840
Tel: (401) 849-0120
Fax: (401) 849-0620
info@njyachts.com

BR, C

Northwest Shipyard

825 Queen Avenue
Hoquiam, WA 98550
Tel: (360) 538-1622
Fax: (360) 538-0225
howard@northwestshipyard.com
www.northwestshipyard.com

B

Notika Teknik Yacht Construction

Tersaneler Cad. G. 50 Sok. No. 3
Tuzla-Istanbul, 81700 Turkey
Tel: +90 (0) 216 493 6227
Fax: +90 (0) 216 493 6228

B, NA, YS, D

Novurania of America, Inc.

2105 South US 1
Vero Beach, FL 32962
Tel: (561) 567-9200
Fax: (561) 567-1056
novuraniainc@novurania.com
www.novurania.com

B

Novurania Rib manufacturer. Featuring luxury yacht tenders from 10ft to 36ft outboards/inboards, gas or diesel.

Nuvolari-Lenard

39a via Della Chiesa
31020 Zerman Treviso Italy
Tel: +39 (0) 0414 57272
Fax: +39 (0) 0414 57393
nlyachts@mpbnet.it

NA, D

Ocean Classic International

Villa #4
Madinat Hassan Mohamed
Pyramid Street Giza Egypt
Tel: +202 (0) 315 2124
Fax: +202 (0) 582 0766
oceancls@mailer.datum.com.eg

O

Oceanco International

Gildo Pastor Center
7 Rue du Gabian
MC 98000 Monaco
Tel: +377 (0) 93 10 02 81
Fax: +377 (0) 92 05 65 99
oceanco@oceanco.mc

O

Oceanfast

18 Clarence Beach Road
Henderson, 6166
Western Australia
Tel: +61 (0) 8 9494 9999
Fax: +61 (0) 8 9494 9900
boats@oceanfast.com.au
www.oceanfast.com.au

B

Also:

Oceanfast, LLC

1515 SE 17th Street Suite 119
Fort Lauderdale, FL 33316
Tel: (954) 522-5353
Fax: (954) 522-5350
oceanfastusa@attglobal.net
www.oceanfast.com

B

Offshore Nautical Limited

La Collete
Le Quai D'Avergne St. Heiler
Jersey, JE2 3NX
United Kingdom
Tel: +44 (0) 1534 514 444
Fax: +44 (0) 1534 514 445
info@offshore-nautical.com
www.offshore-nautical.com

O

Offshore Yachts

1011 Brioso Drive, Suite 102
Costa Mesa, CA 92672
Tel: (949) 645-4159
Fax: (949) 645-0250

B

For over 50 years, Offshore has been a leader in high-performance luxury yachts ranging from 48ft to 90ft. Offshore is renowned for the highest standards in quality, craftsmanship, safety, and innovative design by famed naval architect William Crealock.

Overing Yacht Design

998 Robinson Avenue
Ocean Springs, MS 39564
Tel: (228) 872-1881
Fax: (228) 875-2862
yachtdesigns@bellsouth.net

NA, D

P

Pacific Coast Marine Industries, Inc.

4314 Russell Road
Mukilteo, WA 98275
Tel: (425) 743-9550
Fax: (425) 348-3767
pcmii@compuserve.com

O

Pacific Coast Marine Industries, Inc. (PCM) fabricates custom doors, hatches, windows, and related marine hardware for both commercial and leisure vessels. PCM maintains a large inventory of a wide variety of aluminum extruded shapes.

Pacific Custom Interiors, Inc.

2742 Alki Avenue SW, Suite 200
Seattle, WA 98116
Tel: (206) 938-8700
Fax: (206) 938-8707
pcinteriors@qwest.net

D

Pacific Custom Interiors' yachts are outfitted to the highest turnkey standards and include fine crystal, china, and silver as well as any specific client requests.

Pacific Mariner

P.O. Box 1382
La Conner, WA 98257
Tel: (360) 466-1189
Fax: (360) 466-1147
pacmar@ncia.com

B

Palm Beach Yacht Crew

4200 North Flagler Drive
West Palm Beach, FL 33407
Tel: (561) 863-0082
Fax: (561) 863-4406
donna@yachtcrew.com
www.yachtcrew.com

YS

Yacht Crew Placement & Management agency provides professional qualified yacht crew for all vessels, power and sail, reference checks, longevity, and commitment goals. Also offers worldwide yacht charters and global crew medical insurance. Other locations in Palma de Mallorca, Spain and Queensland, Australia.

Paradigm Yacht Sales & Brokerage, LLC.

14311 Port Comfort Road
Fort Myers, FL 33908
Tel: (941) 454-8484
Fax: (941) 454-8485

BR, C

Experience, integrity, and service guarantee each client the ultimate satisfaction when buying or selling your next yacht.

Pavlik Design Team

1301 East Broward Blvd.
Fort Lauderdale, FL 33301
Tel: (954) 523-3300
Fax: (954) 525-9501
info@pavlikdesign.com
www.pavlikdesign.com

D

Our mission is to develop planning and design solutions that serve the client's strategic objectives. Under the direction of President Seann Pavlik, the yacht division is backed by over 25 employees and specializes in both new construction and vessel refitting. The company has consistently been ranked as one of the top 10 design firms in the country for the past decade.

Pedrick Yacht Design, Inc.

3 Ann Street
Newport, RI 02840
Tel: (401) 846-8481
Fax: (401) 846-0657
pedrickyacht@compuserve.com
www.pedrickyacht.com

NA

Pedrick Yacht Designs is a progressive naval architecture and marine engineering firm offering exceptional quality and diversity of design services. Established in Newport, Rhode Island in 1977, Pedrick Yacht Designs works in both power and sail, being best known for creating extraordinary sailing yachts.

Peer Gynt Yachts

14604 SE 15th Street
Fort Lauderdale, FL 33316
Tel: (954) 763-3565
Fax: (954) 763-2215

B

Performance Paint Yacht Refinishing, Inc.

275 SW 33rd Street
Fort Lauderdale, FL 33316
Tel: (954) 462-1080
Fax: (954) 462-2244
paint@aol.com

YS

Perini Navi SpA

Via Coppino, 114
55049 Viareggio, Italy
Tel: +39 (0) 0584 4241
Fax: +39 (0) 0584 424200
sales@perininavi.it
www.perininavi.com

B, NA, D

This company was founded by Fabio Perini in 1984 and has focused on the engineering, design, and construction of highly automated blue-water sailing yachts capable of being handled by a reduced crew.

Also:

Perini Navi USA, Inc.

One Maritime Drive
Portsmouth, RI 02871
Tel: (401) 683-5600
Fax: (401) 683-5611
perininaviusa@efortress.com
www.perininavi.com

BR, C

Perini Navi USA is the first Perini Navi office outside Italy - and as such is testimony to the importance of the American market for the Viareggio-based yacht builder. Perini Navi USA is managed by Bruce Brakenhoff Jr., and serves the US, Canadian, Central and South American markets.

Permanent Reflections

4400 Route 517
Hamburg, NJ 07419
Tel: (973) 209-2544
Toll Free: (800) 792-3266
Fax: (973) 697-3266
info@permanentreflections.com
www.permanentreflections.com

YS, D

Distinctive etched & carved artwork in glass, appropriate for the finest environments in the world. Specializing in commissioned art glass designed specifically for each individual interior and taste. Applications include railing panels, shower enclosures, partitions, furniture, sculpture and more.

Michael Peters Yacht Design

47 South Palm Avenue, Suite 202
Sarasota, FL 34236
Tel: (941) 955-5460
Fax: (941) 957-3151
mpyd@aol.com

NA

MPYD provides complete naval architecture, design, and engineering for powerboats and motoryachts to 160ft. Specializing in advanced hull designs, MPYD has designed vessels to speeds of 140 knots in wood, aluminum, FRP, and advanced carbon composites.

Phantom Marine

2801 Carleton Street
San Diego, CA 92106
Tel: (619) 221-8184
Fax: (619) 221-8051

YS

Specializing in sales, service, and installation of marine electronics. Factory authorized dealers for Furuno, Simrad, Raytheon, ICOM, and many more. Serving Southern California's boating industry from Marine del Ray to Ensenada. Showrooms located in Newport Beach and San Diego.

Philbrook's Boatyard, Ltd.

2324 Harbour Road
Sidney, BC V8L 2P6
Canada
Tel: (250) 656-1157
Fax: (250) 656-1155

B, O

Philbrook's Boatyard has been building, repairing, and renovating motor and sail yachts since 1950. It is the largest yacht repair facility in the Victoria area with two enclosed work areas accessed

by two marine railways for vessels up to 120ft or 150tons in capacity.

Piening-Propeller

Otto Piening GmbH
Am Altendeich 83
D - 25348 Gluckstadt, Germany
Tel: +49 (0) 4124 91680
Fax: +49 (0) 4124 3716
info@piening-propeller.de
www.piening-propeller.de

O

Piening-Propeller supplies complete propulsion systems for megayachts and high-speed yachts with various types of propellers, from 500nm upwards. Special attention is given for maximum efficiency and high reliability of the propulsion systems.

Platypus Marine, Inc.

102 North Cedar Street
Port Angeles, WA 98363
Tel: (360) 417-0709
Fax: (360) 417-0729
judson@platypusmarine.com
www.platypusmarine.com

YS, O

One of the largest refit centers in the Pacific Northwest.

Pokela Design

2907 Harbor View Drive, Suite P
Gig Harbor, WA 98335
Tel: (253) 853-4240
Fax: (253) 853-4230
pokeladesign@compuserve.com

D

International styling and interior design.

Proteksan-Turquoise Shipyard

Ozel Tersaneler Bolgesi 313
Tuzla 81700
Istanbul, Turkey
Tel: +90 (0) 216 395 8312
Fax: +90 (0) 216 446 0491
proteksan@proteksan.com.tr
www.proteksan.com

B

Puleo International Designs

733 West Las Olas Blvd.
Fort Lauderdale, FL 33312
Tel: (954) 522-0173
Fax: (954) 761-3216
slpuleo@aol.com

D

Premise: "Never say never." Extend the client's dream. Complete renovations and new construction. Exceptional space planning and use. Original architectural designs. Thorough experience in yacht projects internationally. Project problem solving is a specialty.

Q

Quantum Marine Engineering of Florida

4350 West Sunrise Blvd.
Plantation, FL 33313
Tel: (954) 587-4205
Fax: (954) 587-4259
support@quantumhydraulic.com
www.quantumhydraulic.com

YS

Precision design and manufacturing of marine hydraulics and control systems. Sales, service, and repair of stabilizers, deck cranes, and thrusters.

R

Rammer Marine
Ulya Engin I's Merkezi
Atatürk Cad No: 68 K:10
Kozyatag, Istanbul
Turkey
Tel: +90 21 63 86 49 00
Fax: +90 21 63 86 82 40
rammer@ramsa.com.tr
www.ramsa.com.tr
BMA
Turkish distributor for Hallberg-Rassy.

Rayburn Custom Yachts
32860 Mission Way
Mission, BC V2V 5X9
Canada
Tel: (604) 820-9153
Fax: (604) 820-2457
B

Rex Yacht Sales
2152 SE 17th Street, Suite 202
Fort Lauderdale, FL 33316
Tel: (954) 463-8810
Fax: (954) 462-3640
rex@rexyachts.com
www.rexyachts.com
BMA, BR
Rex Yacht Sales has been a yacht brokerage and new-build agent for the past 24 years. Known for its introduction and development of the Cheoy Lee Yacht line, Rex now concentrates on new build representation, coordinating clients' wishes with naval architects, suppliers, and shipyards.

Richleigh Yachts
P.O. Box 267580
Fort Lauderdale, FL 33326
Toll Free: (800) 578-4348
Fax: (954) 236-8822
richard@richleighyachts.com
www.richleighyachts.com
YS, C
Richleigh Yachts offers over 500 luxury crewed charter boats in exotic destinations worldwide that cater to discerning tastes and preferences. Combined 30 years hands-on experience in sailing, chartering, and captaincy.

Rivolta Marine, Inc.
2127 Ringling Blvd., Suite 102
Sarasota, FL 34237
Tel: (941) 954-0355
Fax: (941) 954-0111
rrivolta@rivolta.com
www.rivolta.com
B, NA
Rivolta Marine is a full-service design-build shipyard providing high technology construction and architectural services for both sailing boats and power boats and for private individuals, designers, and manufacturers. Rivolta Marine brings the best in European design and American technology to each project, treating every client individually.

RMK Marine A.S.
Deniz Tasimaciligi Isletmeleri A.S.
81700 Tuzla, Istanbul
Turkey
Tel: +90 216 395 2865
Fax: +90 216 395 4582
cemt@rmkmarine.com.tr
www.rmkmarine.com.tr
B

RNR Yacht Charters
809 SW 9th Street
Fort Lauderdale, FL 33315
Tel: (954) 522-9563
Toll Free: (800) 525-2536
Fax: (954) 463-4525
C

Dee Robinson Interiors, inc.
2755 East Oakland Park Blvd.
Suite 301
Fort Lauderdale, FL 33306
Tel: (954) 566-2252
Fax: (954) 566-2044
deerob@bellsouth.net
D
Specializes in superyacht interior design and execution of all phases of pre-construction and refits.

Roscioli International, Inc.
3201 State Road 84
Fort Lauderdale, FL 33312
Tel: (954) 581-9200
Fax: (954) 791-0958
roscioliyachting@roscioli
   yachting.com
www.donziyachts.com
B

Robin M. Rose & Associates
399 SE 18th Court
Fort Lauderdale, FL 33316
Tel: (954) 525-6023
Fax: (954) 525-0010
rroseyacht@worldnet.att.net
D
Robin M. Rose & Associates, Inc. was established in May of 1989. We specialize in project management, space planning, furniture design, and execution, which all go hand-in-hand. We are proud of the fact that over 90 percent of our business is repeat clientele and referrals.

Cor D. Rover Design
Schoonhovenseveer 19
2964 GB Groot-Ammers
The Netherlands
Tel: +31 (0) 184 609 333
Fax: +31 (0) 184 609 444
cdrd@euronet.nl
D

Royal Denship of America
1500 Cordova Road, Suite #308
Fort Lauderdale, FL 33316
Tel: (954) 525-2709
Fax: (954) 525-2731
info@royaldenshipusa.com
www.royaldenshipusa.com
B, BMA
Also:

Royal Denship
Marselisborg Havnevej 36
DK 8000 Arhus C
Denmark
Tel: +45 (0) 86 18 39 19
Fax: +45 (0) 86 18 39 14
www.royaldenship.com
B

Royal Huisman Shipyard BV
P.O. Box 23
8325 ZG Vollenhove
The Netherlands
Tel: +31 (0) 527 243 131
Fax: +31 (0) 527 243 800
yachts@royalhuisman.com
www.royalhuisman.com
B

Royal Marine Insurance Group
8300 Executive Center Drive
Suite 102
Miami, FL 33166
Tel: (305) 477-3755
Fax: (305) 477-3858
info@royalmarine.com
www.royalmarine.com
O
From initial consultation to complete administration, Royal Marine provides an entire range of products and services to the yachting industry, including yacht management, luxury yachts, charter operations, fleet and owner associations, and many more coverages.

Rybovich Spencer
4200 North Flagler Drive
West Palm Beach, FL 33407
Tel: (561) 844-1800
Fax: (561) 844-8393
service@rybovich.com
www.rybovich.com
YS
A world-renowned service and repair yard with capabilities including a 300 ton and 70ton travelift and 120ton syncrolift. Areas of expertise include carpentry, metal and mechanical, diesel and generator, paint and electrical, and yard crews. A 22 acre facility with over 50 years of experience in refits, extensions, reconstruction, and repairs.

S

The Sacks Group Yachting Professionals
1600 SE 17th Street, Suite 418
Fort Lauderdale, FL 33316
Tel: (954) 764-7742
Fax: (954) 523-3769
info@sacksyachts.com
BR, C

San Juan Composites LLC
502 34th Street
Anacortes, WA 98221
Tel: (360) 299-3790
Fax: (360) 299-2747
sanjuan@sanjuanyachts.com
www.sanjuanyachts.com
B
Builders of advanced composite, downeast styled, express motoryachts for the discerning yacht owner. Unmatched fit and finish, with performance.

Jack W. Sarin Naval Architects, Inc.
382 Wyatt Way NE
P.O. Box 10151
Bainbridge Island, WA 98110
Tel: (206) 842-4651
Fax: (206) 842-4656
jsarin@jacksarin.com
www.jacksarin.com
NA
Jack W. Sarin Naval Architects, Inc. is a full-service naval architectural firm in operation since 1980. In addition to hull design and engineering, the firm provides an in-house staff and facilities to include a full range of interior and lighting design, styling, and complete ship's system coordination during construction.

Sarnia Yachts Limited
P.O. Box 79, La Plaiderie House
St. Peter Port, Guernsey
Channel Islands, GY1 3DQ
United Kingdom
Tel: +44 (0) 14 8170 9960
Fax: +44 (0) 14 8172 6526
info@sarniayachts.co.gg
www.sarniayachts.com
B

Bob Saxon Associates, Inc.
1500 Cordova Road, Suite 314
Fort Lauderdale, FL 33316
Tel: (954) 760-5801
Fax: (954) 467-8909
yachts1@bobsaxon.com
www.bobsaxon.com
YS, C
Private yacht management, charter yacht management, professional crew placement, charter brokerage.

SEA
7030 220th Street SW
Mountlake Terrace, WA 98043
Tel: (425) 771-2182
Fax: (425) 771-2650
salesmktg@sea-dmi.com
www.sea-dmi.com
O
SEA is an American manufacturer of marine electronics including VHF and SSB radiotelephones, satellite products, and GMDSS equipment.

Sea Tel, Inc.
1035 Shary Court
Concord, CA 94518
Tel: (925) 798-7979
Fax: (925) 798-7986
jborchelt@seatel.com
www.seatel.com
YS
SeaTel is the world's leading manufacturer of marine-stabilized antenna systems for satellite communications and satellite television at sea. SeaTel markets its products globally and has a responsive worldwide service support network.

Seabourne
Le Grande Large, 42 Quai
MC 98000 Monaco
Tel: +377 (0) 9797 6888
Fax: +377 (0) 9797 6889

Seafury Propulsion Systems Ltd.
P.O. Box 336
Silverdale Hibiscus Coast
Auckland, New Zealand
YS

Sensation Yachts
11 Selwood Road
P.O. Box 79-020
Henderson, Auckland 8
New Zealand
Tel: +64 (0) 9 837 2210
Fax: +64 (0) 9 836 1775
sensation@sensation.co.nz
www.sensation.co.nz
B
Specializing in large custom sail and power yachts built from all materials.

Setzer Design Group

590 New Waverly Place, Suite 210
Cary, NC 27511
Tel: (919) 859-7014
Fax: (919) 859-7015
setzerdesign@mindspring.com

NA, D

Setzer Design is a full-service naval architecture and design office. We specialize in custom yachts from 70ft to 200ft. Our focus remains to create designs that can be built and are meant to go to sea with style and comfort.

Sharp Design, Inc.

The Loft at Driscoll Boat Works
2500 Shelter Island Drive
San Diego, CA 92106
Tel: (619) 223-4860
Fax: (619) 223-6312
doug@sharpdesign-na.com
www.sharpdesign-na.com

NA, D

Sharp Design is a full service yacht design and consulting company with offices in San Diego, CA and Shanghai, China. Our naval architect and engineer/ designers are involved in all aspects of yacht design from initial concept and hull design through structural and systems design, to final outfit and delivery.

Shipshape Interiors

1670 Mathers Avenue
West Vancouver, V7V 2G7
Canada
Tel: (604) 925-0778
Fax: (604) 922-6205

D

George J. Shull & Associates

801 Seabreeze Blvd.
Fort Lauderdale, FL 33316
Tel: (954) 463-4546
Fax: (954) 463-5531
tcshull@aol.com

O

George J. Shull & Associates specializes in placing multi-million dollar loans on megayachts and aircraft for distinguished clientele. The firm has relationships with some of the world's most respected lending and private banking institutions. With offices at Bahia Mar Marina in Fort Lauderdale, Shull is committed to your service.

Siewert Design, LLC

P.O. Box 601
Charlestown, SC 29402
Tel: (843) 853-6154
Fax: (843) 577-4234
siewertdesign@mindspring.com
www.siewertdesign.com

NA, D

Siewert Design provides its clients with innovative, cost-effective, and enduring yacht design. The office is primarily concerned with the conceptual and detail design of both exterior styling and interior arrangements. It also offers services in illustration and project planning to clients who need assistance in guiding their project to completion.

Skaf Interiors, Inc.

Bahia Mar Yachting Center
801 Seabreeze Blvd.
Fort Lauderdale, FL 33316
Tel: (954) 523-6155
Fax: (954) 532-6156
suzanne@skafinteriors.com
www.skafinteriors.com

O

Skaf Interiors, Inc. specializes in yacht refits and new construction projects, offering a 'turnkey' interior with timeless details designed for both beauty and practicality. On-site management allows maximum level of quality control all the way through to the project's completion. Dedicated to excellence, Skaf offers the finest customer service in the field of interior design.

Larry Smith Electronics

1619 Broadway
Riviera Beach, FL 33404
Tel: (561) 844-3592
Fax: (561) 844-1608
lsei@gate.net

YS

With over 40 years in the marine industry, factory-trained technicians, and in-house CADD department, Smith provides sales, custom installations, and service for discriminating owners of custom-built boats and megayachts. To serve our customers worldwide, there are offices in South Florida, the Pacific Northwest, and Europe.

Paola D. Smith & Associates

300 NE 3rd Avenue
Fort Lauderdale, FL 33301
Tel: (954) 761-1997
Fax: (954) 767-6270
pds@pdsdesign.net
www.pdsdesign.net

D

Paola D. Smith & Associates is among the top leading interior design firms in the industry of megayachts. With over 25 years of experience, their firm's technical support team is classified among the finest in the industry providing complete interior design services, including exterior styling and space planning for both customized new construction and refits.

South Florida Yacht

2010 Avenue B
Riviera Beach, FL 33404
Tel: (561) 844-4109
Fax: (561) 844-7162
sales@southfloridayachts.com
www.southfloridayachts.com

YS

Southern Wind Shipyard/Pegaso srl

Via Corsica, 6
56126 Pisa, Italy
Tel: +39 (0) 50 831 2038
Fax: +39 (0) 50 831 2038
info@pegaso-pr.it

B

Sovereign Yachts, Inc.

23511 Dyke Road
Richmond, BC V6V 1E3
Canada
Tel: (604) 515-0992
Fax: (604) 515-0994
info@sovereign-yachts.com
www.sovereign-yachts.com

B

Also:

Sovereign Yachts Limited

P.O. Box 131
Westpark Marina
West Harbour, Auckland 1008
New Zealand
Tel: +64 9 417 0100
Fax: +64 9 417 0101
info@sovereignyachtsnzltd.co.nz

B

Sparkman & Stephens, Inc.

901 SE 17th Street
Fort Lauderdale, FL 33316
Tel: (954) 524-4616
Fax: (954) 524-4621
brokerfl@sparkmanstephens.com
www.sparkmanstephens.com

BR, C

Also:

Sparkman & Stephens, Inc.

529 Fifth Avenue, Suite 205
New York, NY 10017
Tel: (212) 661-1240
Fax: (212) 661-1235
design@sparkmanstephens.com
brokerage@sparkmanstephens.com
www.sparkmanstephens.com

NA, BR, C

Naval architecture, marine engineering, yacht brokers, marine insurance, worldwide.

Spectro Oil Analysis Company, Ltd.

Palace Gate Odiham
Hampshire, RG29 1NP
United Kingdom
Tel: +44 (0) 12 5670 4000
Fax: +44 (0) 12 5639 3507

O

Jet-Care International, Inc.

3 Saddle Road
Cedar Knolls, NJ 07927
Tel: (973) 292-9597
Fax: (973) 292-3030

O

Spectro is a 27-year-old laboratory that provides engine health monitoring around the world. Services cover oil, fuel, and hydraulic fluid analysis, predicting and highlighting potential technical issues before they become critical. We offer you savings and peace of mind by avoiding long overhauls and costly repairs.

Sponberg Yacht Design, Inc.

P.O. Box 661
8 Fair Street
Newport, RI 02840
Tel: (401) 849-7730
ewsponberg@cs.com

NA

Naval architects and marine engineers designers of offshore racing and cruising sailboats, mono-hulls and multi-hulls, powerboats and motoryachts. Specialists in high-performance wing-masts, free-standing rigs, and engineered boat structures. Service provided in repair engineering and supervision.

St. Augustine Marine, Inc.

404 South Riberia Street
St. Augustine, FL 32084
Tel: (904) 824-4394
Fax: (904) 824-9755
staugmar@aug.com

YS

A full-service yacht yard that can handle up to 200tons on the railway and 100tons on a mobile hoist. Services include painting, extensions, interiors, repowering, and full restorations. Electronics, air-conditioning, and canvas work are available as well.

Donald Starkey Designs

The Studio
2 Richmond Road
Isleworth Middlesex, TW7 7BL
United Kingdom
Tel: +44 (0) 20 8569 9921
Fax: +44 (0) 20 8569 9862
info@dsdyachts.com

D

Designer working on the largest megayachts.

Stodgell Interiors

2300 East Las Olas Blvd.
2nd Floor
Fort Lauderdale, FL 33301
Tel: (954) 527-4456
Fax: (954) 527-5809
designers@stodgellinteriors.com
www.stodgellinteriors.com

D

The Strategic Organization

38 Molasses House
Plantation Wharf
London, SW11 3TN
United Kingdom
Tel: +44 (0) 20 7228 8800

O

Stratos

300 Corporate Avenue
Suite 108
Western, FL 33331
Tel: (954) 217-2256
Fax: (954) 217-2272

YS

Stratos is a leading provider of global mobile satellite communications services and equipment to the yachting and marine industries. Stratos offers a full site of services for remote and offshore communications including voice, data, and fax through iridium, Mini-phone, Inmarsat A, B, M, and Oceancell.

Studio Scanu

Largo Risorgimento 6
55049 Viareggio, Italy
Tel: +39 (0) 0584 943229
Fax: +39 (0) 0584 31879
studioscanu@inwind.it

NA, D

Guided by Paolo Scanu since 1983, this international design team combines Italian style with proven hydrodynamics and applies this to new builds and refits of quality motor and sailing yachts.

Summit Furniture
5 Harris Court
Monterey, CA 93940
Tel: (831) 375-7811
Fax: (831) 375-0940
YS

Sunrise Harbor Marina
1030 Seminole Drive
Fort Lauderdale, FL 33304
Tel: (954) 667-6720
Fax: (954) 667-6730
O

Designed and constructed to cater to the exacting needs of the megayacht community. Located on the Intra Coastal Waterway, the marina features 2,500ft of floating docks in parallel construction that offers side-to docking. Services include electrical hook-up, water, cable television, sewage pump-out connections, and multiple telephone outlets.

Sunseeker USA, Inc.
2001 SW 20th Street, Suite 106B
Fort Lauderdale, FL 33315
Tel: (954) 765-1234
Fax: (954) 765-1931
www.sunseeker.com
B, O

The Sunseeker Company embraces the very latest technology in design, construction techniques, materials, engines, and propulsion systems. It also invests heavily in research and development and in creating the most modern molding and production units.

Super Yacht Technologies
1300 SE 17th Street, Suite 219
Fort Lauderdale, FL 33316
Tel: (954) 761-7934
Fax: (954) 761-3192
info@super-yachts.com
www.super-yachts.com
YS

Project management firm active in new construction, refitting and vessel operations, marine engineering, MCA surveys and regulation consultants, superyacht surveys, safety management, and marina development.

T

Tarrab Yachts
1535 SE 17th Street
Suite 117B at The Quay
Fort Lauderdale, FL 33316
Tel: (954) 462-0400
Fax: (954) 462-4968
www.tarrabyachts.com
B

Tarrab Yachts, Argentina's premier builder of semi-custom fiberglass yachts from 60ft to 125ft+ has been producing yachts of quality for nearly 40 years.

Taylor Made Environmental Systems, Inc.
P.O. Box 15299
Richmond, VA 23227
Tel: (804) 746-1313
Fax: (804) 746-7248
NA, O

Taylor Made Environmental Systems, Inc. (TMES), a member of Taylor Made Group, Inc. was created in 1999 by the merger of Marine Development Corporation, Richmond, Virginia, and Marine Air Systems, Pompano Beach, Florida. TMES is the world's leading supplier of environmental control systems, battery chargers, and refrigerations products for the recreational and commercial marine industry and vehicular markets.

Tilse Industrie & Schiffstechnik GmbH
Projecting-Design
Sottorfalle 12
22529 Hamburg, Germany
Tel: +49 (0) 40 561 014
Fax: +49 (0) 40 563 417
tilse@t-online.de
YS

Titan Hyde & Torrance
81 Akti Miaouli
18538 Piraeus, Greece
Tel: +301 (0) 428 0889
Fax: +301 (0) 418 2834
tht@hol.gr
B, YS, BR, C

Titan Brokerage Corporation offers full management services particularly for megayachts. Fully certified under ISM for management of passenger vessels (including yachts) by the American Bureau of Shipping. Large-scale refit specialists whose attributes include refits of Othelia, Nefertiti, Christina O, and Galeb.

Townsend Bay Marina, LLC
919 Haines Place, P.O. Box 2067
Port Townsend, WA 98368
Tel: (360) 385-6632
Fax: (360) 385-6652
YS

TR Design
P.O. Box 33
Gabriola Island, BC V0R 1X0
Canada
Tel: (250) 247-9315
Fax: (250) 418-5343
tadroberts@shaw.ca
www.tadroberts.com
NA

Trinity Yachts
4325 France Road
P.O. Box 8001
New Orleans, LA 70182
Tel: (504) 283-4050
Fax: (504) 284-7318
info@trinityyachts.com
www.trinityyachts.com
B

Recognized as one of the worldwide leaders in the state-of-the-art construction of megayachts. Trinity designs, engineers, and manufactures custom one-of-a-kind motoryachts in aluminum and steel.

Tripp Design Naval Architecture
144 Water Street
South Norwalk, CT 06854
Tel: (203) 838-2215
Fax: (203) 838-2448
info@trippdesign.net
www.trippdesign.net
NA

Tripp Design specializes in the design of high performance cruising and racing yachts which are speedy, strong and clean. They are developing new solutions to resolve the seeming contradictions of boats with world class sailing speed, and worldwide capabilities, into common gains and ever-higher levels of optimal trade off.

U

Universal Aqua Technologies, Inc.
2660 Colombia Street
Torrance, CA 90503
Tel: (562) 944-4121
Fax: (562) 941-9633
uat1sy@aol.com
YS

UAT manufactures high-quality reverse osmosis sea water desalination systems for yachts, ships, oil rigs, and land-based applications. Equipment sizes range from 200gpd to 16,000gpd. All sizes are available in framed and modular configurations and include a patented Digital Diagnostic Control Panel.

V

Van Cappellen Consultants
Het Vierde Kwartier
De Wederik 12
Papendrecht, 335 5SK
The Netherlands
Tel: +317 (0) 864 11022
Fax: +317 (0) 861 55349
O

Vectorworks, Inc.
805 Marina Road
Titusville, FL 32796
Tel: (321) 269-8444
Fax: (321) 269-8483
hopfk@vectorworks.com
www.vectorworks.com
B, BMA, YS

Vectorworks International provides design, engineering, tooling, and FRP production services to the marine industry. The firm's backbone, however, is production of plugs and molds, utilizing two large CNC 5-axis routers.

Venture Pacific Marine
1101 N. Northlake Way, Suite 201
Seattle, WA 98103
Tel: (206) 547-6161 x16
Fax: (206) 383-1321
lindsayann@worldnet.att.net
YS, O

Venture Yachts International Ltd.
New Zealand
Tel: +64 9 521 3765
Fax: +64 9 521 7302
marketing@ventureyachts.co.nz
www.ventureyachts.co.nz
B

Vernicos Yachts
11 Poseidonos Avenue
GR-174 55
Alimos, Greece
Tel: +30 210 989 6000
Fax: +30 210 985 0130
marketing@vernicos.gr
www.vernicos.com
BR

Vintimar, Inc.
2420 140th Place SE
Mill Creek, WA 98012-1303
Tel: (425) 485-1203
Fax: (425) 316-0250
sales@vintimar.com
www.vintimar.com
YS

Vintimar provides custom shipboard monitoring and control systems, including graphic user interfaces. Our systems interface with fire, security, CCTV, HVAC, lighting, paging, and other shipboard monitoring systems. We also develop custom computer applications, program PLCs, and implement computer networks.

Vitters Shipyard, BV
Postbus 108
8064 9D Zwartluis
The Netherlands
Tel: +31 (0) 38 386 7145
Fax: +31 (0) 38 386 8433
B

Vripack Yachting
Zwolsmanweg 16
P.O. Box 334
8600 AH
8606, KC SNEEK
The Netherlands
Tel: +31 (0) 515 436 600
Fax: +31 (0) 515 436 634
info@vripack.com
www.vripack.com
YS, O

W

The W-Class Racing Yachts
W-Class Yacht Company, LLC
P.O. Box 250
Lyndfield, MA 01940
Tel: (781) 334-7250
Fax: (781) 334-4554
info@w-class.com
www.w-class.com
B, YS, BR

W-Class Yacht Company develops, builds, races, and manages spirit of tradition cold-molded wooden sloops from 46ft to 130ft.

Waite & Morrow Associates
515 Seabreeze Blvd., Suite 226
Fort Lauderdale, FL 33316
Tel: (954) 764-1789
Fax: (954) 764-6867
info@luxuryyachtexchange.com
www.LuxuryYachtExchange.com
O

Also:

Waite & Morrow
135 Marginal Way, Suite 131
Portland, ME 04104
Tel: (954) 764-1789
Fax: (954) 764-6867
info@luxuryyachtexchange.com
www.LuxuryYachtExchange.com
O

Wally
Seaside Plaza, 4 Av. Des Ligures
MC 98000 Monaco
Tel: +377 9310 0096
Fax: +377 9310 0094
sales@wally.com
www.wally.com
B

Wally is the leading builder of advanced composite large cruisers. Both the sail and power boats carrying the Wally brand combine technology with design, resulting with unique and marked characteristics of performance, functionality, and style that became a reference point for the yachting industry. The Monaco-based company controls two shipyards that specialize in advanced composite construction, one joinery facility dedicated to the interior work, and one company that specializes in yachting electrical and hydraulic systems.

Wards Marine Electric
617 SW 3rd Avenue
Fort Lauderdale, FL 33315
Tel: (954) 523-2815
Fax: (800) 297-8240
O

Warwick Yacht Design Ltd.
2B William Pickering Drive
P.O. Box 302 156, North Harbour
Auckland, 1311 New Zealand
Tel: +64 9 410 9620
Fax: +64 9 410 8254
wyd@wyd.co.nz
www.wyd.co.nz
O

Webster Associates
P.O. Box 30038
Fort Lauderdale, FL 33316
Tel: (954) 525-5101
Fax: (954) 525-5103
jim@jimwebster.com
www.jimwebster.com
BR, C
Yacht and charter brokers providing clients with intensive, confidential services.

West Bay SonShip Yachts Ltd.
8295 River Road
Delta, BC V4G 1B4
Canada
Tel: (604) 946-6226
Fax: (604) 946-8722
marketing@west-bay.com
www.west-bay.com
B

Westerbeke Corporation
150 John Hancock Road
Taunton, MA 02780
Tel: (508) 823-7677
Fax: (508) 884-9688
O
Manufacturer of marine engines, generators, and climate control systems.

JS Westhoff & Co.
14006 West 107th Street
Lenexa, KS 66215
Tel: (913) 663-9900
Fax: (913) 663-9949
www.westhoffco.com
O
Westhoff & Co. provides the most comprehensive resource for property management, consulting, engineering, and joinery of megayacht interiors for owners, shipyards, naval architects, and interior designers.

Westport Shipyard, Inc.
P.O. Box 308
1807 Nyhus Street
Westport, WA 98595
Tel: (360) 268-1800
Fax: (360) 268-1900
B
Westport Shipyard specializes in large composite yachts as well as commercial passenger vessels. Supplies composite hulls to builders in the Pacific Northwest.
Also:
Westport Yacht Sales
2957 State Road 84
Fort Lauderdale, FL 33312
Tel: (954) 316-6364
Fax: (954) 316-6365
www.pacificmariner.com
B
Also:
Westport Yacht Sales
2601 West Marina Place, Suite F
Seattle, WA 98199
Tel: (206) 298-3360
Fax: (206) 285-0342
www.pacificmariner.com
B

Westship
1535 SE 17th Street, Suite 202
Fort Lauderdale, FL 33301
Tel: (954) 463-0700
Fax: (954) 764-2675
inquire@westshipyachts.com
www.westshipyachts.com
B, BMA
Westship builds and markets custom fiberglass yachts 98ft to 165ft under the direction of Herb Postma. All Westship yachts encompass advanced composite technology, innovative designs, contemporary exterior styling, and luxurious custom interiors. Each Westship echoes the philosophy of minimum maintenance and maximum luxury with unequalled sea-keeping characteristics. Full marine support services available worldwide.

Wilson Yacht Management Ltd.
18A Hull Road
Hessle, HU13 OAH
United Kingdom
Tel: +44 (0) 14 8264 8322
Fax: +44 (0) 14 8264 8277
allan@wilsonyachtmanagement.com
www.wilsonyachtmanagement.com
YS
Yacht management for professionals, services include crew, accounts, operations, charter, refit and repair management, ISM/MCA compliance.
Also:
Wilson Management Ltd.
77 Impasse des Cabrieres
06250 Mougins, France
Tel: +33 (0) 92 921609
Fax: +33 (0) 93 758969
yachts@wilsonmanagement.com
www.wilsonmanagement.com
YS

Also:
Wilson Management Ltd.
Ataturk Cad Belvu Sit
C Blok Kat 3, No. 19
Kusadasi, Turkey
Tel: +90 (0) 256 613 2679
Fax: +90 (0) 256 613 2977
BR, C
We are worldwide agents for Tecnomar Offshore & Steel Yachts, Predator Marine, Dauphin Marine, ARC 2000 and Libertas. Yacht sales and charter brokers. Management of large yachts. Consultancy and project management for the construction of large yachts.

Andrew Winch Designs Ltd.
The Old Fire Station
123 Mortlake High Street
London, SW14 8SN
United Kingdom
Tel: +44 (0) 20 8392 8400
Fax: +44 (0) 20 8392 8401
info@andrew-winch-designs.co.uk
www.andrew-winch-designs.co.uk
D
Andrew Winch specializes in interior and exterior design of luxury yachts. From concept through to completion, we complete a turnkey operation designing the boat from scratch. This involves working closely with the client to ensure that their dream is turned into reality.

Yacht Engineering Associates
Bunderbos 93
2134 RN Hoofddorp
The Netherlands
Tel: +31 (0) 23562 8156
Fax: +31 (0) 23562 8157
NA, D

Yacht Equipment & Parts
3355 SW 2nd Avenue
Fort Lauderdale, FL 33315
Tel: (954) 463-7222
Fax: (954) 463-9009
O
Full-service sales, installation, and service for frequency converters, stabilizers (Wesmar & Naiad), and bow thrusters.

Yacht Interiors by Shelley
2050 South Federal Highway
Fort Lauderdale, FL 33316
Tel: (954) 525-3111
Fax: (954) 525-0833
yibs@cablemarine.com
O

Yacht Link Engineering
311 Northeast 45th Street
Fort Lauderdale, FL 33334
Tel: (954) 771-2489
Fax: (954) 771-5837
info@yachtlinkpro.com
www.yachtlinkpro.com
O
We sell vessel management programs called Yacht Link Pro, which keep track of inventory, maintenance, purchasing, MCA compliancy, crew suppliers, and custom boat drawings. Another product is called Yacht Link Manager. This is for use in the office of yacht suppliers for inventory, investing, purchasing, and accounting.

Yachting Partners International
28/29 Richmond Place
Brighton, East Sussex, BN2 2NA
United Kingdom
Fax: +44 (0) 12 7357 1720
ypi@ypi.co.uk
www.ypi.co.uk
BR, C
Also:
Yachting Partners International
Avenue de 11 Novembre
06600 Antibes, France
Tel: +33 (0) 493 34 01 00
Fax: +33 (0) 493 34 20 40
ypifr@ypi.co.uk
www.ypi.co.uk
BR, C, O

Dick Young Designs
134 High Street
Lymington, SO41 9AQ
United Kingdom
Tel: +44 (0) 159 068 8912
Fax: +44 (0) 159 067 7134
enquiries@dickyoungdesigns.com
www.dickyoungdesigns.com
D
Dick Young Designs offers a full interior and exterior design service, specializing in both power and sailing yachts for the custom and production boat markets.

Zodiac of North America
540 Thompson Creek Road
Stevensville, MD 21666
Tel: (410) 643-4141
Fax: (410) 643-4491
B, YS
US distributor of Zodiac inflatable boats, semi-rigid yacht tenders, life rafts, and marine evacuation slides. Standard production of semi-rigid inflatable boats for 11ft to 24ft. Inboard and outboard power, including water jets and marine diesel. Custom boats of any size, including aluminum hulls USCG and SOLAS approved life rafts.

Zuretti Interior Designers S.a.r.l.
268, Avenue de la Californie
06200 Nice, France
Tel: +33 (0) 4 93 72 40 60
Fax: +33 (0) 4 93 72 40 66
interiordesigners@zuretti.com
www.zuretti.com
D

Zurn Yacht Design
P.O. Box 110
Marblehead, MA 01945
Tel: (781) 639-0678
Fax: (781) 639-6776
dz@zurnyachts.com
www.zurnyachts.com
NA

Index

Advertisers

Photographers

ANY PHOTOS NOT CREDITED WERE SUPPLIED BY A YARD, BUILDER, OR DESIGNER WITHOUT A PHOTO CREDIT.